W9-ACH-831

An
Ambrose Bierce
Companion

ROBERT L. GALE

GREENWOOD PRESS
Westport, Connecticut • London

Library of Congress Cataloging-in-Publication Data

Gale, Robert L., 1919–
    An Ambrose Bierce companion / Robert L. Gale.
       p.   cm.
    Includes bibliographical references (p.) and index.
    ISBN 0–313–31130–7 (alk. paper)
    1. Bierce, Ambrose, 1842–1914?—Encyclopedias.   2. Authors, American—19th
century—Biography—Encyclopedias.   3. Journalists—United
States—Biography—Encyclopedias.
    PS1097.Z49G35   2001
    813'.4—dc21   00–057657

British Library Cataloguing in Publication Data is available.

Library of Congress Catalog Card Number: 00–057657
ISBN: 0–313–31130–7

First published in 2001

Greenwood Press, 88 Post Road West, Westport, CT 06881
An imprint of Greenwood Publishing Group, Inc.
www.greenwood.com

Printed in the United States of America

The paper used in this book complies with the
Permanent Paper Standard issued by the National
Information Standards Organization (Z39.48–1984).

10 9 8 7 6 5 4 3 2 1

To
S. T. Joshi and David E. Schultz,
Stellar Biercians

Contents

Preface

William Shakespeare occasionally has a character reveal something profoundly relevant to the action of a given play in four terse words. Thus, Cleopatra says, "Not know me yet?"; Hamlet, "The rest is silence"; Macbeth, "Let it come down"; and Othello, "It is the cause." Wily Ambrose Bierce, however, shortchanged Shakespeare, in whose literary abilities he ventured to detect limitations, when he summed up his own philosophy of life in half of four words, thus: "Nothing matters." All this, in a letter dated 15 August 1903 to the so-so poet George Sterling, whose friendship Bierce also soon felt had severe shortcomings. "Nothing matters." What a thing to urge a friend to believe.

But, despite his off-putting disclaimer, Bierce wrote as though much mattered to him. He wrote some of the best war fiction any American ever created, and did so by virtue of horrific combat experience, a sharp eye, an uncanny memory, and a perspective of decades after the Civil War. That does matter. Perhaps the only veterans of that ghastly war whose writings can bear halfway favorable comparison with Bierce's are John Esten Cooke, John William DeForest, and Ulysses S. Grant. The wound Bierce suffered at the battle of Kennesaw Mountain left more than a sharpshooter's rifle ball in his head; it left an unbalance there for the remainder of his curious life.

Once the war was behind him, Bierce in 1867 started a career in journalism in San Francisco. His newspaper columns, which have yet to be completely assembled and published, are among the sharpest, most stinging, venomous, and daring that any American has ever composed. They also matter. Some of them have been published, of course, including many that Bierce himself chose for inclusion in his *Collected Works* (1909–1912). But they all matter. Only two satirical curmudgeons come to mind who are comparably savage. They are Jonathan Swift and H. L. Mencken. When compared to Bierce, Swift had less trouble in his life, wretched though much of it was, but he also had better targets for his satire. Bierce and Mencken, who knew and respected each other personally, were kindred spirits in many compelling ways.

In addition to war fiction and venomous satire, Bierce wrote ghost stories, yarns of horror and oneiric eeriness, and West-based tall tales. In these he rivals Edgar Allan Poe, whom he extolled, and Mark Twain, whose abiding excellence Bierce seemed unaware of—if not possibly jealous of. Bierce's pieces in these subgenres matter. He also wrote poetry. He regarded great poets as the best of the best in the literary pantheon. In my view, he evaluated his own poems more responsibly than some of the later apologists for them have done. To him, they surely did not matter much. Nor to me do they matter much; they usually seem a bit forced and strained, though often as naughty in their bite as his best prose. His favorite poet was probably John Keats. And like Keats some of the time, Bierce seems all of the time "half in love with easeful death." Over most of his fiction, journalistic items, and poetry, death seems to cast its shadow and fling its odor. But, still, something from much of it does matter.

Bierce is a supreme stylist. He is an accomplished wordsmith. He wields an extensive vocabulary, weighted with a multitude of odd words, many tottering past obsolescence. He employs a spectrum of colors, an orchestra of sounds, and arsenal of weapons. Although in his use of similes and metaphors, he is surprisingly stingy, he manages other elements of style and tone with a magic touch. Even when, as is often the case, his topic or his target should have been beneath his contempt, his treatment can be exciting. And nothing was beneath his contempt, certainly not contempt. When he writes about stale subjects or long-forgotten politicians, he invests them with at least momentary importance by virtue of his style. He demands close reading, partly because of the complex tones of his well-modulated voice, but mostly because of his unrelenting syntax, which will confound the would-be speed reader. He teases readers into reading closely, if for no other reason than that the reward is a dose of verbal nastiness, whether relished with gusto or rejected after a sniff. Eventually Bierce, the man of letters, will inspire a respect bordering on awe.

Curiously, perhaps uniquely, Bierce combines stylistic rancor and philosophical cleanliness. The list of topics still controversial that he exposes, rakes over, and explores, often with startling prescience, is a long one. In many surprising ways, he comes down on the "correct" side, according to contemporary advocates of political correctness. He favored minority rights, unrestricted world trade, environmental sanity, superciliousness toward religions, and euthanasia. He absolutely reviled Christopher Columbus and what he did—a popular stand today. He disrespected mergers because they gave too few people too much ill-used power and wealth and also caused massive unemployment. In some ways, he was a revisionist before revisionists began to revise. But Bierce was a better hater than he was an exponent of any positive cause. He regarded as useless or dangerous, or at least something to dislike, the following: formalized educational institutions and programs, organized charities, labor unions, tariffs, yellow journalism, and the entire legal system—including lawyers, judges, courts, namby-pamby treatment of women offenders, frequent avoidance of the death sentence, and prisons themselves. Any statistical analysis of *The Devil's Dictionary*, very likely his most popular work, would show Bierce as negative not positive, as hater not espouser. He praised British and Japanese cultures (at the obvious expense of American culture), rejoiced when Japan defeated Russia in 1905, but warned his fellow countrymen (never say "countrypersons" in his lurking presence), like a veritable California Nostradamus, of the incipient dangers of Japanese and also Chinese commercial invasions. As for Bierce's opinions concerning women, sexuality, and marriage, the once-hot women's suffrage question, and females invading the sacred all-male work force—the less said the better, given today's penchant for political correctness.

If I had known at the outset of my Biercian project half of what I have hinted at above, I would not have approached the task with the innocence I began it with. Once upon a time, I thought that I could reread his stories, his *Devil's Dictionary*, and his *Monk and the Hangman's Daughter*, run through his poetry, and then be similarly impressed and amused upon digging into some minor pieces, which I figured would not be too hard to locate. After all, I had access to Bierce's twelve-volume *Collected Works*, rare and carefully boxed, but able to be checked out from Hillman Library at the University of Pittsburgh. So I was efficiently gnawing my way through the set, with wrong-headed naiveté, when a problem arose. Imagine my surprise when in October 1999 I learned that the definitive bibliography of Bierce had just been published. I did know that earlier ones were dreadful but was not perturbed by the fact. When I made inquiries, the assiduous Bierce bibliographer-scholars S. T. Joshi and David E. Schultz sent me a copy. Only then did I learn to my dismay that Bierce wrote more—much more—than I had ever thought.

Almost at once, I had to decide to make my coverage of Bierce selective, whereas for my previous Greenwood Encyclopedia and Companions—concerning F. Scott Fitzgerald, Dashiell Hammett, Henry James, Sarah Orne Jewett, Herman Melville, and Nathaniel Hawthorne—my coverage was at least 99 percent complete. As was not the case even with James, the most prolific of that sextet, Bierce turned out more wordage than I could hope to embrace and process. After all, under "Contributions to Books and Periodicals," Joshi and Schultz list 3,533 items. In an appendix titled "Newly Discovered Items" they add titles of 70 more. Only a small fraction of these 3,603 pieces are available in book form. Moreover, Joshi and Schultz identify 1,577 letters by Bierce, located in 52 repositories. Random publications of some of Bierce's letters, beginning in 1922 with the pioneering but woefully inadequate selections by Bertha Clark Pope, have been helpful but shockingly minimal. Fortunately in time for me to consult for this Companion have been two recent publications—*The Unabridged Devil's Dictionary*, edited by David E. Schultz and S. T. Joshi (2000), and *The Collected Fables of Ambrose Bierce*, edited by S. T. Joshi (also 2000). Too late for me to incorporate has been Joshi and Schultz's edition of *The Fall of the Republic and Other Political Satires* by Bierce. Surely this may be just as well. I had begun to feel like a stepbrother of Jay Leyda, who called his search for material to go into *The Melville Log: A Documentary Life of Herman Melville* an "endless quest." Bierce is no Melville, nor am I a Leyda; but I have sense enough to know when to call a quest quits.

In fairness to all, I may report that in this companion I have entries on 92 short stories, 161 essays, 19 short dramas, 5 reviews, 3 assemblies of fables, 1 novel, and 57 family members, friends, former friends, enemies, and professional associates. (Cross references are indicated by asterisks.) In truth, I believe, this companion easily concerns itself with a good 90 percent of Bierce's really valuable publications. Let me suggest that yet to be done, however, in service to Bierce devotees are the following: an annotated edition of Bierce's complete fiction, a multivolume edition of his letters with biographical and other notes, an analysis of revisions he made between periodical and book publication of his most strident essays impaling his favorite enemies, a directory of the crowd of people whose lives he touched, and a comprehensive study of his myriad rhetorical weapons.

For help and encouragement of various sorts, I should like to thank my colleagues in the English Department at Pitt who helped me become less illiterate with word processors; my friends at Hillman Library who helped me with research into the lives of Bierce's associates, blessedly few when compared to the hordes who knew Fitzgerald, Hammett, James, Jewett, Melville, and Hawthorne; and my friends in the library who courteously and efficiently handled my many interlibrary-loan requests. Invaluable in helping me interpret Bierce have been S. T. Joshi and David E. Schultz, who are now my esteemed pen pals; Lawrence I. Berkove, who supplied insights, offprints, and his fine book on Bierce's skepticism and dissent; and the late M. E. Grenander, whose pioneering work on Bierce and whose courage are alike memorable. And a hearty thank-you to the good people at Greenwood Press, especially Dr. George F. Butler, Betty C. Pessagno, and Diana Drew, for welcome advice and needed damage control. As always, my love and thanks to my wife Maureen and to our immediate family, John, Jim, Christine, and Bill. I would like to close by wishing peace to the indomitable spirit of Ambrose Gwinnett Bierce, brave soldier and fearless writer, whose astringent honesty is a sterling example, even if many of his conclusions are simply revolting. Readers may detect little adverse criticism of Bierce in my

Companion. There would be more but for my fear that if I griped, he would disturb my predawn sleep more than he has already done. Do agree that Bierce is a memorable man of letters, and should—and will—be seen as a towering figure in the ineluctably dystopian times we all have yet to face.

Chronology

1842	Ambrose Gwinnett Bierce (1842–1914?) born 24 June in Meigs County, Ohio, youngest of ten surviving children of Marcus Aurelius Bierce* and Laura Sherwood Bierce.*
1846	Moves with family to Koskiusco County, Indiana; Bierce attends school, meets Bernice Wright.*
1857	Moves alone to Warsaw, Indiana, and works as a printer's devil for anti-slavery newspaper.
1859	Moves to Akron, Ohio, lives with uncle, Lucas Verus Bierce; attends Kentucky Military Institute, Franklin Springs.
1860	Leaves Kentucky Military Institute, moves to Elkhart, Indiana, works at various odd jobs.
1861	May, enlists in 9th Indiana Volunteers, Union Army, for three-month hitch; proceeds to western Virginia. June, in Civil War battle of Philippi; July, as sergeant major, in battle of Richmond Mountain and Laurel Hill; mustered out, re-enlists for three years, is promoted to sergeant. October, on reconnaissance at Cheat Mountain. December, in battle of Buffalo Mountain.
1862	April, under Colonel William B. Hazen* in battle of Shiloh. December, as second lieutenant, in battle of Stones River.
1863	April, promoted to first lieutenant. May, becomes topographical engineer under General Hazen. September, in battle of Chickamauga. November, in battle of Missionary Ridge. December, on leave to Warsaw, is engaged to Bernice Wright.
1864	February, returns to active duty. May, proceeds to Georgia, in battle of Resaca. June, at battle of Kennesaw Mountain, is shot in head, is hospitalized in Chattanooga. July–September, on leave in Warsaw. Engage-

ment to Bernice Wright is broken. September, returns to active duty. October, briefly captured by Confederate unit near Gaylesville, Alabama. November, in battle of Franklin. December, in battle of Nashville.

1865   January, head wound incapacitates him for active duty; takes job in Treasury Department in Alabama and New Orleans. September, vacations in Panama.

1866   July, joins Hazen's unit to explore forts in the West and on to San Francisco.

1867   Refuses regular army commission as second lieutenant; resigns from army. Works in San Francisco at the U.S. Mint. September–December, publishes first poems and first essays, in *Californian*.

1868   March, first publishes in *San Francisco News Letter and California Advertiser*. December, begins "The Town Crier" columns in *News Letter* (ending August 1873 in *Figaro*).

1869   Publishes extensively in *News Letter* (until March 1872).

1871   Publishes first short story, "The Haunted Valley" (July, *Overland Monthly*). December, marries Mary Ellen ("Mollie") Day (*see* Bierce, Mary Ellen Day) and lives in San Rafael.

1872   March, resigns *News Letter* position. April, leaves with Mollie for England. Writes in London for *Fun* for Tom Hood,* and "Town Crier" and "The Passing Show" columns for *Figaro*. December, son Day Bierce* born.

1873   Lives in Bath and London. July, *The Fiend's Delight*, first book, published by John Camden Hotten.* *Nuggets and Dust* published.

1874   *Cobwebs from an Empty Skull* published. April, son Leigh Bierce* born.

1875   April, Mollie, Day, and Leigh return to California. September: Bierce follows, works again at Mint. October, daughter Helen Bierce* born.

1876   February, father dies.

1877   Becomes associate editor of *Argonaut* (until 1879) and writes "Prattle" column for it. *The Dance of Death* (coauthor Thomas Arundel Harcourt).

1878   May, mother dies.

1880   July to October, works as general agent, Black Hills Placer Mining Company, Rockerville, Dakota Territory. October, goes briefly to New York City.

1881   January, back in San Francisco. March, becomes staff member at *Wasp*, associate editor, and "Prattle" columnist (until May 1886). Writes prolifically. Suffering from asthma, seeks relief outside San Francisco.

1887   March, becomes editorial writer for *San Francisco Examiner*, owned by William Randolph Hearst.* Writes prolifically.

1888   Leaves Mollie over dispute concerning love letters she received.

1889   July, Day Bierce dies. Writes some of his best short stories (until 1909).

1891   September, begins serial publication of *The Monk and the Hangman's Daughter* (coauthor Gustav Danziger*).

1892   *Tales of Soldiers and Civilians* (title of English edition: *In the Midst of Life*) and *Black Beetles in Amber* published.

1893   *Can Such Things Be?* published.

1896   January to November, employed by Hearst in Washington, D.C., to write critically of Collis P. Huntington* in Hearst's *Examiner* and Hearst's *New York Journal*.

1898   Publishes pieces concerning Spanish-American War in *Examiner*.

1899   *Fantastic Fables* published. December, correspondent in Washington for *New York Journal* (later named *American*) and *Examiner*.

1901   March, Leigh Bierce dies.

1903   *Shapes of Clay* (financed by George Sterling*) published.

1904   December, Mollie Bierce files for divorce (but dies 1905).

1905   May, writes for *Cosmopolitan* (until 1909; owned by Hearst).

1906   *The Cynic's Dictionary* (later titled *The Devil's Dictionary*) published.

1908   Begins to assemble works for collected edition.

1909   *The Shadow on the Dial and Other Essays* and *Write It Right: A Little Blacklist of Literary Faults* published. First volume of *The Collected Works of Ambrose Bierce* (twelfth and last volume, 1912), all published by Walter Neale.*

1910   May–October, lives in California.

1911   Summers in Sag Harbor, Long Island, New York.

1912   June–October, revisits California for a final time.

1913   October, leaves Washington to visit Civil War battlefields. November, visits Juarez and Chihuahua, Mexico.

1914   Disappears.

1922   *The Letters of Ambrose Bierce* published.

1936   *Selections from Prattle* published.

1967   *The Enlarged Devil's Dictionary* published.

1980   *Skepticism and Dissent: Selected Journalism, 1898–1901* published.

1995   *Poems of Ambrose Bierce* published.

1998   *A Sole Survivor: Bits of Autobiography* published.

2000   *The Collected Fables of Ambrose Bierce, The Unabridged Devil's Dictionary,*
         and *The Fall of the Republic and other Political Satires* published.

Abbreviations

Berkove	Lawrence I. Berkove, ed. Ambrose Bierce, *Skepticism and Dissent: Selected Journalism, 1898–1901* (Ann Arbor: UMI Research Press, 1986).
Davidson	Cathy N. Davidson. *The Experimental Fictions of Ambrose Bierce: Structuring the Ineffable* (Lincoln: University of Nebraska Press, 1984).
Davidson, *Essays*	Cathy N. Davidson, ed. *Critical Essays on Ambrose Bierce* (Boston: G. K. Hall & Co., 1982).
De Castro	Adolphe De Castro. *Portrait of Ambrose Bierce* (New York and London: Century Co., 1927).
Fatout	Paul Fatout. *Ambrose Bierce: The Devil's Lexicographer* (Norman: University of Oklahoma Press, 1951).
Grenander	M. E. Grenander. *Ambrose Bierce* (New York: Twayne Publishers, 1971).
Hopkins	Ernest Jerome Hopkins, ed. *The Ambrose Bierce Satanic Reader: Selections from the Invective Journalism of the Great Satirist* (Garden City, N.Y.: Doubleday & Company, 1968).
Joshi	S. T. Joshi, ed. *The Collected Fables of Ambrose Bierce* (Columbus: Ohio State University Press, 2000).
Joshi and Schultz	S. T. Joshi and David E. Schultz, eds. *Ambrose Bierce: A Sole Survivor: Bits of Autobiography* (Knoxville: University of Tennessee Press, 1998).
Lindley	Daniel Lindley. *Ambrose Bierce Takes on the Railroad: The Journalist as Muckraker and Cynic* (Westport, Conn.: Praeger, 1999).
McWilliams	Carey McWilliams. *Ambrose Bierce: A Biography* (1929. n.p.: Archon Books, 1967).

Miller   Arthur M. Miller. "The Influence of Edgar Allan Poe on Ambrose Bierce," *American Literature* 4 (May 1932): 130–150.

Morris   Roy Morris, Jr. *Ambrose Bierce: Alone in Bad Company* (New York: Crown, 1995).

Neale   Walter Neale. *Life of Ambrose Bierce* (New York: Walter Neale, 1929).

O'Connor   Richard O'Connor. *Ambrose Bierce: A Biography* (Boston and Toronto: Little, Brown and Company, 1957).

Schaefer   Schaefer, Michael W. "Ambrose Bierce on the Construction of Military History." *War, Literature, & the Arts: An International Journal of the Humanities* 7 (Spring–Summer 1995): 1–13.

Starr   Kevin Starr. *Americans and the California Dream 1850–1915* (New York: Oxford University Press, 1973).

St. Pierre   Brian St. Pierre, ed. *The Devil's Advocate: An Ambrose Bierce Reader* (San Francisco: Chronicle Books, 1987).

Woodruff   Stuart C. Woodruff. *The Short Stories of Ambrose Bierce: A Study in Polarity* (Pittsburgh: University of Pittsburgh Press, 1980).

A

ABERSOUTH, CAPTAIN. In "A Shipwreckollection," he is the captain of the *Mudlark*, out of London. While carelessly reading long novels, he watches his ship get damaged in a storm. He and the narrator toss passengers overboard to lighten the load, and then Abersouth heaves the narrator over as well. In "The Captain of the 'Camel,' " Captain Abersouth commands the *Camel* on a trip toward the South Pole, suffers a calm south of the Equator, proceeds into cold weather, reads some three-volume novels, and dies quoting one of them and frozen into vacuity. In "The Man Overboard," Abersouth is cast into the sea when his ship, the *Nupple-duck*, is lost on a sunken reef. Spotted by the lookout of the *Bonnyclabber*, he makes a raft out of stuff thrown in his direction. The narrator, whom Abersouth calls Claude Reginald Gump, leaves the *Bonnyclabber* and boards the raft. He persuades Abersouth to contribute a finale to sea stories Gump has been writing about him by drowning himself.

ABERSUSH, AMASA. In "The Applicant," he was the philanthropist who gave Grayville the Abersush Home for Old Men, only to be denied a refuge in it when he became impoverished himself and applied.

"ACROSS THE PLAINS" (1890, 1909). Essay. (Original title: "Lieutenant Bierce: Tells How He Earned Promotion to That Rank.") Bierce reports that in 1866 he mainly followed the same route General John Bidwell (1819–1900) had taken in 1841—that is, from the Midwest to California. Bierce enjoyed reading Bidwell's account (*Journey to California*, 1842). But unlike Bidwell, who was a pilgrim, Bierce was an engineer under the command of General William B. Hazen,* whose group also included a cook and a teamster. Hazen was under orders to inspect new military posts from North Platte on west. Bierce was mainly expected to sketch maps and "amuse the general and other large game." They visited Fort Phil Kearny (soon to be the scene of a massacre by Indians), observed some buffalo near Fort C. F. Smith, picked up a cavalry escort, and endured thirst and hunger before getting to Fort Benton on the upper Missouri River. They proceeded to Helena and Virginia City, Montana, to Salt Lake, and on to California. The party was to return to Washington, D.C., via Panama. But Bierce took umbrage at his lowly appointment in San Francisco to a regular-army second lieutenancy, and therefore resigned and stayed in that city.

This essay is a poor example of Bierce's nonfiction. It scarcely begins to detail his trip west with Hazen. Moreover, it is choppy, too short, and padded with excessive quotations from Cyrus Townsend Brady's *Indian Fights and Fighters: The Soldier and the Sioux* (New York: McClure, Phillips & Co., 1904). Bierce's experiences in crossing the Plains provide some background details in his story "A Man with Two Lives."

Bibliography: Rockwell Dennis Hunt, *John Bidwell: Prince of California Pioneers* (Caldwell, Id.: Caxton Printers, 1942); Morris.

"ACTORS AND ACTING" (1882, 1884, 1893, 1911). Essay. Audiences stupidly praise certain actors, for example, Sir Henry Irving and Signor Ernesto Rossi, when motivated by patriotism, affectation, or ignorance of the actors' personal lives. Showy actresses thus glorified may be members of "the world's higher harlotage."

ADAM. In "Hades in Trouble," he is mentioned as an inhabitant, with Eve, of chaotic Earth. Satan sends his fellow devil a message expressing the hope that the troublesome couple will never upset peaceful Hades by arriving there themselves.

ADAMS, SHERIFF. In "The Middle Toe of the Right Foot," he is the sheriff of Marshall. With King and Brewer, he goes to the abandoned Manton house and discovers the body of Manton, who ten years earlier murdered his wife, Gertrude Manton, and their two children there. Brewer identifies footprints in the dusty floor of the house as those of his sister Gertrude.

ADDERSON, JAMES. In "Parker Adderson." *See* Adderson, Sergeant Parker.

ADDERSON, SERGEANT PARKER. In "Parker Adderson, Philosopher," he is a Union Army spy, caught one night by Confederate soldiers under the command of General Clavering and soon to be executed. They are in Clavering's small tent. Sergeant Adderson displays philosophical serenity, and even wit, when downplaying the importance of death in conversation with Clavering, who on the other hand expresses horror at the notion of dying. Clavering surprises Adderson by ordering him to be shot, not hanged, and this very night, not next morning. After protesting, Adderson seizes Clavering's knife and in a confused struggle mortally stabs Captain Hasterlick, Clavering's provost marshal, who tries to rescue Clavering but mortally wounds him instead. Before dying peacefully, Clavering orders the immediate execution by firing squad of Adderson, who is now blubbering and begging for mercy. Parker Adderson's name in the original version of the story is James Adderson.

"AN ADVENTURE AT BROWNVILLE" (1892). Short story. (Original title: "An Occurrence at Brownville.") (Characters: Richard Benning, Maynard, Eva Maynard, Pauline Maynard, Moran.) Moran, the narrator, is a teacher at Brownville, California. He lives in a hotel catering to vacationers. Returning late one evening from school through the moonlit woods, he overhears a woman, later identified as Pauline Maynard, asking a polite-looking man, later named as Richard Benning, if he means to "murder us." When Moran offers to intervene, the pair vanish. Next morning he sees two female newcomers, Pauline and her young sister Eva Maynard, at breakfast. When Moran leaves, he hears an aria from *Rigoletto* rendered in a rich baritone. The singer is Benning, who levels a gaze at Moran combining courtesy with "hatred and dread." Benning and Pauline then seem to disappear. From the landlady, Moran learns that the girls are from San Francisco, that Benning knew their deceased father, that Benning is their well-to-do guardian, and that Eva is here possibly seeking a cure for consumption. A month later Pauline dies in the bedroom she shared with Eva. The authorities say she had heart disease and have her body sent home. A week later Moran eavesdrops on the veranda and hears Eva calmly tell Benning to kill her as he did Pauline and thus leave her in peace. Benning courteously walks out and beyond the garden and is soon heard singing "a barbaric chant." Moran begs Eva to let him help. She replies that he can do nothing, that she and Benning are leaving in two days, that she loved Pauline, and that she loves Benning. But suddenly she asks Moran, now thoroughly in love with her, to walk with her. She turns coquettish and persuades him to meet her at the Old Mill in town the next afternoon. They so meet and then walk to the Eagle's Nest, a spot at a cliff top. Benning suddenly—and affably—joins them, and Eva greets him lovingly. After chatting a while about local flowers, he stares hypnotically at the girl, who smiles angelically but with terror in her eyes, then leaps to her death off the cliff. Benning coolly says she obviously committed suicide. To Moran's accusation that he all but killed her himself, Benning shrugs, walks away to summon the authorities, and is heard singing "La Donna e Mobile" from *Rigoletto*. A careful reader will note that Bierce handles phases of the moon skillfully. However, "La Donna e Mobile" is a tenor, not a baritone, aria. In a note, Bierce, says he wrote "An Adventure

at Brownville" in collaboration with Ina Lillian Peterson. She was the adopted niece of Ina Coolbrith,* the California poet.
Bibliography: Morris.

"ADVICE TO OLD MEN" (1903, 1911). Essay. (Original title: "The Problem of Success for Old Men—A Scamposium.") Don't get drunk before dinner. Be diligent in business to keep young employees from stealing you blind. Study old men rising in the world. They don't kiss girls or play football. Be well-mannered toward youths. Be modest, because "age is peculiarly liable to error through the glamour of experience." Accept advice from the ignorant and the young. Don't try to get something for nothing. Dress lightly.

AEGIDIUS. In *The Monk and the Hangman's Daughter*, he is a Franciscan monk who accompanies Ambrosius and Romanus from Passau to Berchtesgaden.

"AESOPUS EMENDATUS" (1899, 1906, 2000). Part of *Fantastic Fables*. In these prose fables, each short and titled, Bierce introduces Jupiter, Venus, Mercury, and Hercules but generally concentrates on animals, birds, and fish. His favorites are wolves, lions, and vipers, probably because of their reputed viciousness. Often, however, the cocky strong are defeated by the canny weak. For example, in "Lion and Mouse," a lion lets a captured mouse go when the mouse promises to spare the lion's life. Later, when the lion is caught and tied up, the mouse comes by and eats only his tail. Bierce likes to discomfit the reader's expectations; thus, the man with the goose that laid golden eggs finds not only that the dead goose had no internal gold mine but also that the eggs were just ordinary eggs. The two best fables may well be "Hare and Tortoise," in which the tortoise passes the hare and wins, only to be told that the hare really won and returned to cheer the tortoise along; and "Old Man and Sons," in which a man shows his quarreling sons that a bundle of sticks cannot be broken but then separates the sticks and breaks one over the head of each son. Human traits that Bierce exposes to ridicule are cowardice, cruelty, jealousy, lying, pride, selfishness, and trickery.
Bibliography: Joshi.

"THE AFFAIR AT COULTER'S NOTCH" (1889). Short story. (Characters: Coulter, Captain Coulter, Mrs. Coulter, Colonel Harmon, Morrison, Lieutenant Williams.) The colonel in command of Captain Coulter, who lived in the South but joined the Union Army and is an artillery officer, is ordered by their new commanding general to direct Coulter to take one artillery gun at a time to a narrow notch in a mountain pass and fire at twelve Confederate artillery pieces down beyond, in the valley. When the colonel expresses dismay, the general, with a half-smile, replies that "your brave Coulter . . . [is] a whole battery himself." When ordered, Coulter questions the order momentarily, turns pale, but then takes his men and one gun to the notch. Furious firing begins, with deadly effect on both sides. As ordered, Coulter directs special fire at one exposed enemy gun, located near a mansion. Each time one of his artillery pieces is destroyed, he orders up another. A little later, the adjutant general gossips to the colonel that a year earlier the general commanded a division camped near Coulter's home for some weeks and got to know Coulter's wife, who was a Secessionist lady. Complaints caused his transfer to this division, where Coulter's battery is "odd[ly]" assigned. The colonel rushes forward, finds hellish Union carnage, notes the withdrawal of the enemy, bivouacs his brigade near the mansion, and finds it heavily damaged. During supper, an orderly reports something untoward in the cellar. The colonel finds a fiendishly blackened man with a dead woman and a dead baby in his arms. He tells the colonel that this is his house, the dead are his wife and child, and he is Captain Coulter.

Bierce describes the geography surrounding the notch with topographical exactitude. He deliberately leaves unnamed both Coulter's colonel and his new general, perhaps to make the story more parable-like. Will the general ordering Coulter to fire on his house be court-martialed? The likelihood hardly matters under the circumstances. It has been suggested that Coulter's destruction of his home and family parallels Bierce's ruinous reaction to his discovery in 1888 that his wife Mary Ellen Day Bierce,* probably innocent, had some love letters from another man in her possession. In addition, Bierce must have felt indirectly responsible for the death in July 1889 of his son Day Bierce,* after a shootout with Neil Hubbs, who married Day's fiancée Eva Atkins in Chico, California. Bierce and his son had argued shortly before the duel. At any rate, "An Affair at Coulter's Notch," published 20 October 1889 with its loaded title, has a hero who kills both wife and child.
Bibliography: Grenander, Morris.

"AN AFFAIR OF OUTPOSTS" (1897). Short story. (Characters: Captain Armisted, Julia Armisted, the Governor, General Masterson.) In 1861, after the war had started, Armisted asks the Governor of his state for a commission to serve in the Union Army. When the Governor seems concerned that Armisted, a Southern sympathizer, wants to help the North, the young man says he feels that the North is right and further that he wishes to be killed because his wife has proved unfaithful. At the Governor's suggestion that he go kill the other man, his reply is that he does not know who the man is. The Governor authorizes a commission for Armisted as captain with the Tenth Infantry now in Tennessee. Time passes. The scene is now after the battle of Pittsburg Landing and the Confederate retreat to Corinth. The Governor visits the soldiers from his state there and asks General Masterson, in charge, to send him forward to see Captain Armisted. With some difficulty he finds Armisted, looking older and with a couple of battle scars.

Recognizing the Governor, he salutes but does not shake hands. Shots interrupt their talk, and dreadful combat follows. Scurrying back, the Governor badly sprains his ankle. Armisted, with sing-song aplomb, orders survivors of his depleted company to rally and save the Governor. In the confusion, the Governor finds a letter Armisted dropped. Three months old, it is signed "Julia" and contains not only the name of her lover, who deserted her, but also an expression of her "penitence." The Governor pockets the letter, is told that Armisted has been killed, but does not touch his corpse—for fear his hand "would bleed."

Bierce takes exceptional care to provide the historical background of "An Affair of Outposts." He reports that Confederate forces were defeated at Pittsburg Landing (Shiloh, 6–7 April 1862) and retreated to Corinth, after which Major General Ulysses S. Grant, his army having been saved by skillful Major General Don Carlos Buell, was replaced by inexperienced Major General Henry Wager "Old Brains" Halleck; some weeks pass, and high-ranking politicians are lured to the consequent bloody stalemate "to see what they safely could of the horrors of war." Among them were the fictitious, adulterous Governor, whom Bierce based on Indiana Governor Oliver P. Morton and who visited the troops in Tennessee of the Ninth Indiana, an infantry regiment he helped create. Bierce fought at Shiloh and wrote about doing so in "What I Saw of Shiloh." In "An Affair of Outposts" he contrasts romantic and realistic notions of war. His depiction of the action surrounding the Governor's retreat, helplessness, and rescue is extremely gory. It has been suggested that cynical realists may equate the seduction of Julia by a successful politician and the seductive appeal of warmongers to the patriotism of the naive.

Bibliography: Grenander, Morris, Schaefer.

"THE AGE ROMANTIC" (1902, 1911). Essay. Distance tempts us to romanticize past eras as picturesque. Romantic place names help. Mont Blanc is better than White Mountain; Capri, than Goat Island. We inveigh against today's prosaic commercialism, but railroads are better than camels and stagecoaches; steamships, than clipper ships.

AGGIE. In "Hades in Trouble," she is mentioned by Nick as an entrancing woman on chaotic earth. Belial would like her to come to Hades.

AHKOOND OF CITRUSIA, THE. In "For the Ahkoond," he is the gracious majesty who in the year 4591 rules over the descendants of Californians. He sends the narrator on a scientific expedition to the east of what was once called the Rocky Mountains.

AH WEE. In "The Haunted Valley," she was Gopher's Chinese girlfriend until Jo. Dunfer won her in a poker game in San Francisco. In his place out of town, Jo. demeans her, finds her to be seemingly intimate with Gopher, and kills her with an axe. Tardily noting that Gopher was only trying to save Ah Wee from a tarantula, Jo. uses as an excuse for his conduct the fact that she used to cut trees for timber badly. He also tells the narrator that Ah Wee was a man.

"THE A.L.C.B." (1890, 1912). Essay. Bierce says he has founded the American League for the Circumvention of Bores. If a bore is killed, more bores swarm up, including reporters, lawyers, and jurors. So it is better to leave them alive to be tortured by their "own esteem." A league brother being bored by someone can issue a secret distress signal, and a brother will come to the rescue by saying the bored brother's uncle has just fallen and broken his neck. The bored one can then escape.

ALFINGER, NATHAN. In *The Monk and the Hangman's Daughter*, this is the name of the man who was hanged by the hangman. His crime, according to Benedicta, the hangman's daughter, was killing a man because of a woman.

"THE ALLOTMENT" (1888, 1912). Essay. In a dream, a black-and-white angel offers the narrator, after his Thanksgiving dinner, drinks out of three vessels, each holding up to 100 parts. They are rationed 50–50 sweet and bitter, 9–1 sweet compared to bitter, and 90–10 bitter compared to sweet. He says a 50–50 drink is exceedingly rare and implies that the 9–1 vessel, only a tenth full, is for immature people.

"ALPHABÊTES AND BORDER RUFFIANS" (1893, 1911). Essay. Type-founders should not redesign letters, for example, O, M, and U. Nor should borders of pages be decorated. Nor should characters be depicted with white clothes and black faces and hands.

"AMBROSE BIERCE SAYS: AMERICA IS WARLIKE, BUT NOT MILITARY." *See* "Warlike America."

"AMBROSE BIERCE SAYS: A PAINTING CAN NEVER BE BETTER THAN IT LOOKS." *See* "Concerning Pictures."

"AMBROSE BIERCE SAYS: MISSIONARIES CAUSE THE CHIEF TROUBLE IN CHINA." *See* "Religion."

"AMBROSE BIERCE SAYS: NOT ALL MEN DESIRE IMMORTALITY." *See* "Immortality."

"AMBROSE BIERCE SAYS: PUBLIC OPINION IS RESPONSIBLE FOR MANY FALLACIES." *See* "The Game of Politics."

"AMBROSE BIERCE'S PECULIAR VIEW OF THE TURK." *See* "In the Infancy of 'Trusts' " and "The Turko-Grecian War."

"AMBROSE BIERCE WRITES THE MONOLOGUE OF THE MELANCHOLY AUTHOR." *See* "The Author as an Opportunity."

AMBROSIUS. In *The Monk and the Hangman's Daughter*, he is the narrator. Handsome, bright-eyed, and twenty-one, this devout Franciscan monk is ordered to move from Passau to Berchtesgaden, which is near Salzburg. At the monastery there, he meets Benedicta, the hangman's daughter, tries to befriend the proscribed girl, and is criticized by Father Andreas, his superior. Ambrosius warns Benedicta, with whom he has fallen in love, not to be seduced by Rochus. When she professes faith in that unworthy young man, Ambrosius fights Rochus but is defeated. After fasting, Ambrosius gets what he thinks is a message from God, goes to Benedicta, and—failing to dissuade her—stabs her to death to save her soul and is hanged for murder.

"THE AMERICAN CHAIR" (1888, 1911). Essay. American males, but not females, sag forward with feet up when sitting because American chairs from way back have been built to be uncomfortable. The British who ridicule our sitting postures should be more sympathetic.

"THE AMERICAN SYCOPHANT" (1891, 1897, 1901, 1909, 1912). Essay. A certain American writer opines that our republican government has made Americans no longer servile in the presence of royalty. Not so. Americans are servile in seeking social recognition in Europe, refer to Queen Victoria more respectfully than Britons do, doff hats before a Brazilian emperor, and bow before the King of Hawaii. Our president should not debase himself while on tours. We should pay respect only to goodness. When kings or nobleman visit America, their nobility properly drops from them. We should never address them as "your majesty" or "your royalty."

AMULA. In *The Monk and the Hangman's Daughter*, she is the dark, beautiful girlfriend of Rochus, until he turns his attention to Benedicta, the hangman's daughter. Amula becomes jealous and warns Ambrosius, the monk-narrator, about Rochus's amorous ambition. Amula also reviles Benedicta. After Ambrosius is convicted of murdering Benedicta, Amula visits him, to thank him, before his execution.

"THE ANCESTRAL BOND" (1888, 1889, 1909, 1912). Essay. The fact that a man in Ohio discovered another with the same name and with identical handwriting tends to prove the belief that a person "is the sum of his ancestors; that his character, moral and intellectual, is determined before his birth." *The Guardian Angel* by Oliver Wendell Holmes tends to suggest as much. Some ancestors are more determinative than others, with respect to intellect, physical traits, and so on. Racial traits are persistent; so why not congenital ones? We should breed better humans, the way we breed better dogs, horses, and pigeons, instead of preserving "incapables" by unnatural charities. People believing otherwise are "inaccessible" to reason.

"THE ANCIENT CITY OF GRIMAULQUIN: A RECORD OF IN-DUSTRIAL DISCONTENT." *See* "A Revolt of the Gods."

ANDREAS. In *The Monk and the Hangman's Daughter*, he is the superior at the Berchtesgaden monastery. He has been harsh in his treatment of the hangman and Benedicta, the hangman's daughter. When Ambrosius attempts to defend Benedicta, the superior criticizes and punishes him. Andreas precipitates the climactic action when he tells Ambrosius that the Bishop of Salzburg will give Ambrosius holy orders.

ANDREW. In "The Difficulty of Crossing a Field," he is the planter Williamson's overseer.

"THE ANNUAL GOBBLE." *See* "Thanksgiving Day."

"ANOTHER 'COLD SNAP.' " *See* "Another 'Cold Spell.' "

"ANOTHER 'COLD SPELL' " (1887, 1911). Essay. When a learned Coast Survey official discusses earthquakes and storms, we should take notice and not be smug and feel safe. Disaster—perhaps a new glacier age—may be coming.

ANTI-SEMITISM IN BIERCE, ALLEGED. Bierce regularly wrote in defense of minorities in general and in particular. These included African Americans, Chinese, Jews, Mormons, Native Americans, foreigners if in groups, and in a very few cases even women. At the same time, Bierce attacked individuals, regardless of their classifications and affiliations. Therefore, it should not have surprised anyone that he ridiculed the inferior poetry of David Lesser Lezinsky,* a young Jewish writer in San Francisco, in 1893, but also defended Alfred Dreyfus, the young Jewish captain in the French Army unjustly convicted of treason in 1894 and not pardoned until 1899. The "Dreyfus Affair" commanded international attention.

Bierce's printed comments on Lezinsky's weak verses may have contributed to his suicide, which did not disturb Bierce, even though several important San Franciscans, for example, Ina Coolbrith,* turned against him

and accused him of anti-Semitism. In his "Apocryphal Conversations" (San Francisco *Examiner* and New York *Journal*, 25 September 1898), Bierce amusingly pits a bewildered Dreyfus against his unprincipled (and illogical) accuser, Major C. F. Walsin-Esterhazy. In 1899 Bierce criticized with feigned mildness a Jewish rabbi who helped foreign laborers in Hawaii get out of a legal work-for-passage contract (*Examiner* and *Journal*, 1 October 1899). Bierce did not greatly improve his image of impartiality when he wrote "The Jew." In it he calls Jewish people "a peculiar people, peculiarly disliked," and suggests that they ought to pay less attention to "ceremonies and symbolisms of a long-dead past," to define God as "more than . . . [their] private tutor," and to seek to know "why . . . [they are] subject to hate and persecution by the Gentile." Too often, he adds, Jews feel "of . . . superior holiness and peculiar worth." They should renounce "their irritating claim to primacy in the scale of being . . ." and discontinue "racial isolation in a ghetto of . . . [their] own invention." (*See also* Frank, Ray.)
Bibliography: Berkove, Morris.

"APOCRYPHAL CONVERSATIONS" (1900). *See* "A Cabinet Conference," "For Intervention," "An Indemnity," "A Presidential Progress."

"THE APPLICANT" (1892). Short story. (characters: Amasa Abersush, Byram, Deacon Byram, Tilbody, Mrs. Silas Tilbody, Silas Tilbody.) There is an ugly building in Grayville. It is the Abersush Home for Old Men. It was built and endowed by a philanthropist named Amasa Abersush, who made his money in the Boston-China silk and spice trade. He went away on one of his ships and disappeared. Some time passed. Silas Tilbody, the superintendent of the Amasa Home, is anxious to turn it from a charitable institution into a profit-making one. On Christmas Eve, Tilbody is walking toward town to buy some presents when he encounters a tattered old man. He tells the old man that his application for admission to the Home has been denied. The old man walks aimlessly away in the snow. Next morning, the small son of Deacon Byram finds the frozen body of the old man. He is Amasa Abersush.

Several touches in "The Applicant" reveal Bierce's bitterness. For example, he suggests that Abersush's motive in giving the town the Home was to "rob . . . his heirs-in-law." He says that its architect made it ugly so people would not look at it a second time. He says that the tattered old man (Abersush) walks like "a scarecrow blessed with youth, health, and discontent." He calls Santa Claus "the hunch-bellied saint." And he describes Abersush's seemingly aimless final walk in the snow "not as reasonless a proceeding as it looked." Bierce rather spoils "The Applicant" by making its first event the boy's finding something in the snow, before the flashback begins. Every reader possessed of ordinary imagination surely concludes at the outset that the object in the snow is Abersush's corpse.

"ARBITRATION" (1894, 1909, 1912). Essay. Arbitration never works. International arbitration fails because no strong nation will submit to arbitration anything "vital to its honor or welfare." Industrial arbitration fails because inevitable compromise with labor unions is followed by strikes and concessions to the strikers. Employers have to surrender, to avoid risking ruinous stoppages and public animosity. Sympathy strikes are especially villainous. When California railroad owners cheated the public and jailed innocent people, why didn't well-paid railroad workers strike in sympathy? Big strikes result in violence, spoiled businesses, property destruction, and often killings—all reported in hypocritical ways by the press. A person has a right to work but not to quit work to the detriment of others. Managers are not allowed to strike, that is, shut down what they manage. Anyone breaching a labor contract—employer or employee—ought to be jailed. Owners, managers, and workers—and those in related industries—would then be safe. Otherwise, labor contracts are impotent, crimes will increase, capital will be invested elsewhere, and hard times—and worse—will ensue.

ARMAN, ORDERLY. In "The Major's Tale," he is an orderly serving the staff of a division general of the U.S. Army. The general's headquarters are in a civilian home in Nashville. To get even with Lieutenant Haberton, who incessantly boasts of his amorous conquests, his fellow officers outfit Arman in female clothes found in a closet and lead Haberton to "her." He is completely fooled until a Confederate shell explodes upstairs and Arman begins to tear off his encumbering garments. The fun-loving narrator, Major Broadwood, undoubtedly means for his readers to interpret the name Arman as "our man."

ARMISTED, CAPTAIN. In "An Affair of Outposts," he is a Union Army officer. Although his heart is with the South, his head knows that the North is right. He obtained his commission from the Governor, after telling him he wanted to die because his wife has been unfaithful to him with an unknown rival. In the course of the story it is revealed that Armisted learns by a letter from his wife, Julia Armisted, that the Governor was that rival and that he has deserted her. Even so, when the Governor visits the troops, Armisted helps rescue him from danger and dies doing so.

ARMISTED, JULIA. In "An Affair of Outposts," she is the unfaithful wife of Captain Armisted. She later writes him to identify the Governor as her lover, adds that he has deserted her, and expresses penitence.

ARMSTRONG, HENRY. In "One Summer Night," he is buried alive, is dug up by Jess, and sits up. This terrifies two medical students, who thought he was dead. Jess kills Armstrong, delivers his body to the dissecting room, and demands his pay.

"AN ARREST" (1905). Short story. (Originally part of "Some Uncanny Tales.") Characters: Orrin Brower, Burton Duff.) Convicted of murdering his brother-in-law, Orrin Brower is in a Kentucky county jail, waiting to be hanged. He slugs Burton Duff, his jailer, with an iron bar, escapes, runs out of town, and is soon lost in a forest. He encounters a figure, the "visible embodiment of Law," pointing his way back to town. Fearing that he will be shot, Brower turns around and walks along, looking back only once. He sees Duff behind him, his wounded brow livid. Burton meekly re-enters the jail and finds some armed men standing beside Duff's corpse, lying on a table.

"THE ART OF CONTROVERSY" (1889, 1899, 1911). Essay. Most people who argue—for example, lawyers and theologians—are irrational. People engaging in controversies should limit their efforts to entertaining others and gratifying themselves. If you are good at it, you can write in a controversial manner and at the same time be entertaining. And you can also please yourself by preserving your self-respect while at the same time destroying your adversary's self-respect, by making him respect you, and by leading him into blunders.

"ASHES OF THE BEACON" (1888, 1905, 1906, 1909). Essay. Bierce pretends to be a scholar of the far-advanced year of 4930 (3687 in another version) looking far back and analyzing the causes for the "Decline and Fall of the Connected States of America." Bierce reviles some of the beliefs and activities of a partly remarkable population. The very concept of "self-government" is erroneous. There can be no government where what is governed governs. When one is restrained only by agreeing to be restrained, there is no longstanding restraint. We are dominated and motivated by selfishness. Politics is a struggle of clashing interests. Neither patriotism nor respect for the law survives. Americans long ago were a blend of contrary bloods temporarily ruled by "the majority," that is, "the ignorant, restless and reckless." They even thought that the republican form of government was divinely appointed and furthered by "the god Washington, . . . [and then] Gufferson, Jaxon and Lincon." An explorer found some stones evidently from a temple glorifying Washington. A few precious documents have survived. One memoir, dated 1908, indicates that the increasing practice of suicide was proving unnecessary because of the steady increase in the murder rate. Turbulence was widespread by 1920. Witness the massacres in St. Louis, New York, and Washington, D.C., that year. Only Chicago and San Francisco were spared, the latter because it was defended by the Chinese there. In 1995 anarchy took over, when the three presidents abandoned their respective capitals, in Cincinnati, New Orleans, and Duluth.

Having consulted several political and military historians, Bierce wants to discuss "germinal conditions" for America's decline and fall and then "point the awful moral." Earlier republics in Egypt, China, Greece, and Rome—all studied by archaeologists—and then in France and Ireland all failed. Founders of later ventures should not have been "blind and deaf." The idea of majority rule is a mistake. If *A* and *B*, together or separately, pursue a like interest, then it follows that *C*, if differing, will lose. Yet one person can be "right" and his fellows all "wrong"—for example, Galileo. Anarchists proscribed in Europe in the nineteenth century found sanctuary in America because of its belief that those given the right of free speech would merely speak about their beliefs, not go ahead and act on them. However, four of the seven assassinated presidents were killed by anarchists opposed to "law and authority." Anarchists are the most active in that feeblest of governments, that is, republics. Weak stopgaps to anarchy were reform movements and socialism. But why did Americans think human nature was different in the New World?

One cause of the ruin was the determination of educators to inculcate only material values. Wealth became "the touchstone of merit," and literature and science were alike despised. Another cause was America's reverence for the jury system. The twelve so-called "peers" were necessarily residents of the locality where the crime was committed, were prejudiced by gossip about the crime, were subjected to rehearsed testimony that was largely false, and were forced to remain ignorant of relevant evidence legally suppressed. Judges were hardly better, because their existence depended on favoritism. Even judges at the top of the system "had crept to place through the slime of the lower courts." Meanwhile, lawyers juggled facts, were deceptive, and often won by tricks and technicalities. The entire "judicial system . . . was inefficient, disreputable, corrupt."

Bierce turns to one of his favorite subjects—women. In ancient times, women were exempt from political and military duties but were punished if they committed crimes. Not so in nineteenth- and twentieth-century America. Even if arrested, tried, and convicted of murder—all of which was rare—a woman was almost never executed, because "mischievous sentimentalists" contended that women were more emotional and less rational than men; furthermore, they argued that if women could not vote in favor of capital punishment, they should be exempt from it. Bierce casually mentions an earthquake occurring in the year 2342.

Next, Bierce harangues against ancient insurance companies and their attorneys. Fire-insurance agents are "professional gamblers," who "in the long run . . . *must* win." When San Francisco burned in 1906, insurance companies declined to pay in full, on the grounds that the fire was an act of God; they cited an earlier act of God—a cow kicking over a lamp and burning another city. Life insurance is "the most vicious" form of insurance. It got so bad that the dishonest president of a life-insurance company was killed by a mob, news of which then led to the destruction of all such companies.

American religion, during those "crude and primitive" times, was even more ludicrous. These backward polytheistic people made deities of women, their imagined virtues being adulated. Intertribal warfare, however, expunged "[g]yneolatry." Interesting also was the number of railroad deaths—5,000 in 1907—more than casualties of the battle of Gettysburg, about which we know only its name. Great Britain, with "a government that governed," had almost no casualties caused by its trains, which were faster. Republican governments assume their people are honest and intelligent, whereas they are, in reality, vicious and ignorant. It is foolish to assume that a group can be wiser than its wisest member. Majorities rule because of strength, not wisdom. It is blasphemous to think that the people's voice is that of God. After a terrible civil war, the victors did not save the country; they took it. Offenses included expensive public building programs and a protectionist tariff system to keep foreign goods out. National surpluses of money that accrued were vied for by two competing political parties, raided by "political adventurers," and used to build ugly public structures that soon fell down. Wars followed, including one against Japan occasioned by American fear of "Oriental dominion."

"[C]apital and labor" strife was occasioned by women demanding emancipation, equality, and the right to hold jobs. The result was a 30 percent increase in the work force, with women often ruinously replacing male workers, who then sought menial jobs. These events triggered the unemployment of what became "nomadic mendicant tramp[s]," causing "sedition, anarchy and insurrection." A "sophistry" called "the law of supply and demand" kept wages low and prices high, with enriched industrialists then becoming benefactors far and wide, and workers shirking whenever possible, unionizing, and striking—usually making "reasonless . . . demands" supported by hypocritical newspaper editors and fawning politicians. A labor dispute in 1931 paralyzed half the country. Capitalists fought back by employing strike breakers, by bribery, and by merging into "gigantic corporations."

Well-managed industries, even so-called "trusts," could have produced and distributed their goods efficiently, to the benefit of all. But since everyone lacked honesty and intelligence, greed prevailed. Financiers issued overvalued stock, and people who were little better than addicted gamblers rushed to buy—and lose. Suddenly, early in the twentieth century, "an ingenious malefactor managed to combine powerful capital and powerful labor into one rich unit bent on despoiling all others. A riot broke out in St. Louis. When 100 millionaires and 20,000 citizen-workers died, nationwide insurrection followed and lasted 350 years. After "skulking anarchists" died out, only "skin-clad savages subsisting on offal and raw flesh" survived, and then they too "vanished from history."

Bierce concludes by telling of a person promising the "reconciliation" of contending factions. In a "sweet and serious" voice this man, tall and robed, said the following, thrice, to a vast throng at the Capitol: "Whatsoever ye would that men should do unto you, even so do ye also unto them." He went among crowds of people, each of whom said he was near him. Disappointed, they all sought to lynch him; but the stranger was not seen again.

"Ashes of the Beacon," which could be abbreviated with the initials A. B., like Ambrose Bierce's, is a combination of accurate prophecy and rambling poppycock. The work began as "The Fall of the Republic: An Article from a 'Court Journal' of the Thirty-First Century" (1888). Bierce's "The Jury in America" and "Insurance in Ancient America: Translated from the Work of the Future Historian" were incorporated into the larger satirical "Ashes of the Beacon." Bierce spoofs researchers by citing dozens of fictitious historians and scientists with funny names: Bamscot, Bardeal, Bogramus, Bogul, Debrethin, Droyhors, Dumbleshaw, Gakler, Golpek, Professor Golunk-Dorsto, Gunkux, Holobom, Kekler (the younger), Kobo-Dogarque, Macronus, Professor Richard A. Proctor (now Proroctor), Sagab-Joffoy (or Sagab-Joffy), Soseby, and Straman. One is simply named Harley. Bierce names two real authors. He deliberately misidentifies Richard Anthony Proctor (1837–1888), an English astronomer and writer (in the United States from 1881), as "that eminent ancient philosopher, Professor Richard A. Proctor (or Proroctor, as the learned now spell his name)," who wrote on the subject of majority rule. And Bierce identifies Edward Bok (1863–1930), who was the editor of the *Ladies' Home Journal* from 1889 to 1919, as "the only writer of the period whose writing has survived." He quotes Bok on women's emancipation and describes his style as "exceedingly humane, refined and womanly." As Jonathan Swift did in *Gulliver's Travels*, one of his favorite books, Bierce creates bits of an imaginary place in his depiction of America, with population figures, types of currency (called *drusoes*, which replaced dollars, and *prastams*), and classes of people (including *blukuks*).
Bibliography: Anonymous review of *The Collected Works of Ambrose Bierce*, vol. 1, in Davidson, *Essays*, pp. 18–20; Lawrence I. Berkove, "Two Impossible Dreams: Ambrose Bierce on Utopia and America," *Huntington Library Quarterly* 44 (Autumn 1981): 283–292; Joshi and Schultz.

ASHMORE. In "Charles Ashmore's Trail," she is the younger daughter of Christian Ashmore and his wife.

ASHMORE, CHARLES. In "Charles Ashmore's Trail," he is the son, sixteen, of Christian Ashmore and his wife. On 9 November 1878, he goes toward the spring for water but vanishes on the way. Later, his mother hears his voice, recognizes that he is speaking words, but cannot recall them. Other family members and other people also hear his voice, which grows fainter until silence follows.

ASHMORE, CHRISTIAN. In "Charles Ashmore's Trail," he is the father of two grown daughters, the older of whom is Martha, and of a son, Charles Ashmore, sixteen. They live together on their farm near Quincy, Illinois.

When Charles disappears, Christian and Martha follow his tracks in the snow; but the tracks suddenly stop. Although they hear his voice later, they never see him again.

ASHMORE, MARTHA. In "Charles Ashmore's Trail," she is the older daughter of Christian Ashmore and his wife. She and Christian seek Charles by following his tracks in the snow. But he disappears, and they never see him again.

ASHMORE, MRS. CHRISTIAN. In "Charles Ashmore's Trail," she is the wife of Christian, and the mother of their two daughters and their son, Charles. When Charles disappears, his mother seeks him in vain, although she hears his voice. He is speaking specific words, which, however, she cannot recall. Once she dies, she probably knows her son's "fate."

"ASPIRANTS THREE" (1900, 1912). Short drama. "McPresident," who is also called the "Incumbant" (i.e., William McKinley*), a so-called "Born Candidate," and the "Ambitious Mariner" (George Dewey, hero of Manila Bay in the Spanish-American War) discuss Dewey's desire to succeed the president—all in funny heroic couplets. For example, Dewey wonders, "Why, blast my tarry toplights! what's this row? / And which of you is speaking, anyhow?"
Bibliography: St. Pierre.

"AN ASSIGNMENT." *See* "A Fruitless Assignment."

"AS TO CARTOONING" (1899, 1906, 1911). Essay. Cartoonists should moderate their tendency to make their picture "yell" at the audience. Wrongly thinking "incongruity is witty," they distort the human anatomy and anthropomorphize animals and birds. Maps are also spoiled by cartoons of buildings, soldiers, and ships. Cartoonists properly "afflict the Eminent Unworthy" by minimizing pictorial exaggeration.

ATHERTON, GERTRUDE (1857–1948). Author. She was born Gertrude Franklin Horn in San Francisco. After her alcoholic parents' divorce in 1860, she was educated in San Francisco boarding schools, at St. Mary's Hall in Benecia, and at the Sayre Institute in Lexington, Kentucky. In 1876 she married George Henry Bowen Atherton in San Francisco and quickly proved to be the more dominant of the two. After having two children, Gertrude Atherton began publishing, anonymously and pseudonymously at first in the *Argonaut*, in the *Overland Monthly*, and in newspapers. She used the byline Asmodeus as the author of *The Randolphs of Redwoods: A Romance*, which are related stories in serial form (1883). Her marriage, which had soured, ended with her husband's death in 1887. She published two novels,

What Dreams May Come (1888, by "Frank Lin") and *Hermia Suydam* (1889, under her own name). The latter garnered bad reviews as prurient. She moved to New York as the *Argonaut* correspondent, vacationed in London and Paris, and returned to San Francisco in 1890. Then followed a distinguished literary career—with some thirty-eight novels, collections of short fiction, historical and autobiographical books, and miscellaneous writings—during which span of time she often traveled widely.

Her best early novels are *The Doomswoman* (1892), an idealized depiction of a Western woman; *Patience Sparhawk and Her Times* (1897), partly autobiographical and partly a pioneering treatment of female sexuality; *The Californians* (1898), a character-packed, critical depiction of socially long-established San Franciscans, rigid, complacent, and pro-male; *Perch of the Devil* (1914), pitting a brave mining engineer against emerging labor unions; *Black Oxen* (1923), a bestselling, daringly profeminist but antiflapper narrative cast in New York; and *The House of Lee* (1940), presenting life in San Francisco just before World War II. These, and several other novels, many of which have reappearing characters and other narrative interweavings, have been seen as ably chronicling the centuries-long social history of Spanish, Mexican, and American California. Atherton's autobiography is *Adventures of a Novelist* (1932).

Atherton knew many of the same writers and celebrities in San Francisco that Bierce was acquainted with, including Ina Coolbrith,* Jack London,* Joaquin Miller,* George Sterling,* and Charles Warren Stoddard.* Her friendship with Bierce began when he wrote her in 1889 to accuse her (rather loftily) of adopting the publicity-generating fad of feminism to court favorable responses from a despicable public. In reply, she called him "nasty" and defended (a bit hypocritically) the pioneering eroticism in her *Hermia Suydam*. In 1890, back in San Francisco, she wrote to invite him to her apartment; he countered by sending her an invitation to his place in Sunol, in the East Bay. After exchanging more self-serving letters, she visited him early in 1891 for lunch—a bit daringly, given the times. When he said that her writing merely showed promise, she said his was lacking in humanity. When he said that short stories were better than novels, she said character development needed the length of novels. After becoming more polite, they quarreled, she says in her autobiography, when he tried to kiss her. But they continued to correspond, evidently mixing rebukes and self-revelations. Bierce's letters to her, carefully kept, were destroyed in the San Francisco earthquake and fire of 1906. Hers to him are extant.

Atherton's contract to write "Woman in Her Variety," a weekly column in the *San Francisco Examiner* (August–November 1891), put her on a journalistic par with Bierce—only briefly, however, because her columns offended conservative women. She moved to Fort Ross, north of San Francisco, sought Bierce's advice by letter while writing *The Doomswoman*, and even said once that she hoped he would eventually be proud of her.

They were better friends apart and on paper. They agreed that Walt Whitman and William Dean Howells* were poor writers. Atherton praised Bierce in a *Cosmopolitan* article (January 1891). He defined *The Doomswoman* as the best California novel (*Examiner*, 18 June 1893). By then, she was back in New York, where she helped get him published and reviewed. She suggested *Shapes of Clay* as the title for his 1903 book of poems, which Charles Scribner rejected by a courteous letter to Atherton, not Bierce. When she advised him to play up to Eastern critics, he declined and their friendship began to cool, perhaps as a result. In 1895 Atherton moved to England, and a year later Bierce went to Washington, D.C. Their diminished correspondence ended in 1908. His daughter Helen Bierce* said that Bierce regarded Atherton as one of only three women whose minds he admired. The other two were Empress Eugènie and George Eliot. The enigmatic relationship of Bierce and Atherton is close to unfathomable.

Bibliography: Gertrude Atherton, *Adventures of a Novelist* (New York: Liveright, 1932); Helen Bierce, "Ambrose Bierce at Home," *American Mercury* 30 (December 1933): 453–458; Emily Wortis Leider, *California's Daughter: Gertrude Atherton and Her Times* (Stanford, Calif.: Stanford University Press, 1991); Charlotte S. McClure, *Gertrude Atherton* (Boston: Twayne Publishers, 1979); Lois Rather, *Bittersweet: Ambrose Bierce and Women* (Oakland: The Rather Press, 1975).

ATNEY, THE REV. ELIAS. In "That of Granny Magone," he is the respected, well-educated Methodist minister summoned when Sarah Magone dies. He is to conduct the funeral on the following day. That evening, he and other watchers over the corpse see a black cat leap onto Sarah's face. Her right arm hurls it away. Efforts to revive her fail, and she is buried four days later.

"AT OLD MAN ECKERT'S" (1901). Short story. (Original title: "At the Eckert House.") (Characters: Philip Eckert, John Holcomb, Wilson Merle, Andrus C. Palmer.) Philip Eckert, a recluse about whose past nothing is known, lived in a weathered old house three miles outside Marion, Vermont. Called "Old Man Eckert," he became the subject of gossip. Was he once a pirate? One day he simply disappeared. Five years pass, during which stories about his haunted house became so common that three reputatable men decide to investigate. The three are an apothecary named John Holcomb, a lawyer named Wilson Merle, and a teacher named Andrus C. Palmer. They agree to meet at 8:00 one winter evening at Holcomb's house and go on together to Eckert's house. When Palmer does not arrive, Holcomb and Merle proceed without him. They are sitting in Eckert's front room when they hear an inner door open and see Palmer, pale and "distrait," enter, pass by them, and go out the front door—leaving no footprints in the snow. Fifteen more years pass, and Palmer is never seen again. The editor of the local newspaper concludes that Eckert "reached out and pulled him in."

"AT SANTIAGO" (1898, 1912). Short drama. (Originally part of "New 'Imaginary Conversations.' ") Major-General William Rufus Shafter (1835–1906, high-ranking officer during the Spanish-American War) tells General José Toral Vàzquez (1834–1904) that if Toral had not surrendered (17 July 1898), Shafter, his "army . . . rotten with fever," would have done so. Toral, commander of the Spanish Fourth Army Corps at Santiago de Cuba, says that he surrendered out of fear that Shafter would.
Bibliography: Berkove.

"AT THE DRAIN OF THE WASH-BASIN" (1888, 1889, 1912). Essay. Prohibitionists illogically opposed licensing liquor as legal recognition of the liquor trade. Unless declared illegal, liquor is legally recognized with or without licenses. Prohibitionists ought to call the license fee a fine. One drinks water to cure the disease of thirst; but water is impure, sometimes even "hydrate of dead dog." Old age may well be caused by drinking too much dirty water. We drink water because our forebears did not know "the sacred grape." They ate beetles and each other. Should we? Prohibitionist, beware. If he rebukes my wine drinking, "I will fill up his well."

"AT THE ECKERT HOUSE." *See* "At Old Man Eckert's."

AUNTIE. In "A Lady from Redhorse," she is Mary Jane Dement's aunt, companion, and perhaps guardian when the two are living in the hotel in Coronado.

"THE AUTHOR AS AN OPPORTUNITY" (1901). Essay. (Original title: "Ambrose Bierce Writes the Monologue of the Melancholy Author.") The Melancholy Author laments the fact that he is fair game to all readers, including critics, who wrongly think that reading books qualifies them to criticize literature. They are unaware that "books are not literature," which is an art. Every expert except critics serves an apprenticeship. They think themselves certified simply by inspiration. This is the first of five essays in which Bierce casts himself as the Melancholy Author. He combines traits of conceit, sarcasm, world-weariness, and alcoholism.

B

"A BABY TRAMP" (1891). Short story. (Characters: Mrs. Darnell, Parlow, Hetty Brownon Parlow, Joseph Parlow.) In Boston, Hetty Parlow, beautiful, pure, and sweet, marries Parlow, "a young scapegrace." Returning to Blackburg, her hometown, they have a child, Joseph, nicknamed Jo and Joey; but then both parents die of a disease that kills half the citizenry. At age one, Jo "set[s] up as an orphan." One night in May three years later, a dozen young people are driving from Greenton past the Blackburg cemetery when they see Hetty's ghost there, reaching her arms westward and crying "Joey, Joey!" At that moment, Jo, who was adopted, wanders lost in the desert near Winnemucca, Nevada. He is found by Piute Indians and sold to Mrs. Darnell, who is traveling east by train. Arriving in Cleveland, she adopts Jo, who soon wanders off to Whiteville, far from Blackburg. He is grabbed and washed off but escapes through the woods and in due time gets to Blackburg. Behold him standing on a surburban street corner, in a dark, sticky, autumnal rain— ragged, barefoot, cold, hungry—and staring, not knowing where he is. A "bowsing" dog prevents his entering a bright house nearby. He hobbles along the road toward Greenton and next morning is found dead on Hetty's grave—one upturned cheek washed and ready for an angel's kiss. Bierce begins "A Baby Tramp" with a weird description of Blackburg's history for the previous ten or twelve years—complete with a rain of frogs, a blood-colored snowfall, and then the mysterious disease.

"THE BACILLUS OF CRIME" (1892, 1911). Essay. All but moribund physicians know that diseases are caused by bacilli. Since crime is now called a disease, we must find its bacillus. Does one grand bacillus produce assassins, thieves, and congressmen? Or do several smaller ones? If the former, maybe we can find it and thus put sheriffs out of work. *See also* "Crime and Its Correctives."

"A BAFFLED AMBITION" (1900, 1912). Short drama. When Theodore Roosevelt* tells William McKinley* that he wants to be part of the administration, John Hay,* secretary of state, suggests making him part of the cabinet. Roosevelt leaves and pulls a bowie knife on the doorkeeper.

"A BAFFLED AMBUSCADE" (1906). Short story. (Part of "Soldiers and Ghosts," the other story in which was "Two Military Executions.") (Characters: Trooper Dunning, Major Seidel.) One dark night after the battle of Stone River, near Murfreesboro Tennessee, Major Seidel of the Union Army, with a few cavalry soldiers under his command, rides up to check on his sentinels. They are on a road between Readyville and Woodbury. One soldier is missing. He is Trooper Dunning. A soldier reports that Dunning, probably "skeered," went on ahead. The little group continues forward. Midnight passes. Advancing alone, Seidel finds Dunning, dismounted, with a dead man lying across a dead horse. Dunning silently warns Seidel back by pointing toward a cedar forest. Seidel expects Dunning to return soon and report. At dawn Seidel's whole force advances. Seidel finds Dunning dead as a statue, shot hours earlier, and lying on his horse. Evidence leads observers to conclude that a Confederate ambuscade had surely been among the cedars. The reader is to assume that brave Dunning, after being killed, warned his officer. Bierce and a cavalry officer named Major Charles B. Seidel, with other infantry and cavalry soldiers, participated in an abortive ambush in the spring of 1863 near Woodbury, outside Murfreesboro.
Bibliography: Morris.

BAKER, DANIEL. In "Present at a Hanging," he was a farmer in Lebanon, Iowa. In 1853 he evidently lured Samuel Morritz to his house, robbed and murdered him, and buried his body beneath a nearby bridge. Seven years later, in remorse, Baker hangs himself at the bridge. To the Rev. Mr. Cummings, Morritz's ghost points out the scene of the hanging and his own burial beneath the bridge.

"THE BALD CAMPAIGNER." *See* "The Nature of War."

BANCROFT, HUBERT HOWE (1832–1918). Historian and businessman. He was born in Granville, Ohio. At age sixteen, he began to work under his brother-in-law, a book seller in Buffalo, New York. Bancroft took a consignment of books to San Francisco, in 1856, and, financed by family money and admiring New York book dealers, opened a bookstore there. By 1860 his firm, H. H. Bancroft & Co., had made him wealthy enough to expand his business to include office supplies, stationery, printing, and bookbinding. Bancroft gave the reins of his company to his younger brother, Albert Bancroft, and devoted himself to studying history, traveling, and collecting books and documents relating to California and nearby states and countries. Within a decade, his library numbered 16,000 volumes. When he sold it in 1906 to the University of California at Berkeley, it contained 60,000 volumes, together with ancillary materials. Meanwhile, Bancroft employed a small army of researchers to index and read his holdings, and help prepare *The Native Races of the Pacific States of North America* (5 vols., 1874–1875), and thereafter upwards of thirty more volumes of history—of Central America (1882–1887), Mexico (1883–1888), the northern Mexican states and Texas (1884–1889), several western states, the northwest coast, British Columbia, and Alaska, and finally autobiographical volumes mainly concerning his professional research and writing techniques. Bancroft shrewdly reissued *The Works of Hubert Howe Bancroft* (39 vols., 1882–1890), sold by subscription and by traveling salesmen. He followed with *Builders of the Commonwealth* (7 vols., 1891–1892), a vanity series of biographies of numerous persons willing to pay him to include them. Adolph Sutro,* mayor of San Francisco (1894–1896), is included, among countless others. Although critics of Bancroft were quick to point out that he did not write everything in his scattershot *Works*, they had to acknowledge that the series contained countless sources of information that that would have been lost if not for his energetic efforts.

Bancroft's company published *Map of the Black Hills Region, Showing the Gold Mining District and the Seat of the Indian War, Drawn by A. G. Bierce from Surveys Ordered by the War Department* (1877). Thomas Arundel Harcourt (?–1884), who coauthored *The Dance of Death* with Bierce in 1877, had earlier been one of the many writers for low pay in what Bierce called Bancroft's "history mill." As T. Arundel Harcourt, he helped write *The Native Races*, which carried only Bancroft's name on the title page. In several "Prattle" columns for the *Wasp* in the mid-1880s, Bierce lambasts Bancroft for seeking, thus early, to sell his big library to the University of California at Berkeley. In one "Prattle" item for the *San Francisco Examiner*, Bierce avowed that the collection would be worth less to California than "Bancroft's brains to an educated pig" (27 January 1889). All the same, after several legislative setbacks, the collection was sold to Berkeley for $250,000. It became the nucleus of and the magnet for uniquely significant holdings. For a change, Bierce was wrongheaded in his vituperative condemnation of the purchase. *Bibliography:* Harry Clark, *A Venture in History: The Production, Publication, and Sale of the Works of Hubert Howe Bancroft* (Berkeley and Los Angeles: University of California Press, 1973); De Castro; Grenander; Starr; St. Pierre.

"THE BAPTISM OF DOBSHO" (1874). Short story. (Original title: "A Sinful Freak.") (Characters: Henry Barber, Thomas Dobsho, the Rev. Mr. Swin.) The narrator, Henry Barber, and his friend Thomas ("Tom") Dobsho live in Harding, Illinois. The narrator wants to spoof Tom, who, it seems, has found religion during a revival—virtually Rampageanism. Tom is a minor sinner, all right, but now takes pleasure in confessing to a sequence of sins just short of criminal and even hints that he could tell of more if encouraged. Put on probation for a time, he is now to be baptized on Sunday. The narrator goes to the Rev. Mr. Swin, the revival leader, on Saturday, tells him that Tom has been a Plunger (favoring total immersion), suggests that a basin of water over his head might be sufficient, but then says Swin will know best and maybe a tiny sprinkling will be enough provided they can work on Tom later to prevent backsliding. Sunday comes. Tom is nervous. His hair is standing up like porcupine spines. The narrator offers to comb it nicely, sits Tom down, and prepares it. They proceed to the service. Swin approaches with an earthen bowl filled with water but instead of sprinkling Tom pours it wholesale over his head. Since the narrator "had sifted a prodigal profusion of Seidlitz-powders" into Tom's hair, the result is a simmering, steaming, hissing, spurting, flashing "snowbank"—a "sinful shampooing" indeed. As other baptismal candidates leave, Swin shatters the earthen bowl on the narrator's head, declines to judge lest he be judged, but tells him to take that and sin no more.

BARBER, HENRY. In "The Baptism of Dobsho," he is the mischievous friend of Thomas Dobsho, into whose hair he puts effervescent powder so that when the Rev. Mr. Swin baptizes him the results will be spluttery and frothy. In "Corrupting the Press," Henry Barber, the narrator, delivers a $1,000 bribe to silence Sam Henly, editor of the Berrywood *Bugle*. When Sam reports a failed $20 bribe attempt by Barber, that crooked politician leaves Berrywood ahead of a mob.

BARBOUR. In "The Affair at Coulter's Notch," he is the orderly who alerts Captain Coulter's colonel that "there is something wrong in the cellar." The colonel finds Coulter there with his dead wife and dead baby.

BARR, MORTIMER. In "One of Twins," he is Henry Stevens's friendly psychologist and is the recipient of Henry's letter explaining the tragic consequences of his being the identical twin of John Stevens.

BARR, MRS. MORTIMER. In "One of Twins," she is Henry Stevens's psychologist's wife. In his letter to Mortimer, Henry mentions her kindness in nursing him back to consciousness after he discovered the murder of Julia Margovan, the fiancée of Henry's identical twin John Stevens, and also John's suicide immediately thereafter.

BARRITZ, DR. In "A Lady from Redhorse." *See* James.

BARTINE, BRAMWELL OLCOTT. In "John Bartine's Watch," he was Rupert Bartine's father and John Bartine's great-grandfather. Bramwell owned the watch that John now possesses. Bramwell, a wealthy Virginia planter, was a Tory at the time of the American Revolution, was seized by "rebels," and disappeared. The narrator, John's physician and friend, theorizes that Bramwell was hanged at 11:00 one evening.

BARTINE, JOHN. In "John Bartine's Watch," he is the physician-narrator's friend. From Rupert Bartine, his grandfather, John inherited the watch of Bramwell Olcott Bramwell, his great-grandfather. When the narrator challenges John to look at the watch, he does so, thinking it is set safely after the dangerous 11:00 hour. But the narrator, for an experiment, set it just before 11:00, and when John looks at it, he dies. Presumably, Bramwell was hanged shortly before 11:00 one evening.

BARTINE, RUPERT. In "John Bartine's Watch," he was Bramwell Olcott Bartine's son and John Bartine's grandfather. Through Rupert, John inherited Bramwell's watch.

BARTING, LAWRENCE. In "A Cold Greeting," he was a captain in the Union Army during the Civil War. Benson Foley, who knew him then, remembers him when James H. Conway, presenting a letter of introduction, becomes friendly with Foley. Barting and Conway agreed that the first to die would try to communicate with the other. Barting's communication after his death takes the form of bowing at but then ignoring Conway on the streets of San Francisco.

BARTING, MRS. LAWRENCE. In "A Cold Greeting," she is the wife and then the widow of Lawrence Barting, whose photograph she sends Benson Foley shortly after Barting's death.

BARTON, ATWELL. In "Staley Fleming's Hallucination," he was Staley Fleming's neighbor and enemy. He died of stab wounds. His Newfoundland dog found the body and later starved to death at his grave. Three years later, Fleming returns from Europe and awakens night after night seeing a Newfoundland dog watching him earnestly.

BARWELL. In "The Man Out of the Nose," he was a mining engineer working out of Sacramento. He and his attractive wife, Elvira Barwell, had two children. His visits to San Francisco brought him, and Elvira as well, into contact with John Hardshaw and his wife. Hardshaw began seeing Elvira in Sacramento when Barwell was away. This resulted in Hardshaw's imprisonment on a charge of stealing Elvira's miniature portrait. Years later, when the Barwells returned from an absence of two years in Peru, Hardshaw saw Elvira at her window. She leaned out to see him and fell to her death. The Barwell residence is regularly described as once a fine home but now a dingy factory.

BARWELL. In "The Man Out of the Nose," he or she is either of the two children of Barwell and his wife, Elvira Barwell. The children drop out of the story.

BARWELL, ELVIRA. In "The Man Out of the Nose," she was the attractive wife of Barwell, a Sacramento mining engineer. They had two children. Elvira and John Hardshaw fell in love. When he left her home with her miniature portrait, encased in diamonds and probably a gift to him, he was arrested. He called himself John K. Smith and served a prison term for theft. Years later, when the Barwells returned from a two-year stay in Peru, Hardshaw was impelled to walk to her residence. They saw each other at her window. She leaned out and fell to her death. This completed the ruin of Hardshaw's mental health.

BAUMSCHANK, BRIGADIER-GENERAL SCHNEDDEKER. In "Jupiter Doke, Brigadier-General," he is a Confederate Army officer who wants to resign after Brigadier-General Jupiter Doke's mysterious mule attack.

BAYNE, MYRON. In "The Death of Halpin Frayser," he is one of Halpin Frayser's maternal great-grandfathers. He was a poet in colonial Tennessee.

BAYROLLES. In "An Inhabitant of Carcosa," he is the medium to whom Hoseib Alar Robardin "impart[s]" the story. In "The Moonlit Road," Bayrolles is the medium that Julia Hetman, murdered by Joel Hetman, her wrongly suspicious husband, uses in a vain effort to communicate with both Joel and their son, Joel Hetman, Jr.

"THE BEDSIDE TELEPHONE." *See* "For Last Words."

BEELZEBUB. In "Hades in Trouble," he is a bored devil in Hades. He returned from an exploration of chaotic Earth and much preferred Hades. He is one of the host of devils trying to rescue Satan from the earth.

BEESON, HIRAM. In "The Night-Doings at 'Deadman's,' " he is a demented miner, twenty-eight but looking much older and living by himself in a pine shanty in Deadman's Gulch, fourteen miles from Bentley's Flat. Two years before, he and his companions buried their dead Chinese servant under the shanty because the ground was frozen. Beeson wrongly cut off the man's pigtail and nailed it to an overhead beam. The phantom of "the Chinaman" repeatedly comes back for his pigtail, needed for entrance into heaven. These visits ultimately cause Beeson's death. Eerie elements in the story suggest that Death calls on Beeson and shoots him at the order of a San Francisco showman who disappears up the chimney as the phantom swings overhead with his pigtail in his teeth.

"BEHIND THE VEIL: WORK FOR THE SOCIETY OF PSYCH-ICAL RESEARCH." *See* "A Cold Greeting" and "The Isle of Pines."

BELIAL. In "Hades in Trouble," he is a bored, sensual devil in Hades. He is one of the host of devils trying to rescue Satan from the earth.

BEN. In "Perry Chumly's Eclipse," he tries to analyze the composition of a comet with his spectroscope but instead points his instrument at a maid in a dormer window and finds not only carbon and iron but meat, whisky, soap, and hair. Ben's friend, Thomas, the narrator, is initially impressed. William, aware that Perry Chumly once mistook a black man's face for the moon during a solar eclipse, alerts him to reality.

BEN, OLD. In "The Captain of the 'Camel,' " he is the boatswain of the *Camel* who remarks that the only calm "deader" than the one the *Camel* suffers for almost a year occurred when Preacher Jack shouted in a seaman's chapel that the Archangel Michael would put the Devil in the brig.

BENEDICTA. In *The Monk and the Hangman's Daughter*, she is the hangman's daughter, sinless but proscribed by the church in Berchtesgaden. Ambrosius, the monk-narrator, falls in love with her and wants to save her from Rochus, whose ambition is to seduce her. When Benedicta tells Ambrosius that she trusts Rochus, Ambrosius kills her to save her soul.

"A BENIGN INVENTION" (1889, 1911). Essay in two parts. (Original titles: "Talking Back" and "As We See Ourselves.") The phonograph chastens us by requiring us to hear our own voices for a change. But while photographers can retouch portraits to please vain sitters, the phonograph cylinder cannot alter voices. Thomas A. Edison's best invention would be the "theoscope," a device enabling A to see B exactly as B sees himself, that is, with the "supernatural dignity" of god.

BENNING, RICHARD. In "An Adventure at Brownville," he is a middle-aged man, evidently well-to-do, from San Francisco. Tall, dressed in black, and suave, Benning and his wards, Pauline Maynard and her sister Eva Maynard, are vacationing at a hotel in Brownville. The narrator, Moran, discerns that Benning, through his mysterious, hypnotic influence, evidently caused the death of both girls. He is habitually courteous and bland, and is occasionally heard singing. At one point, his stare at Moran is full of "hatred and dread."

BENTLEY, JO. In "The Famous Gilson Bequest," he is the owner of the "gorgeous 'saloon' " in Mammon Hill, where Milton Gilson lost money at faro.

"BEYOND THE WALL" (1907). Short story. (Characters: Mohun Dampier, Parapelius Necromantius.) After years in the Orient, the narrator, now rich and on his way from Hong Kong to New York, stops in San Francisco to see old friends. One is Mohun Dampier, a former schoolmate remembered as strong, handsome, and scholarly. Having written to get back in touch, the narrator takes a cab one winter night and enters, as asked, Dampier's row house. Sequestered in his tower is Dampier, gray, thin, and pale. While they are talking rather gloomily, the narrator hears a gentle, slow, insistent tapping on the wall. Saying that no one is there, Dampier explains: Ten years ago he moved to this Rincon area, once fashionable but now neglected. One morning as he was walking to the street he saw a beatifically beautiful young girl in the garden of the property adjoining his. He doffed his hat in respect but said nothing. She looked at him courteously and went into her house. Two days later he saw her in the neighborhood. Although he had fallen hopelessly in love, he did not pursue her. But he ascertained her name, learned that she was orphaned and depended on a fat old aunt, and decided that her class was beneath his "aristocrat[ic]" status. Further, he felt that marriage to her would spoil the "subtle charm in an impersonal and spiritual relation." The two never met again. When he found out from his gossipy landlady that the girl's bedroom shared a party wall with his tower wall, he surrendered to the "coarse impulse" of tapping on his wall. An hour later he heard—or thought he heard—three replying taps. These signals went on for a while. Then silence. He haunted the streets to see her again. In vain. Then one "fatal night" he heard faint taps, but "the Adversary of Peace" prompted him to punish her for her earlier prolonged silence, and he did not tap in reply. Next morning his landlady told him that the young girl had been ill for weeks, asked last night to have her bed placed against the wall, and then soon died. Dampier feels damned because of his selfishness. The narrator rises, shakes Dampier's hand in sympathy, and departs. Later that night, Dampier dies. It has been suggested that the beautiful girl's "glorious dark eyes" owe something to the beautiful eyes of Mary Ellen Day Bierce,* Bierce's wife, and, further, that overly proud Dampier's inadequate method of communicating with his neighbor may symbolize Bierce's refusal to communicate rationally with his wife after their miserable estrangement. "Beyond the Wall" may owe something to "The Fall of the House of Usher," by Edgar Allan Poe, by whom Bierce alternately said he was and was not influenced.
Bibliography: Miller, Morris.

BIERCE, DAY (1872–1889). Bierce's older son. He was born in Bristol, England. His first name was the maiden name of his mother, Mary Ellen Day Bierce,* known as Mollie. Bierce was an inadequate father to Day, and to his other children, Leigh Bierce* and Helen Bierce,* as well. Day and Leigh, also born in England, accompanied their mother when she returned without Bierce to San Francisco in 1875. Bierce followed in September, a month before Helen was born. Day idolized Bierce, imitated his erect bearing, and grew to become even more handsome. By 1878 Bierce was indifferent to Mollie and usually resided apart from her and their children. In the spring of 1888 he visited her home in St. Helena, California, and argued with Day when he learned that the lad wanted to quit school and become a newspaperman. He evidently had shown talent for writing, and also for drawing. Perhaps he wished to please Bierce by trying to follow in his footsteps and become a reporter. Bierce was unable to persuade him to remain at St. Helena until he was better educated and more mature. Day went to Red Bluff, in northern California, and worked for the *Sentinel* there. Mollie asked Bierce to follow and bring him home, but Bierce refused. When Mollie sent Day some money, he returned it. In the winter of 1888–1889 Bierce had a final rupture with Mollie and abandoned her forever. In April 1889 Day met Eva Atkins, a sexy but stupid cannery worker as young as he, at a picnic in Chico, near Red Bluff. He fell for her, quit his job with the *Sentinel*, and moved into a boardinghouse run by her mother in Chico. In July, two days before Day and Eva were to get married, Eva eloped with Neil Hubbs, Day's best friend. When the newlyweds returned to Chico, Day argued with Neil, and the two drew pistols and fired at each other. Day mortally wounded Hubbs, shot at Eva and clipped her ear, went to an upstairs room, and shot himself. Both young men died on July 27. The Chico *Enterprise*, 12 August 1889, carried Eva's story, perhaps partly untrue. Bierce never wrote about Day's death.

Bibliography: Fatout, Grenander, McWilliams, Morris, O'Connor.

BIERCE, HELEN (1875–?). Bierce's daughter. She was born in San Francisco. Her mother, Mary Ellen Day Bierce,* known as Mollie, returned with her sons, Day Bierce* and Leigh Bierce,* from London to San Francisco in April 1875, without Bierce. He followed in September, to be there when Helen was born in October. It did not take him long to realize that his marriage was unsatisfactory. Helen recalled that when he was home, he often wrote at night and slept during the day, and that the family tiptoed around him. By 1889, when Day committed suicide, the marriage was irreparable. Bierce even sent support money for Mollie through Helen. In 1896 he left Washington, D.C., visited friends in San Francisco, and saw Helen again. In 1901 she attended Leigh's funeral in New York City, saw Bierce on that occasion, and stayed with him for a few weeks when he returned to Washington, D.C. On 27 January 1913, Bierce, old and depressed, wrote Helen, whom he called "Bib," a final letter. In it he transferred a family cemetery plot in St. Helena, California, to her, said that he did not wish to be buried there, and added that she need "not be bothered about the mortal part of/ Your Daddy." A little while later he paid her a visit in Bloomington, Illinois, bringing a trove of personal papers. At that time she was married to a man

named H. D. Cowden and had two stepsons, Henry and Victor, whom
Bierce liked. In 1914, after Bierce's disappearance, Helen sought official help
in locating his whereabouts—without success. Late in his life, Bierce asked
his publisher, Walter Neale,* to transfer to Carrie J. Christiansen* copyrights of some of his writings; then late in her life, Christiansen transferred
those rights to Helen, by then married to her third husband, a man whose
last name was Isgrigg. Helen published recollections of her father in "Ambrose Bierce at Home," *American Mercury* 30 (December 1933): 453–458.
Bibliography: Fatout, McWilliams, Morris, Neale, O'Connor.

BIERCE, LAURA SHERWOOD (1804–1878). Bierce's mother. She was
born in Cornwall, Connecticut, the daughter of a Congregational deacon
who traced his ancestry to William Bradford, a *Mayflower* passenger and
governor of Plymouth colony. At an early age, she moved with her family
to Ohio. She married Marcus Aurelius Bierce* in 1822 in Portage, Ohio,
moved with him in the 1840s to Horse Cave and Circleville, in Indiana, and
then to Warsaw, Indiana. She may have felt that the Sherwood family was
superior to the Bierce family. Only in 1858 did the family get title to the
Warsaw farm, and it was then put in Laura's name only. In 1861 she sold
it and bought a house in Warsaw. In 1865, in effect head of the shrinking
family, she bought farm property near Elkhart, Indiana, and moved from
Warsaw, and in 1869 bought and moved into a house in Elkhart. Ambrose
Bierce evidently felt emotionally rejected by his mother, theorized that she
lacked enough love to share with so many children, disliked her lugubrious
piety, and seems to have actually hated her. In "A Bottomless Grave" (1888),
Mrs. Brenwalter is an evil hypocritically pious murderess and favorite-
playing mother; and in "Oil of Dog" (1890), Mrs. Bings is satirically said to
be zealous in protecting her son from life's temptations. Bierce must have
been thinking of both of his parents when he defined "disobedience" in *The
Devil's Dictionary* as "the silver lining to the cloud of servitude."
Bibliography: Fatout, Morris.

BIERCE, LEIGH (1874–1901). Bierce's younger son. He was born in
Leamington, England. When Bierce's wife, Mary Ellen Day Bierce,* was
expecting their third child, she left England in April 1875 with Leigh and
Day Bierce,* Leigh's older brother, and returned to San Francisco. Bierce
followed and was with the family when their daughter Helen Bierce* was
born. Bierce was never much of a father to any of his children. Leigh studied
art in San Francisco under John Herbert Evelyn Partington* (1843–1899),
whom Bierce knew and who painted Bierce's portrait in 1893. In that same
year, Gustav Danzinger*—then Bierce's literary friend, but not for long—
wanted Partington to illustrate a book of Danzinger's. While only nineteen,
Leigh roomed briefly with George Sterling,* the handsome poet and Bierce's
friend. Danzinger tells questionable stories about Leigh—that Bierce broke

up an affair the teenager was having by lying to the effect that the girl was Bierce's illegitimate daughter, and that Danzinger tried to help Leigh when the lad was hopelessly drunk outside a San Francisco dive. As for his career, Leigh wrote articles for *The Wave*. On orders of William Randolph Hearst,* newspaper magnate and Bierce's employer, Leigh went to Yosemite Valley to send essays on its beauties to the *San Francisco Examiner*. Leigh lived in Los Angeles and was a reporter for the *Record* there. He accompanied Bierce when he went to Washington, D.C., in 1896; Leigh wrote for the *Morning Telegraph* in New York until 1900. He edited *The Bee*, a New York journal, for which he created competent illustrations. Like his father, Leigh was a hard-drinking lover of several women; unlike him, however, Leigh had a weaker constitution and poor taste and was, moreover, indiscreet. He had evidently started an affair in Oakland, California, with an artist's wife and continued the relationship with her in New York. When Leigh was about to marry a pretty girl named Flora, the daughter of his New York boardinghouse proprietress, Bierce noted imperfections in her and accordingly argued with Leigh. Once the two were married, Bierce cut off most contacts with Leigh; however, again according to the less-than-reliable Danzinger, Bierce's feelings toward his son and daughter-in-law softened a little. Leigh planned to write an account for the *Telegraph* about a group planning to dispense toys and provisions to the poor on Christmas Eve 1900; but he stopped at a bar, got drunk, and while accompanying the group began to give items away on the street. He caught a lingering cold and soon contracted pneumonia. Bierce rushed from Washington to sit at the young man's deathbed in March 1901. After Leigh's death, Bierce avoided Flora and her family; but he did send money to them through Helen, his daughter. *See also* "John Mortonson's Funeral."
Bibliography: Fatout, McWilliams, O'Connor.

BIERCE, MARCUS AURELIUS (1799–1876). Bierce's father. He was born in Cornwall, Connecticut, the son of a sergeant in the American Revolutionary army. He went to school at the nearby Litchfield, moved to Nelson, in Portage County, Ohio, near where his father owned land and where Marcus Bierce's younger brother, Lucius Verus Bierce, had preceded him. Lucius Bierce was to become a popular lawyer and politician in Ravenna and Akron. Meanwhile, Marcus married Laura Sherwood (*see* Bierce, Laura Sherwood) in Portage in 1822. About 1840 they moved to Horse Cave, Meiggs County, Ohio, then near Circleville, Ohio, and in 1846 Warsaw, Indiana— where Ambrose Bierce, born in Horse Cave, grew up. The Bierces had thirteen children—each oddly given a first name beginning with "A." Bierce was the tenth child and the youngest to live to adulthood. In chronological order the thirteen were Abigail Bell Bierce, Amelia Josephine Bierce, Ann Maria Bierce, Addison Byron Bierce, Aurelius Bierce (died in 1862), Augustus (Gus) Bierce, Almeda Sophia Bierce, Andrew Bierce (nicknamed "Dime"; after serving in the Navy one year he lived with his parents from 1863 until they died), Albert Sherwood Bierce, Ambrose Gwinnett Bierce, Arthur Bierce (died 1846), and twins Adelia Bierce and Aurelia Bierce (both dying in infancy). Marcus evidently combined farming and storekeeping, and was a poor provider. Bierce felt closest to always-friendly Albert (nicknamed "Grizzly"), who eventually lived in California. Bierce liked, and late in life wrote to, Albert's son Carleton ("Carlt") Bierce's wife Lora Bierce. Gus grew to a weight of three hundred pounds. Addison worked as a strong man in a traveling circus. Almeda became a missionary and died in Africa—perhaps the victim of cannibals, according to a family story. Bierce always disliked Andrew, evidently a favorite with their parents. Aurelius was killed in a carpentry accident, whereupon Bierce called him "Mr. Bildad Snobblepopkin" in a column ridiculing his dying young despite chronic abstemiousness (*San Francisco News Letter*, 25 June 1870). In 1855 Marcus Bierce was named local overseer of the poor and also vice president of an agricultural society. By 1863 he quit all work. In 1865 he and the remnants of his family moved to a farm west of Elkhart. When he died, an obituary in the Elkhart *Observer* identified him as a former private secretary of President Martin Van Buren. No evidence confirms this probably untrue statement. He was also called "colonel" for no legitimate reason.

Bierce later reminisced about his authoritarian father, whose strict orders, including Congregational Sunday-School attendance, he and his siblings obeyed out of fear. As he matured, Bierce enjoyed flouting his father's authority. Although Bierce called both of his parents "unwashed savages," he did praise his father for his library and his considerable scholarship. Marcus Bierce liked to read eighteenth-century essays, Gothic fiction, Lord Byron, and family magazines. It is possible that Bierce got the names he did because his father may have read Douglas Jerrold's *Ambrose Gwinnett; or, A Sea-Side Story* (1828). While in England, Bierce sent London papers home to his father, who gave them to an Elkhart newspaper editor. In "My Favorite Murder" (1873), Bierce describes old Ridley, the narrator Samuel Ridley's father, as "reticent, taciturn," whose advancing years "somewhat relaxed the austerity of his disposition." This sounds like old Marcus. In "Three and One Are One" (1908), Bierce describes the father of the Lassiter family as he might have described his own father—a man whose severe manner and devotion to duty concealed an affectionate nature. Bierce's numerous stories about patricide, however, may indicate a deep-seated revulsion against Marcus and his ways. When he learned of his father's death, however, Bierce wrote his mother that he had not been a good son to a good father and that his eyes were flooded with tears. Given Bierce's weird personality, it is distinctly possible that this letter was insincere.
Bibliography: Fatout, Grenander, Morris.

BIERCE, MARY ELLEN DAY (?–1905). Bierce's wife. Mary Ellen Day was the daughter of Holland Hines Day, a wealthy mining engineer, originally from Illinois but a Westerner from the 1850s, and his socially ambitious wife, who was from New York. Mollie, as Miss Day was called, was an attractive and peppy brunette. She and Bierce met in the summer of 1871, and the outspoken misogynist was soon smitten. After a conventional courtship, during which the two played cards with Ina Coolbrith* and Charles Warren Stoddard,* the San Francisco poets, Bierce and Mollie were married on Christmas Day, 1871, in the Day house in San Francisco. Bierce filled a few funny *San Francisco News Letter* columns with stories about his engagement and wedding. For example, "Female Suffragers and the Town Crier" is a satirical lament about his marriage (30 December 1871). Holland Day, who liked and was liked by Bierce, left his Utah mine to be happily present at the ceremony; Mrs. Day, however, opposed the marriage from the start. Holland Day promised to stake the newlyweds to a trip to England. In the summer of 1872 Bierce and Mollie went to London, where he met several literary men, notably Tom Hood.* The Bierces moved to Bristol, and in December 1872 Mollie gave birth to their first son, Day Bierce.* In 1873 the Bierces moved to Bath and then back to London. Mollie's mother visited them for a prolonged period of time, much to Bierce's displeasure. The Bierces were living in Leamington when Mollie gave birth to their second son, Leigh Bierce,* on 29 April 1874. In April 1875 Mollie, Day, and Leigh moved to San Francisco; Bierce, distressed when he received news that Mollie was pregnant again, followed in September. On 30 October 1875, their daughter, Helen Bierce,* was born. An unsatisfactory regimen was soon established, with Bierce working in San Francisco and elsewhere, while Mollie and the children stayed in nearby San Rafael and then St. Helena. By 1878 Bierce was of the conclusion that he and Mollie were badly paired. Only part of his problem concerned the too-frequent presence of Mollie's mother over the years and sometimes also that of James Day, Mollie's brother. Moreover, James Day got himself entangled in a love affair with the daughter of an old preacher with whom Bierce and his family, and Holland Day and his wife as well, had been friendly. When the old reverend committed suicide because of the scandal, Bierce gave his brother-in-law the cold shoulder from that point on. Until then, Bierce called Mollie, James Day, and their mother "the Holy Trinity."

When his asthma bothered him, Bierce went alone to nearby resorts. In 1888, he recognized that his separation from Mollie would be permanent. He distressed her by visiting her at her home and arguing with Day. The lad wanted to quit school and be a reporter; so he ran away to Red Bluff, California, and worked on a newspaper there. Distraught over Bierce's attitude, Mollie sent Day money, but he returned it. In the winter of 1888–1889 Bierce discovered some love letters from a stranger addressed to his neglected Mollie, wrongly assumed his wife's infidelity, and abandoned her forever. Day broke his mother's heart, and his father's as well, when he argued in Chico, California, in July 1889, over his worthless fiancée's quick marriage to his best friend; the upshot of an ensuing gunfight was the death of each young man. Bierce and Mollie met only once after Day's funeral, and then simply by chance. In 1896, while Bierce was visiting friends in Los Angeles and Mollie was there taking care of her senile mother, he rebuffed efforts at a reconciliation. He sent checks for Mollie's support but only through their daughter Helen. When Leigh died in New York City in 1901, Mollie was unable to leave her ailing mother and attend the funeral. Helen advised her mother to divorce Bierce and marry again, but she said she could love no one but him. In 1904 Mollie heard that Bierce wanted a divorce and therefore filed for one in December; she died, however, on 27 April 1905, before the decree was final.

Bierce, who rarely wrote about Mollie, did mention her in at least four letters to Charles Warren Stoddard,* written from England in 1873, 1874, and 1875. In the letters he merely calls her "wife" and "Mrs. B." and reveals nothing of his feelings. He did, however, tell their daughter Helen in 1896 that Mollie was the only woman he ever loved.

Bibliography: Fatout, Joshi and Schultz, McWilliams, Morris, O'Connor.

THE BIG FOUR. Four California railroad monopolists: Charles Crocker,* Mark Hopkins,* Collis P. Huntington,* and Leland Stanford.* During the Gold Rush Days, the four, all of whom were born in the East, migrated separately to Sacramento, California, to become merchants, politicians, and railroad magnates. Their mentor, Theodore Dehone Judah (1826–1863), was the first to plan a transcontinental railroad, starting from California and proceeding to Reno, Nevada. He persuaded Crocker, Hopkins, Huntington, and Stanford to incorporate the Central Pacific in 1861, while he went to Washington, D.C., to lobby an aid bill in Congress, succeeding in 1862. After buying Judah's interest in 1863, the Big Four lobbied, bribed, and dishonestly lured and cheated investors for the next several years. In 1868 the Big Four bought the Southern Pacific Railroad. On 10 May 1869, the Central Pacific Railroad, organized by the Big Four, connected at Promontory Point, Utah, with the Union Pacific Railroad, which had started at Omaha, Nebraska. Hopkins's death in 1878 reduced the Big Four to three. By 1883 their Southern Pacific had pushed into Arizona, Texas, and Louisiana. In 1885 they merged the Southern Pacific and the Central Pacific, controlled coastal business, bought California politicians, and made enormous profits through exorbitant commercial and agricultural freight charges.

In 1881 Bierce began to edit the *Wasp* in San Francisco, looked around for satirical targets, and settled on Crocker, Huntington, and Stanford, whose dishonesty in Sacramento was odious to him. He leveled many diatribes at the men he called "railrogues."

Bibliography: Oscar, Lewis, *The Big Four: The Story of Huntington, Stanford, Hopkins, and Crocker, and of the Building of the Central Pacific* (New York and London: Alfred A. Knopf, 1941); Lindley.

BILLOWS, MAJOR-GENERAL DOLLIVER. In "Jupiter Doke, Brigadier-General," he is a Confederate Army officer who exaggerates casualty figures after Brigadier-General Jupiter Doke's mysterious mule attack. Brigadier-General Schneddeker Baumschank mistakenly reports Billow's death. The name "Billows" may have derived from that of Gideon Johnson Pillow (1806–1878), Confederate Army general.

BINGS. In "Oil of Dog," he manufactures dog oil by boiling dogs in a cauldron. His wife disposes of unwanted babies. Their son, Boffer Bings, is the narrator. He helps his father by bringing him dogs, and he helps his mother by disposing of babies she has knifed to death. Bings sells physicians *ol. can.*, which they profitably prescribe. Once, when pursued by the police, Boffer escapes into his father's factory and tosses a dead baby into the oil cauldron. The resulting oil is of higher quality. When town leaders object and their business falters, Boffer's parents fight. His mother stabs his father, who grabs her and leaps with her into the boiling cauldron.

BINGS, BOFFER. In "Oil of Dog," he is the narrator and helps his father, a dog-oil manufacturer, by bringing dogs, and helps his mother, a baby killer, by bringing babies. Once, when pursued by the police, Boffer escapes into father's factory and tosses a dead baby into the oil cauldron. This inspires his mother to join forces with his father. But when the authorities object and their business falters, the mother and father fight. Mortally wounded, the father leaps with the mother into the pot. Boffer moves to Otumwee and writes his memoirs. He is sorry that by tossing the baby into the pot he indirectly caused his beloved parents' demise.

BINGS, MRS. In "Oil of Dog," she is a baby killer. Her husband makes dog oil. Their son, Boffer Bings, helps her by supplying many babies and then disposing of her "debris" and helps her husband by bringing him dogs. When Boffer happens to dispose of a dead baby by tossing it into his father's pot and the resulting oil is better, Mrs. Bings realizes that she can join forces with her husband. Authorities, however, object to the resulting raids on babies and even older people. Bings and his wife fight. She stabs him badly. He grabs her and leaps with her into his boiling cauldron.

BIRD, JOEL. In "Corrupting the Press," he is a candidate for governor of Missouri. Sam Henly, editor of the Berrywood *Bugle*, publishes damaging reports about Bird until bribed by Henry Barber for $1,000. Then Henly publishes an account of his refusing Barber's $20 bribe.

"BITS OF AUTOBIOGRAPHY" (1909). Eleven autobiographical essays Bierce assembled for inclusion under this title in *The Collected Works of Ambrose Bierce*. The essays are "On a Mountain," "What I Saw of Shiloh," "A

Little of Chickamauga," "The Crime at Pickett's Mill," "Four Days in Dixie," "What Occurred at Franklin," " 'Way Down in Alabam'," "Working for an Empress," "Across the Plains," "The Mirage," and "A Sole Survivor."

"A BIVOUAC OF THE DEAD" (1903, 1912). Essay. There is a valley in Pocahontas County, West Virginia. Through it flows the calm Greenbrier River. There is a farm house with a post office where the valley road crosses the Stanton-Parkersburg Turnpike. Once a tavern, the house is now called Travelers' Repose. Close by are Confederate fortification lines. Bierce's Union regiment fought there. A dozen or so were killed on each side. Union dead now rest, with comrades killed elsewhere, in a national cemetery at Grafton. Between eighty and a hundred "forgotten" Confederate dead lie in "rows of shallow depressions" behind their earthworks near Travelers' Repose. Only two have evidently been reburied near their homes. All should be given "the tribute of green graves." They fought for ideas fomented by "political madmen" and did not live to read "the literary bearers of false witness," thus never "impair[ing] . . . the dignity and infinite pathos of the Lost Cause." This moving tribute ends with a sonorous sentence, which is in iambs and includes a tiny rhyme: "Give them, these blameless gentlemen, their rightful part in all the pomp that fills the circuit of the summer hills." The haunting title for this essay comes from "The Bivouac of the Dead" (1847), a poem by Theodore O'Hara (1820–1867) commemorating American soldiers killed in the battle of Buena Vista (22–23 February 1847).

BLACK BEETLES IN AMBER (1892). The first collection of poems by Bierce in book form. When *Tales of Soldiers and Civilians* (1891) proved popular, he thought of assembling his poems as *Black Beetles in Amber*, which a friend thought might better be called *Red Peppers in Vinegar*. Publishing houses evinced little interest; so Gustav Danziger* suggested that he and some friends establish the Western Authors Publishing Company and issue it. Joaquin Miller* and William Chambers Morrow* agreed to help. The resulting book reprinted items from Bierce's columns in the *Argonaut*, the *San Francisco Examiner*, and the *Wasp*, and even included seven dramas, all short, satirical, and in verse. The book failed to make money but did make enemies—namely, the objects of Bierce's poetic invective. Targets ranged from important men to others now known mainly because of Bierce's blasts. *See also* Poetry by Bierce. Gustav Danziger,* who heard that William Ewart Gladstone, prime minister of England, had relished Bierce's *Cobwebs from an Empty Skull*, sent him a copy of *Black Beetles* without Bierce's knowledge. When Gladstone wrote to thank Bierce for it, Bierce wrote him to apologize and then blasted Danziger in a "Prattle" column (*San Francisco Examiner*, 3 July 1893).
Bibliography: O'Connor.

"BLATHERING BLAVATSKIANS." *See* "The Death Penalty."

BLOBOB, DR. In "For the Ahkoond," he supplies the narrator with essential "Condensed Life-Pills."

"THE BOARDED WINDOW" (1891). Short story. (Full title: "The Boarded Window: An Incident in the Life of an Ohio Pioneer.") (Characters: Murlock, Mrs. Murlock.) In 1830, Murlock, a young pioneer, lives in a one-window log cabin with his loving wife in the forest near where Cincinnati later developed. His wife contracts a fever, and he nurses her tenderly. But after three days, observing her death, he grieves soundlessly beside her body, which, prepared for burial next day, lies on a table. While resting his head beside her, he seems to dream of a cry, feels the table shake, hears the soft padding of footsteps, and senses something falling to the floor and a scuffle. He seizes his rifle, fires aimlessly, and by the flash sees a big panther dragging the woman toward the window. In the darkness Murlock loses consciousness. Awakening to sunlight and bird songs, he sees his wife's corpse, with blood at her throat and a piece of the animal's ear between her teeth. The narrator got this story from his grandfather. When Murlock was fifty he looked seventy; he continued to live in his cabin, its window curiously boarded up, until he died. The place was thereafter considered haunted. Bierce was familiar with this Ohio region until he moved with his family in 1846 to a farm in northern Indiana. Bierce's earlier story, "That of Granny Magone," is partly a rehearsal for "The Boarded Window." It may have been slightly influenced by Edgar Allan Poe's "The Premature Burial" and is one of Bierce's most frequently anthologized stories.
Bibliography: Grenander, Miller.

"BODIES OF THE DEAD: ADDITIONAL INSTANCES OF PHYSICAL ACTIVITY AFTER DEATH." *See* "A Creature of Habit" and "A Light Sleeper."

"BODIES OF THE DEAD: SOME AUTHENTIC ACCOUNTS OF THEIR SEEMING CAPRICES." *See* "A Cold Night," "Dead and 'Gone,' " "The Mystery of John Farquharson," and "That of Granny Magone."

BOLTRIGHT, THE REV. MR. In "A Providential Intimation," he is a San Francisco clergyman. Stenner sends him $100 and advice to buy Sally Meeker, which Stenner thinks is the name of a horse. Sally Meeker, however, is a mine. Boltright invests in it, makes $25,000, but does not share his profits with Stenner.

BOOJOWER, MONSHURE DE . In "The Captain of the 'Camel,' " he is mentioned by Captain Abersouth as a character in a novel by Mary Elizabeth Braddon (1837–1915) that he is reading.

"A BOTTOMLESS GRAVE" (1888). Short story. (Full title: "A Bottomless Grave: How a Good Mother Reared Noble Sons and Daughters.") (Characters: Brenwalter, Brenwalter, George Henry Brenwalter, John Brenwalter, Mary Maria Brenwalter, Mrs. Brenwalter.) John Brenwalter, the narrator, is the son of an alcoholic inventor and his totally vicious, amoral wife. When the father receives a patent for a device to break open safes soundlessly by means of hydraulic pressure, his wife evidently engineers his death and explains to John and his siblings, including George Henry Brenwalter and Mary Maria Brenwalter, that it is better that their father is dead. Mrs. Brenwalter circumvents an autopsy by ordering John to "go and remove the Coroner," which he willingly does. Arrested, he is defended by the coroner's brother, an attorney who had quarreled with the coroner over a land deal. He now praises the prosecuting attorney, insults the judge, gets John off, and the next day disappears forever. Once John's father is buried in the back yard of the family home, the remaining Brenwalters must seek work. The mother opens a private school for criminals. George Henry plays the bugle in an asylum for deaf mutes. Mary Maria sells oil for flavoring mineral springs. John gilds gibbet crossbeams. Their tiny siblings, well taught, steal items from shop fronts. The whole family also decoys travelers into their cellar, nicely stocked with liquor and food, and bury them there. One night, while burying the mayor of a nearby town, Mary Maria sees their father, ten months gone but risen and drunk. Terrified, the Brenwalters all rush out, gather their possessions, set fire to the house, and decamp. The mother dies years later. After ten years pass in all, John sees fit to return, to gaze once more on his "beloved" father's face, and also to retrieve the man's enormous diamond ring—that is, if the dishonest police, who searched the ruins with spade and shovel, have found nothing more than bones. While digging at his father's grave site, John falls down into a drain, creeps through it, and emerges in the cellar area. Father must have been buried alive, fallen through, escaped, and—sensing he was not welcome at home—survived on food and drink in the cellar. John labels him a thief for taking "our food" and "our wine." Wanting companionship at last, he obviously blundered and let his survivors see him.

"A Bottomless Grave" is a variation of Bierce's numerous stories of patricide; in this case, the father's wife apparently commits the would-be murder. Critics should not make too much of Mrs. Brenwalter's hypocrisy in saying, like a pious Victorian, that her husband is better off dead. Bierce is mainly writing a grimly entertaining horror story, with satire unaccompanied by many chuckles, and lacing it with too many expressions of subhuman callousness; for example, the Brenwalters give the murdered mayor "the solemn offices of Christian burial," complete with gothically flickering candles. *Bibliography:* Davidson.

"LA BOULANGÈRE" (1889, 1911). Essay. The American actress, Mary Anderson, baked wonderful bread and gave her recipe to the London *Times.* Colonial women during the American Revolution baked bad bread, simply because they refused to use old-world recipes. Women on both sides of the Civil War continued the tradition of making bad bread. Bread-baking reform will mitigate America's current "dyspepsia." Mary Antoinette Anderson (1859–1940) was born in Sacramento, starred in Shakespearean roles, married Antonio de Navarro in 1889, and settled in England.

BOWLES, JEROME. In "Mr. Swiddler's Flip-Flap," he is to be hanged for murdering an Indian. His friend Swiddler gets pardon papers from the governor but is stopped from delivering them from Swan Creek, the capital, to Flatbroke, the scene of the execution, when Jim Peasley disorients Swiddler in the act of doing a somersault. Swiddler walks back to Swan Creek instead of proceeding to Flatbroke.

BRADING, JENNER. In "The Eyes of the Panther," he is an attorney in a village near a western forest. Irene Marlowe rejects his proposal of marriage on the grounds of her insanity. He doubts that her dementia was caused because her mother saw the eyes of a panther at their cabin window. But Brading then sees panther eyes at his window, fires his revolver at them, and kills Irene.

BRADY, WILL. In "A Story at the Club," he tells Dr. Dutton that he saved a man from being killed by a railroad train but could not inherit the grateful man's fortune because he, Brady, was already dead.

BRANSCOM. In "The Death of Halpin Frayser." *See* Larue.

BRAYLE, LIEUTENANT HERMAN. In "Killed at Resaca," he is an aide-de-camp under the Union Army general commanding the brigade in which the narrator serves as a topographical engineer. Brayle is motivated to behave with ostentatious and suicidal bravery because Marian Mendenhall, the love of his life, has sent him a horrible letter. In it she tells him that Winters said Brayle was cowardly during a battle in Virginia and that she could bear to hear of his death but not evidence of his cowardice. Brayle is killed showing off at Resaca.

BRAYTON, HARKER. In "The Man and the Snake," he is an athletic-looking bachelor, thirty-five and scholarly. He returns from a trip abroad and accepts the hospitality of Dr. Druring, a San Francisco scientist and collector of live snakes. In a guest room, Brayton reads about the hypnotic power of snakes, scoffs at the notion, but then sees snake-eyes staring at him. He crawls toward them, screams, and dies in a fit. Druring enters and discovers a stuffed snake, with shoe-button eyes, under his guest's bed.

"BREACHES OF PROMISE" (1888, 1911). Essay. Preferable to being awarded damages for a breach of a promise to marry should be obtaining recompense for a promise to marry, because real damage follows such a promise. A man liable for pain caused by breaking his promise should be paid for the joy he gave by making his promise. Since a woman profits plenty in being rid of him, he ought to be able to file a counterclaim. What does he get during courtship that she does not also enjoy? Let her prove any promise by validating it in writing. No such document means the man had no such intent. Wealthy men would be less preyed upon. Men "in love" could change their minds; such changes would always be improvements.

BREE, BARNEY. In "A Holy Terror," he was a saloon swamper and grave digger in Hurdy-Gurdy, California. He wrote Jefferson Doman a grotesquely slangy letter to the effect that when he buried Scarry (*see* Murphy, Manuelita), he found gold in the earth beneath. Bree died of alcoholism soon after.

BREEDE, CHARLES. In "The Suitable Surroundings," he committed suicide in his Copeton woods house, according to James R. Colson. The house, ten or so miles outside Cincinnati, has remained empty and is now considered haunted. Because of a pledge given Breede, Colson plans to kill himself four years later but does not. Breede's son-in-law conceals part of Colson's written explanation.

BRENTSHAW, HENRY CLAY. In "The Famous Gilson Bequest," he is the sheriff of Mammon Hill. He caught Milton Gilson stealing Harper's horse, for which he was arrested and hanged. It is discovered that Gilson willed his considerable estate to Brentshaw, provided no one within a period of five years could prove Gilson was ever a criminal. Brentshaw spends all he might have inherited bribing various people, including Harper, in an effort to prove Gilson's innocence. When Brentshaw goes to the cemetery and sees Gilson's ghost stealing ashes from nearby coffins, unearthed by a flood, he dies—probably shocked by his gullibility.
Bibliography: Davidson, Morris.

BRENWALTER. In "A Bottomless Grave," he is the father of John Brenwalter, the narrator. He is an alcoholic inventor. Seeing possibilities in his patented device to break open safes, his wife evidently tries to engineer his death. The family bury him, unaware that he is not dead, in their back yard. Unbeknownst to them, he falls into a drain, crawls through it up into the family cellar, and survives for a time on food and wine left there. Wanting companionship, he emerges one night while the family is burying another victim, and scares them into burning the house down.

BRENWALTER. In "A Bottomless Grave," he or she is any of John Brenwalter's two or more siblings too young to do more than steal items from shop fronts, as they are trained to do.

BRENWALTER, GEORGE HENRY. In "A Bottomless Grave," he is John Brenwalter's oldest brother. When times are bad for the family, he gets a job playing a bugle in an asylum for deaf mutes.

BRENWALTER, JOHN. In "A Bottomless Grave," he is the narrator. He, his mother, and his siblings, including George Henry Brenwalter and Mary Maria Brenwalter, engage in totally amoral and hypocritical lives of crime. They bury the father, not aware that he is still alive, in the back yard; rob and kill others and bury them in their cellar; and commit other awful acts. John later wants to retrieve his father's diamond ring; so he tries to dig up his corpse, falls into a drain, and thus learns that his father did the same and survived for a time.

BRENWALTER, MARY MARIA. In "A Bottomless Grave," she is John Brenwalter's sister. She is the first to see their supposedly dead and buried father in the family cellar. After this, times turn bad for the family; so she gets a job taking orders for Professor Pumpernickel's Essence of Latchkeys, with which to flavor mineral springs.

BRENWALTER, MRS. In "A Bottomless Grave," she is the mother of John Brenwalter, the narrator, and his siblings, including George Henry Brenwalter and Mary Maria Brenwalter. Mrs. Brenwalter, a heartless criminal, evidently tries to kill her husband and then sees to his being buried in the back yard of the family home. She continues to lead her children into lives of crime. On her deathbed years later and in a foreign land, she regrets only that they did not collect insurance after torching their house.

BREWER. In "The Middle Toe of the Right Foot," he is the brother of Gertrude Manton. She and her two small children were murdered by her husband, who then disappeared. Ten years later, Brewer, who is her heir, accompanies Sheriff Adams and King to the abandoned Manton home and identifies the footprints in the dusty floor leading to Manton's corpse as those of his sister, because of the missing middle toe of the right foot.

BRILLER, JOEL, ESQ. In "Jupiter Doke, Brigadier-General," he is the cousin of Brigadier-General Jupiter Doke, who gives Briller his proxy.

BRISCOE, SERGEANT WILLIAM ("BILL"). In "A Man with Two Lives," he is the sergeant at Fort C. F. Smith who tells Private David William Duck that Duck is dead and that Briscoe was a member of the party that buried him.

BROADWOOD, MAJOR. In "The Major's Tale," he is the narrator. He is on the staff of a division general headquartered in a civilian home in Nashville. To play a joke on ladies'-man Lieutenant Haberton, Broadwood and other staff officers dress Orderly Arman as a girl and lead Haberton to her in the office of Lawson, the adjutant-general. The ruse succeeds until an enemy shell bursts upstairs and Arman, startled along with the others, begins to disrobe.

BRONSON, ZENAS. In "A Psychological Shipwreck," he was William Jarrett's partner in the New York mercantile firm of Bronson & Jarrett. When it failed in 1873, Bronson, unable to endure poverty, died.

BROSKIN. In "Mr. Masthead," he was formerly the physician in charge of a mental hospital in Warm Springs, Missouri. Now he is a candidate for the Kansas legislature running against Johnson's brother-in-law, Jefferson Scandril. He identifies Masthead, the editor of Johnson's Claybank newspaper, as the father of one of his former mentally disturbed patients.

BROUGH, COLONEL. In "George Thurston," he takes command of the narrator's regiment when its general is wounded. Colonel Brough brings along his aide-de-camp, First Lieutenant George Thurston.

BROWER, ORRIN. In "An Arrest," he is convicted of murdering his brother-in-law and waits in county jail in Kentucky to be hanged. He slugs his jailer, Burton Duff, and escapes into a forest, only to be forced by a figure resembling Duff to return. When he re-enters the jail, he finds a group of armed men watching over Duff's corpse.

BRUNE, DRAMER. In "The Story of a Conscience," he is a former Ohio private with the Union Army who had a change of political convictions, became a spy for the Confederates, but was caught and arrested by Captain Parrol Hartnoy when on picket duty. Their conversation next morning in camp brings the following to light: Brune had been arrested in Virginia in 1861, was sentenced to execution, and was guarded by Hartnoy, who fell asleep. Instead of escaping and thus causing Hartnoy's execution for sleeping on duty, Brune woke him up and only later escaped. Hartnoy owes his life to Brune but orders his execution to proceed and then kills himself.

" 'THE BUBBLE REPUTATION' " (1886). Short story. (Full title: " 'The Bubble Reputation': How Another Man's Was Sought and Pricked.") (Characters: Eliza, Inhumio, Longbo Spittleworth.) Forward to San Francisco, Autumn 1930, 11:00 P.M., stormy. Employees of the gas works are on strike, because the manager's cousin subscribed to the San Francisco *Daily Malefactor*, a newspaper censuring a merchant whose in-laws were rich. Evidently to deflect public opinion, the *Malefactor* editor sends Longbo Spittleworth, a reporter he calls 216, to the Sorrel Hill cemetery to get some dirty news about Inhumio, its superintendent. Since doing so will gain a bubble of reputation for Spittleworth, out he goes, in slouch hat, black cloak, and jack boots, and armed with a poniard. A few days later the *Malefactor* features a full-page article with garish headlines about all kinds of hellish activities in connection with the Sorrel Hill cemetery.

"BUCKING WALRUS, THE." In "My Favorite Murder." *See* Ridley, Mrs.

BURLING, CAPTAIN. In "George Thurston," he is the officer in command of the narrator's mapping expedition. First Lieutenant George Thurston goes along as an observer.

BURNS, HAMERSON. In "An Unfinished Race," he is a photographer in Leamington. He, Barham Wise, and an unnamed man follow James Burne Worson, who has bet the unnamed man that he can run to Coventry and back. On the way, the three see Worson suddenly vanish. Back in Leamington, they tell about his disappearance but are not universally believed.

BUSHROD, ALBRO. In "Three and One Are One," he is a friendly schoolmate whom Barr Lassiter knew when both were boys near Carthage, Tennessee. After two years of service in a Union Army cavalry regiment from Kentucky, Barr returns home for a visit. Bushrod accompanies him and tardily explains that the Lassiter dwelling was destroyed a year earlier by a Union shell.

BUXTER, MAJOR-GENERAL GIBEON J. In "Jupiter Doke, Brigadier-General," he is a Confederate Army officer who says in his report that Brigadier-General Jupiter Doke's mysterious mule attack was really a tornado. He also exaggerates his casualty figures. Major-General Dolliver Billows mistakenly reports Buxter's death.

BYRAM. In "The Applicant," he is the small son of Deacon Byram. The boy finds the frozen body of Amasa Abersush in the snow on Christmas morning in Grayville.

BYRAM, DEACON. In "The Applicant," he is the chairman of the board of the Abersush Home for Old Men in Grayville. He and Silas Tilbody, its superintendent, evidently agreed that a certain old man's application for admission to the Home should be rejected. The old man turns out to be Amasa Abersush, the philanthropist who donated the Home to the town some time earlier.

C

"A CABINET CONFERENCE" (1900, 1912). Short drama. (Originally part of "Apocryphal Conversations.") John Hay* (secretary of state) calls Elihu Root (secretary of war) and John D. Long (secretary of the navy) for a secret little cabinet conference. They do nothing but drink, then leave. The press then enters and issues a false summary of what was said.

CAIN. In "Hades in Trouble," according to Nick, Satan's son, Cain is Nick's uncle on earth.

CALAMITY JIM. In "A Lady from Redhorse." *See* Jim, Calamity.

"A CALIFORNIAN STATESMAN" (1888, 1912). Essay. Henry Vrooman, a state senator from Alameda County, gets himself re-elected term after term by lugubriously stating that he is just about to die. Constituents figure there is no harm in voting him back in. Vrooman was a friend of Leland Stanford* and helped get him elected as a U.S. senator.
Bibliography: Norman E. Tutorow, *Leland Stanford: Man of Many Careers* (Menlo Park, Calif.: Pacific Coast Publishers, 1971).

"A CALL TO DINNER." *See* "The Religion of the Table."

CAMERON, GENERAL. In "One Kind of Officer," this Union Army officer orders Captain Ransome to fire on any troops in front of him. When Ransome asks for details, Cameron tells him he is not to know anything but is simply to obey. Cameron learns from his superior, General Masterson, that Cameron's flank has been reinforced by General Hart's troops. Ransome in foolish obedience fires on Hart's troops. By the time Ransome would like Cameron to clarify orders for Masterson's enlightenment, Cameron has been killed.

CAPTAIN, THE. In "The Stranger," he is the leader of a half dozen gentlemen adventurers out West. He explains that he found the bodies of Berry Davis, Ramon Gallegos, William Shaw, and George W. Kent.

"THE CAPTAIN OF THE 'CAMEL' " (1875?). Short story. (Original title: "A Nautical Novelty.") (Characters: Captain Abersouth, Old Ben, Monsure de Boojower, Preacher Jack, Pondronnummus, Angelica Thundermuzzle.) Captain Abersouth, formerly captain of the *Mudlark*, on which the narrator sailed earlier, now takes the *Camel* on a voyage of discovery toward the South Pole in 1864. They cross the Equator, and heat increases. They are becalmed for almost a year. Abersouth placidly reads stacks of three-volume novels. To move the *Camel*, the sailors have a bullock, taken aboard, push mightily against the mast. They tack due south. Food grows sparse; so they eat the ship's tackle, leather stuff, oaken, tar, sails, and finally Abersouth's reading material. Absorbing its contents, they begin to speak fictive diction—even "the technical slang of heraldry"—and act out fictive plots—including "broadsword combat." The narrator plays cards with the first and second officers, kills them when they dispute his winning hand, and tells Abersouth that he has assumed control of the *Camel*. When Abersouth complains that the temperature is 190°F and that the heat is warping the ship, the narrator replies that it is supposed to be hot in July in this latitude. The instant Abersouth doubts this explanation and sends the narrator below, an icy wind blows, snow and icebergs appear, and the sailors freeze and fall dead. Abersouth stares vacantly, murmurs a quotation about this delightful place where they are passing the rest of their lives, and also dies.

About the only thing to recommend "The Captain of the 'Camel' " is Bierce's implicit criticism of the suffocating diction of Victorian fiction. Bierce, who disapproves of hackneyed language, reports that Captain Abersouth's reading fare includes works by Ouida (Marie Louise de la Ramée, 1839–1908) and Mary Elizabeth Braddon (1837–1915).

"A CARGO OF CAT" (1885). Short story. (Full title: "A Cargo of Cat: A True Story of the Mediterranean.") (Character: Captain Doble.) On 16 June 1874, Captain Doble takes the *Mary Jane* out of Malta "heavily laden with cat." The 127,000 cats are not in bales but loose in the battened-down hold. The mate feels that they need water and pumps a quantity at them. The 6,000 cats in the bottom level drown, soon swell up, strain the *Mary Jane* into a dangerous shape because of "feline expansion," and cause planks at the water line to start. Before the narrator can suggest a remedy to his indolent captain, the cats explode through the hatch in a volcanic column.

It is cohesive because the cats have all clawed themselves firmly together. The ship's chaplain prays. For three days and nights the cats, holding tight, sing a hymn in seventeen octaves. Since all provisions are in the unapproachable hold, the men soon grow hungry and begin to draw lots to start cannibalizing procedures. But suddenly the cats spot southern Italy, in the shape of a boot. Wanting to avoid having it flung at them, the "songsters" release their collective grip, thud 121,000 strong back down onto the deck, spring spitting into the sea, and head for Africa.

"CATS OF CHEYENNE" (1887, 1911). Essay. (Original title: "The Cats of Cheyenne.") The sudden development of insanity in the formerly level-headed cats of Cheyenne is surprising. The epidemic started when Wyoming winds blew over dry grass, charged itself with electricity, and sparked up the cats. Cheyenne citizens get shocks when they shake hands. The musical yowling of Cheyenne cats may soon grow memorable.

"A CAUTION TO PROPHETS." *See* "The Hour and the Man."

"CERTAIN AREAS OF OUR SEAMY SIDE" (1888, 1912). Essay. (Original title: "Theft versus Blackmail.") Ostentatiously displaying wedding presents, together with donors' names, is a subtle form of extortion, and sneak thieves who steal such gifts deserve our praise. Repugnant also are showoffs who parade their coats of arms, boast of their fancy ancestors, and decorate their chests with military medals.

"THE CHAIR OF LITTLE EASE" (1891, 1892, 1912). Essay. We wrongly complained when the Shah of Persia recently boiled someone in oil. For a long while, all European rulers inflicted the same type of punishment. Nor was burning at the stake a "superior" form of execution. Death by electrocution may be excruciatingly painful, despite protestations to the contrary by physicians, who are as ignorant as toads. Criminals thus dispatched should have the courtesy to leave diaries detailing their pains.

"CHARITY" (1894, 1909, 1912). Essay. Although professional charity-fund handlers protest, there is much to be said for direct giving. True, professionals tap reluctant givers, but it does nothing to lessen the poor's hate of the rich. Christ never spoke of giving to the indigent through intermediaries. At the Last Judgment, "Munniglut" will not advantageously say he heard that A was needy and so he gave to B. The poor will always be with us. Best it is to give, sincerely and "with both . . . hands," to the nearest needy.

"CHARLES ASHMORE'S TRAIL" (1888). Short story. (Originally part of "Whither? Some Strange Instances of Disappearance.") (Characters: Ashmore, Charles Ashmore, Christian Ashmore, Martha Ashmore, Mrs. Christian Ashmore.) Christian Ashmore lives on his farm near Quincy, Illinois, with his mother, his wife, their two grown daughters, and their son, Charles Ashmore, sixteen. About 9:00 P.M. on 9 November 1878, Charles leaves their house to get water from a nearby spring. When he does not return, Christian and Martha, the older daughter, take a lantern to see what has happened. They follow Charles's tracks in the snow. But they simply stop, with snow ahead unmarked. No snow is falling. They find the spring covered with old ice. Four days later, Charles's distraught mother goes to the spring, soon returns, and says she heard Charles's voice, speaking distinct words which, however, she cannot recall. For months, not only family members but also others hear the same voice and identify it as Charles's, from a distance. Again, his words cannot be recalled. In time the voice grows more faint, until in midsummer silence follows. Probably the mother, now dead, is aware of her son's "fate." Bierce complicates "Charles Ashmore's Trail" by beginning it with the report that the Ashmores lived in Troy, New York, moved in 1871 or 1872 to Richmond, Indiana, and then a year or two later went on to Quincy.

"CHICKAMAUGA" (1889). Short story. (Characters: none named.) One sunny afternoon in autumn a boy, about six, strays from his plantation home into a forest. He has seen his father's military books and pictures, has made himself a wooden sword, and, having inherited bellicose tendencies from generations back, marches boldly to a creek bank. Scared by a rabbit, however, he sobs himself to sleep. He awakens in twilight and sees a swarm of men in a misty clearing with a few trees. The boy moves among the crawling mass. Some men are dead. Others have faces gouted with red like painted circus clowns that the boy recalls. He tries to ride piggyback on one creeping soldier, who tosses him off and snarls out of a mouth with a lower jaw missing. The men resemble silent beetles. The glow of a fire on ahead tinges them pink. The boy waves his sword and leads them forward. Detritus of war is all about. Footprints point to both an advance and a retreat. The boy heads for the fire, comes upon his own burning house, flings his sword into it, recognizes his surroundings, and turns dizzy. He comes upon his mother, dead from a shell that splattered her brains. The boy emits animal-like cries. He is a deaf mute.

Bierce took part in the battle of Chickamauga, in northwest Georgia and southern Tennessee. In this story he describes the terrain accurately, as a combination of vine-cluttered woods and open farm acreage. Bierce summarizes his military actions in an essay titled "Chickamauga" (retitled "A Little of Chickamauga," *San Francisco Examiner*, 24 April 1898), and, revised, in "Bits of Autobiography" (1909). In this story, Bierce has the boy duplicate General William S. Rosencrans's military error at Chickamauga when he incautiously advanced south from Chattanooga, by having his boy hero "commit . . . the common enough military error of pushing the pursuit to a dangerous extreme" and getting too quickly to the menacing brook. Some readers, revulsed by Bierce's gory descriptions here, have called him bloodthirsty. In reality, however, "Chickamauga" is as powerful an antiwar document as "The War Prayer" (1923) by Mark Twain. The terror here is ironic, because the child is unaware of danger. "Chickamauga" may have influenced an episode in George Washington Cable's *John March, Southerner* (1894), in which John, age seven, plays at killing Yankees with a bayonet on a stick.

Bibliography: Lawrence Berkove, "A Possible Influence of Bierce Upon Cable," *Markham Review* 7 (Spring 1978): 59–60; Davidson; Grenander; Morris; Eugene E. Reed, "Ambrose Bierce's *Chickamauga*: An Identity Restored," *Revue des Langues Vivantes* 28 (January–February 1962): 49–53; Eric Solomon, "The Bitterness of Battle: Ambrose Bierce's War Fiction," pp. 182–194 in Davidson, *Essays*; Glenn Tucker, *Chickamauga: Bloody Battle in the West* (Indianapolis: Bobbs-Merrill, 1961); Woodruff.

CHRISTIANSEN, CARRIE J. ("Norrie") (1874–?). Friend from Napa, California. Bierce met Norrie Christiansen in Angwin, California. The entire Bierce family befriended her, and he sent her to the normal school at Berkeley and also tutored her. When he moved to Washington, D.C., in 1896, she followed him, and he helped her obtain a teaching position in a high school there. He called her his "Ugly Duckling." Until he went south and disappeared, the two usually lived in nearby rooms in the same apartment building. The publisher Walter Neale,* their mutual friend, theorized that it was possible, though unlikely, that the two got married; if so, Neale adds, it would have been secretly so that young Christiansen could keep her teacher's position and salary as a hedge against early widowhood. There is, however, no evidence that the two were ever married. Christiansen was his companion, confidante, nurse, secretary, and well-chaperoned fellow traveler. Bierce sometimes visited her during her summer vacations at Sag Harbor, Long Island, New York. When Bierce asked Neale to accompany him and Christiansen on an extensive tour of Civil War battlefields, Neale declined, which both disappointed and offended Bierce. After Bierce's disappearance, Christiansen, who shared his safety-deposit box in a Washington bank, obtained a court order to have the box opened. At Bierce's request, Neale transferred to Christiansen copyrights of *The Collected Works of Ambrose Bierce*, published by Neale, together with some minor works he also published, and their royalties as well. But in 1914 he declined to pay Christiansen royalties, which soon dwindled to nothing anyway. She obeyed Bierce's request to destroy his letters to her. She did transcribe part of what was evidently the last letter he wrote to anyone (Chihuahua City, Mexico, 26 December 1913), and two others have survived. After Bierce's disappearance, Christiansen returned to California and settled in Napa. She ultimately transferred her nominal rights to Bierce's works to his daughter, Helen Bierce,* who was then Mrs. Isgrigg.

Bibliography: Grenander, McWilliams, Morris, Neale, O'Connor.

"CHRISTMAS AND THE NEW YEAR" (1877, 1883, 1884, 1911). Essay. Some aspects of our observing Christmas go back to heritages now meaningless. An example is Santa Claus, "patron saint of deceived children," whose name combines a Spanish feminine title and a German nickname. We wonder who will present what gifts. Children observe adults acting like idiots. Then comes New Year, with unkept, unkeepable resolutions.

CHUMLY, PERRY. In "Perry Chumly's Eclipse," William tells Ben and Thomas how Perry Chumly once climbed down a well to observe a solar eclipse, and briefly mistook the aperture above for the sun and a black man's face for the moon. When he realized the truth, he screamed, fainted, and drowned.

"THE CITY OF THE GONE AWAY" (1888). Short story. (Original title: "The Gone Away: A Tale of Medical Science and Commercial Thrift.") (Character: Badelina Fatti.) The unnamed narrator at age twenty-three leaves the drudgery of farm life with his "poor because honest parents," vows never to make an honest wage again, and goes to what is called "the City of the Gone Away." With a forged medical-school diploma, he sets up as a physician, kills numerous patients, develops a flourishing funeral parlor, a burgeoning private cemetery, some marble works, and a flower garden. He sends for his parents, and his father prospers as a fence handling stolen goods. Countless people bring sick relatives, unwanted spouses and children, paupers, lunatics, and the like to the narrator for quick treatment and disposal. The city profits and expands. The aldermen declare his cemetery a health hazard, plan a park there, and insist on moving his corpses elsewhere. The narrator accepts an exorbitant fee and plans to decamp. A solemn ceremony inaugurates the removal of bodies—robed mayor, hundred-voiced choir, sacrificial pig, apt sermon and dramatic digging for the first corpse. The narrator leaves. Later, he gets the rest of the story by letter from his father, written shortly before that man's execution. All through the day and well into the torch-lit night, frenzied citizens seek corpses but, alas, find none. It seems that the narrator buried none, but instead sold some to medical colleges while he processed others in his "extensive and thoroughly appointed soapworks." The renowned soprano, Badelina Fatti, once wrote the narrator that she liked his "Toilet Homoline."

"CIVILIZATION" (1878, 1889, 1891, 1894, 1909, 1912). Essay. We wrongly call a group uncivilized if its standards, often unknown to us, differ from ours. We have in our culture savagery identical to that in cultures we call uncivilized. Civilizations are built on the "blood and bones" of their victims. We kill our enemies. Cannibals kill and eat theirs. So? The best part of American civilization came from Europe, but we have created our own "errors and mischiefs." The English are our intellectual and therefore our moral superiors. Whereas their schools are superb, ours are "a means of dispensing formulated ignorance." English aristocrats may have their faults, but their excellent education enables them to handle their institutions well. It is patriotic of us but stupid to fault and attack civilizations different from ours. Our systems have produced so-called "free institutions" but a diseased "body politic" with "criminals and dunces" in control. "[T]yranny, insurrection, combat" will follow. History gives us reason to hope, but not by relying on any majority, because most people are "neither good nor wise." We falsely believe that later generations are better than earlier ones. But we know that savages camp on glorious ruins. Although our nation is heading toward oblivion, we need not hasten the process. The "unappeasable rich," "lazy workmen," "foul anarchists," "imbecile politicians," and "writers and thinkers unread" should heed this: "All things whatsoever ye would that men should do to you, do ye even so to them." Otherwise, this "pick-pocket civilization" will soon be quenched.

"CIVILIZATION OF THE MONKEY" (1893, 1911) Satirical essay. What we need is more civilization. The Chinese, Southern ex-slaves, persecuted Indians, and others resist our attempts. By studying the "sibilants and gutterals," we may learn to communicate with monkeys and get them into our civilization—with its military ingenuity, urban lights and noises, and sewer and other pollution problems. Next, we can enfranchise monkeys.

THE CIVIL WAR AND BIERCE. Shortly after the Civil War began in April 1861, Bierce enlisted, out of his home in Warsaw, Indiana, for three months of service with the 9th Indiana Volunteers. On 29 May, he left for the western part of Virginia (*see* "A Horseman in the Sky" and "The Mocking-Bird"). On 3 June he was in combat during the battle of Philippi. On 11 July he fought in the battles of Rich Mountain and Laurel Hill; during the latter engagement, he carried a buddy, with a mortal neck wound, to safe ground. Late in July Bierce was mustered out but re-enlisted for a period of three years, and was promoted to sergeant major. He returned to Virginia, on 3 October did reconnaissance duty at Cheat Mountain (*see* "A Bivouac of the Dead" and "A Tough Tussle") and in December was in the battle of Buffalo Mountain. Early in 1862, at Nashville, Bierce joined General William Nelson's 4th Division of the Army of the Ohio, commanded by General Don Carlos Buell. Bierce met William B. Hazen,* then a colonel serving under Nelson and commanding not only the 9th but also the 6th Kentucky and 41st Ohio. Hazen's unit was the 19th Brigade. On 6–8 April, Bierce was in the battle of Shiloh (*see* "An Affair of Outposts," "Two Military Executions," and "What I Saw of Shiloh"). The 9th (called "the Bloody Ninth") suffered the greatest number of casualties of all Union regiments involved on 6–7 April. On December 1, Bierce was promoted to second lieutenant. On December 31, he was in the battle of Stones River (*see* "A Baffled Ambuscade" and "A Resumed Identity"). In March 1863, Hazen assigned Bierce to brigade headquarters, as provost marshal (*see* "Parker Adderson, Philosopher"). On 25 April, Bierce was promoted to first lieutenant. In May he became an acting topographical officer on the staff of Hazen, who was promoted to brigadier general in June and placed in command of a brigade of five regiments (from Illinois, Indiana, Kentucky, and Ohio)—all part of a division commanded by General John M. Palmer, under Major General William S. Rosecrans's Army of the Cumerland. On 19–20 September, Bierce fought during the battle of Chickamauga (*see* "Chickamauga"), endured the siege of Chattanooga, and on 23–25 November was in the victorious battle of Missionary Ridge. In December he went on furlough to his home in Warsaw, Indiana. During this time he became engaged to Bernice Wright.* In February 1864, Bierce returned to duty. In May, his unit was part of the Army of the Cumberland, which moved to Georgia. On 14–15 May, he was in the battle of Resaca (*see* "Killed at Resaca.") On 27 May he fought at Pickett's Mill (*see* "The Crime at Pickett's Mill.") On 27 June, during the battle of Kennesaw Mountain, Bierce was shot in the head by a Confederate sniper (*see* "One of the Missing.") From July to September, he was hospitalized and then on furlough in Warsaw, during which time his engagement to Bernice Wright was broken. In late September Bierce returned to duty as a topographical officer in Hazen's brigade, which was then commanded by Colonel P. Sidney Post. In October, Bierce was captured by Confederate soldiers near Gaylesville, Alabama, but soon escaped (*see* "Four Days in Dixie"). On 30 November, he participated in the battle at Franklin (*see* "What Occurred at Franklin.") In November he designed and supervised the construction of a fortification at Pulaski, Tennessee. On 15–16 December, he was in the battle of Nashville (*see* "George Thurston," "The Major's Tale," and "Three and One Are One"). On 16 January 1864, Bierce was declared unfit for further military service because of his head wound and was discharged. He took a job on 19 January as a Treasury Department agent in Alabama (*see* " 'Way Down in Alabam' ").

The Civil War was without a doubt the most significant event in Bierce's life and provided controlling elements in his later life, his activities, and his best writings. In October 1913, old and sad, Bierce revisited intimately known battlefields, notably Chattanooga, Chickamauga, Stones River, Franklin, and Shiloh. He went on briefly to Texas, penetrated into Mexico, and disappeared from accurate historical record.

Bibliography: David Bosse, "From Maps to the Macabre: Ambrose Bierce as Topographer," *Geography and Map Division Bulletin* 144 (June 1986): 2–15; Paul Fatout, "Ambrose Bierce, Civil War Topographer," *American Literature* 26 (November 1954): 391–400; William B. Hazen, *A Narrative of Military History* (Boston: Ticknor & Company, 1885); Joshi and Schultz; Morris.

CLAVERING, GENERAL. In "Parker Adderson, Philosopher," he is a Confederate Army officer whose men capture Sergeant Parker Adderson, a

Union Army spy, one night. Knowing that he is to be executed, Adderson shocks Clavering, who hates the notion of death, by his serenity and wit. But when Clavering orders the execution to be by firing squad at once and not by hanging the next morning, Adderson goes berserk and grabs Clavering's bowie knife. In the ensuing struggle, the tent collapses on the two, and also on Captain Hasterlick, Clavering's provost marshal, who is mortally stabbed. In the end, Adderson is kneeling and begging ineffectually, while Clavering, also stabbed, passes away peacefully and with a smile.

CLEMENS, SAMUEL LANGHORNE. *See* Twain, Mark.

CLIPPER. In "A Providential Inimation," this is the name of Budd Doble's horse.

"THE CLOTHING OF GHOSTS" (1902, 1911). Essay. People have faith in their belief in ghosts because ghosts have long been believed in. But this is not logical. People used to believe the sun moved around the steady earth. People united in one belief are not credible witnesses. People who say that they have seen ghosts never say the ghosts were naked but in their regular clothes or in cerements. But we cannot believe that cloth immaterializes like ghost flesh. A ghost can credential himself only by appearing nude.

COBWEBS FROM AN EMPTY SKULL (1874). Collection of Bierce's *Fun* contributions, published under the pseudonym Dod Grile, with "The Fables of Zambri, the Parsee" revised and with one original item ("Stringing a Bear"). Bierce's first two books, *The Fiend's Delight* and *Nuggets and Dust Panned Out in California* had been published in London by his mercurial friend John Camden Hotten,* an unprincipled opportunist. *Cobwebs from an Empty Skull* was published by the respected George Routledge & Sons, London and New York. Its contents are a little less wild. William Ewart Gladstone, prime minister of England, read *Cobwebs*, and pronounced it a work of genius. An abridged edition, simply called *Cobwebs*, was issued by the *Fun* office (1884).
Bibliography: De Castro, O'Connor.

"A COLD GREETING" (1888). Short story. (Originally part of "Behind the Veil: Work for the Society of Psychical Research.") (Characters: Lawrence Barting, Mrs. Lawrence Barting, James H. Conway, Benson Foley.) In the summer of 1881, in San Francisco, James H. Conway of Franklin, Tennessee, presents a note of introduction to the narrator, Benson Foley, from Lawrence Barting. Foley knew Barting as a Union Army captain during the Civil War. At dinner one day, Conway tells Foley that he and Barting agreed that whoever died first would try to communicate with the other. A few weeks later when Foley meets Conway on the street, he is treated curtly.

Next day, Foley sees Conway again, is rebuffed again, and requests an explanation. Conway reveals that he saw Barting a few moments before he saw Foley those two times and was rudely treated. He therefore feels that he does not deserve Foley's continued "civility" since Barting has become unfriendly toward Conway. But Foley says that Barting died four days before and shows him letters he has received announcing the fact. Conway suggests that maybe the man he saw was not Barting, since the man lacked "Barting's mustache." Foley does not show Conway a very recent photograph of Barting that his widow included in her letter to Foley—it too lacked a mustache. Bierce presents "A Cold Greeting" in the form of a story "told by the late Benson Foley of San Francisco."

"A COLD NIGHT" (1888). Short story. (Originally part of "Bodies of the Dead: Some Authentic Accounts of Their Seeming Caprices.") (Characters: None named.) A Union sergeant is shot in the center of his forehead after the first day of the "battle at Stone River," and lies on his back with a probe, placed by a surgeon as a joke, through his wound. His steel-rigid body is covered with a blanket, which a fellow soldier later removes to use for himself and the narrator. In the morning the two find the sergeant lying curled up on one side, with his hands thrust, seemingly for warmth, into his jacket.

THE COLLECTED WORKS OF AMBROSE BIERCE (1909–1912). Walter Neale,* a publisher and a long-time friend, suggested in 1908 that Bierce assemble much of his writings for a collected edition, initially projected at ten volumes. Within two months Bierce had scissored and pasted enough newspaper items for five volumes. Neale issued a detailed prospectus of the edition. From the start, Bierce worried about what to include and how extensively to revise many of his selections. He was soon writing elaborate letters to Neale to complain about how the printers were mishandling his texts, especially with regard to punctuation. In 1911 Neale decided to add two volumes. Critics are generally of the opinion that the edition preserved far too much. Neale decided to print 1,250 sets as a first run. An "Autograph Edition," 250 in all, with the first volume of each signed by Bierce, sold by subscription for $120 per set. These sets were skillfully bound by a German named Walter Roache, whose shop was in New York City and whose material was unpolished, brown Levantine leather, silk lined and with ornaments and lettering in 22-karat gold. A "Half Morocco Edition," each volume slipcased, sold for $72 a set. A "Cloth Edition," also slipcased, cost $30 a set. Despite the fact that in 1966 Gordian Press reprinted all volumes in facsimile, an original set now commands a price in excess of $3,500. Volume 1 (1909), containing *Ashes of the Beacon* and much else, has 25 items, some of which are political satires, and others which are memoirs. Volume 2 (1909) contains *Tales of Soldiers and Civilians*, numbering 26 stories. Here Bierce presents in final form his war stories and his nonsupernatural civilian stories. Volume 3 (1910) has 42 stories from *Can Such Things Be?* These are supernatural yarns. Volume 4 (1910), *Shapes of Clay*, presents 284 poems, reorganized from the 1903 book, with some omissions, some additions (some from *Black Beetles in Amber*), and minor items under the subtitles "Some Ante-Mortem Epitaphs" and "The Scrap Heap." Volume 5 (1911), *Black Beetles in Amber*, has 246 poems and 2 verse plays. This volume reorganizes the 1892 edition, with omissions, additions, and a few poems from *Shapes of Clay*. Volume 6 (1911) includes *The Monk and the Hangman's Daughter* and 295 fables under these rubrics: *Fantastic Fables, Old Saws with New Teeth*, and *Fables in Rhyme*. Some fables are revised from the 1899 edition, and many new fables are added. Volume 7 (1911) is a revision of the 1906 version of *The Devil's Dictionary*. Changes in it are extensive and complicated. Volume 8 (1911), titled *Negligible Tales, On with the Dance*, and *Epigrams*, contains 29 items in all. Volume 9 (1911), called *Tangential Views*, contains 56 pieces. Some were originally unsigned editorials; others, new combinations of old separate pieces. Volume 10 (1911), titled *The Opinionator*, presents 50 items under "The Opinionator," "The Reviewer," "The Controversialist," "The Timorous Reporter," and "The March Hare." These are mostly snide comments on authors and their writings. Volume 11 (1912), called *The Penultimata*, has "The Shadow on the Dial" (partly revised) and 39 other pieces. And Volume 12 (1912), titled *In Motley*, is divided into "Kings of Beasts," "Two Administrations," and "Miscellaneous," with 69 items in all. The first section consists of revised and recombined "Little Johnny" sketches; the second, short dramas in verse and prose lampooning presidents William McKinley* and Theodore Roosevelt,* among others; the third, essays and brief fictions. In all, *The Collected Works* contains some 1,164 works—fewer than a third of all his titles, though in number of words considerably under that of his total wordage, if one includes his letters as well as scattered journalistic pieces. The most grievous omissions are his characteristic columns in the *Argonaut*, the *San Francisco Examiner*, the *San Francisco News Letter*, and the *Wasp*.

This collection, especially the *édition de luxe*, was derisively and, at times, witlessly reviewed, owing to the countless enemies Bierce had managed to make in the literary establishment over the decades. But even as dreadful reviews of the first volumes were spewing forth, Neale and Bierce pressed on. The worst descriptions of the contents of the volumes, despite their sumptuous exteriors, are contained in the following: "a depressing assemblage of worn-out and fly-blown stuff" (H. L. Mencken*); "except from the upholsterer's point of view, they are not books at all"; "potatoes set in platinum"; "that formidable mausoleum" (Wilson Follett); "pure piffle in plush pants"; "pure vanity" (Carey McWilliams); "turnips in Tiffany's window"; and "twelve-volume behemoth" (Richard O'Connor). Neale spent more than $40,000, including $7,500 in borrowed funds, on the lavish publishing venture; in under six months the loan had been repaid, and in time all expen-

ditures were recouped. Bierce invested $2,000 in Neale's company. Neale says that by 1914 he paid Bierce and "his assigns" $2,229.29 and an additional "considerable sum" by January 1915. Eventually, Neale sold all rights to the edition to the publishers Albert and Charles Boni.
Bibliography: Davidson, *Essays*; Wilson Follett, "Ambrose, Son of Marcus Aurelius," pp. 81–95, in Davidson, *Essays*; Joshi and Schultz; McWilliams; Morris; Neale; O'Connor; St. Pierre.

COLSTON, JAMES R. In "The Suitable Surroundings," he is a writer who has published some ghost stories in the Cincinnati *Messenger*. He challenges Willard Marsh, a businessman, to read, in manuscript, one of his stories in an eerie setting and chooses Charles Breede's deserted house as the place for Marsh to do so. Colston predicts that the story will kill him. Marsh reads it there and dies, thinking he has seen and heard a ghost. Colston's manuscript contains an explanation that Breede killed himself in that house four years earlier, that Colston plans to commit suicide also, and that he will haunt Marsh later. Colston is taken into custody before he can kill himself and is now in an insane asylum.

"COLUMBUS" (1892, 1911). Essay. Discoverers are treated too much like heroes. Columbus was an ignorant pirate, lusted for gold, and terrorized "harmless and hospitable peoples" he found. It does no good to say that Columbus was no worse than scoundrels of his time. Heroes of various epochs have been better than sinners around them. Columbus's expedition failed in its purpose, which was to find India. He missed by eight or ten thousand miles but died still deluded. Saying that he discovered America is also false. Lief Ericsson and his "Northmen" did so. The Columbia Exhibition, incidentally rife with looted appropriations, is a monument to our stupidity. The lips of every statue of Columbus should say, "I am a lie!"
Bibliography: Fatout; Morris; Foster Provost, *Columbus: An Annotated Guide to the Scholarship on His Life and Writings, 1750 to 1988* (Detroit: Omnigraphics, 1991).

"COMFORTABLE PENANCES." *See* "The Death Penalty."

"COMPULSORY MILITARY SERVICE." *See* "Warlike America."

"CONCERNING GHOSTS." *See* "A Ghost in the Unmaking."

"CONCERNING NOSES." *See* "Some Privations of the Coming Man."

"CONCERNING PICTURES" (1887, 1901, 1911). Essay. (Original title of one part: "Ambrose Bierce Says: A Picture Can Never Be Better Than It Looks.") Great artists, from the Italian Renaissance to modern times, have been adept in more than one field of endeavor. In a discerning artist's work, objects in nature display activities and expressions comparable to those of humans. Rich patrons and governments pay exorbitant prices for works of art later proved to be spurious. But the works of masters, which we selfishly covet and collect, are better than those of their imitators.

CONFEDERATE SECRETARY OF WAR, THE. In "Jupiter Doke, Brigadier-General," he receives an erroneous report from Major-General Gibeon J. Buxter.

CONWAY, JAMES H. In "A Cold Greeting," he comes from Franklin, Tennessee, to San Francisco in 1881, for his health. He presents a letter of introduction to Benson Foley from their mutual friend, Lawrence Barting. Conway tells Foley that he and Barting agreed that whoever died first would try to communicate with the other. Conway twice sees Barting on the streets and is rebuffed. Foley explains that at the time of those sightings Barting was dead. Foley lets Conway think that the person he saw, who was clean shaven, could not have been Barting, who wore a mustache. But not so. In his latest photograph, sent Foley by Barting's window, he also lacked a mustache.

COOLBRITH, INA (1841–1928). Poet and librarian. She was born Josephine "Ina" Donna Smith in Nauvoo, Illinois, the daughter of Don Carlos Smith, the younger brother of Joseph Smith, the founder of Mormonism and its prophet, and Agnes Coolbrith Moulton Smith. In 1846 Ina's widowed mother married a lawyer and printer named William Pickett. The family moved to St. Louis in 1851 and by 1855 were located in Los Angeles, where Pickett established a good law practice. Ina attended school only briefly (1855–1858) and published a few poems in the *Los Angeles Star* (beginning 1855). She married Robert Carsley in 1858, a minstrel performer and an ironworks official. When he foolishly called Ina a prostitute in 1861 and attacked her, Pickett shot him in the hand. Ina divorced Carsley, moved in 1862 to San Francisco, and began calling herself Ina Donna Coolbirth. In 1868 Anton Roman founded the *Overland Monthly*, of which Bret Harte* was first editor, with Charles Warren Stoddard* and Ina as coeditors until 1871. Meanwhile, Coolbirth was publishing in Eastern journals, joined the Bohemians of San Francisco, and became friendly with dozens of writers, eventually including Gertrude Atherton,* Mary Austin, Isadora Duncan, Jack London,* Edwin Markham,* John Muir, George Sterling,* Joaquin Miller,* and Bierce.

Coolbirth and Bierce first met in the *Overland* office in 1869. When he was courting Mary Ellen Day (*see* Bierce, Mary Ellen Day) in 1871, he organized card games in San Rafael, California, with Miss Day, Coolbirth, Stoddard, and Bierce himself. In print Bierce praised Coolbirth's poem "Commencement Ode" (1871) and identified her superb sonnet "Beside the

Dead" (1875) as her best. He lauded her poem "Our Poets" but said that she ought to have written a dirge instead, since California poets were all dead or should be (1883), and suggested renaming the periodical in which she had published it the *Warmed-Overland Monthly*. He turned sarcastic in discussing her "Unattained" (1883), wondering when after fifteen years of publishing she was going to "attain" success and commenting on "this dainty writer's tiresome lugubriousness." Once again, Bierce used his bitter pen to spoil yet another friendship. Coolbirth was saddened but probably not surprised. She joined forces with those who fancied that his criticism of David Lesser Lezinsky,* the San Francisco poet, had contributed to the young man's suicide.

Coolbirth experienced many misfortunes in the 1870s and later. Her stepfather, Pickett, disappeared. In 1872 she made a home for Calli Shasta, the natural daughter of Joaquin Miller, whose name she had persuaded him to change from Cincinnatus Hiner Miller. When her sister died in 1874, Coolbirth adopted the woman's son and daughter. Bierce did not increase Coolbirth's regard for him when he allegedly tried to seduce that niece in the 1890s. Coolbirth was a dedicated, underpaid librarian at the Oakland Free Library from 1874 until her dismissal in 1892 because of budget difficulties. She visited the World's Columbian Exposition in Chicago in 1893. After failing financially as a lecturer in California, she worked at the Mercantile Library of San Francisco in 1898–1899 and then part-time at the Bohemian Club until about 1907—the only woman there. She was distressed when Stoddard used her as a model for Elaine, a sad, droopy librarian, dubbed "Our Lady of Pain," in his 1903 novel *For the Pleasure of His Company*. Coolbirth worked hard on a literary history of California, only to have her notes, manuscripts, three thousand books, and furniture destroyed in the San Francisco earthquake of 1906. Her many friends' generosity enabled her to continue her literary salon, and in 1915 she helped convene writers for the Panama-Pacific International Exposition and was named California's poet laureate. Although her health worsened from 1919, she continued to write. Her four books of poetry, the most representative one being *Songs from the Golden Gate* (1895), are historically valuable. She is best remembered as an unselfish friend of writers having more talent than she, and as a hostess in whose home they were always welcome.

Bibliography: Morris; O'Connor; Josephine De Witt Rhodehamel and Raymund Francis Wood, *Ina Coolbirth: Librarian and Laureate of California* (Provo, Utah: Brigham Young University Press, 1973).

"COOL CORRESPONDENCE." *See* "The Failure of Hope & Wandell."

CORONER, MR. In "The Damned Thing," he conducts an inquest into the cause of Hugh Morgan's death. After hearing William Harker's testimony, the jury decides that a mountain lion killed Morgan. When alone, the coroner learns from Morgan's diary about an opaque but invisible creature that was the object of Morgan's fear. The jury foreman calls the coroner Mr. Coroner.

CORRAY, MARGARET. In "The Realm of the Unreal," she is the fiancée of Manrich, the narrator. He is hypnotized by Dr. Valentine Dorrimore into believing that she and her mother left their home in Oakland and visited Manrich in Auburn, and further that Dorrimore wooed her away from Manrich and beat him up in a cemetery. Once Manrich realizes that he has been hypnotized, he returns to San Francisco and later marries Margaret.

CORRAY, MRS. In "The Realm of the Unreal," she is Margaret Corray's mother. The two live in Oakland. Dr. Valentine Dorrimore hypnotizes Manrich, the narrator and Margaret's fiancé, into believing that the two women visited him in Auburn.

"CORRUPTING THE PRESS" (1874). Short story. (Characters: Henry Barber, Joel Bird, Sam Henly, Hooker.) When Joel Bird is running for governor of Missouri, Sam Henly, editor of the Berrywood *Bugle*, prints lies about him but then, worse, starts writing truthful stories about him. So Henry Barber, the narrator, is asked to bribe Henly into silence. A political committee raises $1,000, which Barber hands Henly in one clean note. All rejoice, except a man from Jayhawk named Hooker, who says that he is "dubersome." Barber says he will be the corpse at a fancy funeral if Henly is proved dishonest. Suddenly a mob is after Barber, because the *Bugle* reports that Barber tried to bribe Bird with $20, now donated to the orphanage. The committeemen believe that Henly is honest, as Barber has asseverated. Barber escapes into a forest outside Berrywood, to which he plans unselfishly never to return, even though if he did so he could look after his political and other matters. Bierce had a low opinion of most newspapermen, as proved by this story of an editor expensively bribed into silence and then lying in print about refusing a smaller bribe.

CORWELL, JOHN WHITE. In "Present at a Hanging," he and Abner Raiser accompany the Rev. Mr. Cummings to the bridge, where they find Daniel Baker hanged and the bones of the murdered Samuel Morritz.

COULTER. In "The Affair at Coulter's Notch," he or she is Captain Coulter's dead baby. Coulter finds both his wife and his baby in the cellar of their home, killed by the artillery fire he was ordered to direct there.

COULTER, CAPTAIN. In "The Affair at Coulter's Notch," he is a Southerner, slim, alert, and no more than twenty-three, serving in the Union Army as an artillery officer during the Civil War. His colonel is ordered by their newly arrived general to direct Coulter to fire at a rear-guard Confederate Army artillery position near a mansion. Although the enemy force is stronger, Coulter bravely does so. It turns out that Coulter's wife was a Secessionist living in the mansion and further that the general made advances toward her. Whether he was welcomed or spurned is not stated. Coulter's fire kills both his wife and their baby.

COULTER, MRS. In "The Affair at Coulter's Notch," she is the wife, a Secessionist, of Captain Coulter, a Union Army artillery officer. He obeys the order to direct artillery fire at their mansion. His doing so killed her and their baby. His general had, or wanted to have, an affair with Mrs. Coulter; complaints caused his transfer to the division in which Coulter serves.

"THE COUNTRY PAPER." *See* "The Rural Press."

"THE COUP DE GRÂCE" (1889). Short story. (Full title: "The Coup de Grâce: An Uncanny Occurrence in the Chicahominy Woods.") (Characters: Major Creede Halcrow, Sergeant Caffal Halcrow, Captain Downing Madwell.) Major Creede Halcrow is the commanding officer of a Union Army infantry regiment in 1862 or soon thereafter. The unit is on outpost duty a mile in advance of the main body. He orders Captain Downing Madwell to advance and hold a ravine until recalled. The two men have a longstanding and burning hatred of each other. So, turning sarcastic, the major says that the captain can order a subordinate officer to do the job if he is afraid. The captain replies that he will take personal command and, with equal sarcasm, expresses the hope that the major will come along, preferably on horseback so as to present a conspicuous target for the enemy. A half hour after the ordered advance, Madwell and his company are scattered in retreat, having suffered horrible casualties. Madwell finds himself alone, amid some trees, until he comes upon Sergeant Caffal Halcrow. He is Major Halcrow's brother, Madwell's close friend from their civilian days together in Massachusetts, and now a hideously wounded casualty. His abdomen has been torn open, his intestines partly exposed and evidently gnawed by swine, some of which are still nearby. In "giant agony," Sergeant Halcrow is pleading with his eyes for "the rite of uttermost compassion, the *coup de grâce*." Hesitating, Madwell observes a horse with its leg smashed by a shell and quickly steps up and shoots it with his revolver. Returning, he tries to shoot Caffal as well, but he finds that he has spent his last cartridge on the horse. With sudden resolution, he thrusts his sword down through the man's heart and into the ground, almost stumbling in the act. In his death throe, Caffal tries to pull the sword out with his right hand, until it bleeds—

just as three men approach. Two are stretcher bearers; the third, Major Halcrow.

Characteristically, Bierce structures this superb story in three parts: First, he describes the casualties that have resulted from combat action; second, he sketches the unstable relationships involving his three characters, in a flashback followed by the sarcastic exchange between the two officers; and third, he presents the mercy killing, disastrously observed. Irony weaves through the story. A burial squad must "tidy up." Figures of the enemy dead are inflated to make the victory seem greater than it was. Did Madwell let more of his men die than necessary to prove his major's order to have been a stupid one? Was the major's order motivated in the first place by a desire to blast his brother's friendship with Madwell, regardless of costs? Finally, why did Caffal grab the sword even as he asks for death? Bierce makes much of the fact that military protocol keeps Captain Madwell and Sergeant Halcrow, though friends, mostly apart because of their differences in rank. (*See also* "On the Uses of Euthanasia" and "What I Saw of Shiloh.")
Bibliography: Davidson, Morris, Woodruff.

"A COWARD." *See* "One Officer, One Man."

"A CREATURE OF HABIT" (1888). Short story. (Originally part of "Bodies of the Dead: Additional Instances of Physical Activities after Death.") (Characters: Dreyfuss, Henry Graham, Dr. Arnold Spier.) In 1865, at Hawley's Bar, a mining camp outside Virginia City, Montana, a gambler named Henry Graham has a dispute with a miner named Dreyfuss. The next day Graham invites Dreyfuss to have a drink. Unsuspecting, he agrees, but at the bar Graham shoots him dead. The vigilantes seize Graham, hang him in public view, and after half an hour lower him again. Graham prances away, head wobbling, tongue lolling, and blood frothing from his mouth. Many in the crowd scatter. But a bunch of men grab the rope, still attached to Graham; they are eager to complete the execution. Dr. Arnold Spier walks up purposefully, however, cuts the rope, and sees to it that Graham is placed on his back on the ground. The body, neck broken, is rigid enough in death. Spier explains that corpses, being "creatures of habit," will walk when placed on their feet but lie peacefully when made to lie down.

CREEDE. In "A Jug of Sirup," this is the last name of the tiny daughter of Alvan Creede and Jane Creede. The child asks if Eddy can play with the jug when it is empty.

CREEDE, ALVAN. In "A Jug of Sirup," he is a respected banker in town. He evidently purchases a half-gallon jug of maple syrup from Silas Deemer, the local merchant, three weeks after Silas has died. When he thinks about the purchase, he fears that he is insane. Later he waits outside Silas's store when a crowd mobs it.

CREEDE, EDDY. In "A Jug of Sirup," he is presumably the little brother of the tiny daughter of Alvan Creede and Jane Creede. Their daughter innocently asks whether Eddy may play with the jug when it is empty.

CREEDE, JANE. In "A Jug of Sirup," she is the wife of Alvan Creede, the respected town banker. He asks her where the jug is that he just bought from Silas Deemer, who is dead and buried at the time. She tries to comfort him in his evident derangement.

"CRIME AND ITS CORRECTIVES" (1881, 1892, 1894, 1899, 1900, 1903, 1905, 1909, 1912). Essay. (Original titles of parts: "The Bacillus of Crime" and "When One's Friend Is under Fire.") Essay. The essay begins with a revised version of "The Bacillus of Crime." The suggestion that incurable criminals, drunkards, idiots, and lunatics should be eliminated has caused criticism but seems to be gaining in popularity, since "mental and moral diseases" are advancing the world over. These unfortunates ought to prefer death to more suffering. We deplore roguery but socialize with rogues, especially rich ones, and forgive them in print. Remember that Christ felt kindly toward transgressors but flogged money changers. You cannot advise hating sin but not the sinner because the sinner commits the sin and sin is only an abstraction. Universal forgiveness will not work. Abandon your friend if he has caused the trouble he is in; his friendship disgraces you. " 'Principles, not men,' is . . . the noise of the duper duping on his dupe."

"THE CRIME AT PICKETT'S MILL" (1888, 1909). Essay. (Full title: "The Crime at Pickett's Mill: A Plain Account of a Bad Half Hour with Jo. Johnston.") Bierce begins by saying that certain events "are foredoomed to oblivion." Few know, he says, that "the name Pickett's Mill suggest[s] acts of heroism and devotion performed in scenes of awful carnage to accomplish the impossible." General William T. Sherman ordered it but ignores it in his memoirs. General Oliver O. Howard planned it but gives it only one sentence in his general account of the campaign. Bierce sketches the background of the battle. In May 1864, Sherman and Confederate General Albert Sidney Johnston were opposing each other near Dalton, Georgia. On 27 May Howard planned a rear or at least a flanking attack. General William B. Hazen,* Bierce's superior, was ordered to lead his "single sunken brigade" without support. Bierce pauses to ridicule Howard as Stonewall Jackson's inferior opponent at Chancellorsville, Virginia, and then praises Hazen, who by nothing but a look revealed his awareness that the order was a "criminal blunder." Hazen, with Bierce as one of his staff officers, advanced against masses of the enemy. Johnston later reported that "hundreds of [Union] corpses" soon lay within twenty paces of his "Texans." Bierce pauses to define a "dead-line" as the front row of such casualties, then continues his description of the slaughter, the wounded, the retreat, and the skulkers. He based much of this on Johnston's published account. Bierce concludes: ". . . just forty-five minutes had elapsed, during which the enemy had destroyed us and was now ready to perform the same kindly office for our successors." *Bibliography:* William B. Hazen, *A Narrative of Military History* (Boston: Ticknor & Company, 1885); Morris; Schaefer.

"THE CRIME OF INATTENTION" (1902, 1911). Essay. (Original title: "The Curmudgeon Philosopher.") The Curmudgeon Philosopher complains verbosely to the Timorous Reporter that egotism prevents people from paying attention to others. He recalls that when he used to make witty comments at a club or a tavern, fellows there either kept talking or turned away.

"THE CRIME OF 1902." *See* "A Possible Benefactor."

CROCKER, CHARLES (1822–1888). American financier. Crocker was born in Troy, New York, heard about the Gold Rush, and went overland to California in 1852. He settled in Sacramento (1852), and in due course was in charge of the construction of the Central Pacific Railroad (1863–1869). President of the Southern Pacific Railroad from 1871, he helped engineer its merger with the Central Pacific Railroad (1884). Crocker was one of the so-called Big Four,* the others being Mark Hopkins,* Collis P. Huntington,* and Leland Stanford.* Crocker handled construction and labor relations, Hopkins was the bookkeeper, and Stanford was a political liaison man. Huntington took the lead in lobbying Congress beginning in 1862 and continuously rearranging terms with respect to money and bond subsidies and land grants. Bierce denominated the four as "railrogues." Although his most prolonged fire was aimed at Huntington and Stanford, Bierce sided with a Chinese neighbor of Crocker's who declined to sell his land to Crocker. The magnate tried to get even by building a thirty-foot-high fence all around the Chinese cottage. Bierce pretended in an *Argonaut* column (3 November 1877) to sympathize with Crocker, whose nice place was jeopardized by lawless neighbors. But in "The Birth of the Rail" (*Wasp*, 21 October 1881), a satirical verse drama, Bierce presents Crocker as a road agent named Cowboy Charley. In two "Prattle" columns in the *Wasp* Bierce blasted Crocker in straight invective. In one, he says that Crocker inherited his streak of selfishness from an ancestor who dug Mount Calvary postholes (5 July 1882); in the other, he judged that the corpulent Crocker outweighed a recently discovered mushroom with a nine-foot circumference, even if his fat, belonging to the public, were subtracted (2 February 1885). Years after Crocker's death, Bierce referred to the man in a *San Francisco Examiner* item

when he theorized that corrupt rich men praise work as a virtue but really toil on only because of their avarice (25 July 1897).
Bibliography: Hopkins, Lindley, Morris, St. Pierre.

"CRUISE OF THE 'MUDLARK.' " *See* "A Shipwreckollection."

CUMMINGS, THE REV. MR. In "Present at a Hanging," he is driving past Daniel Baker's farm house near Lebanon, Iowa, one night, when the ghost of Samuel Morritz points to a bridge. Returning with John White Corwell and Abner Raiser next morning, he finds Baker hanged and the bones of Morritz in the ground beneath.

"THE CURMUDGEON PHILOSOPHER." *See* "The Crime of Inattention," "Fetishism," "The New Penology," and "Our Audible Sisters."

"CURRIED COW" (1874?). Short story. (Characters: The Rev. Berosus Huggins, Patience Huggins, Phoebe.) The unnamed narrator's widowed Aunt Patience has a small farm in Michigan and a cow named Phoebe that gives neither milk nor veal. Instead, Phoebe is a phenomenal kicker. She can put several domestic animals into the air simultaneously. Seeming to be blissfully chewing her cud, she once lashed out at a big, ignorant hog and sent him "beyond the distant hills" like a meteor. Aunt Patience requires her servants to curry Phoebe, which regularly kicks them entirely out of Patience's employment. The farm grows neglected. So she announces her desire to wed again. To avoid her, men quickly marry elsewhere in droves, some widowers even taking their mothers-in-law to the altar. Many a man swears he has wives in Indiana. Finally a funereally garbed Methodist minister, the Rev. Berosus Huggins, proves eligible and willing. One day after their wedding, Patience orders Berosos to start a two-year job of rendering the farm "ship-shape generally." When he is upbraided into agreeing to curry Phoebe, he securely fastens his seven-foot, cast-iron pump, which Patience has efficiently taken from his parsonage, to some barnyard planks and dresses it in his long frock-coat and low-crowned black hat. Phoebe saunters by, tacking this way and that, noses her way forward, and with lightning speed fetches the pump, which resembles a scarecrow, a furious, forceful kick. It does not move, but Phoebe spins about like a top, begins "to sway and wabble," and faints, legs up. Patience, puzzled and sympathetic, nurses her to seemingly "tractable and inoffensive" health. But then one day Patience approaches Phoebe with some turnips, and—"Gad! how thinly she spread out that good old lady upon the face of an adjacent stone wall! You could not have done it so evenly with a trowel."

THE CYNIC'S WORD BOOK. See *The Devil's Dictionary.*

D

"THE DAMNED THING" (1893). Short story. (Characters: Mr. Coroner, William Harker, Hugh Morgan.) The coroner, called Mr. Coroner by the jury foreman, is conducting an inquest into the death of Hugh Morgan, a hunter in a region of farmers and woodsmen. He asks William Harker, Morgan's friend, to testify. Harker is a local newspaperman and a would-be fiction writer. Harker reads from a prepared report. He and Morgan were hunting one day when they saw a field as it was being trampled by something invisible. Calling it the Damned Thing, Morgan shot at it, rushed at it, and was mauled and killed. Harker is excused, and the jury of seven votes that Morgan was killed "at the hands of a mountain lion." By himself again, the coroner reads parts of Morgan's diary, in which he wrote that he saw stars on the crest of a hill briefly blotted out by something invisible. He theorized that just as birds hear sounds unheard by humans, so certain colors are outside the spectrum of colors visible to humans. He feared the Damned Thing, of a color invisible to him.

Shortly after the death of his friend, the British poet and editor Tom Hood*, in England in 1874, Bierce was returning to his home in Leamington when he felt the spirit of Hood rushing past him in the dark. Memory of the eerie sensation remained with Bierce for years and perhaps inspired Hugh Morgan's uneasiness in the presence of "the Damned Thing." In the *San Francisco Examiner* (27 May 1894), Bierce first sarcastically defends himself against the charge that he plagiarized this story from Fitz-James O'Brien's 1859 short story "What Was It?"; Bierce goes on to express his belief that animals can be opaque but of a color outside the range of human vision.

Bibliography: Joshi and Schultz, Morris.

DAMPIER, MOHUN. In "Beyond the Wall," he is the unnamed narrator's melancholy friend. He tells the narrator that he fell in love with a gloriously beautiful young girl next door to the house he rented in San Francisco. They communicated only by tapping on their party wall. When she tapped again but only after a prolonged silence, Dampier sought to punish her by not replying. Later that night she died. Ten years have passed, and while the narrator and Dampier are talking, the tapping resumes. Later that night, Dampier dies.

THE DANCE OF DEATH (1877). Literary hoax, written under the pseudonym of William Herman. Ballroom dancing, especially the waltz, had become all the rage in San Francisco. So Bierce and a friend named Thomas Arundel Harcourt (?–1884) wrote the 131-page treatise, which purported to condemn such dancing as lascivious. Harcourt's father-in-law, a photographer named William Herman Rulofson, was distressed by his wife's addiction to ballroom dancing. He financed the publication and even provided the pen name. The book caused an uproar in San Francisco because of its titillatingly libidinous descriptions of controversial dance movements. Bierce, straightfaced, reviewed the book adversely and suggested that William Herman should be exposed and shot (*Argonaut*, 23 June 1877). One rebuttal, *The Dance of Life*, as by Mrs. J. Milton Bowers, defended ballroom dancing. It has been suggested that Bierce even wrote *The Dance of Life*, in order to keep up the fun; but this seems unlikely. Bierce did write his friend and publisher Walter Neale* that he was coauthor of *The Dance of Life*. It was popular enough to merit a second edition (also 1877), which included quotations from reviews.
Bibliography: Fatout; Joshi and Schultz; Morris; O'Connor; Vincent Starrett, *Ambrose Bierce* (Chicago: W. M. Hill, 1920).

DANZIGER, GUSTAV (1859–1959). (Full name: Gustav Adolphe Danziger.) German-born migrant to California. He was a rabbi, journalist, lawyer, dentist, diplomat, author, and translator. His writings include short stories, poetry, a film script, newspaper articles and columns, and unpublished works that include novels, a Talmudic history, and an autobiography (titled *All I Care to Tell*). He met Bierce in 1886 through a *San Francisco Examiner* reporter and soon wanted to be his collaborator. He followed Bierce when he was on vacation outside San Francisco in 1888, played up as an invalid to him, and soon charmed and impressed him. Bierce praised Danziger in the *San Francisco Examiner* and caused some of his poetry to be published there. Danziger says that in 1889 he read Richard Voss's *Der Mönch von Berchtesgaden*, prepared two modified and slightly abridged translations of it as "The Monk and the Hangman's Daughter," and showed both to Bierce. To eliminate what Danziger called "Germanisms" in it, Bierce rewrote the whole story. It was published serially in the *Examiner*, under the byline "Dr. G. A. Danziger and Ambrose Bierce." Danziger paid all costs, and the profits accruing from its newspaper appearance were to go two-thirds to Danziger and one-third to Bierce. A Chicago firm published the novel in 1892, but soon after collapsed and paid the authors nothing. Meanwhile, Bierce and Danziger argued over the newspaper royalties, and Danziger aroused Bierce's verbosely defensive ire by claiming that he had been swindled (*Examiner*, 8 May 1892). Still, Danziger persuaded two mutual friends, the poet Joaquin Miller* and the fiction-writer William Chambers Morrow,* to start the Western Authors Publishing Company. It was a subsidy publishing business, partly financed by a $500 advance from Bierce. Danziger published Bierce's *Black Beetles in Amber* (1892) but lost money and Bierce's friendship yet again, partly because the book failed but mostly because Danziger soon claimed that he sold copies at auction at a loss and had to borrow money to pay the printer's bill. Bierce was so outraged that he allegedly broke his cane over Danziger's head, kept the pieces, and called them a reminder of friendship. He also inveighed against Danziger in *Examiner* columns, saying at one point that the fellow had "a dual individuality like that of a two-headed calf . . . saint and sinner . . . a layman for lying and a minister for fighting" (23 July 1893). The success of Danziger's *In the Confessional and the Following* (1893), a short-story collection his publishing company issued, overshadowed Bierce's 1892 book, undoubtedly angering Bierce some more. Danziger tried, without success, to have the British-born painter John Herbert Evelyn Partington (1843–1899)—Bierce's close friend in San Francisco—illustrate his *In the Confessional*.

Soon after Bierce moved to Washington, D.C., in 1896, Danziger, then living in New York City, wrote seeking a reconciliation. Bierce replied that he was not interested unless Danziger had acquired a new personality. In 1900 Danziger tried to regain Bierce's admiration by trying to broker a reconciliation between Bierce and his son Leigh Bierce,* who was then on the staff of the *New York Morning Telegraph*. Danziger also briefly interested Bierce in having someone convert *The Monk and the Hangman's Daughter* into a New York play; the idea intrigued Bierce but bore no fruit. After a trip to Europe, Danziger returned to New York in 1902—to be greeted by a letter from Bierce asking him to explain some bills he had left for Bierce to pay, and also "to show . . . you are not an irreclaimable crook" (19 July 1902). Bierce never spoke or wrote to Danziger again.

In 1921 Danziger legally changed his name to Adolphe Danziger de Castro (de Castro being an ancestral family name). Two years later he wrote Francisco "Pancho" Villa, received a reply (14 March 1923), and says he went to Mexico and interviewed Villa shortly before Villa was assassinated (20 July 1923). De Castro published "Ambrose Bierce as He Really Was" (*American Parade*, October 1926), in which he reports that Villa said he turned against Bierce because he wanted to join Venustiano Carranza, Villa's opponent. In 1927 or 1928, De Castro paid H. P. Lovecraft, science-fiction writer, editor, and reviser, $16 to revise De Castro's "Clarendon's Last Test," a story from his 1893 collection. It appeared as "The Last Test"

(*Weird Tales*, 1928). In 1927 De Castro tried, without success, to interest Lovecraft in revising a book he was calling "Bierce and I." Lovecraft suggested a young writer named Frank Belknap Long, who agreed on condition that he could write a signed introduction. Lovecraft reluctantly read the revision and made some suggestions, gratis. The result, called *Portrait of Ambrose Bierce* (1928), has some historical value and presents Bierce's personality; but much of it is uncorroborated, erroneous, and suspicious, while even more of it is grossly self-aggrandizing. Danziger is especially inaccurate when he discusses Bierce's detestation of Michel Henry de Young,* the owner-editor of the *San Francisco Chronicle*.

Oddly, Lovecraft improved another of De Castro's stories: "The Automatic Executioner" (1893) became "The Electric Executioner" (*Weird Tales*, 1930). De Castro translated into Spanish an altered version of *The Monk and the Hangman's Daughter* but could not find a publisher. Innumerable later literary efforts also failed. Though surprisingly tolerant, Lovecraft called De Castro egotistical, loquacious, pompous, tedious, unctious, pestiferous, wily, and queer in letters to an aunt. No wonder Bierce was both attracted to and repelled by him.

Bibliography: De Castro; Fatout; Grenander; Lindley; McWilliams; Neale; O'Connor; Chris Powell, "The Revised Adolphe Danziger de Castro," *Lovecraft Studies* No. 36 (Spring 1997): 18–25.

DARNELL, MRS. In "A Baby Tramp," she adopts Joseph Parlow in Cleveland, only to lose him when he wanders off.

DAVENPORT, HOMER CALVIN (1867–1912). Political cartoonist. He was born in Silverton, Marion County, Oregon, the son of a politically minded farmer. His mother died when the boy was three. He grew up on the farm and then failed in some business ventures. He began drawing assertive, pen-and-ink cartoons for the Portland *Oregonian*, after which he succeeded with the *San Francisco Examiner* (1892–1895). Its owner, William Randolph Hearst,* assigned him to New York (1895), where his cartoons for the *New York Evening Journal* were popular and effective. A sharp, savage observer, Davenport commanded a high salary. His cartoons influenced voters during the free-silver campaign (1896), the Spanish-American War (1898), and the re-election campaign of William McKinley* for the presidency (1900). Transferring to the *New York Evening Mail*, Davenport shed Hearst's bias against Theodore Roosevelt* and helped his 1904 presidential campaign with the sensationally popular "He's Good Enough for Me," a cartoon showing Uncle Sam with an approving hand on Teddy's meaty shoulder. Also influential were his cartoons of Ohio politician Mark Hanna, often called "Dollar Mark," in a checkered suit full of dollar signs; his brutal depiction of the bloated, greedy, generic figure labeled "Trust" and "Trusts"; his cartoons of the railroad-magnate Collis P. Huntington* as bloated and ugly; and his portrayal of the San Francisco boss figure Sam Rainey as callous. One of Davenport's positive cartoons showed Admiral George Dewey, a Spanish-American War hero, pictured as deserving of a nation's gratitude. Davenport went to Rennes, France, in 1899 to attend the second trial of Captain Alfred Dreyfus, unjustly convicted earlier of treason, and to make sketches of various people involved in the Dreyfus Affair. Returning home, Davenport drew for the *New York American* and also lectured on the value of cartooning. He published several books: *Cartoons* (1898), *The Bell of Silverton* (1899), *Other Stories of Oregon* (1900), *The Dollar or the Man?* (1900), and *The Country and the Boy* (1910). Long a horse fancier, he received a gift of twenty-seven Arabian horses as a result of President Roosevelt's request sent to the Sultan of Turkey; Davenport then wrote *My Quest of the Arab Horse* (1909).

Bierce worked hand in hand with Davenport when the two were first in Washington, D.C. Later, they enjoyed convivial reunions with mutual friends in New York City and Atlantic City, New Jersey (1906). Bierce, who was also interested in the Dreyfus case, wrote an article critical of the French "method" (*San Francisco Examiner* and *New York Journal*, 17 September 1899).

Bibliography: Fatout; Ann Gould, *Masters of Caricature from Hogarth and Gillray to Scarfe and Levine* (New York: Alfred A. Knopf, 1981); William Murrell, *A History of American Graphic Humor*, 2 vols. (New York: Whitney Museum of American Art, 1933–1938); 2 vols. (New York: Cooper Square Publishers, Inc., 1967); O'Connor.

DAVIDSON, PROFESSOR. In "My Favorite Murder," he is an "authority in matters seismic" who avers that when Samuel Ridley's uncle, William Ridley, was butted high into the air and fell to the ground, the vibrations went "from north to southwest."

DAVIS, BERRY. In "The Stranger," he is the stranger who enters the hunters' camp and tells how Berry Davis, Ramon Gallegos, William Shaw, and George W. Kent were attacked by Apaches and driven into a cavern. Gallegos, Shaw, and Kent committed suicide. It turns out that the stranger is the ghost of Davis, who also died in the cavern.

"THE DAWN OF A NEW ERA." *See* " 'To Elevate the Stage.' "

DAWSON, EMMA FRANCES (1851–1926). Short-story writer and poet. Emma Dawson was born in Massachusetts, moved to San Francisco as a young adult, and continued to live in California. She supported herself by teaching school and giving piano lessons. Thoroughly aware of Eastern American and European culture, she combined *fin-de-siècle* poetic and prose effects in her fiction while basing her subject matter on regional topics and folklore. In *An Itinerant House and Other Stories* (1896), Dawson integrates ten stories by tracing several suicides in one often-moved haunted house back to a single terrifying incident. In "A Gracious Visitation," a sea-captain's widow is pleasantly visited by ghosts of former Russian settlers in San Francisco. Other stories present opium-induced visions in Chinatown, sisters attracting the Devil, the ghost of a suicide visiting his cold girlfriend, a ghost spiriting away her betrayer, and similar eldritch events. The San Francisco earthquake of 1906 destroyed most copies of *An Itinerant House*, which is now therefore a collector's item. Rumor had it that Dawson's death, which occurred in Palo Alto, was caused by starvation.

Inevitably admiring Dawson's work, Bierce made her one of his many protégées. Some of the stories collected in *An Itinerant House* first appeared in the *Argonaut* and the *Wasp*. Bierce reviewed the collection. (*See* "Emma Frances Dawson.") Dawson also published *Ballads of Liberty and Other Patriotic Verse* (1917). A reprint titled *A Gracious Visitation* (1921) includes an old "appreciation" by Bierce. Ina Coolbrith,* who knew Dawson, called her "Old Glory."
Bibliography: The Penguin Encyclopedia of Horror and the Supernatural, Jack Sullivan, ed. (New York: Viking, 1986).

"DEAD AND 'GONE' " (1888). Short story. (Originally part of "Bodies of the Dead: Some Authentic Accounts of Their Seeming Caprices.") (Characters: Reid, George J. Reid, Mrs. Reid.) On 14 August 1872, George J. Reid, age twenty-one, enters the dining room of his parents' home in Xenia, Ohio, walks toward a window, but falls down lifeless. His parents, two sisters, and a young cousin, who were all at breakfast, get him to a bedroom, fail to resuscitate him, send the cousin for a physician, cover the body with a sheet, and wait outside the room. When the physician arrives twenty minutes later, they enter the bedroom, but George is gone. His clothes are in a heap on the floor. His body's outline is visible under the sheet. The bedroom has only one window, which is locked, and only one door. After an investigation, George is declared simply "dead and 'gone.' "

"A DEAD LION" (1899, 1911). Essay. (Original titles: "The Dead Lion (Again) and the Living Professor" and "Ingersoll, the Dead Lion.") Essay. The late agnostic, Robert G. Ingersoll, is here defended first against the attempted rebuttal by an unnamed editor whose illogical criticism resembles the sincere braying of "a wild ass," and then against the more temperate, better expressed, but disappointing strictures of Harry Thurston Peck, a professor of Latin and a publishing scholar, though a "not very profound thinker." Peck concedes that Ingersoll was of decent character but wrongly feels that personal morality is based exclusively on pronouncements in the Bible. He is also wrong to criticize Ingersoll for tearing religion down without building something else up, wrong to criticize Ingersoll's style and ignore

his message, wrong to accuse him of lecturing for money, and surely wrong
to wonder whether, when dying, Ingersoll repented too tardily.

"THE DEAD LION (AGAIN) AND THE LIVING PROFESSOR." *See*
"A Dead Lion."

DEATH, BIERCE'S. Bierce was self-dramatizing much of the time. Circumstances surrounding his death make that final event no less dramatic and
mysterious. Facts and speculations about it are frequent. On 10 September
1913 Bierce, in Washington, D.C., wrote to Lora Bierce, the wife of his
brother Albert Bierce's son Carleton ("Carlt") Bierce, that he planned to go
to Mexico and "probably to South America." On the same day, he wrote a
California friend, Josephine McCrackin, of his plan to go to Mexico and
South America, adding, "if I can get through [Mexico] without being stood
up against a wall and shot as a Gringo." Then he noted, "But that is better
than dying in bed, is it not?" On 1 October he wrote Lora that he regarded
being shot in Mexico as "a pretty good way to depart this life. It beats old
age, disease, or falling down the cellar stairs. To be a Gringo in Mexico—
ah, that is euthanasia!" Bierce then followed a benedictory visit to several
Civil War battlefields by proceeding to New Orleans (23 October). A journalist for the *States* in that city, which Bierce loved, interviewed him and
reported the following: Bierce, dressed in black and ramrod straight, said
that he planned to observe the fighting in Mexico, to ascertain whether
Americans are in much danger there; to avoid risks; to travel by horseback
southwest; and then to sail to South America, cross the continent via the
Andes if he could, and return home. He said that his trip might take some
years. When pressed, he turned wistful and added that though old and in-
active he might turn to writing again later. On 6 November he wrote a final
letter to Lora, mailed from Laredo, Texas, concluding that he would not be
there long enough for her to write him, and closing thus: "Guess it doesn't
matter much."

Once in Mexico, Bierce, according to the diary of his close friend Carrie
Christiansen,* went twenty or thirty miles south of Juarez (13 November)
and then wrote her a final time from Chihuahua (26 December) to say that
he was leaving the next day for Ojinaga, Mexico, immediately south of Pre-
sidio, Texas, and would be traveling with the revolutionary forces of Pancho
Villa, who was cordial toward him and had furnished him with credentials.
M. E. Grenander, a distinguished Bierce scholar and editor, concludes that
Bierce was most probably killed at the Battle of Ojinaga (11 January 1914).
Other theorists, however, disagree. Did Bierce act as a spy to report to
friends in official intelligence circles in Washington, D.C., on possible military actions by Japanese and Mexican forces against the United States or a
possible inimical German plot against the Panama Canal, then nearing com-
pletion? An authority on Frederick Albert Mitchell-Hedges,* a swashbuck-

ling explorer-scientist, asserts that Mitchell-Hedges and Bierce were fellow espionage agents, and that when the pair finished spying they proceeded together to British Honduras, whereupon Bierce stayed on alone—and disappeared from record. Still another theory, first advanced by Walter Neale,* Bierce's friend and publisher, suggests that Bierce wrote a good deal of nonsense about penetrating into Mexico, with all of its dire dangers, only to conceal his true plan, which was to disappear, whether from Mexico or Texas, proceed to the Grand Canyon, and commit suicide in a remote spot therein. Joe Nickell, a private detective, has sifted through all available evidence and also favors the suicide explanation.

Bibliography: Fatout; Grenander; M. E. Grenander, "Ambrose Bierce," pp. 28–39, in *Nineteenth-Century Western American Writers*, Robert L. Gale, ed. *Dictionary of Literary Biography*, vol. 186 (Detroit: Gale Research, 1997); Carey McWilliams, "The Mystery of Ambrose Bierce," *American Mercury* 22 (March 1931): 330–337; Sibley Morrill, *Ambrose Bierce, F. A. Mitchell-Hedges and the Crystal Skull* (San Francisco: Cadleon Press, 1972); Morris; Neale; Joe Nickell, *Ambrose Bierce Is Missing and Other Historical Mysteries* (Lexington: University Press of Kentucky, 1992).

"THE DEATH OF HALPIN FRAYSER" (1891). Short story. (Characters: Myron Bayne, Frayser, Frayser, Halpin Frayser, Holker, Jaralson, Larue, Catherine Larue.) One midsummer day Halpin Frayser gets lost while hunting in the Napa Valley, falls asleep dreamlessly, and suddenly wakes up uttering the name "Catherine Larue"—a name unknown to him. Asleep again, he dreams of walking on an evil-seeming road; he comes upon a pool, dust in his path, and trees, all loaded with blood caused by some puzzling crime or sin that he feels he committed. He vainly shouts, tries to write a penitent confession in his notebook with a blood-dipped twig, and hears a loon-like laugh. He tries but fails to appeal to benign powers, drops his notebook, and suddenly looks into his dead mother's eyes.

It seems that Halpin Frayser worried his parents, when they were all living together in Nashville, Tennessee. After Halpin completed law studies, his father wanted him to go into politics, and his mother, who spoiled the lad, had to conceal the fact that she liked the idea that her son wanted to be a poet like Myron Bayne, one of his maternal great-grandfathers, a published poet in Tennessee back in colonial times. Son and mother, whom he affectionately called Katy, enjoyed a singularly close relationship. When Halpin suddenly said that he was going to California on a legal case, his mother dreamed that Myron half approved the move but also dreamed that her son was choked. She thought of accompanying him for treatment in medicinal springs in California for her supposedly pain-stiffened fingers. But she remained at home with her rather indifferent husband. Once in San Francisco, Halpin was shanghai-ed, spent six years in the South Pacific, and returned to the Mount St. Helena region with another sailor, to await news and money from home. Then he went out alone—to hunt, camp, and dream.

Now he stares, as in a dream, at something like, and unlike, his mother—a body without a soul. The apparition charges at him; they grapple; Halpin feels choked, falls back, and dreams that he is dead. Morning comes. Earlier the previous afternoon a ghostly, foggy cloud appeared on the western slope of Mount St. Helena. Now, Holker, a Napa deputy sheriff, and Jaralson, a San Francisco detective, are seeking a man named Branscom, wanted for cutting the throat of his wife, whose body is buried in the White Church graveyard outside the town of St. Helena. A reward has been posted for Branscom, whose real name is something else—perhaps Pardee, Holker vaguely recalls. Jaralson says he theorized that the killer was hiding near his wife's grave, went there, and found the man, who, however, chased him away with a weapon. Returning armed, Holker and Jaralson now find the graveyard, abandoned and decayed, and also spot the corpse of a horribly strangled man. They identify him as Halpin Frayser by his notebook, which contains a funeral narrative poem. Jaralson remarks that it resembles the dismal poetry of Myron Bayne. When they find a rotting headboard with the name Catherine Larue on it, Holker recalls that Branscom's real name was Larue and that his murdered wife's maiden name was Frayser. Out of the distant fog comes "a low, deliberate, soulless laugh."

"The Death of Halpin Frayser" is one of Bierce's most intriguing stories. It has long puzzled and confounded critics. It is a story of the supernatural but with facts not explainable by blaming anything supernatural. Halpin's dream is composed of horrifying symbols. Or is he is awake and thus the victim of a visitation? Did Halpin, possibly a throwback to Bayne, write poetry? That particular poem? If so, when? Of what significance is Bierce's careful statement, given during his discussion of the early "consanguinity" of Halpin and his "Katy," about "the dominance of the sexual element in all the relations of life"? In describing the mountain and forest scenes, Bierce once again shows his military topographical expertise. (*See also* "Visions of the Night.")

Bibliography: Grenander; William Bysshe Stein, "Bierce's 'The Death of Halpin Frayser:' The Poetics of Gothic Consequences," *Emerson Society Quarterly* 18 (1972): 115–122.

"THE DEATH PENALTY" (1888, 1895, 1897, 1900, 1909, 1912). Essay. (Original titles of parts: "Blathering Blavatskians" and "Comfortable Penances.") Bierce begins by asserting that "a life for a life" is a "just principle." This admonition to would-be killers must not be a mere threat. Where executions are swift, murder rates are down. "A man's first murder is his crime, his second is ours." A hanging deters the hanged. Imprisoned killers can kill inside their prisons. Executions do not cause bloodthirstiness in society. The eye-for-an-eye option is justice, not revenge. If execution is called illogical because it does not restore the life of a murdered victim, life imprisonment is also illogical; it does not restore the victim's life either. If people can legally defend themselves against a murderous attacker, society must also defend them. God doubtless chose to make us aware of good by knowledge of evil; hence some crime is probably good for society, because awareness of it creates "warm and elevated sentiments" in us. Modern women oppose the death penalty because they are convinced that "whatever is is wrong." Prisons are more comfortable than some criminals' homes. If we make executions more pleasant—say, by rose-leaf smothering or poisoning by rich foods—would-be suicides may be tempted to murder, get caught, and be gently dispatched. Ignorance, poverty, and hatred of authority were more prevalent in ages past and hence generated more horrible forms of execution than are needed now. Authorities and criminals alike, then, were more unreasonable and barbarous than we are. But we must watch out, because lax detective work, low conviction rates, and mild penalties all add up to trouble. Bierce imagines visiting the world a century hence. A warden shows him one of twelve prisons, each housing honest citizens leading happy lives, thus protected from rogues outside, who—as always—manage commerce. Bierce advances to the gate, wanting in, and turns to ask the warden. But he has disappeared, as has the prison. All about is a level, sandy desert.

"DECADENCE OF THE AMERICAN FOOT" (1892, 1911). Essay. (Original title: "The Decline and Fall of the American Foot.") Modern science points out that the human foot, with toes, arch, sole, is not proof of "an intelligent Designer," since bears' feet and horses' hooves serve their mobile owners well. Furthermore, human feet resemble monkeys'. If the scientist and the "religionist" will compromise, one can conclude that human feet were designed by God for our "arboreal future." But American feet will be left behind, since we have surrendered walking to the streetcar and the elevator. Soon we may have "the moving sidewalk" and "tubes" for sucking us about. Rural inhabitants will lose their feet more slowly, but American inventiveness will eventually cause their disappearance in time.

De CASTRO, ADOLPHE. This became the pen name of Gustav Danziger,* legally changed in full to Adolphe Danziger de Castro in 1921. Danziger was a friend of Bierce's for a while. He called himself Adolphe de Castro when he wrote "Ambrose Bierce as He Really Was," *American Parade* 1 (October 1926): 28–44 and *Portrait of Ambrose Bierce* (New York: Century, 1929).

"THE DECAY OF THE NOSE." *See* "Some Privations of the Coming Man."

"THE DECLINE AND FALL OF THE AMERICAN FOOT." *See* "Decadence of the American Foot."

DEEMER. In "A Jug of Sirup," this is the last name of either of the two grown daughters of Silas Deemer and his wife. The family lives together in Hillbrook until his death.

DEEMER, MRS. SILAS. In "A Jug of Sirup," she is the wife of Silas Deemer, the hard-working merchant. The couple, with their two grown daughters, live together in Hillbrook above his store. When he dies, a merchant buys his goods *en bloc*, and the three women leave town.

DEEMER, SILAS. In "A Jug of Sirup," he was a town merchant who worked conscientiously, day and night, and lived with his wife and two grown daughters above his store in Hillbrook. He dies on 16 July 1853 and is soon buried. His goods are sold, and his family leaves town. But his ghost continues to mind the store, even selling a half-gallon jug of maple syrup three weeks later to Alvan Creede, the town banker. Deemer is calmly looking over his salesbook as a frightened mob of citizens storms his store and creates a riot inside. His "fixity and invariety" cause the town humorist to call him "Old Ibidem."

DELUSE, HERMAN. In "The Isle of Pines," he has just died, on 4 November 1867, in his four-room house near Gallipolis, Ohio. He is rumored to have been a pirate in possession of gold from the Spanish Main. Greedy neighbors dig around his house but find nothing. On 10 November the Rev. Henry Galbraith says that he stopped at Deluse's house, not knowing the man was dead, stayed there overnight, and saw him vainly looking for something evidently while sleepwalking. The next night, Galbraith, his son, and a friend named Robert Mosely Maren enter the house and something kills young Galbraith, who is found with a bag of gold.

DEMENT, MARY JANE. In "A Lady from Redhorse," she is staying in a hotel in Coronado. While there, she writes five letters to Irene. In them she reveals that she is physically unattractive but has inherited a million dollars from her father, Calamity Jim, who struck it rich in the mining fields. She knows Jack Raynor, would have married him but for his being too short, is happy that Jack persuaded Barritz to go from Vienna to Coronado, falls in love with Barritz, and is delighted when Barritz turns out to be the man whom they called Dumps in the mining field and who is now to be called James. The two love each other. Bierce may have named Mary Jane Dement as he did to suggest her manifest dementia.

"THE DEMON'S DICTIONARY." See *The Devil's Dictionary*.

DENNEKER. In "Staley Fleming's Hallucination," he is the author of *Meditations*, in which Dr. Halderman, while treating Staley Fleming in Fleming's home, is reading about the interpenetration of spirit and flesh when a thud upstairs prompts him to look in on Fleming. In "A Psychological Shipwreck," both Janette Harford and Gordon Doyle, separately, read in Denneker's *Meditations* about kindred souls leaving their respective bodies and going along intersecting paths.

"DETHRONEMENT OF THE ATOM" (1903, 1911). Essay. (Original title: "An Infant Crying for the Light.") Essay. As science advances, it destroys illusions. Darwinism did so. Now "depedestaled," the atom has been divided into tiny electrons. In the absence of scientific explanations about all this, we "believe without comprehending."

"THE DEVIL AT YERBA BUENA." *See* "The Discomfited Demon."

THE DEVIL'S DICTIONARY (1881, 1906, 2000). Collection of definitions. Bierce published definitions of words beginning with "A," in what he called "The Demon's Dictionary" in the *San Francisco News Letter* (11 December 1875). Then the real start began, with more "A" words, in "The Devil's Dictionary" in the *Wasp* (5 March 1881). His intention with these definitions was to be witty, not humorous, and savagely witty at that, but also to improve his readers. In the process, he scorned the misguided beliefs and actions of foolish, hypocritical, and villainous people for their conceited, deceptive, fraudulent, immoral, intolerant, phony, selfish, sinful, smug, stupid, and trivial thoughts and conduct. He employed a variety of styles—corny, dialectal, homiletic, pedantic, poetic, preachy, scholarly, scientific, and terse. The *Wasp* entries ended with "L" words (14 August 1886); Bierce left the paper later in 1886. Joining the *San Francisco Examiner*, owned by William Randolph Hearst,[*] in 1887, Bierce resumed in it with more "L" words, this time under the title "The Cynic's Dictionary" (4 September 1887–29 April 1888), a title he disliked.

Bierce published no more definitions until more "A" words, under the same title "The Cynic's Dictionary," appeared in Hearst's *New York American* (26 June 1904) and were repeated a week or so later in the *Examiner*. Under the same title and in the *American* more "A" words followed (9 July 1904). Bierce jumped to "M" (23 July 1904) and so on steadily into "P" (*American*, 27 January 1905), most entries being repeated in the *Examiner*. Bierce assembled his various definitions, through "L," for *The Cynic's Word Book* (published October 1906), a title he also disliked. Between manuscript submission and publication, Bierce offered more "Cynic's Dictionary" and "Cynic's Word Book" definitions in the *American* and the *Examiner* (22 February to 11 April, 30 May to late July 1906).

The Devil's Dictionary, the title Bierce preferred, became volume 7 (1911) of *The Collected Works of Ambrose Bierce* (12 vols., 1909–1912), published by his friend Walter Neale.[*] For it, Bierce revised *The Cynic's Word Book* entries, included unused entries from newspaper columns, and completed entries through "Z." *The Devil's Dictionary* has proved more popular than anything else Bierce ever wrote, with the exception of five or six of his most compelling Civil War stories. The reader's response to his devilish definitions, typically, combines howls of offended outrage and wicked pleasure. The book bitterly targets organized religion, idealism, love and marriage, commerce, education, political corruption, science, philosophy, literature, and much else. Bierce's well-sharpened weapons are the grotesque joke, the sadistic practical joke, and black humor. The lexicon can become dreary if read at one sitting or even in large doses. It is better to dip into it and be shocked at every turn of Bierce's rhetorical knife.

Any reader can select a hundred favorite definitions. Exigencies of space here, however, permit only thirty or so examples, many chosen for their brevity, while others are incompletely quoted here. "Abdication, *n.* [1.] An act whereby a sovereign attests his sense of the high temperature of the throne. . . . [2.] The surrender of a crown for a cowl, in order to compile the shin-bones and toe-nails of saints." "Alone, *adj.* In bad company." "Bachelor, *n.* A man whom women are still sampling." "Beauty: *n.* The power by which a woman charms a lover and terrifies a husband." "Birth, *n.* The first and direst of all disasters." "Bore, *n.* A person who talks when you wish him to listen." "Bride, *n.* A woman with a fine prospect of happiness behind her." "Brute, *n.* See *Husband.*" "Cribbage, *n.* A substitute for conversation among those to whom nature has denied ideas. See *EUCHRE, PEDRO, SEVEN-UP, etc.*" "Cynic. *n.* A blackguard whose faulty vision sees things as they are, not as they ought to be." "Dad, *n.* A father whom his vulgar children do not respect." "Dance, *v.i.* To leap about to the sound of tittering music, preferably with arms about your neighbor's wife or daughter." "Ghost, *n.* The outward and visible sign of an inward fear." "Grapeshot. *n.* An argument which the future is preparing in answer to the demands of American Socialism." "Guillotine, *n.* A machine which makes a Frenchman shrug his shoulders with good reason." "Hers, *pro.* His." "History, *n.* An account mostly false, of events mostly unimportant, which are brought about by rulers mostly knaves, and soldiers mostly fools." "Husband, *n.* One who, having dined, is charged with the care of the plate." "Insane, *n.* Addicted to the conviction that others are insane." "Lacteal Fluid, *n.* (*Reporterese.*) Milk." "Lawyer, *n.* One skilled in circumvention of the law." "Nudity, *n.* That quality in art which is most painful to the prurient." "Once, *adv.* Enough." "Opportunity, *n.* A favorable occasion for grasping a disappointment." "Peace, *n.* In international affairs, a period of cheating between two periods of fighting." "Pleasure, *n.* [1.] The least hateful form of dejection. [2.] An emotion engendered by something advantageous to one's self or disastrous to others." "Positive, *adj.* Mistaken at the top of one's voice." "Promise, *n.* A form of incantation to conjure up a hope that is to be exorcised later by inattention." "Really, *adv.* Apparently." "Religion, *n.* A daughter of Hope and Fear, explaining to ignorance the nature of the Unknowable." "Senate, *n*. A body of elderly gentlemen charged with high duties and misdemeanors." "Truce, *n*. Friendship." "Truthful, *adj*. Dumb and illiterate." "Un-American, *adj*. Wicked, intolerable, heathenish." "Vanity, *n*. The tribute of a fool to the worth of the nearest ass."

Bierce, proud of his reading background, casually names a number of authors and also quotes a few non-English passages—mostly Latin, some spurious. Authors are both real and made up. Real ones include Anacreon, Omar Khayyam, Victor Hugo, Dr. Weir Mitchell (spoonerized into Dr. Meir Witchell [in "Laughter"]), William Shakespeare, and Ella Wheeler Wilcox (semi-spoonerized into Bella Peeler Silcox ["Leonine"]). Bierce's made-up ones include Armit Huff Bettle, Oogum Bem, Pollo Doncas, J. Milton Sloluck, and Suffer Uffro, among dozens. One of the silliest names, offered probably because of its dotted letters, is Jijiji Ri, in the nonsense-story added to "Scimeter." Bierce appends little essays to some definitions, for example, on scrofula ("King's Evil"). He often intrudes with his own poems as well. Fortunately, they are usually short, but occasionally they are wearisomely long, for example, Porfer Poog's "Safety-clutch," which contains fifty-two mangled lines. Nor can Bierce resist punning. Thus, "The Exile of Erin" ("Exile"); "harangue-outang" ("Harangue"); Mercy on her knees in court has "no standing here" ("Law"). Morbid though he is, Bierce can be sidesplittingly funny. For one randomly chosen example: "Sir Boyle Roche . . . held that a man cannot be in two places at once unless he is a bird" ("Ubiquity"). Bierce, like Jonathan Swift, one of his favorite authors, can range from philanthropy to misogamy and misogyny and misanthropy, and from idealism downward. He burlesques by using Hudibrastic diction, the lampoon, the mock-epic, and parody. What he steadily despises, as is made clear in *The Devil's Dictionary*, are hypocrisy, legalized venality, and pusillinamity. Incidentally, Sir Boyle Roche (1743–1807) was a flamboyant Irish politician. Bierce mentions him again in "A Sole Survivor."

In general, *The Devil's Dictionary* was not well reviewed. In 1925, however, it began to be reprinted, for a total of twenty-three times, the last time resulting in the best and only complete edition—*The Unabridged Devil's Dictionary* (2000).

Bibliography: B. S. Field, Jr., "Ambrose Bierce as Comic," *Western Humanities Review* 31 (1977): 173–80; James Milton Highsmith, "The Forms of Burlesque in *The Devil's Dictionary*," pp. 123–135, in Davidson, *Essays*; Morris; David E. Schultz and S. T. Joshi, eds., *The Unabridged Devil's Dictionary* (Athens and London: University of Georgia Press, 2000).

DE YOUNG, MICHEL HENRY (1849–1925). Newspaper publisher. He was born Michel Henry De Young, Jr., in St. Louis. His father, originally Meichel De Jong, was a Dutch Jew who changed his name when he migrated to the United States. He died in 1854 while trying to move to California with his family, including Charles De Young, a son two years older than

Michel. When they were established in San Francisco, the brothers began in 1865 to publish a playbill called *Dramatic Chronicle: A Daily Record of Affairs, Local, Critical and Theatrical*. It expanded to include news items and articles, including early pieces by Bret Harte,* Charles Warren Stoddard,* and Mark Twain.* After the *Chronicle* scooped other local papers in reporting Abraham Lincoln's assassination, the De Youngs turned it into a regular newspaper, called the *Daily Morning Chronicle* (1868). It featured scandalous news, diatribes against local celebrities, but also temperate editorials. Renamed the *San Francisco Chronicle*, the paper criticized the Rev. Isaac S. Kalloch, leader of the Workingman's Party in municipal elections in 1879. When his ticket won, Kalloch became mayor and *Chronicle* editorials became more rancorous. From his bully pulpit, Kalloch rebuked Charles in 1880. Charles entered Kalloch's church, shot at him, and wounded him in the leg. Kalloch's son pursued Charles to his office, and shot and killed him. When he became sole proprietor of the *Chronicle*, Michel De Young, continued gossipy editorials and in 1880s inveighed against the Spreckels family, which had amassed a fortune in Hawaiian sugar cane and owned the rival *San Diego Union-Tribune*. Adolph Spreckels, taking a cue from the Kallochs, visited De Young's office and took a quick shot at him, which missed.

In later years, De Young editorialized in support of reforms to fight political and commercial corruption, to establish a commission to regulate railroads, and to advance the cause of organized labor. When the railroad moguls (*see* The Big Four) lobbied to restrict freedom of the press, De Young, among other newspaper editors, successfully fought back. Less liberally, his *Chronicle*, along with newspapers under the control of William Randolph Hearst,* sought to restrict the influx of Asian immigrants, especially Chinese, whose low-paid labor greatly enhanced the wealth of what Bierce called "the railrogues." In 1890 the *Chronicle* moved into a ten-story building. In 1892 De Young vigorously sought the Republican nomination for the U.S. Senate, but without success. He was active in civic and cultural affairs, and served on the commissions of several national and international expositions, including the San Francisco Exposition of 1894. He favored high tariffs and opposed America's interference in Cuba, until the Spanish-American War began. In 1905 he built a seven-story tower atop the *Chronicle* building, which was destroyed a year later by the San Francisco earthquake. He quickly recouped. His paper was the first to print daily cartoons ("Mutt and Jeff," by Bud Fisher, from 1907). In 1913 he bought the *San Francisco Call*, a Spreckels-owned morning daily, and withdrew it from publication. In 1880 De Young married Katherine I. Deane, a Roman Catholic, and later converted to her faith. She died in 1917. After his death, their four daughters began to run the durable *Chronicle*. De Young was also called Meichal Harry De Young, Michael Henry De Young, and simply M. H. de Young.

Bierce closely watched activities of the Workingman's Party, which put Kalloch in as San Francisco's mayor. He editorialized to the effect that Kalloch was a "moral pirate . . . pitch-forked into power" (*Wasp*, 6 May 1881). Bierce, however, also disliked De Young, and blasted him in vicious prose and also in now-forgotten poetry, which he tried to keep alive in two editions of *Black Beetles in Amber*. He despised De Young for taking bribes to support corrupt sugar-plantation owners in Hawaii. He chronically insulted and reviled De Young, who only smiled and became a millionaire. Bierce was distressed to see a museum in Golden Gate Park named after De Young. In his biography of Bierce, Gustav Danziger* gives preacher Kalloch and his son the name Strong and says that Charles was a better writer than "Mike." In a poem called "A Lifted Finger" (*Wasp*, 21 October 1881), Bierce invites De Young to live long enough to see into actuality Bierce's "dream of broken necks and swollen tongues/The whole world's gibbets loaded with de Youngs!" Danziger, amid added anecdotes, quotes "A Lifted Finger" and other poems by Bierce, some of which helped squelch De Young's senatorial ambitions. Bierce also inveighed against De Young's appointment as a commissioner to the Paris Exposition (Danziger's *San Francisco Examiner*, 18 January 1900). Danziger's account of the Bierce–De Young feud is not to be completely trusted. For example, his report that "Mike" once shortchanged Bierce for a *Chronicle* column, thus infuriating him forever, is now regarded as based on uncorroborated hearsay.

Bibliography: De Castro; Fatout; Joshi and Schultz; McWilliams; Doris Muscatine, *Old San Francisco: The Biography of a City* (New York: Putnam's, 1975).

"A DIAGNOSIS OF DEATH" (1901). Short story. (Characters: Dr. Frayley, Hawver, Dr. Mannering.) Hawver, a seemingly healthy violinist, tells his friend Dr. Frawley that physicians label as ghosts what are merely hallucinations or apparitions. Hawver feels that a person can so impress his personality on his immediate environment as to reappear there after being long gone. The previous summer, to avoid the heat, Hawver had gone to Meridian and had rented the vacant house of Dr. Mannering, who had lived in it for ten years and, according to the village physician, had written a book theorizing that one could forecast the death of a seemingly healthy person as much as eighteen months in advance. One night in the rented house, Hawver saw Mannering, who looked just like his oil portrait, which was in his study. Mannering walked in, lifted his right forefinger, and disappeared. Hawver adds that Mannering could not be dead because Hawver saw him in town earlier this day. Frayley asks if Mannering raised a forefinger this very day, adding that Mannering used such a gesture when he would announce the result of a diagnosis. Hawver replies that Mannering did raise his finger; startled, he asks whether Frayley knew Mannering, to which Frawley says that he knew both the man and his book about foretelling death, and, further, that he attended Mannering in his fatal illness three years ago. When Hawver asks Frayley's advice, Frayley suggests that he should go home and play something light on his violin. Next day Hawver is found dead, his violin in his hands, and the music of Chopin's funeral march open before him.

"DID WE EAT ONE ANOTHER?" (1873, 1911). Essay. Human beings are carnivorous. Human flesh, whether fat or thin, is superior to beef. Our former habit of eating one another is proved by such sayings as "sweet sixteen," "she is . . . a peach," and so on.

"THE DIFFICULTY OF CROSSING A FIELD" (1888). Short story. (Originally part of "Whither? Some Strange Instances of Mysterious Disappearance.") (Characters: Andrew, Sam, Williamson, Williamson, Mrs. Williamson, Armour Wren, James Wren.) One morning in July 1854, Williamson, a planter living near Selma, Alabama, tells his wife he forgot to inform Andrew, his overseer, about some horses. Armour Wren has sold him a few horses, to be delivered this day. In their carriage on the road, Wren and his young son, James, see Williamson walk across his lawn, over the road, and into his pasture beyond. Wren tells his son that he forgot to tell Williamson about the horses, which were to be delivered this day but are delayed until the following day. So they turn back to inform him. But Williamson has disappeared. During a legal inquiry into Williamson's estate, Wren deposes thus: When James asked what had become of Williamson, Wren looked about but could not see him. James was astonished, as was Sam, Wren's "little black" servant. Mrs. Williamson rushed out, crying that her husband was gone. Wren says that he never saw Williamson again. James confirms almost all of these particulars. Mrs. Williamson soon loses her reason. Efforts to find Williamson fail. None of his field hands in the pasture saw him approach them, but they start some "grotesque fictions" about the matter. The courts pronounce Williamson deceased and distribute his estate properly.

"A DIPLOMATIC TRIUMPH" (1905, 1912). Short drama. (Originally part of "The Views of One.") John Hay,* secretary of state, informs President Theodore Roosevelt* that he warned the minister from China, which has behaved in a non-neutral fashion, by telling him of the advent of a ship with "a very large mast"—clearly meaning a "big stick." Other ministers, after being summoned and informed, leave with the door open—signifying the American Open Door policy. Bierce often ridiculed Hay's positions, but his Open Door policy is now regarded as wise.
Bibliography: Berkove.

"THE DISCOMFITED DEMON" (1870). Short story. (Original title: "The Devil at Yerba Buena.") (Characters: None named.) The narrator watches one stormy night as skeletal remains are removed from a cemetery to be reinterred in less valuable land. He pockets a few bones as souvenirs, trips, gets to his feet, and is told by a stranger sitting on a tombstone to get off his tail. The two have seen each other at the coroner's office. The stranger gives his address as Asphalt Avenue in Hades. So the narrator calls him the devil but is branded in return a ghoul. When the narrator admits that he is called "the Fiend in Human Shape" in newspapers, the stranger scampers away.

"DISINTRODUCTIONS" (1902, 1911). Essay. In our democratic country, we are carelessly introduced to others so often that we are in danger of meeting the devil himself, who is a citizen of all countries. A friend—let's call him Smith—meets you on the street and introduces you to a friend, who may be a thief or even your enemy, for all Smith knows. Such introductions invade your rights. Citizens or other countries are also "promiscuous" in this way, even the French, though not the Spanish or the Japanese. Someone of social importance should initiate a program of disintroductions. You could say to an acquaintance you wish to dump, "Charmed to unmeet you, sir."

"A DISSERTATION ON DOGS." *See* "Dog."

DOANE, JOHN. In "A Story at the Club," he lives in Peequeegan, Maine, and inherited $750,000 from a man whom he rescued from rowdies fifteen years earlier. The newspaper account of Doane's story inspires Will Brady to tell his friend Dr. Dutton about his nearly inheriting money for rescuing someone.

DOBLE, BUDD. In "A Providential Intimation," he is the owner of Clipper, a horse.

DOBLE, CAPTAIN. In "A Cargo of Cat," he is the captain of the *Mary Jane*, with a cargo of 127,000 cats out of Malta, in the battened-down hold. He is indifferent when 6,000 of the cats drown when given water, then swell and cause damage to his ship.

DOBSHO, THOMAS ("TOM"). In "The Baptism of Dobsho," he is the narrator Henry Barber's friend. When Tom Dobsho gets religion, confesses to more sins than he could possibly have committed, and prepares to be baptized, the narrator puts effervescent powder in Tom's hair. The Rev. Mr. Swin pours water generously over Tom's head, which naturally turns spluttery and frothy.

"DOG" (1883, 1889, 1893, 1896, 1897, 1901, 1909, 1912). Essay. (Original titles of parts: "A Dissertation on Dogs," "The Dog as a Motor," "In the Interest of Dog," and "Two Kinds of Hydrophobia.") Dogs, a "dismal anachronism," used to bring meat to humans. Now feeding them cheats poor people. Dogs have not evolved. They house fleas and smells. They are loyal to sinful masters. Women foolishly love dogs, often instead of men. Women, including that "absurd" dog-defender, Louise Imogen Guiney (1861–1920), who kiss their dogs should remember that dogs sniff out other dogs first. Parents often cherish rabid dogs that kill their children. Some physicians argue that "pseudo-hydrophobia," not hydrophobia, is the real cause of such deaths. An American diplomat in Belgium reports that dogs there are forbidden to loaf but are made to carry things, and adds that Americans ought to put dogs to similar use. Let us keep the dog, lest he escape, join the uncivilized wolves and coyotes far away, and cause us to miss his barks, bites, and the wistful look when hungry that we mistake for lovelight in his eye. Among many enumerated ways to keep dogs from howling so much would be to stop reading novels in dialect in their presence.

"THE DOG AS A MOTOR." *See* "Dog."

"DOGS FOR THE KLONDIKE" (1898, 1911). Essay. In the wake of greedy men rushing to the Yukon gold fields may come civilization, even camels, and perhaps palm trees and pineapple groves. Meanwhile, long-haired dogs are in such demand in Dawson that the rest of the country may soon be rid of the pampered creatures. Let the flea-ridden Newfoundland and the bicycle-bumping Great Dane be summoned to Alaska. Ladies' pampered lapdogs could also go here—and be eaten. Canned spaniel meat could be sent ahead as samples.

DOKE, BRIGADIER-GENERAL JUPITER. In "Jupiter Doke, Brigadier-General," he is the ineffective, pompous Union Army officer. A political appointee, he does everything wrong but is praised by Congress. Only Major-General Blount Wardorg criticizes him.

DOKE, JABEZ LEONIDAS. In "Jupiter Doke, Brigadier-General," he is Brigadier-General Jupiter Doke's son.

DOKE, MRS. JUPITER. In "Jupiter Doke, Brigadier-General," she is Brigadier-General Jupiter Doke's wife and the cousin of Joel Briller, Esq.

DOMAN, JEFFERSON ("JEFF"). In "A Holy Terror," he left his girlfriend, Mary Matthews, in Elizabethtown, New Jersey, to seek gold in California. Although he promised to return for her, she took up instead with Jo. Seeman. He cut her face, a photograph of which she sent Jeff to break off their relationship. Years later, Jeff, when informed by a letter from Barney Bree about gold located under the grave of Scarry (*see* Murphy, Manuelita) in Hurdy-Gurdy, California, goes there, hoping for a strike to share with Bree. But when Jeff finds Scarry's skull, he confuses it with Mary's face and falls dead.

DORBLEY. In "For the Ahkoond," he was a specialist through whom the narrator learned that "our ancestors" domesticated horses long ago.

DORRIMORE, DR. VALENTINE. In "The Realm of the Unreal," he is a hypnotist from Calcutta, called Professor Dorrimore. He has Oriental manners, a cynical and contemptuous smile, and what is described as a "disagreeably engaging" manner. Five years before in San Francisco, he hypnotized Manrich, the narrator, into believing that Dorrimore was stabbed to death on the street and then came to life. Now he encounters Manrich on his way from Newcastle to Auburn, and rides with him there. Once in Auburn, Dorrimore hypnotizes Manrich into believing that Manrich's fiancée, Margaret Corray, has become fond of Dorrimore; the two men fight, and Manrich winds up injured in his hotel room. None of these events can be confirmed.

DOUB, CATHARINE. In "That of Granny Magone," she is a witness confirming the story that Sarah Magone, though pronounced dead, fought a black cat off her face. Four days later, Sarah, never reviving, was buried.

DOYLE, GORDON. In "A Psychological Shipwreck," he met William Jarrett in Liverpool and sails for New York with him aboard the *City of Prague*. Doyle intends to marry Janette Harford. To avoid detection by the wealthy Harfords, her Devonshire parents, she sails for New York aboard the *Morrow* and is never heard from again. Doyle tries to make sense of Jarrett's story that he was aboard the *Morrow*, met Janette, and tried unsuccessfully to rescue her from drowning when the *Morrow* sank. The careful reader may wonder how Gordon Doyle is able to tell Jarrett that Janette grew up never knowing she was adopted.

DRURING, DR. In "The Man and the Snake," he is a hospitable scientist in San Francisco. His mansion has a wing called the Snakery, which houses live snakes. He offers a guest room to Harker Brayton, just back from foreign travel. When Brayton dies in a fit, thinking he is being hypnotized by a snake and is about to be attacked, Dr. Druring finds under his guest's bed a stuffed snake with shoe-button eyes.

DRURING, MISS. In "The Man and the Snake," she is any of the daughters of Dr. Druring and his wife. They all live together in San Francisco.

DRURING, MRS. In "The Man and the Snake," she is Dr. Druring's wife. The two are in the library when they hear their guest Harker Brayton's dying scream.

DRUSE. In "A Horseman in the Sky," he is Private Carter Druse's father. The father, a staunch Virginian, fights on the Confederate Army side. The son, a Union Army soldier, sees his father on horseback at a cliff edge scouting Union forces, shoots the horse, and causes his father to plunge to his death.

DRUSE, MRS. In "A Horseman in the Sky," she is Private Carter Druse's mother, who, according to Carter's father, was soon to die.

DRUSE, PRIVATE CARTER. In "A Horseman in the Sky," he tells his pro-Confederate father of his intention to join the Union Army in Grafton, Virginia. Later, he sees his father, fighting for the Confederate side, on horseback at the edge of a cliff and scouting Union troops. Remembering his father's injunction to do his duty as he conceives it to be, he shoots his father's horse and causes both man and mount to fall to their deaths.

"A DUBIOUS VINDICATION" (1887, 1911). Essay. Cannibals have been unjustly slandered. Why call a cannibal a murderer? It is better to kill your dinner before than while eating him. Although the Rev. Mr. Hopkins, a Methodist missionary back from the South Pacific islands, avers that he never felt in danger of being eaten, his testimony lacks weight, because he was obviously inedible. When asked sarcastically about his colleague, the Rev. Mr. "Fatty" Dawson, Hopkins swore that the native king invited Dawson to dinner but did not dine on him. Only "the most impenitent calumniator" would suggest that Hopkins may have eaten Fatty.

DUCK, PRIVATE DAVID WILLIAM ("DEAD DUCK"). In "A Man with Two Lives," he was a soldier at Fort Phil Kearney. After the Fetterman Massacre of 21 December 1866, Private Duck was ordered to take dispatches to Fort C. F. Smith. According to Sergeant William Briscoe, Duck was killed by Indians and was buried by Briscoe and some fellow soldiers. But according to Duck, he survived and is now living in Aurora, Illinois. Duck was nicknamed "Dead Duck" by soldiers who regarded him as dead.

DUDLEY, LIEUTENANT WILL. In "Two Military Executions," he is Private Bennett Story Greene's superior officer in an incompletely trained U.S. Army unit. The two were schoolmates in civilian life. Greene strikes Dudley, which he would not have done with more experience. Dudley reports the incident, and Greene is court-martialed and executed. Weeks later, however, a voice answers Greene's name at roll call and a rifle shot from far away kills Dudley.

DUFF, BURTON. In "An Arrest," he is the jailer, in a county jail in Kentucky, whom the murderer Orrin Brower slugs, after which he escapes. But once he is in a forest outside town, a figure resembling Duff orders Brower back to jail, where Brower sees Duff's corpse.

DUMPS. In "A Lady from Redhorse." *See* James.

DUNFER, JO. ("WHISKY JO."). In "The Haunted Valley," he is the loquacious owner of a place in the West, between Hutton's and Mexican Hill. It is half-residence and half-saloon. One day he gets drunk and tells the Eastern narrator about Ah Wee. He says that he hired Ah Wee, who he says was a Chinese man; but then Jo. got religion and turned properly anti-Chinese. He says that Ah Wee used to cut trees badly. When he suddenly sees what he regards as the deceased Ah Wee's black eye staring at him through a knot-hole in the saloon wall, he turns frantic. Years later the narrator learns the truth from Gopher, another of Jo.'s employees. He explains that Jo. won Ah Wee, Gopher's girlfriend, in a poker game, demeaned her for a long time, and killed her when he wrongly suspected her of being intimate with Gopher. He turned "anti-coolie," became popular, and was elected county justice of the peace. But shortly after he drank with the narrator he fell ill, asked Gopher to bury him next to Ah Wee near Jo., and soon died. Unable to resist punning, Bierce says at one point that Dunfer is done for.

DUNNING, TROOPER. In "A Baffled Ambuscade," he was a brave Union Army cavalry soldier who, after being shot dead, warned his commanding officer, Major Seidel, by a silent gesture, of a possible Confederate ambuscade lurking in a nearby cedar forest outside Murfreesboro.

DUTTON, DR. In "A Story at the Club," he mentions, to his friend, Will Brady's account of saving a man from being crushed by a railroad train but not being able to inherit a bequest from the man because he, Brady, was already dead.

E

ECKERT, PHILIP ("OLD MAN ECKERT"). In "At Old Man Eckert's," he was a recluse living just outside Marion, Vermont. He is the subject of gossip. Five years after he disappeared, three men enter his house to investigate. One of them, Adrus C. Palmer, walks out of the house, perhaps following Eckert's spirit, and is never heard from again.

"EDWIN MARKHAM'S POEMS" (1899, 1900, 1911). Review. "The Wharf of Dreams," a sonnet by Edwin Markham,* contains two supremely fine lines: "And from lost ships, homing with ghostly crews, / Come cries of incommunicable news." Recently Markham has slipped from interpreting nature well to interpreting art unsuccessfully. He writes badly about labor problems. Gertrude Atherton* properly criticized Markham for groveling to mobs. The structure of "The Man with the Hoe" is stiff; its blank verse, monotonous; its non-naturalistic message, silly. In truth, the humble multitudes remain ignorant, fickle, cruel, and sour. Markham has been foolishly "inciting a strike against God and clamoring for repeal of the laws of nature," thought he could save society, but through sales of his poetry has achieved "the smug prosperity that he reviles in others." Bierce hopes that Markham will grow disillusioned and write some more good poetry.

ELDERSON. In "The Secret of Macarger's Gulch," he is the narrator. After hunting one summer day in 1874, he sleeps in a deserted cabin in Macarger's Gulch, dreams about a stranger named Thomas MacGregor and his wife in Edinburgh, notes their physical characteristics, and awakens to the sound of a dying woman's scream. But the cabin is empty. Years later, a friend named Morgan tells him that Thomas Morgan moved from Edinburgh with his wife to the region of the Gulch. They lived in a cabin there, and he evidently killed his wife, whose skeleton Morgan found a year earlier in the wind-ravaged cabin.

ELIZA. In " 'The Bubble Reputation,' " a gross headline in the San Francisco *Daily Malefactor* says that in her dying words Eliza asked her mother to feed her to the pigs.

"EMANCIPATED WOMAN" (1893, 1894, 1896, 1909, 1912). Essay. Far from women having to enter the workplace to fill spots vacated by alcoholic men, the advent of such working women increases poverty and crime. Job opportunities for women do not help women as a group but only individual female employees, and also their ruthless male employers, who underpay them and swell their own paunches with the savings. Staying competitive, such employers rationalize that they "cheat to eat." To be polite, little should be said of the fact that girls working in factories are less "moral" than better-protected society girls. God does not assure female virtue; seclusion does.

"EMMA FRANCES DAWSON" (1894, 1897, 1911). Review. *An Itinerant House and Other Stories* is "a work of supreme genius" by Emma Frances Dawson.* It presents unearthly characters in an unearthly environment while making no demands on the reader's feelings or admiration. One hopes that it will survive when much popular fiction is forgotten. Dawson has a knack of disposing of her characters indifferently. Her stories stress the supernatural more than the natural, and many include effective if random verse by her fictive poets. Her scene, always San Francisco, becomes a predawn, childless "dream city . . . of wraiths," of dirge-singing winds, and of pranksters. One story in particular, "A Gracious Visitation," is unsurpassably fine.

"ENGLAND'S LAUREATE" (1902, 1911). Essay. (Original title: "Concerned One Beslubbered." Alfred Austin, poet laureate (from 1896), is not great, but two of his sonnets, "Love's Blindness" and "Love's Wisdom," should never be laughed at. A poet, like an athlete or a racehorse, should be judged by his best performance, not his poorest.

EPIGRAMS (1911.) For *The Collected Works of Ambrose Bierce*, volume 8, Bierce assembled numerous brief and salty definitions, terse statements, and bits of mordant dialogue that he had published from 1871 to 1909 in *Cosmopolitan*, the *San Francisco News Letter and California Advertiser*, the *New York American*, the *New York Journal*, and the *Overland Monthly*. The epigrams are almost always about human failings, with respect to pretended virtues and real vices, the vanity of ambitions of various sorts (amatory, cultural, financial, military, physical, political, social), and the dangerous consequences of such ambitions. Many concern the battle of the sexes. The following are especially notable: "For study of the good and bad in woman

two women are a needless expense." "Woman would be more charming if one could fall into her arms without falling into her hands." "Of two kinds of temporary insanity, one ends in suicide, the other in marriage." "A sweetheart is a bottle of wine; a wife is a wine-bottle." And "He best gets on with women who best knows how to get on without them." Two epigrams tend to throw unique lights on Bierce himself, whether he would agree with such a surmise or not: "These are the prerogatives of genius: To know without having learned; to draw just conclusions from unknown premises; to discern the soul of things"; and "That you can not serve God and Mammon is a poor excuse for not serving God."
Bibliography: Grenander.

EVE. In "Hades in Trouble," she is a troublesome creature, Adam's mate, on the earth. Satan sends a message to his fellow devils expressing the hope that the couple will never be introduced to his peaceful abode. Belial, however, rather likes what he hears about Eve.

"THE EVOLUTION OF A STORY" (1874, 1912). Essay. (Original title: "A Novel.") Evidently to criticize Edward Bok (1863–1930), editor of the *Ladies' Home Journal*, Bierce weirdly connects disparate plot elements of a story. They are a frog eaten by a serpent, which goes to a highway, near which is a gameskeeper, who is fired at by a poacher, within earshot of a baby that walks abandoned to a hotel, with a note saying its royal benefactor will have gems like warts on a toad, which is as celibate as a piano, which its owners would never split open for gold so heavy that horses would be needed to carry it. Horses will be the subject of the next chapter.

"EXTRACTS FROM THE BEST-SELLING NOVELS OF THIS AFTERNOON." *See* "The Sample Counter."

"THE EYES OF THE PANTHER" (1897). Short Story. (Characters: Jenner Brading, Baby Marlowe, Charles Marlowe, Irene Marlowe, Mrs. Charles Marlowe.) Mrs. Charles Marlowe urges her husband, Charles Marlowe, not to leave her and their little daughter, Baby Marlowe, this night and hunt for meat. She has had an upsetting dream. He goes anyway. She imagines that she sees the eyes of a panther at their window. When Charles returns, his wife is frantically hugging dead Baby. Three months later she dies giving birth to a second daughter, Irene Marlowe. Years pass. Jenner Brading, an attorney in the village, proposes marriage to Irene, but she declines, saying that she is insane. He doubts that the sight of the eyes of a panther could have caused her dementia. When she goes to the cabin that she shares with her sad old father, Brading follows her, sees a panther, and warns her as Irene disappears. That night Brading sees the eyes of a panther at his cottage window, draws his revolver, and fires at the sight. Men rush up and find blood. Brading goes alone into the forest and stumbles over Irene's corpse. For years thereafter, Charles mourns at his dead child's grave—both are finally at peace.

Bierce does not tell this macabre story, involving past and present action, in ordinary chronological sequence. He heightens suspense by beginning with Irene's rejection of Brading's proposal, continues by relating in his unnamed narrator's own words Irene's tardy and reluctant story of how she became insane, then introduces details of Irene's present position, and concludes with Brading's seeing the panther and shooting at it—with fatal human consequences.

F

FABLES. Bierce wrote at least 846 fables from 1872 to 1911. Although he read the fables of Aesop, Jean de La Fontaine, and Eastern writers at an early age, he was highly original from the outset in producing his own mordant fables. His earliest efforts in this line are "The Fables of Zambri, the Parsee," in *Fun* (1872–1873), which he revised for inclusion in *Cobwebs from an Empty Skull* (1874). More of his fables followed, in several San Francisco periodicals (1883–1904) and in several New York ones (1898–1907). Bierce collected many for the two editions of *Fantastic Fables* (1899, 1911). His *Fun* fables are written under the pseudonym of Dod Grile. Some later fables, when they are not signed with his name, are signed by full or partial initials. Others, though unsigned, are attributed to Bierce by internal and other evidence.
Bibliography: Joshi.

FABLES FROM "FUN" (1872–1873, 1911, 2000). Fables. These untitled fables in prose originally appeared in *Fun*, the weekly London humor magazine partly edited by Bierce's friend Tom Hood,* and were revised for republication. The implicit moral in most of these fables is that stupid behavior—especially verbosity, boasting, and rationalizing—is dangerous. For example, the owner of a parrot that is proud of speaking Greek advises it not to talk like Socrates. And when an ass, told by an ox to bellow instead of braying, replies that aesthetic judgment of their different voices is a matter of taste, the ox judges the ass's lecture to be "in bad taste."
Bibliography: Joshi, Joshi and Schultz.

FABLES IN RHYME (1901, 1911). Fables. Seven short, titled poems, in iambic tetrameter or irregular anapestic dimeter, concern animals and point acerbic morals. A calm tiger turns an ill-tempered bull "into chyle." When

a dog-bitten man loses his lawsuit, the dogs are free to release "hydrophobia's sap" all over "the map." The gods shut up a "Protagonist of slang."
Dray horses regard the stripes on a zebra to be an indication that its crime
was stealing a man. A speedy cat boasts to a tortoise. A steer wrongly thinks
he has saved a jackass from a lion. A windy speaker got "three cheers," but
then a hungry "tiger [pun!]" followed.

"THE FABLES OF ZAMBRI, THE PARSEE" (1872, 1873, 2000). Fables, untitled and in prose (except #115). Bierce's purpose is usually to ridicule immorality, poke bitter fun at alleged family values, and satirize
religiosity, politicians, scientists, and would-be philosophers. Here are examples, with animals and birds usually monopolizing the talk. A rat, to prevent a cat from eating him, fibs about swallowing poison to die; but the cat,
disbelieving him, eats him up anyway. Moral?—"A rat gets no profit by
lying" (#2). A fox saves her life by leaving her cub, with a thorn in its foot,
as food for pursuing dogs, and nimbly running off. Moral?—"Humanity does
not . . . enjoy a monopoly of paternal affection" (#31). A peasant throws
stones at an ostrich, is impressed when it eats them, thinks it is a god, follows
it, and is gobbled up (#15). Bierce satirizes Fabian socialism by telling how
a bear lies down, lets bees exhaust themselves by stinging him, plans then
to get their honey, but dies and "a fresh bear" gains the sweets (#44). A
robin tells a woodpecker that it cannot succeed in hammering an idea into
thick-headed naturalists (#102). A pig admires the evident ecstasy of a philosopher reading his Zend-Avesta but, all the same, prefers to wallow in his
"cauldron of cold slops" (#62). Puns are rampant. Two are buried in the
following fabulous introduction: "A certain terrier, of a dogmatic turn, asked
a kitten her opinion of rats, demanding a categorical answer" (#128). Ever
since a plowed-up stone talked to a "lump of earth" that would not answer
the stone's attempt at conversation, "it has been customary to call a stupid
person 'a clod' " (#13). A body tells its argumentative organs that he does
not take sides but will make an exception of sides of bacon (#82). A physician
tells a sick crab that he will cure it—by pickling (#92). A hungry wolf
"drawl[s]" at a dog-pursued hare that he plans to do some "hare-splitting"
(#113). Bierce gains humor in several ways: (1) by ornate introductions, for
example, "A herd of cows, blown off the summit of the Himalayas, were
sailing some miles above the valleys, when one said to another . . ." (#72),
and "A wild cat was listening with rapt approval to the melody of distant
hounds tracking a remote fox" (#76); (2) by having one creature identify a
foe with lumbering verbosity, for instance, "my adipose censor" (ass to ox,
#110) and "insolent marsupial" (bear to opposum, #121); and (3) by inflated
speech indicators, such as "replied the prisoner, with a reverential gesture,
repeated at intervals" (#61), "Thus craftily did he inveigle the vain bird"
(#99), and "grunted the sententious scholar, pausing in his mastication of a
Chaldaic root" (#132). Bierce sometimes concludes his fables with surprising

abruptness; but more often he does so by pointing out an obvious moral, by mentioning something irrelevant, by verbosely saying a conclusion is unneeded, or, occasionally, by starting the ending with *fabula docet* or *fabula ostendit*, or alluding to his limitations when it comes to translation. His sense of humor is never better illustrated or more stylish than in these fables, many of which were written early in his long career.
Bibliography: Joshi.

FAHERTINI, MADAME. In "A Shipwreckollection," the narrator recalls that she supplied his mother with "patent palpitators."

"THE FAILURE OF HOPE & WANDEL" (1874). Short story. (Original title: "Cool Correspondence.") (Characters: Jabez Hope, Pike Wandel.) Jabez Hope and his partner, Pike Wandel, of Hope & Wandel, a wholesale boot and shoe company in New Orleans, exchange letters, dated from 27 December 1877 to 3 April 1878. In Chicago, Hope writes Wandel about shipping ice from Lake Michigan and selling it in New Orleans. In New Orleans, Wandel replies, saying that Hope's blotchy letter did not contain the promised sample of ice but adding that he has enclosed a draft of money realized from selling their company. Hope reports that he has built a warehouse to collect ice. Wandel writes about orders taken and wonders about salty ice for cooking but fresh ice for juleps. Hope's final letter reports failure. His warehouse full of ice, built on frozen Lake Michigan, broke loose and wrecked a Milwaukee schooner. He rebukes Wandel for his silly questions about salty and fresh ice. This satirical piece has little to recommend it.

"THE FALL OF THE REPUBLIC: AN ARTICLE FROM 'A COURT JOURNAL OF THE THIRTY-FIRST CENTURY.'" *See* "Ashes of the Beacon."

"THE FAMOUS GILSON BEQUEST" (1878). Short story. (Characters: Jo. Bentley, Henry Clay Brentshaw, Milton Gilson, Moll Gurney, Harper, Carpenter Pete.) Henry Clay Brentshaw, sheriff of Mammon Hill, has just brought in Milton Gilson, a disreputable character suspected of robbing sluice boxes of nearby gold miners—since he always had "clean dust" to lose at Jo. Bentley's faro table—and now caught stealing Harper's horse. Next day Gilson is tried and convicted. He writes a will bequeathing his worldly goods to Brentshaw, on condition that Brentshaw will "plant . . . [his body] white." After being hanged, he is placed in a pine coffin by Carpenter Pete. In Gilson's vest pocket is found a codicil saying that if others can prove, within a period of five years, that he robbed them they are to divide his estate; if not, Brentshaw gets all. It is soon discovered that Gilson had valuable property and big bank deposits back in the East. Miners immediately begin to lay claim to parts of Gilson's estate. So Brentshaw places an ornate stone over Gilson's shallow grave and bribes various people, including Harper, to swear to Gilson's honesty. Five years pass. A sudden flood topples Gilson's marker and unearths his coffin and other coffins as well. Brentshaw, now stooped, gray, doddering, close to insanity, and believing in the supernatural, wanders to Gilson's grave and in the watery moonlight sees, or fancies he sees, Gilson's ghost—panning ashes out of soggy coffins and depositing the findings into his own coffin. Next morning golden sunshine gently falls upon Brentshaw, "dead among the dead."

"The Famous Gilson Bequest," which is about true perceptions and deliberate misperceptions, dramatizes the power of easy money to corrupt an entire community. Bierce strikes deliberately out-of-place sentimental tones amid his usual verbosities; for example, he makes his moon feminine and his sun masculine. Some readers have detected odd religious overtones in this story. It has been noted that the name Milton Gilson calls to mind both the name John Milton, the author of *Paradise Lost*, and also the word *gill*, an early Christian fish sign. Gilson lived in New Jerusalem before proceeding to nearby Mammon Hill. The gallows on which he is hanged is repeatedly called "The Tree." This story anticipates "The Man That Corrupted Hadleyburg" (1899) by Mark Twain,* a considerably similar satire exposing civic righteousness and avarice.

Bibliography: Davidson, Grenander, Morris, O'Connor.

FANTASTIC FABLES (1899, 1906, 2000). Fables. These short, titled fables, all in prose, point sardonic morals, one after another. Subsections are titled "Aesopus Emendatus," "Fables in Rhyme," and "Old Saws with New Teeth." Bierce targets many objects of his contempt. Heading any tabulation would be politicians (including inept diplomats), closely followed by policemen, lawyers, and judges. Other objects of his verbal barbs are government officials—legislative, executive, and judicial—at all levels. He also derides lovers of both sexes (but women more often); church leaders of various stripes; policemen; military and naval personnel; persons supposedly in positions of trust, for example, kings, physicians, bankers, prison wardens, and journalists (especially editors); and writers and would-be writers, most often those of the poetasting persuasion. Bierce often makes his points by introducing animals, most frequently lions, jackasses, and ostriches; they, as well as their associates, reveal characteristics all too human—notably cunning, greed, stupidity, ferocity, misplaced trust, pride, and indolence. Bierce's overarching conclusions are that money wins over morality, venality over idealism, headstrong action over rational conduct (especially war instead of peace), cruelty over kindness, forgetfulness over gratitude, corruption over probity, doing nothing over action—in short, as one might put it, death of various sorts over what we call life. Naming only three real persons, Bierce ridicules the spiritualist Elena Petrovna Blavatsky (1831–1891) (in "The

Ashes of Madame Blavatsky") and the lawyer-statesman Elihu Root (1845–1937) (in "Saint and Soul"), and uniquely praises the Filipino leader Emilio Aguinaldo (1869–1964) (in "A Born Leader"). Utterly typical, here, are Bierce's criticism of spiritual-intellectual pretensions and alleged juridical-political pomposity, and his lonely praise of an anti-American military-political pragmatist.

Bierce's style in *Fantastic Fables* is more absorbing than his content, which grows tedious and predictable. Immediately striking is his habit of slowing the reader and forcing his reader's attention by capitalizing key words, usually nouns. (In this, he anticipated the humorous writings of George Ade [1866–1944], who was more popular, who usually gets credit for this cute device, and whose work Bierce disliked.) Examples: in "Noser and Note," a suspicious official is called "Noser into Things"; a man pursuing the subject of "A Devoted Widow" is "Engaging Gentleman"; a crooked politician in "The Hardy Patriots" is "Dispenser-Elect of Patronage." Bierce modifies place names for humorous effect: thus, "Damnasia" (in "Uncalculating Zeal") and "Despotamia" ("A Chained Eagle"). Bierce's diction is often remarkable. Examples: In "The City of Political Distinction," an aspirant is "half strangled and dreadfully beslubbered by the feculent waters"; a leaping kangaroo in "The Australian Grasshopper" is seen "tracing against the sunset sky a parabolic curve spanning seven provinces"; during a naval bombardment in "Aftermath," "the music of guns lulls like the evensong of a mermaid in the gloaming." Bierce is not above employing puns. Examples: when in "Fogy and Sheik" religious rivals agree, the Fogy extends his hand and says, "Sheik"; a former lawmaker in "Legislator and Citizen" says that he was not a senator but only "a member of the Slower House"; "A Weary Echo" features women writers "hailing the down of a new era."
Bibliography: Joshi.

FARQUHAR. In "An Occurrence at Owl Creek Bridge," he or she is any of the children of Peyton Farquhar and his wife.

FARQUHAR, MRS. PEYTON. In "An Occurrence at Owl Creek Bridge," she is the sweet and loving wife of Peyton Farquhar. His dying thought is of her.

FARQUHAR, PEYTON. In "An Occurrence at Owl Creek Bridge," he is an Alabama planter, slaveowner, and politician, about thirty-five. An ardent secessionist, he dreams romantically of glorious military achievements. When a Union Army scout, pretending to be a Confederate soldier, tells him that the Union-held bridge at Owl Creek, thirty miles away, could be set ablaze, Farquhar takes the bait, tries, is caught, and is hanged. At the moment of his death, he imagines that he escapes and gets home to his wife and children.

FARQUHARSON, CHARLES. In "The Mystery of Charles Farquharson," he knew both William Heyner Gordon and Charles Richter when all three were boys. Farquharson, who became a Parsee, dies in Bombay in the summer of 1843 and his body is consumed by buzzards, in accordance with Parsee practice. When Richter sends Gordon a daguerreotype of Farquharson as an adult, his features match those of the corpse Gordon stumbled on in his room in Philadelphia. In a later version of this story, titled "The Mystery of John Farquharson," Charles is called John.

FARQUHARSON, JOHN. *See* Farquharson, Charles.

"FAT BABIES AND FATE" (1889, 1912). Essay. (Original title: "Fatlings of the Flock.") Essay. The original purpose of baby shows was to identify unacceptable infants to toss down a cliff. Today, baby contests have bad consequences. The fattest babies win. The race is not improved by raising kids with noses and knuckles obscured by fat. Winners eventually lose out when they grow to fat adulthood. Losers are forever frustrated. Mothers of losers turn angry, bitter, sour, ugly. Fathers mainly evince a bit of shame. Matronly contest judges are proscribed by society.

"FATLINGS OF THE FLOCK." *See* "Fat Babies and Fate."

FATTI, BADELINA. In "The City of the Gone Away," she is the world's most famous soprano. She wrote the unnamed narrator to praise "Toilet Homoline," a fine product that he made using human corpses in his soap factory. The gifted soprano's name is an obvious takeoff on that of coloratura soprano Adelina Patti (1843–1919). In a "Prattle" column (*San Francisco Examiner*, 28 June 1891), Bierce comments that both Henry Ward Beecher and Patti "found a certain kind of soap efficacious for washing the conscience." Bierce was hinting that both had committed adultery. Patti evidently had not done so.
Bibliography: Joshi and Schultz.

FESTORAZZI, SIGNORINA. In "The Night-Doings at 'Deadman's,' " when the muffled stranger partially disrobes for the night, Hiram Beeson notes that he resembles Signorina Festorazzi, an Irish woman six feet tall, fifty-six pounds in weight, and a San Francisco sideshow freak.

"FETISHISM" (1902, 1911). Essay. (Original title: "The Curmudgeon Philosopher.") Essay. The Curmudgeon Philosopher tells the Reporter that modern civilization, like a palimpsest, reveals people's new fetishes covering old ones. For example, empty cemetery urns holding no ashes of the dead, whereas valid urns used to contain them. Primitive religionists worshipped rocks. Today we venerate Plymouth Rock, although its connection with the Pilgrims' landing is spurious. Ditto the Liberty Bell.

THE FIEND'S DELIGHT (1873). Bierce's first book, written under the pseudonym of Dod Grile. It was published in London by the disreputable John Camden Hotten.* The book is a collection of columns, often carefully revised, that Bierce had written in the *San Francisco News Letter and California Advertiser.* The title page illustration is of a happy Englishman roasting a baby over a fire. The book includes short narratives, satirical sketches, and little squibs, mostly violent and gruesome. In his preface, Bierce blames Mr. Satan, his collaborator, for the ugly contents. He warns his British readers that he writes in the American language and that if they have trouble understanding it they might do well to visit the United States. In an unsigned review (*Figaro,* 17 July 1873), Bierce enjoyed blasting his own book, calling it ignorant and conceited blackguardism.
Bibliography: McWilliams, Morris, O'Connor.

FINCH, ANTONIO. In "A Fruitless Assignment," he is mentioned as having quarreled with Henry Saylor in Covington and having killed him.

"FIN DE SIÈCLE" (1894, 1911). Essay. Horses at the end of century may continue to resemble those of other times; but for people involved in thought, the arts, moral matters, and politics, the end of the century is marked by "the note of despair, more accurately, desperation." Sounding the phrase *fin de siècle* evokes a self-fulfilling prophecy. The end of a century is wrongly thought to be the end of a straight series of events and an end of opportunity. Foolish people struggle for quick advantages. Only scientists keep their heads, knowing that the new century will not differ from the old one.

FLEMING, STALEY. In "Staley Fleming's Hallucination," he was the neighbor and enemy of Atwell Barton. After Barton was stabbed to death but by no one whom the authorities could identify and nab, Fleming went to Europe. Three years later he returns, has nocturnal visions of a dog, summons Dr. Halderman for advice, and describes the dog to him. Dr. Halderman says that it resembles Barton's dog, now dead. When Fleming equivocates about Barton, Dr. Halderman advises him to retire in his unlocked bedroom while Dr. Halderman will read downstairs. In the night a thud sends Dr. Halderman upstairs, where, after breaking door the door, he finds Fleming dying of fang wounds in the jugular. No animal is around.

FLOOD, MAJOR-GENERAL SIMMONS B. In "Jupiter Doke, Brigadier-General," he is a Confederate Army officer, whose death Major-General Gibeon J. Buxter mistakenly reports.

"A FLOURISHING INDUSTRY" (1889, 1911). Essay. (Original title: "Lean Kine.") A Long Island industry has grown up around a scheme of purchasing valueless cattle, inoculating them with pneumonia and tuberculosis, and collecting the "indemnity" when they are killed by officials. Western ranchers are also getting in on this fledgling business. Instead of watching their herds develop in a chancy way, they send them to Eastern "infectionaries" for profitable disposal. Soon skinny cattle will be imported from South America, possibly with congressional encouragement of such a nicely developing American enterprise.

FOLEY, BENSON. In "A Cold Greeting," he is a San Franciscan who becomes friendly with James H. Conway of Franklin, Tennessee, when that man presents a letter of recommendation from their mutual friend, Lawrence Barting. Conway grows confused when Barting evidently rebuffs him on the street, and more so when Foley reports that Barting died before Conway saw him on the street. Foley, who knows better, lets Conway believe that he saw a man only resembling Barting.

"THE FOOL" (1912). Short drama. A fool is involved with a philosopher, a doctor, and a soldier in discussions about truth, happiness, political economy, physical ailments, and war.

"FOR BREVITY AND CLARITY" (1887, 1912). Essay. It would be advantageous to condense long phrases into single new words. Thus, "joined in the holy bonds of wedlock" could become "jedlock"; "much-needed rest," simply "mest." Since "not either" has become "neither," cannot "No Irish" be "Nirish"? And so on. A curving mark resembling a smiling mouth could be a new punctuation mark, signaling it is time to laugh at humorists' alleged witticisms and thus save them from embarrassment.

"FOR INTERVENTION" (1900, 1912). Short drama. (Originally part of "Apocryphal Conversations.") A representative of the Boer Republic, being defeated by the British, visits President William McKinley* and asks in broken English: "But, your Egcellenza, shall ve haf der onterventions already yet?" As he is shown out, voices—perhaps those of congressmen—praise the Boers.

"FOR LAST WORDS" (1888, 1912). Essay. (Original title: "The Bedside Telephone.") Useful would be a telephone beside a dying person whose disease his telephoners would thus avoid catching. They could also kid him by saying, "Is that you?" Last words of the dying, which would otherwise remain unrecorded by indifferent doctors and nurses, could be preserved. Whether such words would be banal, reminiscent, historical, charitable, or idiotic, the telephone would stand ready for faithful transmission.

"FOR STANDING ROOM" (1911). Essay. Overpopulation in civilized countries has resulted in augmented discussion of capital-labor relations. "Conquest and commerce" have enabled the powerful nations to control the world. Industrial and scientific advances have improved the quality and length of life. More people are interested in enjoying life. So? Along comes overpopulation, followed inexorably by war, famine, disease, anarchy, decivilization—in short, by depopulation. Note the cycle: The goal of competing civilized countries is barbarism, with industrial production leading to competition, leading to labor discontent, leading to a bigger army rationalized as protection against outside aggressors.

"FOR THE AHKOOND" (1888). Short story. (Full title: "For the Ahkoond: The Unknown Land Beyond the Ultimate Hills.") (Characters: Ahkoond of Citrusia, Dr. Blobob, Dorbley, Prof. Nupper, Simeon Tucker.) The narrator has accepted the commission of the Ahkoond of Citrusia, majestic ruler of descendants of Californians, in the year 4591, to explore the unknown region east of the Ultimate Hills (once called the Rocky Mountains). The narrator proceeds by magnetic tube from Sanf Rachisco to the summit of the Hills, where Kikago, capital of Nevraska, once was. For four months he descends the eastern slope through forests and over stagnant lakes. Studying both fauna and flora, he finds tablelands and also horses long thought extinct. Oddly, the creatures had no horns nor forked tails, as he had read they had; instead, they had rear-end tassles. Other animals resemble those he had found earlier in the forgotten continent of Darkest Europe. Flocks of pterodactyls fight in the air. He shoots one of them with his electric rifle and roasts its tasty toe pads. He rafts over a lagoon to a broad rock, checks its surface by petrochronologue and nymograph, and identifies it as Pike's Peak, worn by northern glacier action ending in 1945. Observations enable him to conclude that he is near Denver, once occupied by Galoots. With his aerial isochronophone he sends the first of his reports to the Ahkoond—at his patron's very dinner hour, by prearrangement. The message concerns artistic, preglacial tribes dating back to 1920, "almost within historic times." Instead of proceeding north below sea level, the narrator continues east, now walking fast by his "double-distance telepod," into regions of sparse soil, then barren rock, and finally near a north-south depression formerly called the Mississippi Valley, where, as he reports, the once-prosperous, now-extinct Pukes lived. Cyclones destroyed everything, beginning about 1860, lasting a century, and by coincidence ending when glaciers obliterated the Gahoots and their neighboring tribes. The Ahkoond's reply includes a request that the narrator find and try to revive the Puke king with his patent resuscitator. With his politoscope, the narrator learns that the Puke nation was a republic; so he ignores the request. Six months later, he is above the site of Buffalo, former capital of the powerful Smugwumpia nation, in which, according to his archaethermograph, he discerns that nineteenth-century summers grew shorter but hotter while winters developed killing frosts. A final hot spell ignited the city, then "winter reigned eternal." The Smugwumps headed for California but were fatally snowed over in 1943. A few weeks later, the narrator reports from the Fiery Gulf far southwest of Buffalo. According to his ethnograph, the region was populated in the twentieth century by Whites ("Crackers") and Blacks ("Coons") in "about equal numbers" and having "about equal moral worth." The area is nicely warm and rankly fertile. The extinct humans have been replaced by savage animals, venomous snakes, and ugly birds. According to his necrohistoriograph, the people were "extirpated contemporaneously with the disastrous events," namely, yellow fever onslaughts that eliminated Galoots, Pukes, and Smugwumps together. By 1946 all were "dead and damned." The Ahkoond, having changed his dinner hour, responds by cursing the narrator and threatening to kill him. "For the Ahkoond" has been rightly ignored by almost all Bierce critics.

"FOUR DAYS IN DIXIE" (1888, 1909). Essay. (Full title: "Four Days in Dixie: The Difference Between One Side of a River and the Other.") In October 1864, during a lull in action after the fall of Atlanta, Bierce is on the staff of an easygoing commander, Colonel Henry Kumler McConnell (d. 1898), near Gaylesville, Alabama. For a bright Sunday morning lark, Bierce, an officer named Lieutenant Cobb, and three Union privates cross a river by boat but are soon seen by Confederate cavalrymen. Three are caught, but Bierce and one other man hide separately until night, which proves to be safely moonless. Bierce moves through a cornfield, tries but fails to find the boat they used earlier, detours around a sleepy group of enemy soldiers beside a campfire, is suddenly shot at, and waits by the river until dawn. He wades over to a low island, prepares to swim back to territory he called "Shermany," but falls unconscious—owing to his having been wounded in the head the previous June. Regaining consciousness, he makes a raft of logs and vines, but before sailing he is captured by a Confederate "home guard," fed at a farm house, and put to bed. Next day he and another prisoner are taken by two armed guards fifteen miles to a farm house, where they stay for the night. Once all careless guards are asleep, Bierce tiptoes out, unpursued save by dogs, soon called back by their old civilian owner. Bierce goes through brambles and over streams, leaving parts of his skin "decorating" thorns, boughs, and rocks "along my sylvan wake." By late afternoon he finds the river, swims across, and encounters two Union soldiers and a stolen pig. That evening he makes it back to camp. Cobb is there to haul him in, scrutinize him, and describe him to their unconcerned, unflappable colonel as something dead.

FRANK, RAY (1861–1948). Jewish religious leader. She was born Rachel Frank in San Francisco, California, the daughter of a peddler and fruit vendor, and his religious wife. Frank graduated from Sacramento High School (1879), taught school in Ruby Hill, Nevada (1879–1885), and then returned to her family in Oakland. She tutored in literature and elocution, published in a few periodicals, taught Sabbath classes at the First Hebrew Congregation, and became superintendent of the religious school there. In the 1890s she was a traveling correspondent for Oakland and San Francisco newspapers. On the evening of Rosh Hashanah in 1890, she led the first Jewish service in Spokane Falls (now Spokane), Washington. The service, conducted at the opera house, soon led to the building of a synagogue. Frank continued to combine journalistic work, preaching, and lecturing in the West. In 1893 she took classes for one term at the Hebrew Union College in Cincinnati, Ohio, and addressed the first Jewish Women's Congress held in conjunction with the World's Fair in Chicago. She continued speaking and writing until her marriage in 1901 to Simon Litman, an economics professor at the University of California, Berkeley. In 1908 the couple moved to Champaign-Urbana, at which time he began teaching at the University of Illinois. Frank continued to lecture and also taught postbiblical Jewish history, until her death in Peoria, Illinois.

Frank met Bierce in 1895, when she was active as a lecturer and preacher. The two corresponded frequently from April 1895 until January 1900, when Bierce was in California, then Washington, D.C., and elsewhere in the East. He responds encouragingly to manuscripts of short stories she submitted to him for his criticism, praises her efforts at doing good work through her speeches and prayers, invites her to visit him, complains about his health, remembers Western scenery nostalgically, mentions his reading and writing, and discusses her travels in England in 1898. In one letter, he addresses Frank as "most earnest of all possible girl Rabbis and prettiest of the land" (5 May 1895); in another, he says, "May God be very good to you" (14 January 1900). Bierce's letters to Frank reveal a man of belief, consideration, patience, and gentility. (*See also* Anti-Semitism in Bierce, Alleged.)
Bibliography: Simon Litman, *Ray Frank Litman: A Memoir* (New York: American Jewish Historical Society, 1957).

FRAYLEY, DR. In "A Diagnosis of Death," he knew Dr. Mannering, his book about foretelling death, and the meaning of his gesturing with his right forefinger. He attended Mannering during the man's final illness three years earlier. When Hawver tells Frayley that he saw Mannering's ghost but then later saw him alive, Frayley advises Hawver to go home and play something light on the violin. But the next day Hawver is dead.

FRAYSER. In "The Death of Halpin Frayser," he is the father of Halpin Frayser. He would like to be a politician in his hometown of Nashville, Tennessee. He neglects both his wife and his son, and laughs at their close relationship.

FRAYSER. In "The Death of Halpin Frayser," any of Halpin Frayser's siblings, all older than he.

FRAYSER, HALPIN. In "The Death of Halpin Frayser," he is the son of Frayser, a would-be politician in Nashville, Tennessee, and Catherine Frayser, who spoils her compliant son. The young man would like to be a poet, goes to San Francisco, is shanghai-ed, spends six years in the South Pacific, and returns to California. Near Mount St. Helena, he hunts, gets lost, and dreams a dream that involves his mother and that kills him. Or is he the waking victim of a visitation?

FRAYSER, MRS. ("KATY") In "The Death of Halpin Frayser." *See* Larue, Catherine.

FRENCH, NORA MAY (1881–1907). Poet. She was a young writer, beautiful and blonde. She knew George Sterling,* the San Francisco poet. When she was his guest, and that of his wife, Caroline Rand Sterling, in their home in Carmel, California, she committed suicide. Rumors of an amorous relationship between Miss French and Sterling, a known philanderer, circulated but were probably false. Sterling later wrote poems about her, including a sonnet about how lonely and mysterious she was. Nora French's *Poems* was published in 1910 by the Strange Company of San Francisco. Through his friendship with Sterling, Bierce came to know and admire Nora French.
Bibliography: Thomas E. Benediktssen, *George Sterling* (Boston: Twayne Publishers, 1980).

"FROSTING A BUD" (1900, 1912). Short drama. William McKinley* tells John Hay,* secretary of state, that Mark Hanna (1837–1904, a presidential adviser with a questionable background) ridiculed Hay when McKinley wondered whether Hay would be a good vice president. Hanna enters. McKinley leaves. Hanna asks if Hay would accept the nomination as vice president. Hay shivers. The title sounds like a beer ad.

"A FRUITLESS ASSIGNMENT" (1889). Short story. (Original title: "An Assignment.") (Characters: Antonio Finch, Roscoe, Henry Saylor.) In 1859 the city editor of the Cincinnati *Commercial* tells Henry Saylor, a reporter, to go to the deserted Roscoe house on Vine Street and spend the night in it. Last occupied by an old woman, it is now reputed to be haunted. Many people claim to have seen unfamiliar figures pass in and out of it. Asked to make a two-column report on anything untoward, Saylor goes in, locks all outside doors, and waits. Suddenly a crowd outside yells. He sees a male figure approach, hears footfalls going upstairs, draws his pistol, hears steps in an upper chamber, and goes up and enters it. In the dark, he happens to kick the decapitated head of a woman and lifts it by the hair to examine it.

Suddenly a crowd surrounds him, and he drops the head. People laugh insanely and kick the head from wall to wall and out the door, which closes. He is alone again, and the street is empty. When dawn comes, he reports to his sleepy editor, who stares and asks what happened at the house. "Nothing whatever" is his reply. Bierce unaccountably begins "A Fruitless Assignment" by saying that Henry Saylor quarreled in Covington with Antonio Finch and was killed by him.

FUDDY-DUDDY. In "The Haunted Valley," this is the name by which Gopher addresses his brace of oxen. He also calls one Fuddy and the other Duddy. He also calls at least one of them Terrapin and Geranium.

"THE FUTURE HISTORIAN" (1908, 1909, 1912). Essay. Long ago, sometime after 1813, Hiram Perry Maximus's invention of a silent, invisible firearm led to the fall of the Christian civilization. Widely dispersed, it was soon used to kill military officers, statesmen, then sinister Caucasians' enemies. Panic, plunder, and barbarism followed. Back "in the year 369 Before Smith," two-dollar aeroplanes were used for travel until they caused traffic jams. They were useless in war. Gas also became too expensive for dirigibles. When the electric leg was invented, air traffic diminished. In the so-called nineteenth century, nothing was known of Africa until Tudor Rosenfelt, of Wyo Ming, a Chinese province, hunted there and wrote about it. Aspects of his autobiography "are curiously entangled with those of an earlier hero named Hercules."

"THE FUTURE OF THE HORSE AND THE HORSE OF THE FUTURE." *See* "The Passing of the Horse."

G

GAGE, STEPHEN THORNTON (1831–1916). Railroad executive. Gage was born in Ashtabula, Ohio, and lived on his father's farm until he was twenty-one. He left with four yoke of oxen and after a hundred days was in Hangtown (now Placerville), California, where he mined and clerked. In 1855 he became the youngest member elected to the California legislature. In 1860 he started a freighting business between California and Nevada. In the Civil War he helped keep Nevada loyal. While serving as U.S. collector of revenues, Gage was approached by promoters of the transcontinental railroad, including Leland Stanford,* whose assistant he became for the Southern Pacific Railroad. For forty years, Gage was a railroad developer. In addition, he managed the extensive Iron and Cattle Ranch at Iona, California (1890–1905). He died in Oakland. Bierce in an untitled fable (*San Francisco Examiner*, 28 November 1891) ridicules Gage for professing a total loss of memory when questioned by a grand jury; the jury foreman's immediate response is to check to make sure he still has his wallet.
Bibliography: Joshi.

GALBRAITH. In "The Isle of Pines," he is the son of the Rev. Henry Galbraith and his wife. He accompanies his father and their friend, Robert Mosely Maren, to investigate the house of the recently deceased Herman Deluse, rumored to have been a pirate. Young Galbraith enters a back room ahead of the other two men. When they follow, they find Galbraith dead and clutching a bag of gold.

GALBRAITH, MRS. HENRY. In "The Isle of Pines," she is the Rev. Henry Galbraith's wife. She triggers his strange narrative by asking him where he spent the previous night.

GALBRAITH, THE REV. HENRY. In "The Isle of Pines," he is a minister in Gallipolis, Ohio. After a month in Cincinnati, he is returning home on 10 November 1867, when a storm forces him to find shelter in the house of Herman Deluse, a recluse suspected of having been a pirate. Deluse, however, died on 4 November 1867. Once inside the house, the front door of which is unlocked, Galbraith sees Deluse walking around and looking in vain for something. The next day, Galbraith, his son, and a friend named Robert Mosely Maren break into the Deluse house, the front door of which is locked. Young Galbraith walks on ahead of them into a rear room, and when the other two men follow they find him dead and clutching a bag of gold.

GALLEGOS, RAMON. In "The Stranger," he committed suicide in the cavern when trapped by Apaches.

"THE GAME OF BUTTON" (1892, 1911). Essay. The button is indestructible, perhaps immortal. It is useful, but the hook-and-eye is comparably so. Anyone inventing something better will be highly lauded. Women use the hook-and-eye but mainly in dress backs. Martin Luther said dresses should be hooked up in front so that women would not be enslaved to men who dressed them from the rear. Vestiges of Calvinist thought persuade some women to fasten backwards. But most women are slow to use the front hook-and-eye, and all men still use buttons. (It is a pity Bierce did not live to see, adopt, and write about the pleasures and pains of zippers.)

"THE GAME OF POLITICS" (1895, 1896, 1898, 1900, 1903, 1904, 1912, 1919). Essay. (Original titles of parts: "Ambrose Bierce Says: Public Opinion Is Responsible for Many Fallacies" and "Rhetorical Monke-Shines.") Calling oneself a Democrat or a Republican is meaningless. We vote as we like without fear of loss of party standing. Europeans laugh at our national political conventions, which are full of "inflated" oratory, including worn-out metaphors. It is stupid to believe that any reform is possible by the introduction of voting machines. It is also stupid to believe that the power of oratory is passé. Witness William Jennings Bryan, who combined tongue work and animal magnetism. We are in trouble if we follow public opinion, because the average person is a mediocre thinker, with little knowledge and less logic. If you say that the people's voice reflects God's, you have to agree that God flip-flops in successive national elections. It is simply that the stronger party gains the majority. A nominee's being expected to answer questions implies that he is too obscure to run. Unfortunately, people love fakes and rogues. A representative should not be expected to fight merely for his constituents' capricious wants but instead to listen to his conscience. Poetically eulogizing deceased congressmen hides their faults and immorally holds them up as role models for the young. The *Congressional Record* should become "a book of bathos."

GENERAL X. In "A Son of the Gods: A Study in the Present Tense," he is the officer ordered to send skirmishers to learn the strength of the enemy. A young officer volunteers to ride on ahead to do so, and to return with a report. But he knows that he will be killed and that his sacrifice will be proof that the enemy is there.

"THE GENESIS OF A NATION" (1903, 1912). Short drama. (Originally part of "Unauthenticated Dialogues.") When a senator telephones John Hay,* the secretary of state, to tell him that Panama has seceded from Colombia, Hay expresses surprise and orders preplanned naval action to proceed.

"GENIUS AS A PROVOCATION" (1908, 1912). Essay. Yoni Noguchi (1875–1947) is justified when he asserts that the letters of the late Lafcadio Hearn (1850–1904), the versatile writer who recently died in Japan, should not be published. Families of important dead persons should not publish their letters without permission; they often do so only to derogate and profit. The son of Robert Browning and his wife, as well as the family of Alfred, Lord Tennyson behaved improperly in publishing personal letters left in their care. It would be best if a man could grow great without friends and leave no letters behind. It is wrong to think that the letters of an author are as deserving of publication as words he wrote for the public are. Bierce closes by hoping that his correspondence is never published and adds that none of his love letters was ever sincere.

GENTHE, ARNOLD (1869–1942). Photographer. Genthe was born in Berlin, the son of a professor of Latin and Greek. He earned his doctorate in philology, specializing in medieval Latin literature, at the University of Jena in 1894. By this time, he had published *Deutsches Slang: beine sammlung familiärer Ausdrücke und Redensarten* (1892), on German slang. In 1895 Genthe migrated to San Francisco, to tutor the son of a German nobleman who had married the daughter of a wealthy American businessman. Genthe purchased a small camera to take pictures of California scenes to send home to his family. He became adept at portrait photography and soon opened his own studio. Intrigued by Chinatown, he took the only photographs, about 200 in number, depicting the region between 1896 and 1906. The San Francisco earthquake of 1906 destroyed his studio, but he borrowed a camera and photographed the devastation in 180 priceless pictures. Reestablished, Genthe soon made stunning, often romantic-looking pictures of local and visiting celebrities. Over the years, including his career in New

York from 1911, he captured the moody visages of Gertrude Atherton,* Mary Austin, Sarah Bernhardt, Isadora Duncan, Greta Garbo, Sinclair Lewis, Jack London,* Edwin Markham,* Frank Norris, Anna Pavlova, John D. Rockefeller, Theodore Roosevelt,* George Sterling,* and many other noted literary, political, and theatrical people. In 1908 Genthe experimented with color photography; five years later, his image of a rainbow in the Grand Canyon was the first color photograph on the cover of an American magazine (*Collier's*, 1911).

In his beautifully illustrated autobiography, Genthe memorably describes a drinking party that he, Bierce, London, and Sterling enjoyed over a campfire in California in 1910. He notes that during the course of the boozy, talk-filled evening, Bierce's derby, an unusual garb then, tilted precariously. Genthe won many prizes for his portrait and landscape photographs. His professional travels took him to Mexico and Central America, several countries along the Mediterranean, and Japan. Never married, he suffered a fatal heart attack in Connecticut while visiting friends.

Bibliography: Arnold Genthe, *As I Remember* (New York: Reynal and Hitchcock, 1936); Toby Gersten Quitslund, "Arnold Genthe: A Pictorial Photographer in San Francisco" (Ph.D. dissertation, George Washington University, 1988).

"GEORGE THE MADE-OVER" (1899, 1902, 1911). Essay. Since the American Revolution was of more importance to Americans than it was to the English, the latter have a more sound opinion of George Washington. Americans have made him too virtuous to be human, hence artificial. The natural Washington, also great, was a swearing, drinking "lady-killer." Sadly, all portraits of Washington are idealized. Next, historians inflated his abilities in thought and war. He is now "the public prig," far inferior to Alexander Hamilton.

"GEORGE THURSTON" (1883). Short story. (Characters: Colonel Brough, Captain Burling, First Lieutenant George Thurston.) Casualties in the Union Army brigade in which the narrator serves as a topographical engineer have caused Colonel Brough and his aide-de-camp, First Lieutenant George Thurston, to be assigned to the brigade temporarily. The men do not like Thurston, because he is "unsocial." But he gains the narrator's respect when he asks to accompany the narrator on a dangerous mission, as an unarmed "spectator." Thurston sits on his horse bravely, with his arms folded across his chest. The horse is killed under him. He would have been sabered to death by a tough Confederate, who, however, got shot down first. Later Thurston was badly wounded, recovered in a hospital in Nashville, Tennessee, and returned to duty. A quartermaster theorizes that Thurston is trying to overcome a tendency toward cowardice by bravado. Here is how he dies. In a forest encampment, someone hangs a hundred-foot swing from an immense tree. Thurston swings on it intrepidly—back and forth, higher,

higher—until he falls, arms folded, to a bone-mangled death. This was the first Civil War story Bierce published. In it he describes the dangerous duties of a topographical engineer; he was one himself.
Bibliography: Morris.

"A GHOST IN THE UNMAKING" (1887, 1912). Essay. (Original title: "Concerning Ghosts.") Many people have a general and comforting belief in ghosts, but without much faith in their virtues. Most feel that ghosts aim to upset one's thoughts and disturb one's sleep. On a lonely road one night in Sedalia, Missouri, a woman encountered a being that said that she was the spirit of the woman's husband's deceased first wife and that the second wife should "beware!" At this, the woman beat up the "ghost," which turned out to be the dead woman's irate sister.

"THE GIFT O' GAB" (1891, 1912). Essay. John Goss's *Forensic Eloquence* aims to teach young people "the art of saying things in such a way as to make them pass for more than they are worth." Such spouting is "mischievous because dishonest and misleading." Regular eloquence is all right, being like pleasant ornateness in writing. But forensic eloquence helps tricksters and rogues get ahead. Speakers such as Cicero and Patrick Henry are examples; they use "cunning expedients" irrelevant to their subjects. High-flown speeches, being "turgid and tumid," make poor reading. Trying to imagine one's ear being addressed by the long-gone speaker does not help much.

GILSON, MILTON. In "The Famous Gilson Bequest," he was a disreputable character driven out of Mammon Hill and thought to be a robber of sluice boxes of nearby gold miners. Caught stealing Harper's horse by Sheriff Henry Clay Brentshaw, Gilson is hanged. According to his will, he bequeaths everything to Brentshaw if within five years no one proves him guilty of any crime. A codicil of Gilson's will reveals that he has considerable property and money back in the East. So Brentshaw bribes various people to prove the innocence of Gilson. When Brentshaw sees Gilson's ghost in the cemetery robbing other coffins, all unearthed by a sudden flood, he dies.

GILSTRAP, PETE. In "The Hypnotist," he was a murderer, now deceased, who operated out of a shanty between Succotash Hill and South Asphyxia. The narrator John's parents lived at South Asphyxia. He caused their deaths near the Hill.

"GODS IN CHICAGO" (1890, 1912). Essay. A man named W. J. Gunning, who went around the world collecting gods for the World's Fair in Chicago, has just died and will be missed. He has advanced theological studies, and his "goddery" will prove attractive. Foreign visitors can find the deities of their fathers. There may be a danger, however, in setting up multiple gods in a city tolerating none.

GOPHER. In "The Haunted Valley," he lost his Chinese girlfriend Ah Wee to Jo. Dunfer in a poker game in San Francisco. Even so, Gopher and Ah Wee, who became Jo.'s faithful girl, worked for Jo. at his place near a cool valley. When Jo. wrongly thought the two were intimate, he killed Ah Wee and almost killed Gopher. Unrepentent upon learning that Gopher was innocently trying to protect Ah Wee from a tarantula, which bit him badly, Jo. was acquitted of murder. Years later, however, Jo. is fatally frightened when Gopher looks at him through a knot-hole in Jo.'s saloon; soon dying, Jo. persuades Gopher to bury him near Ah Wee. The narrator, who learns the truth from Gopher, regards him a "luny," which Gopher agrees he is.

GORDON, WILLIAM HEYNER. In "The Mystery of Charles Farquharson," one dark summer night in Philadelphia in 1843, Gordon gets up from bed, stumbles on a corpse in his room, and subsequently learns, through correspondence with his boyhood friend Charles Richter, who now lives in Bombay, that its features exactly resemble those of Charles Farquharson, their mutual friend who has just died in Bombay and whose daguerreotype Richter has sent Gordon. Richter adds that the body of Farquharson, a Parsee, was consumed by buzzards. When Gordon gets permission to open the coffin of the man he stumbled over, he finds it empty.

GORHAM. In "Two Military Executions," he is a soldier answering roll call in Lieutenant Will Dudley's company.

GOVERNOR, THE. In "An Affair of Outposts," he is the governor of the state in which Captain Armisted and his wife Julia live. When Armisted learns of his wife's infidelity with an unknown man, he obtains a commission to serve in the Union Army. The Governor, who was Julia's lover, grants the commission, later visits Armisted after the battle of Pittsburg Landing, and is rescued from danger by Armisted and his men. This, even though Armisted recently received a penitent letter from Julia naming the Governor as her whilom lover. Bierce based part of "An Affair of Outposts" on history, including the fact that Governor Oliver P. Morton of Indiana visited his Ninth Infantry regiment in Tennessee after the battle of Pittsburg Landing. *Bibliography:* Morris.

GRAFFENREID, CAPTAIN ANDERTON. In "One Officer, One Man," he is a Union Army officer whose friendship with the governor of his state held him to desk duty for two years, despite his military education. When he gets the command of a company of veterans, he is happy, wants to impress a girlfriend back home, and tries to endure the snickers of his men. The enemy begins firing, and Graffenreid becomes so terrified that he commits suicide by falling on his sword in front of his sergeant.

GRAHAM, CAPTAIN. In "The Story of a Conscience," he is the Union Army officer whom Captain Parrol Hartnoy directs, through a lieutenant, to supervise the execution of Dramer Brune by firing squad.

GRANIER, HENRI. In "The Mystery of Charles Farquharson," he lives in a room adjoining that of William Heyner Gordon. When Gordon finds a corpse in his room one dark summer night in 1843, his shriek brings Granier, who tries to be of help but can do nothing to solve the ensuing mystery.

GRATTAN, CASPAR. In "The Moonlit Road." *See* Hetman, Joel. Curiously, a superb scholar named C[linton] Hartley Grattan (1902–1980) wrote *Bitter Bierce: A Mystery of American Letters* (1929). Grattan is an unusual name.

GRAYROCK. In "Two Military Executions," he is a soldier answering roll call in Lieutenant Will Dudley's company.

GRAYROCK, JOHN. In "The Mocking-Bird," he is the twin brother of Private William Grayrock of the Union Army. The two have long been out of touch with one another. John has joined the Confederate Army. While on picket duty one night, William hears a sound, shouts a warning, and then shoots and kills John.

GRAYROCK, PRIVATE WILLIAM. In "The Mocking-Bird," he is a soldier in the Union Army. One night on picket duty, he hears a sound, cries "Halt!", and fires accurately at the sound. Disoriented, he does not join the other pickets in a retreat and is regarded as a hero for holding his position. The next day William returns to find what he shot at, but fails to do so, and sits down to rest. He falls asleep and dreams about John Grayrock, his twin brother, with whom he has long been out of touch. Awakening to the beautiful song of a mocking-bird, William walks on and finds his twin's corpse, shot through the chest. He then kills himself.

"THE GREAT STRIKE OF 1895" (1895, 1912). Essay. (Original title: "The Strike of 1899.") The American Authors' Guild struck in 1895. In New York, a non-union author who took some manuscripts to a publisher was beaten up and died. A popular author led a mob to the Astor Library. Another was shot and is delirious. In Boston, some novelists demanded higher royalties; Pinkertons were posted to guard a publishing firm. In Chicago, a mob rescued an author jailed for killing a publisher. In New York a publishing house was burned, with loss of life; bookstores were closed. Readers began to suffer from deprivation of novels. In Philadelphia, the militia fired on strikers. In New York, the guild treasurer promised to continue financial aid to strikers' families, and other unions sent money to help out. Violent sympathy strikes began. In Chicago, accountants of a Methodist book company were killed. In New York, the strike collapsed, publishers promise never to rehire any striking author, and arrests continue. Bierce names many literary victims in this rather foolish sketch, including Richard Harding Davis, Julia Ward Howe, and Mark Twain.*

"GREEDY-GUT." In "The Hypnotist," this was the little girl whom the narrator John hypnotized into regularly giving him her lunch. Although she was made to think she had eaten, she complained of being hungry in the afternoon and was therefore called "Greedy-Gut."

GREENE, PRIVATE BENNETT STORY. In "Two Military Executions," he is a U.S. Army soldier in an incompletely trained unit in the spring of 1862. He strikes Lieutenant Will Dudley, his superior officer, which he would not have done later. Even though Dudley and Greene were schoolmates in civilian life, Dudley reports the incident, and Greene is arrested, court-martialed, convicted, and executed. A few weeks later, however, when Dudley's first sergeant, through force of habit, sings out the name "Greene," a voice answers, "Here!" Twice more the sergeant calls the name, and twice more a voice answers. A moment later a rifle shot from far away kills Dudley.

GROSSMITH. In "The Middle Toe of the Right Foot." *See* Manton.

GRUBER, THE REV. J. In "A Vine on a House," he is a minister in Norton, Missouri. He and Hyatt, an attorney from Maysville, first observe the trembling of the vine covering Robert Harding's house near Norton. They alert townspeople in Norton.

GUMP, CLAUDE REGINALD. In "A Shipwreckollection," "The Captain of the 'Camel,'" and "The Man Overboard," he is the narrator. His name is revealed only in "The Man Overboard." He writes sea stories that combine autobiographical facts and also fictional elements of the sort his contemporary readers lap up. In "A Shipwreckollection," he sails with Captain Abersouth aboard the *Mudlark*, survives a storm by suggesting that they toss heavy passengers overboard, and is tossed overboard himself by the captain. Memories flash across his mind. He then survives. In "The Captain of the 'Camel,'" he goes on a voyage of discovery (1864–1865) with Abersouth aboard the *Camel*, which becomes icelocked when it gets into the South Polar Sea—at least according to the narrator's story. In "The Man Overboard," Gump survives the wreck of the *Nupple-duck*, captained by Abersouth. After adventures aboard the *Bonnyclabber*, run by Captain Billy Troutbeck, he argues with Samuel Martin, first officer, and both go into the water. Gump gets aboard Abersouth's raft, made of floatables tossed at him from the *Bonnyclabber*. He persuades Abersouth, for the good of Gump's sea stories, to drown himself. The alleged humor of these stories stems from Gump's intriguing diction as he mixes the facts of his life, his imagined exploits, and spillovers from soppy Victorian fiction into his own verbosity.

GURNEY, MOLL. In "The Famous Gilson Bequest," she runs an establishment, called a "deadfall," in Mammon Hill. It is less reputable than Jo. Bentley's saloon, where Milton Gilson used to lose at faro.

H

HABERTON, LIEUTENANT. In "The Major's Tale," he is a Union Army officer. A division of which he is a part is headquartered in a civilian home in Nashville. His associates are so tired of hearing him boast of his successes with the ladies that they dress up Orderly Arman as a girl and eavesdrop on his flirting with "her"—that is, until an enemy shell explodes upstairs in their headquarters. When Arman begins to pull off his garments, Haberton offers a sick grin and says they could not fool him.

"HADES IN TROUBLE" (1888). Short story. (Characters: Adam, Aggie, Beelzebub, Belial, Cain, Eve, Mammon, Moloch, Nick, Satan, Time, Zel'y.) The devils, notably Belial, Mammon, and Moloch, are bored in Hades, also called Pandemonium and Sheol. Their lives are aimless, dull, monotonous. They are thinking of having Time come in to divert them, when Beelzebub enters and reports that he saw the devil in chaos, that is, the earth. He also saw Adam and Eve there. He reports that hell is a better place than the earth. Belial says that he would like to pursue Eve, whereas Satan would rather go after Adam. Beelzebub suggests leaving the human pair where they are, because if they come down here they will make hell too hot. When asked to predict the future, Time says that he sees a snake detain Eve, whisper to her, and cause her to blush. Offered an apple, she takes a bite, but then grabs a stick and drives the snake into the brush. The snake was Satan, who leaves his calling card and returns home through chaos. Rebuking Time, Beelzebub, Belial, Mammon, Moloch, and some other devils are lolling about while they await Satan's return, when a handsome youth enters with a written message from him, still on earth. Beelzebub is to get smart, Moloch to turn vengeful, Mammon to get greedy, and Belial to aid Satan. Their happy home must not be ruined by the advent of Adam and Eve. Belial is especially abjured to keep Eve away. As for Adam, Satan says that the fellow initiated him into conduct which, if practiced in hell, would ruin the place. Now that Adam and Eve have had progeny, Beelzebub must keep them out, for they are greedy for fun. Satan assigns his own son to his devilish brethren's care; they must help Nick forget the earth, where he has just been born, and instead be at peace in happy Hell. Satan also asks his fellow devils to visit him on earth, but to be wise, persevere and pity him, forgive and help him. Don't listen to wily Eve, whatever she calls herself. And don't believe what these earthly creatures say in criticism of Satan. The youthful messenger, now identifying himself as Satan's boy Nick, asks for a drink, expresses approval of Hell, and says that he is supposed to stay. He expresses strong doubts when told that Satan runs Hell. He comments on Moloch's strength, Mammon's calculating nature, and Belial's affability. But he is surprised that these fellows do not know how to mix cocktails. Drinking a good bit more, Nick is about to tell his audience about Aggie and Zel'y, and what happened when his father first met Eve, when wine overpowers him and he falls asleep. Belial and Beelzebub agree that they must follow Satan's orders, go to the earth and rescue him, and keep Adam and Eve out of hell. Summoning many assistants, they proceed. But the narrator concludes that their mission has not been successful to date.

Bibliography: Lawrence I. Berkove, " 'Hades in Trouble': A Rediscovered Story by Ambrose Bierce," *American Literary Realism 1870–1910* 25 (Winter 1993): 67–84.

HAÏTA. In "Haïta the Shepherd," he is a young shepherd who learns the hard way that Happiness comes only when unsought and remains if neither questioned nor doubted.

"HAÏTA THE SHEPHERD" (1891). Short story. (Characters: Haïta, Happiness, Hastur.) Haïta, an innocent young shepherd, prays to Hastur, his god, tends his flocks well, and see minor sylvan dieties only out of the corner of his eye. As he ages, he grows sad at the thought of decay. So he decides to defy the gods and seek knowledge. A beautiful, radiant maiden appears, invites his companionship, but when he asks her name rebukes him and vanishes. Returning the next day, she tells him to do his duty and commends him for protecting his flock from the wolves. When he expresses a wish that she were a boy so he could wrestle with her, she leaves again— this time to the accompaniment of a threatening storm. He goes to a hermit who is his long-time friend, and carries him to safety. The next day the maiden returns; but when he asks her to stay, she leaves and fierce bears rush near him. The hermit listens to Haïta's complaints and explains that the maiden is Happiness and that she comes only when unsought and will not stay if questioned or doubted.

HALCROW, MAJOR CREEDE. In "The Coup de Grâce," he is a Union Army infantry regiment commander. He is the brother of Sergeant Caffal

Halcrow and the mortal enemy of Captain Downing Madwell, both of whom are in Major Halcrow's regiment and both of whom are close friends. Major Halcrow orders Captain Madwell into a dangerous combat situation, during which Sergeant Halcrow is badly wounded. While Madwell is killing Caffal, out of compassion, Creede and two stretcher bearers chance to see the merciful but illegal act.

HALCROW, SERGEANT CAFFAL. In "The Coup de Grâce," he is Major Creede Halcrow's brother. Caffal is Captain Downing Madwell's close friend, from their civilian days in Massachusetts. Caffal, though having "nothing military in his taste or disposition," joined the army because of friendship with Downing. Caffal is now in a Union Army infantry company commanded by Madwell, in the infantry regiment commanded by his brother. During an engagement with the enemy, Caffal is horribly wounded through his intestines. Madwell finds him and, in an act of compassion, stabs him to death.

HALDERMAN, DR. In "Staley Fleming's Hallucination," he is Staley Fleming's physician. Fleming summons Dr. Halderman to his house and tells him about seeing a Newfoundland dog at his bed night after night. Dr. Halderman says that the dog is probably the faithful pet of Fleming's neighbor and enemy, Atwell Barton, who three years ago was found by his dog stabbed to death. Later the dog was observed to be dead of starvation on his master's grave. Dr. Halderman says that he has a theory about these matters and wonders if Fleming has one as well. When Fleming equivocates about Barton, Dr. Halderman advises him to retire, leave his door unlocked, and ring for him if necessary. He will be reading downstairs. A thud in the night alerts Dr. Halderman, who rushes upstairs. He breaks down Fleming's locked door and finds his patient dying of a throat wound, caused by the fangs of a beast, now gone.

HALEY. In "Moxon's Master," he is Moxon's machinist assistant and toils in Moxon's workshop. When Moxon is killed by something resembling a chess-playing automaton, it is possible that Haley is the killer. Haley tells the narrator, who is recovering from the fire which destroyed Moxon and his house, that he rescued the narrator.

HALI. In "An Inhabitant of Carcosa," he is the supposed source of the epigraph concerning types of physical and spiritual death.

"HALL CAINE AND HALL CAINING" (1905, 1911). Essay. The first sentence of *The Christian* (1897), the popular novel by bestselling novelist Hall Caine, has twelve prepositions and is otherwise wretchedly composed. Caine regards patient industry, which includes writing slowly and rewriting, as necessary even for a genius like himself, since inspiration is perfected only unhurriedly. Better than all this advice would be for one not to write at all. Caine cruelly makes death even more terrifying when he confesses that he has not yet produced his best (i.e., most profitable) work.

HAMILTON. In "One Kind of Officer," he is General Masterson's provost-marshal. Hamilton receives the sword that Captain Ransome hands to him shortly before Ransome is to be executed by firing squad.

HAPPINESS. In "Haïta," she is a radiantly beautiful maiden who visits Haïta unexpectedly, disappears when he grows curious, and remains only when unsought and unquestioned.

HARDING. In "A Vine on a House," he or she is either of the two young children of Robert Harding and Matilda Harding.

HARDING, MATILDA. In "A Vine on a House," she was the unmarried Julia Went's sister, and was the wife of Robert Harding and the mother of their two young children. They all lived together outside Norton, Missouri. It was reported that in 1884 Matilda, who lacked a left foot, left home to visit her mother in Iowa. She was never heard from again. In 1886, Harding, his children, and Julia left permanently for parts unknown. Four or five years later, townspeople discover that the root system of a huge vine covering the Harding house is in the form of a human body with a missing left foot.

HARDING, ROBERT. In "A Vine on a House," he was the stern, taciturn husband, about forty, of Matilda Harding, the father of their two young children, and the brother-in-law of Matilda's unmarried sister, Julia Went. They all lived together in a house outside Norton, Missouri. Town gossip had it that Harding and Julia were intimate. In 1884 it was said that Matilda went to Iowa to visit her mother. She was never heard from again. In 1886 Harding and Julia, together with his children, left for parts unknown.

HARDSHAW, JOHN. In "The Man Out of the Nose," he is the neatly garbed, white-haired, demented resident, about fifty-seven, of the blank-faced shanty on Goat Hill in San Francisco. His love affair thirty years earlier with Elvira Barwell, a mining engineer's wife, cost him not his faithful wife but a prison sentence in San Quentin—on a rigged charge of theft. When, much later, something impelled him to wander back to Elvira's residence, he saw her at a window. She leaned out to look at him and fell to her death. This, added to his miseries, made Hardshaw, once a physician, a complete mental wreck. *See also* Johnson; Smith, John K.; and Spoony Glum.

HARDSHAW, MRS. JOHN. In "The Man Out of the Nose," she is the faithful wife of John Hardshaw, once a reputable San Francisco physician.

His love affair with Eliva Barwell resulted in a prison sentence, after which Mrs. Hardshaw loyally stood by him, helped him, took in laundry to support him, and tenderly watches him wander daily to the former home of Elvira, now deceased, in a vain search for her.

HARFORD. In "A Psychological Shipwreck," he and his wife, who are rich and live in Devonshire, England, adopted the daughter of William Jarrett and his wife, of South Carolina, when that couple died. The girl thus became Janette Harford. The Harford couple oppose her friendship with Gordon Doyle, so the two plan to elope.

HARFORD, JANETTE. In "A Psychological Shipwreck," she was the daughter of William Jarrett and his wife, of South Carolina. They were living in England when the girl's mother was killed in a fall off a horse while hunting. The girl's father, consumed by grief, killed himself the same day. Knowing nothing of her real parents, the girl was adopted by a rich Devonshire couple named Harford and grew up as Janette Harford, their daughter. Janette fell in love with Gordon Doyle, and when the Harfords opposed their relationship, the two young people planned to elope. Doyle sails for New York aboard the *City of Prague*; she, aboard the *Morrow*, which is never heard from again. In an inexplicable experience, the narrator, who is another man named William Jarrett, imagines that he cannot save Janette from drowning as the *Morrow* sinks.

HARFORD, MRS. In "A Psychological Shipwreck," she is the wife of a rich Devonshire man. William Jarrett, his wife, and their daughter were in England when both parents died. The Harfords adopted the girl, who grew up as Janette Harford. When Janette and Gordon Doyle planned to marry, the Harfords' opposition forced them to elope.

HARKER, WILLIAM. In "The Damned Thing," he is a reporter and a would-be fiction writer, age twenty-seven. He hunted with his friend, Hugh Morgan, who was mauled to death evidently by a beast that was opaque but of a color invisible to human sight. In testifying at the inquest to determine the cause of Morgan's demise, Harker reads an account of their hunting, their shooting at something that trampled the field before them, and Morgan's horrible death.

HARMON, COLONEL. In "The Affair at Coulter's Notch," he is an infantry officer whose subordinate officer asks Captain Coulter's colonel to permit rifle fire at the enemy. But Coulter's colonel has been ordered by their general not to use such fire.

HARPER. In "The Famous Gilson Bequest," he is the owner of the horse that Milton Gilson stole. Henry Clay Brentshaw caught him red-handed.

But after Gilson, who is hanged for the crime, left his estate to Brentshaw on the condition that no one would be able to prove any crimes against Gilson, Brentshaw bribed various people, including Harper, to clear Gilson's name.

HARPER, DR. In "A Watcher by the Dead," he is a young physician in San Francisco. He is a friend of Dr. Helberson and Dr. William Mancher. Harper arranges the bet as to whether Jarette, his rich gambling friend, can stay all night in a dark room with a corpse and not be affected. When the bet goes awry with Jarette's death, Harper and Helberson run off to Europe and become gamblers, evidently with money that Jarette had Harper hold for the wager. Seven years later, in New York, Harper and Helberson run into Mancher, who has assumed Jarette's name. Mancher jokingly calls Dr. Harper "Dr. Sharper."

HART, GENERAL. In "One Kind of Officer," he is a Union Army officer whose forces General Masterson orders forward in support of General Cameron's flank. Captain Ransome fires on Hart's men.

HARTE, BRET (1836–1902). Author. Born Francis Brett Hart in Albany, New York, he joined his widowed, remarried mother in San Francisco in 1854. His first published work was a poem that appeared in the *Golden Era* in San Francisco in 1857. He held a series of jobs—later fantasizing that he had held still more—married Anna Griswold in San Rafael, California, in 1862, and contributed to and occasionally edited the weekly *Californian*. After more publishing and editing, he was the founding editor of the *Overland Monthly*, to which many of his friends contributed. Several of his early stories appeared in the *Overland* (1868–1870), including "The Luck of Roaring Camp," "The Outcasts of Poker Flat," and "Tennessee's Partner," as well as his most famous poem, "Plain Language from Truthful James" (also called "The Heathen Chinee"). Nothing Harte later wrote during his long literary career matches these immensely popular works. He, his wife, and their three children lived in the East (1871–1878), during which time he collaborated with Mark Twain* on *Ah Sin* (1877), a silly play produced in New York. Harte spent all of his remaining years abroad, away from his wife and their three children, first as a commercial agent for the American government in Crenfeld, Prussia (1878–1880), then as U.S. consul in Glasgow, Scotland (1880–1885), and finally in private life in London. Harte died of throat cancer in Surrey, England.

Harte first met Bierce in 1867 at the U.S. Mint in San Francisco, where both men worked. As editor of the *Overland*, Harte accepted early works by Bierce and several of Bierce's acquaintances in San Francisco, including Ina Coolbrith,* Joaquin Miller,* Twain, and Charles Warren Stoddard.* Bierce contended that he advised Harte to publish "Plain Language from Truthful

James" in the *Overland*, rather than in Bierce's *News Letters*, to which Harte had modestly submitted it. (Bierce validated this account in an *Examiner* piece, 3 March 1899.) When Harte went east in 1871, Harte wrote gloatingly to Bierce early in March, and to others, that he was under contract to write exclusively for the *Atlantic Monthly* and *Every Saturday*, for a minimum of twelve contributions in one year for $10,000. Amused neither by the enormous sum nor by the resulting stories, Bierce called them "Warmed-overland monthly." It has been suggested that Bierce's "The Haunted Valley" reflects some of the local color in Harte's humorous mining-camp yarns.

Bibliography: Morris; O'Connor; Gary Scharnhorst, *Bret Harte* (New York: Twayne Publishers, 1992); St. Pierre; Stanley T. Williams, "Ambrose Bierce and Bret Harte," *American Literature* 17 (May 1945): 179–180.

HARTNOY, CAPTAIN PARROL. In "The Story of a Conscience," he is a Union Army officer. While on picket duty in Tennessee, he arrests Dramer Brune, who was a private with the Union Army but became a Confederate spy. In the course of their conversation, Hartnoy is reminded that he was ordered to guard Brune upon his being arrested earlier in Virginia but fell asleep and was kept from being executed for dereliction of duty by Brune's remaining, awakening him, and escaping only later. Hartnoy is astonished when Brune tells him that just as Hartnoy recognizes Brune so Brune recognizes Hartnoy. Brune seems to think that Hartnoy will spare his life. Instead, Hartnoy orders Brune to be executed and then shoots himself to death. The two men are buried without military honors.

HASSMAN, CORPORAL. In "One Kind of Officer," he is a soldier under Captain Ransome's command. He and Gunner Manning tell Sergeant Morris that the enemy is approaching.

HASTERLICK, CAPTAIN. In "Parker Adderson, Philosopher," he is a provost-marshal serving under General Clavering in the Confederate Army. He tries to come to Clavering's rescue when his prisoner, Union Army spy Sergeant Parker Adderson, attacks him with a bowie knife. But Adderson stabs Hasterlick to death by a thrust into his throat.

HASTUR. In "Haïta," he is the god of shepherds, to whom Haïta prays.

"THE HAUNTED VALLEY" (1871). Short story. (Characters: Ah Wee, Jo. Dunfer, Fuddy-Duddy, Gopher.) The young narrator, from the East, is intrigued by a valley running through Jo. Dunfer's premises somewhere in the West. It seems to the narrator that the valley is about to impart a secret. Jo. started to build a cabin in it, abandoned the idea, and instead built a place that is half residence and half "groggery." While drinking, the narrator learns from loquacious Jo. that he hates the Chinese. He says that five years earlier he hired one named Ah Wee and set the black-eyed fellow, with his white worker, Gopher, to cut some trees, which Ah Wee exasperatingly cut around the stems, Chinese-fashion, instead of by cuts on two sides, American-fashion, to make them fall right. Jo. adds that one day he got religion, turned properly prejudiced against non-Christians, and was talked into running for elective office. He gets quite drunk while talking and suddenly stares at a knothole in his bar wall. Both men see a huge black eye staring back. When Gopher enters, the narrator leaves, rides his horse into the cool valley, hopes it will yield an enlightening message, and comes upon Jo.'s abandoned cabin. Nearby is a grave, with a headstone marked Ah Wee but identifying the deceased as a woman. Four years pass. The narrator, back near the valley again, hitches a ride from a little fellow driving a brace of oxen. He turns out to be Gopher, who asks the narrator what he did with "W'isky," his nickname for Jo. The narrator is surprised at the query but remains silent. The two men drive on, to Jo.'s cabin, and the narrator sees a large grave near Ah Wee's. Gopher explains that Jo. got so mad when he found Ah Wee and Gopher lying down together that he hit both of them with an axe. Tardily noting that Gopher was non-amorously trying to remove a tarantula from Ah Wee's sleeve, Jo. kneels beside Ah Wee, who, dying, reaches up to hold Jo.'s head fondly. Jo. was acquitted of murder, since he was a proper Caucasian, and was even elected justice of the peace. Gopher explains: Nine years ago Jo. won Gopher's girlfriend Ah Wee from him in a poker game in San Francisco; she loved Jo. faithfully; he would not "treat 'er white"; he killed her; Gopher kept the secret; when he and the narrator were drinking, Gopher stared at them through the knothole. Gopher suspects the narrator of having poisoned Jo., who, dying soon after his drinking bout with the narrator, asked Gopher to bury him next to Ah Wee. The narrator judges Gopher, who fears dead Jo., to be "luny."

"The Haunted Valley," Bierce's first published short story, appeared in the *Overland Monthly* when it was edited by William C. Bartlett, not Bret Harte,* as is often stated. The story owes much to the early Western tales of both Harte and Mark Twain.* Jo.'s humorous Western lingo is grotesquely out of tune with the story's tragic burden.
Bibliography: Morris.

"HAVE WE A NAVY?" *See* "A War in the Orient."

HAWVER. In "A Diagnosis of Death," Hawver believes in ghosts, as he tells his friend Dr. Frayley. But after Hawver saw Dr. Mannering's ghost last summer and then says that he saw the man alive on the street, he concludes that Mannering cannot be dead. Frayley, however, knows that Mannering is dead, interprets Mannering's gesture with a lifted right forefinger as his prediction that Hawver is soon to die, and advises Hawver to go home and play something light on the violin. The next day Hawver is found dead, his violin under his chin, and with the music of Chopin's funeral march open in front of him.

HAY, JOHN (1838–1905). Politician and author. John Milton Hay was born in Salem, Indiana, earned a master's degree at Brown University (1858), was President Abraham Lincoln's assistant private secretary (1861–1865), and was assigned to diplomatic missions in Paris, Vienna, and Madrid (1865–1867, 1869–1870). Hay engaged in various kinds of writing, as an editor, poet, novelist, and biographer of Lincoln. President William McKinley* appointed him ambassador to England (1897–1898), after which he became secretary of state in McKinley's cabinet and that of President Theodore Roosevelt* (1898–1905). Hay's most important diplomatic successes were developing the Open Door Policy (1900), which prevented the partitioning of China, and negotiating treaties (1901, 1903) making the Panama Canal possible.

Bierce puts Hay in eight short dramas, always in demeaning little ways. The plays are "A Baffled Ambition," "A Cabinet Conference," "A Diplomatic Triumph," "Frosting a Bud," "The Genesis of a Nation," "An Indemnity," "A Twisted Tale," and "A Wireless Penultimatum." Here is an example of Bierce's silly superficiality. When in "An Indemnity" Hay says that he is praying for McKinley's health, the president replies, "Ah, yes, I suffer from Hay fever." In "A Twisted Tale," Hay calls himself "a sizable galoot"—mainly to rhyme with "brute" in the previous line.

Bibliography: Kenton Clymer, *John Hay: The Gentleman as Diplomat* (Ann Arbor: University of Michigan Press, 1975); Robert L. Gale, *John Hay* (Boston: Twayne Publishers, 1978).

HAZEN, WILLIAM B. (1830–1887). (Full name: William Babcock Hazen.) Soldier. Hazen was born in West Hartford, Vermont. He and his parents, who were both farmers, moved in 1833 to a place near Hiram, Ohio, where he knew James A. Garfield, the future president. Hazen was a cadet at the U.S. Military Academy at West Point, graduating in 1855 despite a demerit-earning contentiousness. He served as a second lieutenant in the Oregon Territory (1855–1858) and was in combat in the Southwest against Comanches along the Nueces River in southern Texas (1858–1859). Wounded in the right side of his chest, causing slight permanent disability (1859), he was on sick leave and then taught briefly at West Point (1861). During the Civil War (1861–1865), he fought gallantly in many engagements—Shiloh, Stones River, Chattanooga, Chickamauga, Missionary Ridge, Atlanta, Jonesboro, Sherman's March to the Sea, and into South and North Carolina. Despite his intermittently obstreperous and even defiant behavior, he was promoted to major general. After the war, Hazen commanded a small army group on a fact-finding tour of western forts in Montana and Wyoming (1865–1866). Reverting to the rank of colonel in the regular army, he toured Europe as a government representative (1866–1867), served in the Far West, was an observer during the Franco-Prussian War (1870–1871), was assigned to the Far West again, disputed with George Armstrong Custer about the political value of western lands, and was a military attaché in Vienna during the Russo-Turkish War (1877). Hazen was involved in political imbroglios leading to his being court-martialed in 1879, was totally exonerated, and became chief signal officer of the Signal Corps with the rank of brigadier general (1880). He was criticized for financial irregularities in the corps but was subsequently cleared of all charges (1886). He organized a relief mission to rescue a scientific expedition in the Arctic (1881) and criticized governmental delays in expediting it (1883). Blunt and irascible to the end, he died in Washington, D.C., of diabetic and renal maladies.

Hazen was Bierce's kind of man. In 1862, the 9th Indiana Volunteers, of which Bierce was a sergeant major, was assigned to duty under Colonel Hazen's 19th Brigade. After the war, Bierce accompanied Hazen during part of his western fort–inspecting tour (*see* "The Civil War and Bierce"). In "The Crime at Pickett's Mill," Bierce describes Hazen vividly, in part thus: "General W. B. Hazen . . . was the best hated man that I ever knew . . . Grant, Sherman, Sheridan and a countless multitude of the less eminent luckless had the misfortune . . . to incur his disfavor, and he tried to punish them all. . . . He convicted Sheridan of falsehood, Sherman of barbarism, Grant of inefficiency. He was aggressive, arrogant, tyrannical, honorable, truthful, courageous—a skillful soldier, a faithful friend and one of the most exasperating of men. Duty was his religion, and like the Moslem he proselyted with the sword."

Bibliography: Paul Fatout, "Ambrose Bierce, Civil War Topographer," *American Literature* 26 (November 1954): 391–400; William B. Hazen, *A Narrative of Military History* (Boston: Ticknor & Company, 1885); Joshi and Schultz; Marvin E. Kroeker, "William B. Hazen: A Military Career in the Frontier West, 1855–1880" (Ph.D. dissertation, University of Oklahoma, 1987); Morris.

"THE HEAD OF THE FUTURE." *See* "Some Privations of the Coming Man."

HEARST, WILLIAM RANDOLPH (1863–1951). Publisher. Hearst was born in San Francisco, the son of George Hearst, a mine owner and later a U.S. senator. His mother, Phoebe Apperson Hearst, became a notable philanthropist. Young Hearst enrolled at Harvard College (1882), haunted the offices of the Boston *Globe*, and was expelled from Harvard during his junior year because of rowdiness (1885). In 1886 he was given control of the weak *San Francisco Examiner*, which his father owned and which young Hearst converted into a popular and commercial success. In 1895 he bought the

New York Morning Herald. He spent enormous sums to hire competent liberal journalists, and also to acquire works of art. By the 1910s, Hearst owned seven daily newspapers, which sold well because of sensational, racy, and occasionally fraudulent "yellow journalism." He also controlled several magazines, including *Cosmopolitan, Good Housekeeping, Harper's Bazaar,* and *Motor Boating,* and also news services and a movie company.

Hearst was anti-British and anti-Chinese, and pro-Irish and pro-German, and supported the efforts of Cuban rebels to throw off Spanish rule. After the still-unexplained sinking of the U.S. battleship *Maine* in the Havana harbor 15 February 1898, Hearst's strident jingoism helped precipitate the Spanish-American War. Hearst had political aspirations. As an enormously wealthy Democrat, he effectively supported labor, favored progressive taxes and municipal ownership of utilities, and inveighed against trusts. He was a two-term, dilatory member of the U.S. House of Representatives (1903–1907). In 1903 he married Millicent Willson, a young dancer; the couple had five sons despite an often miserable marriage. During the Democratic National Convention, held in 1904 in St. Louis, to choose the party's presidential nominee, Hearst came in second to Alton B. Parker, who lost to Theodore Roosevelt* in the election. In 1919 or so, Hearst met Marion Davies, a Broadway chorus girl and later a Hollywood actress. They soon began an amorous relationship lasting until his death and symbolized by San Simeon, their multimillion-dollar dream-estate monstrosity south of San Francisco.

In his later years, Hearst failed in bids for various political offices. He fell out of favor with the public during the first years of World War I for supporting Germany, in the 1920s for praising the Bolshevik revolution in Russia, and in the 1930s for admiring Adolf Hitler and Benito Mussolini. He was not criticized, however, for voicing wariness of the Japanese from the 1890s on. He supported Franklin D. Roosevelt in 1932 but soon called his New Deal the "Raw Deal." Hearst's final years were marked by an extravagant lifestyle in California, including financial troubles caused by recklessness, ill-conceived pacifism in 1939, and a diminution of his still-potent but often-criticized newspaper empire.

Bierce met Hearst in March 1887 when the new owner of the *Examiner* tapped at the author's front door in Oakland. In "A Thumbnail Sketch," the subject being Hearst, Bierce later wrote one of his most often-quoted passages:

I found a young man, the youngest man, it seemed to me, that I had ever confronted. . . . I said, "Well" and awaited the answer.

"I am from the San Francisco *Examiner*," he explained in a voice like the fragrance of violets made visible, and backed a little away.

"Oh," I said, "you come from Mr. Hearst." And then that unearthly child lifted its blue eyes and cooed: "I am Mr. Hearst."

Hired at $35 a week—soon raised to a permanent $100—Bierce became the chief editorial writer for Hearst's *Examiner*, began at once to write two "Prattle" columns a week, other work in the *Examiner* for additional pay, and independent work for other publishers. This initiated an association with Hearst lasting until Bierce broke it off in 1909. Bierce began his Hearst columns by attacking old money, its undeserved power and privilege, political and police chicanery, and much else. All of this helped boost circulation and delighted Hearst. Some of Bierce's most virulent satirical writing blistered mining and railroad magnates, especially Collis P. Huntington* and Leland Stanford,* whose initials Bierce regularly converted to £ and $. Hearst bought the New York *Morning Journal* in 1895 and launched the New York *Evening Journal* a year later. In 1895 Bierce was writing in opposition to war with Spain over Cuba. In 1896 Hearst assigned him to Washington, D.C., to lobby against a funding bill favoring Huntington. Hearst also sent Homer Calvin Davenport,* the talented political cartoonist, to underline the criticism. When Hearst began whipping up a pro-war frenzy in his *Evening Journal*, Bierce turned briefly silent on the subject of war. Hearst may have ordered him to do so, although, given Bierce's stubborn love of autonomy, this is unlikely. In addition, Bierce hated war, even though it fascinated him and became a focus of much of his writing; he also despised hypocritical patriots who were often motivated by political ambition and greed. Moreover, he figured that the Cuban populace, being for the most part black in his view, were not worth fighting to free anyway. Bierce alternately boasted that the American army—not the navy—would easily defeat the Spanish in Cuba and ridiculed not only American political leadership but also American war correspondents sent to Cuba. In addition, he presciently warned of long-term complications in the Philippine Islands and regarded American ambitions there as veiled colonial expansionism. At the same time, Bierce shared Hearst's dislike of William McKinley,* president since 1896. Hearst loathed his pacifism; Bierce, his protectionist tariff policy, among other policies.

In February 1900 Kentucky governor-elect William Goebel was shot to death in an election quarrel. Bierce inconsiderately wrote the following poem, quickly published in the *Journal*:

> The bullet that pierced Goebel's breast
> Can not be found in all the West;
> Good reason, it is speeding here
> To stretch McKinley on his bier.

When McKinley was assassinated a year and a half later by a young anarchist named Leon Czolgosz, Hearst and Bierce were both subjected to violent journalistic abuse. Bierce lamely explained that his poem was designed to warn presidents of the dangers of assassins. He hardly needed to add that he had long despised anarchy and anarchists. Hearst's ambitions to become governor of New York and then president of the United States were effectively ended.

In 1905 Hearst persuaded Bierce to discontinue newspaper writing and prepare a monthly feature containing comments on current events instead. It was called "The Passing Show" and appeared in Hearst's *Cosmopolitan*, which Hearst had just purchased for $400,000. Arguing with its sequence of editors, Bierce wrote and fumed, resigned in 1909, and never associated with Hearst again. In the *Devil's Dictionary*, Bierce lampoons Hearst under the entry called "Diary"; he has Hearst die and the Recording Angel read his diary and scoff at its "shallow sentiment and stolen wit." In "A Thumbnail Sketch," Bierce says that he wrote in Hearst's publications for "the millions of readers to whom Mr. Hearst is a misleading light." So much for loyalty. Bierce is reported to have said that "A Thumbnail Sketch" was to be part of a long work he would write on Hearst but not publish during the lifetime of Hearst's mother, whom Bierce admired.

Bibliography: Berkove; Joshi and Schultz; Morris; David Nasaw, *The Chief: The Life of William Randolph Hearst* (Boston: Houghton Mifflin, 2000); Richard O'Connor, *Ambrose Bierce: A Biography* (Boston and Toronto: Little, Brown and Company, 1967).

"AN HEIRESS FROM REDHORSE: TOLD IN LETTERS FROM CORONADO TO SAN FRANCISCO." *See* "A Lady from Redhorse."

HELBERSON, DR. In "A Watcher by the Dead," he is a well-established physician, about thirty, in San Francisco. He theorizes that everyone is in awe in the presence of death. He bets his young friend Dr. Harper's rich, gambling friend Jarette that he cannot remain overnight in a dark room with a corpse and emerge unaffected. The bet goes awry when Dr. William Mancher, a friend of the two physicians, plays the corpse in the room, which is upstairs in an empty house Helberson owns. When Helberson and Harper visit the room early the next morning, they find a repulsive corpse and see Jarette escaping. Helberson and Harper run off to Europe and become gamblers, evidently on money from Jarette's lost wager. Seven years later they encounter Jarette, who is in reality Mancher. Jokingly, Mancher calls Helberson "Dr. Hell-born."

HELL-BORN, DR. In "A Watcher by the Dead." *See* Helberson, Dr.

HENLY, SAM. In "Corrupting the Press," he is the editor of the Berrywood *Bugle*. He publishes reports damaging to Joel Bird, who is running for governor of Missouri. Henry Barber gives Henly $1,000 to stop, whereupon Henly publishes a report that he refused Barber's $20 bribe.

HERSHAW, JOHN. In "That of Granny Magone," he is a witness confirming the story that Sarah Magone, though pronounced dead, fought a black cat off her face. Four days later, Sarah, never reviving, was buried.

HETMAN, JOEL. In "The Moonlit Road," he is a businessman living near Nashville. He suspects his innocent wife, Julia Hetman, of infidelity; so he sets a trap for her. Returning early from a supposed business meeting in town, he sees something leave the house by the rear, grows murderous, and wrongly kills Julia. He suffers terribly thereafter, haunted by her ghost, getting amnesia, changing his name to Caspar Grattan, and dying soon after. He says the number 767 is associated with him. This may mean that he was assigned this number in either an asylum or a prison. If the latter, he may be facing imminent execution.

HETMAN, JOEL, JR. In "The Moonlit Road," he is the son of Joel Hetman, a Nashville businessman. Young Joel is called back home from Yale when his beloved mother, Julia Hetman, is found murdered. He believes his father's account of events but is present on the moonlit road when an apparition (that of Julia) frightens the older man into disappearing. Julia's spirit tries in vain to communicate with her son, "lost . . . forever."

HETMAN, JULIA. In "The Moonlit Road," she is the innocent wife of Joel Hetman and the mother of their son, Joel Hetman, Jr. Before her husband murders her in her bedroom, she fancies she hears "a monster of the night" approaching her. After her death, she tries to communicate her love and pity for her husband and her love to their son. But forever in vain. With his nocturnal "monster," Bierce evidently wishes to personify utter, implacable evil.

HIKE, BEN. In "The Night-Doings at 'Deadman's' " Hiram Beeson tells the muffled stranger that Ben Hike was shot by Baldy Peterson. The stranger's emphatic nod intimates that the stranger is Death.

HILLQUIT, MORRIS (1869–1933). (Original name: Morris Hillkowitz.) Socialist leader and attorney. Hillquit was born in Riga, Latvia (then part of Russia), moved with his family to the United States in 1886, joined the Jewish-American labor movement, and joined the Socialist Labor Party a year later. He earned a law degree from New York University in 1893 and helped found the Socialist Party of America in 1901. A leading socialist theoretician and historian, Hillquit found favor with trade unionists because of his progressive-reform ideas. He was general counsel for the International Ladies' Garment Workers' Union (1913–1933), regarded World War I as a capitalist conflict, served as legal adviser to the Soviet Government Bureau in the United States (1918–1919), but then opposed its pro-Lenin stance.

He ran unsuccessfully for Congress (1906, 1908, 1916, 1920) and for mayor of New York City (1917, 1932) but polled a substantial number of votes.

In 1906 William Randolph Hearst,* the newspaper magnate whose payroll Bierce was on, persuaded Bierce to participate in a debate in a New York hotel on the subject of "Social Unrest," with an emphasis on unemployment and poverty. Hearst's *Cosmopolitan* sponsored the event and reported it in July. Hillquit, a skillful debater and orator who spoke German and Russian in addition to English, was also invited, as was Robert Hunter (1874–1942), whose *Poverty* (1904) was proving to be a popular and influential book. Hillquit and Hunter were well-known socialists. Bierce spoke vigorously in favor of capitalism, the intellectual elite, and the economic elite, and against socialism. His opponents were happy when he admitted that poverty and inequality existed, but they were nonplussed when he countered their hope in socialism by saying that the rich are on top because they are smart. When his opponents asked how he felt about those who merely inherit their wealth, Bierce said that they should be eliminated, most easily if the have-nots got together and voted for changes in laws and systems. When his opponents said that revolution might cure the adverse conditions of the poor, Bierce, ever the pessimistic reactionary, expressed the feeling that the people might revolt and shed blood, but would then get back into their former supine position; he added that the poor resemble ants in an anthill and that he was happy when he looked at successful capitalists. After the debate, Bierce took Hillquit to a bar, bought him a drink, and scared him by saying he would like to hang him by his attractive neck.

Bibliography: McWilliams; O'Connor; Norma Fain Pratt, *Morris Hillquit: A Political History of an American Jewish Socialist* (Westport, Conn.: Greenwood Press, 1979).

HOLCOMB, JOHN. In "At Old Man Eckert's," he is an apothecary who, together with Wilson Merle and Andrus C. Palmer, investigates the haunted house of Philip Eckert. He and Merle see Palmer walk past them and simply disappear.

HOLKER. In "The Death of Halpin Frayser," he is a Napa deputy sheriff. He and Jaralson, a San Francisco detective, pursue Larue, who murdered his wife, Catherine Larue. They find her grave and also the body of Halpin Frayser, Catherine's son.

HOLT. In "A Wireless Message," he is William Holt's brother. William is visiting him in central New York state when he learns by telegram of the death by fire of his wife and child.

HOLT. In "A Wireless Message," he or she is the child of William Holt and his wife. Mother and child burn to death in their Chicago home.

HOLT, MRS. WILLIAM. In "A Wireless Message," she is the wife of a wealthy Chicago manufacturer. An argument in 1895 caused him to abandon her and their child and go to central New York state to visit his brother. In the summer of 1896 she and her child burn to death in their Chicago home. As she is dying, she appears to her husband in a fiery vision holding their child in her arms.

HOLT, WILLIAM. In "A Wireless Message," he is a wealthy Chicago manufacturer. Some "infelicities" in 1895 caused him to leave his wife and child. In the summer of 1896, while he is visiting his brother in central New York state, he has a vision of his wife and child in the air, glowing red, above him. The next morning he learns by telegram that they died in a fire in their Chicago home.

"A HOLY TERROR" (1882). Short story. (Full title: "A Holy Terror: The Story of an Open Grave by Moonlight.") (Characters: Barney Bree, Jefferson Doman, Manuelita Murphy, Porfer, Mary Matthews Porfer.) Hurdy-Gurdy, now a California ghost town, was populated two years earlier by a few thousand gold miners and a dozen women. A man reported a gold strike there but was shot when it was later determined that he had lied. One day Jefferson ("Jeff") Doman, of nearby Red Dog, rides his ass into Hurdy's cemetery, seeks and finds a grave marked Scarry, and stakes a claim immediately around it. It seems that his friend Barney Bree, saloon swamper and grave digger, wrote him a letter—which he mislaid and read only two years later—that he had found gold at the spot where he was burying Scarry, a disfigured camp follower. Meanwhile, Barney died of overdrinking and could not share the find with Jeff. As for Jeff, six years earlier he left his girlfriend, Mary Matthews, in Elizabethtown, New Jersey, to find gold in California. He promised to return for her, but she took up with Jo. Seeman, a New York gambler who argued with her, at one point, cut her face badly, and went to prison for the deed. Mary sent Jeff a photograph showing her ruined face and breaking off their relationship. Now Jeff is at the grave of Scarry, whom rumor called "a holy terror." He laboriously digs out her coffin, finds the body buried face downward, and tilts the coffin upright in the moonlight. He stares at, and through, the coffin bottom with its rusted name plate, seems to see Scarry's decomposed face, and contrasts it with that of his beloved Mary, whose photographs—before and after her being cut—he has with him. He breaks open the coffin and stands face to face with the scary-looking Scarry. A few months later Porfer, a former mining-town faro dealer and now a well-to-do San Franciscan, and his invalid wife happen to be passing through Hurdy with friends on their way to Yosemite Valley. Porfer tells the group that he was briefly in Hurdy back in 1852, but he does not add that when he left he did so a step ahead of the vigilantes. They find Scarry's torn-up grave, her skull there, a plate with the name Manuelita

Murphy, and another skull. Porfer pronounces the glitter down in the grave to be fool's gold. Mrs. Porfer chances upon a jacket, from the pocket of which she takes a bundle of letters postmarked Elizabethtown, New Jersey, and two photographs of the same beautiful girl, one showing a cut and one with Jefferson Doman's name on the back. Mrs. Porfer—full name, Mrs. Mary Matthews Porfer—falls dead. The time scheme of "A Holy Terror" is hard to follow, and in addition its prose contains some of Bierce's most tortured syntax, an element of which is a colossal number of prepositional phrases.

HOOD, TOM (1835–1874). (Real name: Thomas Hood.) British humorist and illustrator. He was born in Wanstead, Essex, the son of Thomas Hood the humorist and poet, and author of the famous 1843 "Song of the Shirt." (Tom Hood is often erroneously referred to as Tom Hood the Younger.) After traveling abroad with his parents (1835–1838), Tom Hood attended a private school, the University College School, a grammar school in Lincolnshire, and Pembroke College, Oxford University, but left from there without a degree. Hood published his first poem in 1853 and his first book, *Pen and Pencil Pictures*, four years later, and did editorial work in Cornwall, where he lived until 1860. He was a clerk in the War Office in London (1860–1865), and then became editor of *Fun*, a comic newspaper, for which he provided jokes, verses, and engravings. His later books are *Rules of Rhyme, Guide to English Versification* (1869), the novel *Captain Masters's Children* (3 vols., 1865), and *Tom Hood's Comic Annual* (1867 and later). Hood and his sister, Frances Freeling Broderip, also wrote children's books. Hood died suddenly in his cottage at Peckham Rye, Surrey. His *Favourite Poems* was posthumously published in Boston in 1877, with an informative introduction by his sister.

Hood liked to befriend American writers in London. For example, in 1870 he met Joaquin Miller,* the minimally talented poet from San Francisco, and advised him to wear his hair long and dress like a California cowboy to advertise himself to Londoners. Shortly after Bierce arrived in London in 1872, Hood welcomed him. He liked Bierce's *San Francisco News Letter* essays and invited him to write for *Fun*, which Bierce did, beginning in July with some "fables," under the pseudonym of Dod Grile. Hood introduced Bierce to many of his hard-drinking cronies in the bar of the Ludgate railroad station in London; they included W. S. Gilbert, of Gilbert-and-Sullivan fame, Captain Mayne Reid, whose adventure novels for youths Bierce had lapped up in Indiana, and George Augustus Sala,* the journalist, editor, and author. When Bierce's son Day Bierce* was born, Hood wrote a letter of congratulation and punned that Bierce would probably like to make Day a Knight. Bierce asked Hood to befriend Charles Warren Stoddard* upon his arrival in London in 1873. When Hood felt that he was near death, he summoned Bierce, and the two agreed that whoever died first should try to

communicate with the other. Shortly after Hood died, Bierce felt, he said, the rush of his friend's spirit past him in the dark. For some time afterwards, Bierce was unable to write. Bierce liked England less after Hood's passing. Bierce's 1893 story, "The Damned Thing," owes much to his professed encounter with Hood's spirit.
Bibliography: McWilliams, Morris, O'Connor.

HOOKER. In "Corrupting the Press," he is a political committeeman in Berrywood, Missouri. He is suspicious when Henry Barber reports that Joel Bird, the editor of the *Bugle*, will stop publishing reports about Joel Bird, who is running for governor of Missouri, because Barber has bribed Bird with $1,000 to be silent. Henly's dishonest editorial that he refused Barber's $20 bribe makes Hooker's unfounded suspicions seem valid, and Barber is run out of town.

HOPE, JABEZ. In "The Failure of Hope & Wandel," he is Pike Wandel's partner in a foolish scheme to ship ice from Lake Michigan to New Orleans, for sale there.

HOPKINS, MARK (1813–1878). Railroad magnate. He was born in Henderson, New York. After the 1828 death of his father, who owned a merchandizing store, Hopkins left school, clerked, read for the law, but then did sales and bookkeeping work in New York and Ohio. News of the Gold Rush inspired him to form the New England Trading & Mining Company, to invest $1,000 in it, and to set sail for California. He settled in Sacramento and hauled and sold goods to miners in Placerville. In 1854 he returned to New York City and married his cousin, Mary Frances Sherwood. They had no children. Once he was back in Sacramento, he went into partnership with Collis P. Huntington,* selling iron and hardware. He soon met Charles Crocker* and Leland Stanford.* Crocker, Hopkins, Huntington, and Stanford, soon known as The Big Four,* organized the Central Pacific Railroad Company in 1861, with Hopkins as its treasurer—a position he held with great skill until he died. In the meantime, he added to his personal fortune by canny business ventures and investments. When he died, his original $1,000 had grown to $20 million, which collateral heirs and alleged heirs fought over until at least 1928.

By the time Bierce began vilifying the crooked moguls he called "rail-rogues," in 1881, Hopkins was dead and was therefore spared. But his reprehensible commercial strategies helped Crocker, Huntington, and Stanford on their nefarious ways and thus made them targets for Bierce.
Bibliography: Hopkins, Lindley.

"A HORSEMAN IN THE SKY" (1889). Short story. (Original title: "The Horseman in the Sky: An Incident of the Civil War.") (Characters: Druse,

Mrs. Druse, Private Carter Druse.) Soon after the Civil War began, Carter Druse most courteously informed his father that he was going to enlist with a Union Army regiment at Grafton, Virginia, near their mountain home. His father, who was a Confederate sympathizer, told him to do his duty as he saw fit but not to disturb his dying mother with his decision. Now it is the autumn of 1861 and Private Carter Druse is sleeping on sentry duty in western Virginia, near his home. Five regiments, of which he is a part, plan a surprise attack on the enemy that night. He is posted in a clump of laurel by a road and can see a flat rock jutting northward, from which an enemy might observe Union forces in the valley below, bottle them up, and wreak havoc. Fate whispers to Druse, and its finger unseals his eyes. Awakening, he looks at the cliff and is surprised to see in sharp outline a mounted scout in gray, looking like a Greek equestrian statue. The horseman turns, seems to be peering at Druse, looks down, and sees the sinuous lines of careless Union men and horses. Druse reluctantly concludes that to save his cohorts this noble foe must be shot. He fires. A Union officer happens to see a horse galloping in the air and carrying its rider crashing a thousand feet down to his death. A sergeant, hearing a shot, creeps forward, asks Druse what he shot at. A horse, is the answer. Was there a rider? Yes, my father, is the answer.

To an unusual degree, Bierce describes the setting with a topographical engineer's thoroughness. For whatever reason, Bierce wrote too many stories about sons killing fathers, as evidenced by stories in his so-called "Patricide Club." Two intriguing questions arise from this story: Would the father approve of the son's shooting him? And if both men survived the war, could they ever have become reconciled?

Bibliography: Grenander, Morris.

"THE HORSEMAN IN THE SKY: AN INCIDENT OF THE CIVIL WAR." *See* "A Horseman in the Sky."

HOSKIN, JOHN. In "A Light Sleeper," he is a man who has lived happily with his wife in San Francisco. In the spring of 1871 she dies while visiting relatives in Springfield, Illinois. Her embalmed body, placed lying on the back with arms at her sides, was sent from Springfield. In San Francisco, Hoskin first sees the body on its right side, before arranging for its burial, suspects foul play, but when returning sees the body on its left side. He goes insane and dies years later in a Stockton asylum.

HOSKIN, MRS. JOHN. In "A Light Sleeper," she was the beautiful, loving wife of John Hoskin of San Francisco. While visiting relatives, including her father, Martin L. Whitney, in Springfield, Illinois, she dies of heart disease, is embalmed, placed on her back with her arms at her sides, and sent home. Hoskin finds the body lying on the right side, later lying on the left side,

and goes insane. A California physician determines that the body was embalmed in Springfield.

HOTTEN, JOHN CAMDEN (1832–1873). British publisher, born in
Clerkenwell, London. At age fourteen, be began clerking for a bookseller in
Chancery Lane and acquired a love for rare books. After spending several
years in the United States (1848–1856), he returned to London and became
a bookseller and publisher. He produced his *Dictionary of Modern Slang, Cant,
and Vulgar Words* (1859). His biggest effort was titled *Handbook of Topography
and Family History of England and Wales, Being an Account of 20,000 Books*
(1863). When the distinguished Moxon publishing firm withdrew Algernon
Charles Swinburne's controversial *Poems and Ballads* (1866), Hotten published it, as well as Swinburne's rejoinder to his critics. In the 1860s and
early 1870s, Hotten pirated several humorous books by American writers,
notably Bret Harte,* Oliver Wendell Holmes, James Russell Lowell, Mark
Twain,* and Artemus Ward. In the absence of an international copyright,
Hotten paid the Americans nothing. When he published two books as
Twain's writing—but, in reality, his own—Twain was incensed. Hotten also
wrote short biographies of Charles Dickens and William Makepeace Thackeray, and other works, translated works by Erckmann-Chartrian (i.e., Emile
Erckmann and Alexandre Chartrian), edited works by others, and also pub-
lished many illustrated books of pornography. When Hotten died, his widow
sold the business to the publishing firm of Chatto & Windus, Andrew
Chatto having been Hotten's business manager.

While Bierce was living in London, he met Hotten in 1872. They quickly
struck up a friendship and Hotten contracted to pay Bierce £75 for what
became his first book, *The Fiend's Delight*, a collection of California pieces,
written under the pseudonym of Dod Grile. Hotten also contracted to publish, again pseudonymously by Dod Grile, *Nuggets and Dust Panned Out in
California*, a collection mostly from the *San Francisco News Letter and California Advertiser*. Delaying all he could, Hotten finally gave Bierce a postdated check in the amount of £100, for *The Fiend's Delight* and *Nuggets and
Dust*, but then died a day before the check came due. According to Bierce,
he rushed toward the bank to cash the check before authorities would cancel
it but was waylaid by friends, including the humorist Tom Hood,* for some
drinks. They beerily composed epitaphs for Hotten, whom they all disliked.
By the time Bierce got to the bank, the check was invalid. The best Hotten
epitaph, by Bierce's drinking friend, the journalist-author George Augustus
Sala,* was "Hotten /Rotten/Forgotten." Chatto & Windus published *Nuggets
and Dust* (1873).

Bibliography: M. E. Grenander, "Ambrose Bierce, John Camden Hotten, *The Fiend's
Delight*, and *Nuggets and Dust*," *Huntington Library Quarterly* 28 (August 1965): 353–
371; Steven Marcus, *The Other Victorians: A Study of Sexuality and Pornography in
Mid-Nineteenth-Century England* (New York: Basic Books, 1964); Morris.

"THE HOUR AND THE MAN" (1887, 1911). Essay. (Original title: "A Caution to Prophets.") Popular belief has it that in a crisis a great leader will come to the fore. Not so. A potentially great leader may remain mute, go unrecognized, be killed by chance, or be hurt by a capricious woman. Some thinkers feel that in tumultuous times the current of events is more important than individuals. However, military history would be different if certain great soldiers, for example, Frederick the Great, Napoleon, and John Sobieski, had died or had been transferred before certain momentous battles.

HOWELLS, WILLIAM DEAN (1837–1920). Author and editor. Howells was born in Martin's Ferry, Ohio, was a typesetter as a youth, moved to Columbus and became a reporter, and wrote the campaign biography of Abraham Lincoln (1860). Rewarded for it, Howells served as the American consul in Venice, Italy, during the entire Civil War. Home again, he began a long and distinguished career as an editor, of the *Nation* (1865–1866), the *Atlantic Monthly* (1866–1881), and *Cosmopolitan* (1892), and also as a prolific author, of fiction, plays, books of travel, and autobiographical works. His best novels include *A Modern Instance* (1882), *The Rise of Silas Lapham* (1885), *A Hazard of New Fortunes* (1890), and *A Traveler from Altruria* (1894). His best travel books are *Venetian Life* (1866), *Italian Journeys* (1867), and *Seven English Cities* (1909). His many books of criticism include *Criticism and Fiction* (1891), *My Literary Passions* (1895), *Literary Friends and Acquaintance* (1902), and *My Mark Twain*[*] (1910).

Howells's three closest literary friends were John Hay,* Henry James, and Twain. Howells's brand of realism is tame, even pallid, when compared to theirs and to that of younger novelists and short-story writers gaining fame all around him, notably Stephen Crane, Henry Blake Fuller, Hamlin Garland, Frank Norris—and Bierce. Howells favored depicting the common, ordinary aspects of human endeavor and downplaying the sordid and the sensual. He avowedly pitched his prose mainly at a decorous female readership. In "On with the Dance! A Review," Bierce calls Howells "Miss Nancy Howells" and his friend James "Miss Nancy James, Jr." In a *Wasp* column, he calls the pair "Two eminent triflers and cameo-cutters-in-chief to Her Littleness the Bostonese small virgin" (17 February 1883). When Howells lectured to the effect that Bierce was one of America's three best writers, Bierce is said to have ungraciously replied that Howells surely regarded himself as the other two. For inclusion in volume 10 of *The Collected Works of Ambrose Bierce* (1911), Bierce assembled earlier essays to make up "The Short Story," in which he reviled Howells yet again, calling him Cato at the head of a small senate and deploring his lack of imagination and inability to handle words properly. Not surprisingly, Bierce a year later declined an invitation to attend a dinner in New York to celebrate Howells's seventy-fifth birthday. *Bibliography:* Davidson, *Essays*; Kenneth E. Eble, *William Dean Howells*, 2nd ed. (Boston: Twayne Publishers, 1982); Fatout; Joshi and Schultz; Kenneth S. Lynn, *William*

Dean Howells: An American Life (New York: Harcourt Brace Jovanovich, 1971); McWilliams.

HOWES, SILAS ORRIN (1867–1918). Poet living in Galveston, Texas. In the late 1890s Howes began to write Bierce to request criticism of his writings. Bierce welcomed him into his coterie. In 1904 Howes visited Bierce in Washington D.C., to discuss the possibility of editing some of Bierce's antisocialist essays, which were gathering dust in old newspaper files. Bierce pretended to warm to the idea only with reluctance. In 1907, Bierce, together with their mutual friend Percival Pollard,* the literary critic, visited Howes in Galveston, where their host made Bierce the center of social and literary attention. In 1909 Howes's edition of *The Shadow on the Dial* by Bierce was published. Over the years, the two men developed an enormous correspondence, of which no less than 138 letters by Bierce have survived. *Bibliography:* Fatout, Joshi and Schultz, McWilliams.

"HOW I WORKED FOR AN EMPRESS: A SINGULAR BIT OF LITERARY HISTORY." *See* "Working for an Empress."

"HOW TO GROW GREAT" (1909, 1911). Essay. (Original title: "The Uses of Adversity.") The Bald Campaigner opines that a nation can grow great by suffering military defeat. Prussia and other German states lost to Napoleon, but look at Germany now. Americans, strong now, forget that we were defeated in the War of 1812 by a comparatively small British force. Historians of beaten people present "heroic" explanations, for example, those in the post–Civil War South, in France after Germany won, in Spain after 1898, and in Russia after the Japanese won in 1905. If we are defeated again, Americans will realize that they owe their country some time in military service, and we will build a strong defensive army and navy. When the Timorous Reporter complains that a big standing army may render civil authority subordinate, the Campaigner says he sounds like a Founding Father.

HUGGINS, PATIENCE. In "Curried Cow," she is the unnamed narrator's widowed aunt. She owns a farm in Michigan and on it Phoebe, her pampered, fractious cow. She insists on having Phoebe curried, thus losing servants when the cow kicks them viciously. Patience wants to marry again, to have someone to tidy up her farm, but almost no one wants to challenge Phoebe. Patience finally collars and marries the Rev. Berosus Huggins, who soon sabotages Phoebe by draping his clothes over a tall, iron pump. Phoebe makes the mistake of attacking it.

HUGGINS, THE REV. BEROSUS. In "Curried Cow," he is the tall, cadaverous-looking Methodist minister who marries the narrator's Aunt Patience. To avoid having to curry Phoebe, her vicious cow, he disguises a tall, cast-iron pump to resemble himself. Phoebe kicks it, hurts herself, and stops bothering the Rev. Huggins.

HUNTINGTON, COLLIS P. (1821–1900). (Full name: Collis Potter Huntington.) Railroad builder and financier. He was born in Harwinton, Connecticut, left school at thirteen, and for some years was an itinerant peddler. Beginning in 1842, he and his brother ran a hardware store in Oneonta, New York. In 1844 Collis Huntington married Elizabeth T. Stoddard; the couple had no children but adopted a daughter of Elizabeth's deceased sister. Huntington went alone to California in 1849 and soon settled with his small family in Sacramento, where he developed a profitable hardware business and later partnered with Mark Hopkins* in the hardware business. The two, together with Charles Croker* and Leland Stanford,* combined to establish the Republican Party in 1856. Known as The Big Four,* they launched the Central Pacific Railroad in 1861. The Pacific Railway Act of 1862—along with later legislation, federal generosity, and unprincipled bribery—enabled them to build eastward and dramatically link with the westbound Union Pacific in 1869. In his New York office, Huntington displayed the necessary fiscal wizardry and chicanery, while his partners managed the engineering and politicking in California. Huntington was also active in financing and planning a railroad line between Chesapeake Bay and the Ohio River, which was completed in 1873. He built locomotive shops at a site in West Virginia that he named Huntington.

Widowered in 1883, Huntington a year later married Arabella Duval Yarrington Worsham, a widow whose son he adopted. Huntington organized the Southern Pacific Railroad in 1884 and became its president in 1890. He was an active, bribe-spreading lobbyist from 1870 to 1880 in Washington, D.C., to secure legislation benefiting his railroad lines. In 1882 he founded Newport News, Virginia, and established a shipbuilding and drydock company there. He overextended his rail lines with terminal points including Cincinnati, Ohio, Richmond, Virginia, and New Orleans, Louisiana. This resulted in his complex holding company, established in 1884, going into receivership four years later. He kept his Newport News facilities and extended his grip on his burgeoning railroad holdings in California, mainly around San Francisco and Los Angeles.

Through complicated and often dishonest maneuvering, Huntington thwarted all competition, absorbed the Central Pacific Railroad into his Southern Pacific, and by 1887 had run one line to Yuma, Arizona, and New Orleans, and another up to Oregon. *The Octopus: A Story of California*, Frank Norris's naturalistic 1901 novel about Huntington's stranglehold on everything involving politics and economics, especially involving the railroad freight business, in California, only partially suggests the man's arrogant and duplicitous ruthlessness. In 1887 the Central Pacific, along with other companies, was the object of a U.S. Pacific Railroad Commission investigation.

Huntington did all he could to deceive commission investigators, but their report concluded that the Big Four had profited unscrupulously at the expense not only of the government—through loans illegally obtained—but also of minority stockholders deprived of dividends. Huntington was finally unsuccessful in lobbying against refunding bills requiring him to repay the government, which he reluctantly agreed to do in 1899. "The Man with the Hoe" (1899), the dangerously prolabor poem by Edwin Markham,* disturbed Huntington so much that he offered to pay $750 for the most effective literary rebuttal.

Huntington was an odious example of the robber barons' delight in exploitation and conspicuous consumption. After his 1884 wedding ceremony, he gave $4,000 to Henry Ward Beecher, the officiating minister. For his first wife's niece, whom he had informally adopted, Huntington bought a husband; the $2 million bridegroom was a worthless German prince. Huntington had a falling out with Stanford and later jeered at "Stanford's circus"—that is, Leland Stanford University in Palo Alto, California, founded in Leland Stanford Jr.'s memory and opened in 1891. In 1871, Huntington hired his nephew, Henry Edwards Huntington (1850–1927), to start working for him in a series of positions. He made the younger man a successful California railroad executive by 1881 and eventually willed him substantial stock. In 1873 Henry Huntington married the sister of his Uncle Collis's adopted daughter. The couple had four children but got divorced in 1906. Then in 1913 Henry Huntington married his Uncle Collis's widow. Over the years, Henry Huntington also amassed a fortune, part of which he used to buy books and art treasures both in the United States and abroad. These holdings became the nucleus of the fabulous Huntington Library in San Marino, California, which he endowed with at least $8 million worth of stock in 1919.

Bierce cast Huntington in a satirical verse drama titled "The Birth of the Rail" as a road agent named Happy Hunty and had him deplore the entrance of a devil called Sootymug as unwanted competition. Bierce, who regularly reviled "the railrogues" and referred specifically to Stanford as "£eland $tanford," went to Washington, D.C., in 1896, sent by William Randolph Hearst,* owner of the *San Francisco Examiner* and numerous other newspapers. Bierce was to send dispatches to the *Examiner* detailing Huntington's efforts to lobby Congress to let him delay—by eighty-three years, no less— repaying the $60–75 million debt owed to the government by his Southern Pacific and Central Pacific railroads.

Bierce filed more than sixty articles (February–May 1896) blasting Huntington in a style often demonstrating his most acerbic invective. He noted that his quarry's "dromedary head . . . [has] tandem bumps of cupidity and self-esteem overshadowing like twin peaks the organ that he is good with, in the valley between." The man has "one leg in the grave, one arm in the Treasury and one eye on the police." In building and running his railroads, he has committed "enormous robberies" and plans "still greater robberies." Bierce remarked that "[o]f the modern Forty Thieves, Mr. Huntington is the surviving thirty-six." He knew many a "prominent citizen with a thoughtful pocket known to entertain kindly sentiments toward theft." When Huntington was deposed before the appropriate Senate committee, he "took his hand out of all manner of pockets long enough to hold it up and be sworn." In his halting testimony (Huntington had recently suffered a stroke), he "merely sought to promote plunder by perjury." Bierce's most vicious comment, perhaps, was that Huntington "deserves to hang from every branch of every tree of every State and Territory penetrated by his railroads, with the sole exception of Nevada, which has no trees." He answered questions "with every evasion of which his faulty intelligence was capable." When Bierce got word that Huntington also hoped for government money to build a harbor near Santa Monica, California, where there were Southern Pacific railroad interests, Bierce labeled his adversary's unsuccessful cohorts "[b]rakebeam statesmen and jailbird petitioners," including "the very scum of the earth" and committing "felonious act[s]." When Huntington finally failed, Bierce gloated that "[h]is hundreds of thousands of dollars paid to half-a-hundred high-priced lobbyists has been absolutely wasted." He can now "gnaw his gold-worn fingers in impotent rage and curse mankind." In short, "this promoted peasant with a low love of labor and an unshakable thirst for gain, being already so rich that he stinks—this Huntington person is dead until December." Defiant to the end, Huntington lived until August 1900.

Bibliography: Hopkins; Joshi and Schultz; David Lavender, *The Great Persuader* (Garden City, N.Y.: Doubleday & Company, 1970); Oscar Lewis, *The Big Four: The Story of Huntington, Stanford, Hopkins, and Crocker, and of the Building of the Central Pacific* (New York: Alfred A. Knopf, 1938).

HYATT. In "A Vine on a House," he is an attorney from Maysville, near Norton, Missouri. He and the Rev. J. Gruber, of Norton, first notice the trembling of the vine covering the Hardings' house near Norton. They alert townspeople in Norton.

"HYPNOTISM" (1901, 1912). Essay. Everyone can hypnotize another to some degree. Success depends on your degree of hypnotic power, opportunity, and the other's susceptibility. Some men succeed in love affairs because of so-called "personal magnetism." Success in oral arguing is a matter of hypnotism. Converting heathens is accomplished by hypnotism, not talk. In the twenty-first century, legislators will never be elected unless they are able to hypnotize opponents.

"THE HYPNOTIST" (1893). Short story. (Original title: "John Bolger, Hypnotist.") (Characters: Pete Gilstrap, Greedy-Gut, John.) John, the narrator, can hypnotize people, read their minds, and so on; yet he tells his friends that he does not care to study the principles of hypnotism. Once in school, at the age of fourteen, he recalls that he forgot his lunch and therefore hypnotized a little girl into giving him hers in a basket. He did so daily, taking her lunch, enjoying it secretly, and destroying the basket. Though hypnotized into believing that she had lunched, she began to complain of being hungry. Not being believed, she was nicknamed Greedy-Gut. This delighted John as well as his selfish parents, who were happy not to have to provide his lunches. Finally tiring of all this secrecy, John caused the girl to die, after which he went to prison. This curtailed his practice of hypnotism, since he was often in solitary confinement. On being released, he stared at the warden and told him he was an ostrich. The poor fellow soon died trying to eat a door knob. John felt vengeful concerning his parents, because of their "niggard economy" about lunches. So he sought them out. When they primly refused to share their lunch with him, he told them off, hypnotized them into believing they were wild horses, and watched as they kicked each other to death and made him an orphan. For the last fifteen years John's attorney has been handling his defense against a charge of disturbing the peace. Whether a bad person might employ "hypnotic suggestion . . . for an unworthy purpose," John cannot say.

I

"I DECLINE TO ANSWER." *See* "Some Features of the Law."

"IF REFORM REFORMED." *See* "Poverty, Crime and Vice."

"IMAGINARY CONVERSATIONS." *See* "Two Conversations."

"IMMORTALITY" (1899, 1901, 1909, 1912). Essay. (Original titles of parts: "Ambrose Bierce Says: Not All Men Desire Immortality" and "Immortality and Reincarnation.") Since sleep, which may be called "virtual annihilation while it lasts," is a pleasure, permanent annihilation should also be acceptable. Those who want permanent annihilation think they will have it. Those seeking immortality are rather certain they are immortal. The few thinkers in between these poles don't fuss much about the question. Although the topic is big, knowledge about it is miminal; so it is a matter of one's faith. Camille Flammarian (1842–1925), the French astronomer, illogically says this: God has caused everyone to want perfect happiness; it is unattainable here; therefore, there is immortality. One may logically reply thus: God may not have caused this human desire; the desire, even if divinely "implanted," may not necessarily be fulfilled. Certainly, "pre-existence is a [baseless] dream," without evidence of topography. Testimony as to afterexistence is open to dispute. A knock on the head may deprive one of awareness of events between yesterday and tomorrow, but upon awakening I am the same, recognizable person. Not so in the interval between "Heretofore" and the "Hereafter."

"IMMORTALITY AND REINCARNATION." *See* "Immortality."

"AN IMPERFECT CONFLAGRATION" (1886). Short story. (Characters: None named.) The narrator casually says that he murdered his father

one morning in June 1872. After executing a nice burglary together, they argued in their library over dividing the spoils. Wanting a beautiful music box his father lied about having, the narrator brained him with an axe. Since his mother would soon be coming in anyway, he quickly "removed[d] her also." Advised by the chief of police, "himself an assassin of wide experience," the narrator hid the bodies in a tall bookcase his father had purchased from a "cranky inventor," took out an insurance policy on the house, and burned it down. He established a suitable alibi and rushed back with a crowd to the burning house, where they found the bodies miraculously unburned behind the bookcase glass doors. Witnesses were dumbstruck, and even the narrator was "greatly affected." Three years later, on some counterfeiting business in New York, the narrator happened upon a bookcase like his father's. The dealer explained that it was fireproofed by being built of wood containing alum and having windows of asbestos. The narrator would never buy it, because having it would kindle "memories that were exceedingly disagreeable." Bierce's repeated theme of patricide is undoubtedly owing to his chronic unease with respect to memories of both of his parents.
Bibliography: Grenander, Morris, Woodruff.

"AN INDEMNITY" (1900, 1912). Short drama. Before leaving the room, President William McKinley* tells John Hay,* the secretary of state, to tell the Turkish minister to "pay up" or face naval action in the Dardanelles. The minister agrees to pay at once instead of helping Hay by delaying until November-election time. The sultan of Turkey asks the Russian czar for money to bribe some Americans with. Refusing, the czar says that he cannot deflect the American ultimatum from the Turks, whom the Americans will talk to death.

"INDUSTRIAL DISCONTENT" (1892, 1894, 1900, 1909, 1912). Essay. Two antagonists in America are capital and labor. If muscular labor, hypocritically praised, is so desirable, why do people shun it for more intellectual employment? Our "no government" condones murderous strikes, thieving trusts, and bad tariff and free-silver laws. Discontent in industries is rife. Labor leaders want unions, by any means, to control everything, so that manual laborers—only if they are union members—can be richer than those who work with their heads. Employers seek to grab all the property and resources they can, and hire workers only to make them, their families, and their homes dependent on wages that are lowered when advantageous to employers. Struggles at such places as Homestead and Coeur d'Alène are over interests, not principles. This is revolution, and employer versus employee would be more accurately called master versus slave. In ancient Egypt, when workers were paid insufficient amounts of grain and oil, they revolted and many were probably killed by the Pinkertons of the time. Discontented workers today are getting organized, and capitalists must beware, because "adjustment[s]" may involve "cracked crowns." When immigrants, oppressed back home, swarmed in, America turned into "the most lawless [country] on the face of the earth," and our "eagle became a buzzard." It is wrong for America to be "an asylum for the oppressed." They get even for the wrongs they fled from, particularly in southeastern Europe, by wreaking vengeance on those providing them sanctuary. Such lowly workers have their grievances, including low wages (only twice what they got back home) and high prices for necessities. But when they act riotously against owners and independent-minded fellow workers, they should, nay, must, be shot. When civil authorities remain feeble, the National Guard is called out but is soon cowed by mobs. Inexcusable riots follow. The people have only what protection they merit. Killing rioters and lynchers a generation ago would have spared the deaths of many today. Lawlessness in a republic causes new evils and cures no old evils. Machine politicians, mutually flattering each other, control the not-very-dangerous masses by dividing them.

"AN INFANT CRYING FOR THE LIGHT." *See* "Dethronement of the Atom."

"INGERSOLL, THE DEAD LION." *See* "The Dead Lion."

"AN INHABITANT OF CARCOSA" (1886). Short story. (Characters: Bayrolles, Hali, Hoseib Alar Robardin.) The narrator finds himself in a sere region, with sentient rocks and blasted trees. He observes an ancient graveyard and wonders how he made his way out of the famous old city of Carcosa. His hands seek his wives and sons. A lynx approaches from the desert. A tattered man appears, with torch, bow, and arrow, and does not answer the narrator's request for directions back to Carcosa. Feeling suddenly alert and vigorous, the narrator sits by an ancient tree. It has grown up from under a rotting stone slab and has carried it up in its trunk. On the face of the stone is carved the narrator's name, together with his birth and death years. The sun rises but does not cast the narrator's shadow onto the tree. Wolves howl. The narrator recognizes the ruins of Carcosa.

"INHUMIO." In "The Bubble Reputation," he is the superintendent of the Sorrel Hill cemetery. Longbo Spittleworth's reports in the *San Francisco Daily Malefactor* viciously and grotesquely malign Inhumio.

"INSURANCE IN ANCIENT AMERICA: TRANSLATED FROM THE WORK OF THE FUTURE HISTORIAN." *See* "Ashes of the Beacon."

"AN INSURRECTION OF THE PEASANTRY" (1907, 1911). Essay. Adverse critical responses, in the form of "indifference, indignation, ridicule," to "A Wine of Wizardry" by George Sterling* were predictable. This is so because the poem is unusual, and people do not like the unusual. Displaying "moral unworth" are the following critics of Sterling: George Harvey and Ina Coolbrith,* who complain that Sterling uses too many distinguished passages and vivid images; Gertrude Atherton,* who would have preferred something on California and says that Sterling is too bookish; Joaquin Miller,* who finds Sterling hard to categorize; and Arthur Brisbane, who complains of Sterling's use of the word "gyre." Critics should applaud Sterling's depictions of "the realm of the unreal," since other daring poets have done so.

"IN THE INFANCY OF 'TRUSTS' " (1897, 1911). Essay. (Original title: "Ambrose Bierce's Peculiar View of the Turk.") The battle against the "trust" will fail and ought to do so. Modern civilization tends toward "combination aggression." Actions involving labor, big money, newspapers, department stores, hotels, farms, railroads, cities, the United States with respect to countries to the south and European powers—all illustrate this trend. International conventions, treaties, and arbitration groups do so as well. *See also* "The Turko-Grecian War."

"IN THE INTEREST OF DOG." *See* "Dog."

INXLING. In "Why I Am Not Editing 'The Stinger,' " this is any of the five children of Henry Inxling and his wife.

INXLING, HENRY. In "Why I Am Not Editing 'The Stinger,' " he is the bookkeeper of Peter Pitchin, editor of *The Stinger*. When asked to eject Muskler, Inxling replies that the man has a revolver and he, Inxling, has a wife and five children.

INXLING, MRS. In "Why I Am Not Editing 'The Stinger,' " she is the wife of Peter Pitchin's bookkeeper and the mother of their five children.

IRENE. In "A Lady from Redhorse," she is the recipient of Mary Jane Dement's letters.

"THE ISLE OF PINES" (1888). Short story. (Originally part of "Behind the Veil: Work for the Society of Psychical Research.") (Characters: Herman Deluse, Galbraith, Mrs. Henry Galbraith, the Rev. Henry Galbraith, Robert Mosely Maren.) On 4 November 1867, Herman Deluse dies in his house near Gallipolis, Ohio. He is suspected of having been a pirate; so his neighbors dig around his premises in a vain search for gold from the Spanish Main. During a sudden storm on 10 November, the Rev. Henry Galbraith, returning from a month in Cincinnati, stops on his way home to his family in Gallipolis—so he says later—at Deluse's house, which showed a light, to rest overnight. He rapped at the door, got no response, let himself into the front room, heard Deluse's footsteps in a locked adjoining room, called out again vainly, and lay down on the floor to rest. Suddenly Deluse opened the locked door, entered—apparently sleepwalking—and seemed to be looking for something. Imagine Galbraith's astonishment the next morning when his family and Robert Mosely Maren, visiting them from Columbus, tell him that Deluse is dead. Maren concludes that Deluse did not sleepwalk but that Galbraith had a dream. Late the next night, Galbraith, his son, and Maren go to Deluse's house to investigate. While outside, they see a light and hear sounds of sword and gun combat. But when they break in the locked front door and enter, all turns dark and silent. They examine the dusty place. Young Galbraith ventures into the rear room. His father and Maren follow and find him dead, clutching some old Spanish coins in a bag obviously taken from a cavity in the wall exposed by a board torn from it and now lying beside young Galbraith's body. Inquests conclude that both young Galbraith and old Deluse died by "visitation of God." The story gets its title from the Rev. Galbraith's joking statement to his astonished family that he spent the previous night with Deluse at the Isle of Pines, which was once a famous rendezvous of pirates.

"IS THE HUMAN RACE DECREASING IN STATURE?" *See* "Revision Downward."

J

JACK, PREACHER. In "The Captain of the 'Camel' " according to Old Ben, Preacher Jack shouted in a seaman's chapel that the Archangel Michael would put the Devil in the brig and whip him.

JACKHIGH, COLONEL. In "The Race at Left Bower," he is the owner of a bony horse that defeats the cocky Englishman's thoroughbred. Bierce hints at a diabolical aspect in Jackhigh when he calls him "the fiend" and his mount "the incarnate nightmare."

JACKSON. In "The Thing at Nolan," he is either of the two Jackson brothers. They overhear John May saying that his father Charles May will die because he struck John. When Charles is missing, the brothers tell what they heard, thus prompting John's trial for murder.

"THE JAMAICAN MONGOOSE" (1892, 1911). Essay. Human beings foolishly disturb the balancing act of nature, which is ever in the process of conserving and destroying life on our planet. Examples are rife. Australians, short of donkeys, imported rabbits in the foolish hope that they would grow, learn to carry loads, and bray. Americans killed off Indians, only to see their natural food, grasshoppers, multiply, with incalculable danger to our crops. Australian ladybugs were brought in to eat fruit pests but ate fruit instead. Someone in Jamaica disliked the rats there, imported mongooses, only to see rats disappear but ticks, to which mongooses are "immune," abound. Moreover, mongooses ate up Jamaica's tick-eating lizards. Ticks are now in control.

JAMES. In "A Lady from Redhorse," this is evidently the real name of the handsome, courteous gentleman known in Coronado as Dr. Barritz and thought to be a magician with connections to India. Earlier, Mary Jane Dement knew him as Dumps in the mining fields and heard that he had been killed while driving a stage in San Juan Smith. James has long been in love with Mary and is encouraged by their mutual friend Jack Raynor to return from Vienna to Coronado to see her, where she finally returns James's love.

"JAMES ADDERSON, PHILOSOPHER AND WIT." *See* "Parker Adderson, Philosopher."

JARALSON. In "The Death of Halpin Frayser," he is a San Francisco detective. He and Holker, a Napa deputy sheriff, pursue Larue, who murdered his wife, Catherine Larue. They find her grave and also the body of Halpin Frayser, her son.

JARETTE. In "A Watcher by the Dead," he is a rich gambler from New York. Dark-haired and confident, he accepts a bet that he can stay overnight in a room with a corpse, with nothing but a short candle for temporary light, and not be affected. His friend Dr. Harper holds the large sum wagered; and Dr. Helberson, a San Francisco physician, bets against him. At night stationed in a room in which the physicians' friend Dr. William Mancher, who somewhat resembles Jarette in appearance, plays the corpse, Jarette grows increasingly uneasy. When Mancher comes to life, the two struggle, Mancher kills Jarette, whose corpse turns white-haired, and escapes by dressing in Jarette's clothes.

JARRETT, MRS. WILLIAM. In "A Psychological Shipwreck," she was the wife of William Jarrett; both were from South Carolina. They had a daughter. When both parents died in England—she by falling off a horse while hunting; he, consumed by grief, by committing suicide—Harford and his wife, a rich couple in Devonshire, adopted the girl and raised her as their daughter, Janette Harford.

JARRETT, WILLIAM. In "A Psychological Shipwreck," he and his wife were both from South Carolina. While in England, Mrs. Jarrett fell off a horse while hunting and died. Grief-stricken, William Jarrett committed suicide the same day. They left a daughter, adopted by Harford and his wife, residents of Devonshire.

JARRETT, WILLIAM. In "A Psychological Shipwreck," he, the narrator, is the surviving partner in the mercantile firm of Bronson & Jarrett of New York. In the summer of 1874, having concluded some business in Liverpool, he sails aboard the *Morrow* for New York. A fellow passenger is Janette Harford, a young Englishwoman. Curiously attracted to her, though not amorously so, he is puzzled when she tells him that her servant, "a middle-aged negress" now accompanying her aboard ship, was left with Janette's parents by William Jarrett and his wife, both from South Carolina, when the two died the same day in England. Jarrett, the narrator, seems to see what must be family members of the deceased William Jarrett staring at him from behind Janette's eyes. He continues his narration by saying that the *Morrow* sank and that he tried to save Janette from drowning but could not. He wakes up in the *City of Prague*, on which Gordon Doyle, whom the narrator recently met in Liverpool, is a passenger. Doyle says that he and Janette are eloping to New York aboard separate ships. The *Morrow*, with Janette aboard, is never heard from.

JARVIS, ALGERNON. In "A Providential Intimation," he is a bad-tempered San Franciscan whose coat Stenner steals. In it he finds a telegram about the purchase of Sally Meeker. He thinks Sally Meeker is a horse, but it is a mine.

JESS. In "One Summer Night," he is a grave robber, described as "a gigantic Negro." When he digs up Henry Armstrong, presumably dead, Armstrong sits up, thus terrifying two medical students who are Jess's latest customers. They flee in terror; but Jess dispatches Armstrong with a blow of his spade, delivers the body to the students, and demands his pay.

"THE JEW" (1898, 1911). Essay. A certain rabbi has said that mixed marriages "are accursed" on the ground that through assimilation and inter-marriage Judaism risks extinction. Well, other well-credentialed religions have decayed and been effaced. The good rabbi should not have argued so negatively. Jews are disliked and persecuted not because of their commercial success but because they claim "advantageous relations" with God and preserve "racial and religious isolation." At its best, "the Jewish character" should be respected, and persecution of Jews should be detested. In the past, however, strong Jewish rulers have lorded it over their weaker Gentile neighbors. There is something a bit comic in the mostly tragic Christian-Jew distrust. Jews must learn that justice does not exist but that it can be approximated if they quit feeling holier than others. *See also* "Anti-Semitism in Bierce, Alleged."
Bibliography: Berkove, Morris, Neale.

JIM, CALAMITY. In "A Lady from Redhorse," he was the father of Mary Jane Dement. He struck it rich in the Redhorse mining field, died, and left her a million dollars.

"JO DORNAN AND THE RAM" (1877). *See* "My Favorite Murder."

JOHN. In "The Hypnotist," he is the narrator. He recalls hypnotizing a little girl at school into giving him her lunch. When he tired of the necessary secrecy involved, he killed her, went to prison, and upon being released hypnotized the warden into thinking he was an ostrich. The warden died trying to eat a door knob. Annoyed that his parents profited from not having to provide him with school lunches, he hypnotized them into thinking they were wild horses. Their kicking each other to death resulted in John's being charged with disturbing the peace—a charge his attorney has been fighting for fifteen years.

"JOHN BARTINE'S WATCH" (1893). Short story. (Full title: "John Bartine's Watch: A Story Written from Notes of a Physician.") (Characters: Bramwell Olcott Bartine, John Bartine, Rupert Bartine.) The narrator, an unnamed physician, is talking to John Bartine, who is a guest in his apartment after the two had dinner at the club. When the narrator asks him the time, Bartine grows nervous, hands over his big old-fashioned watch, and reluctantly offers this explanation. The watch belonged to Bramwell Olcott Bartine, his great-grandfather a wealthy Virginia planter, who was seized during the American Revolution "by that damned traitor, Washington, and his ragamuffin rebels" because of his Tory sympathies. He was never heard from again. Weeks later the watch mysteriously turned up on the family porch wrapped in a paper bearing the name Rupert Bartine, John's grandfather. Now, whenever the watch hands indicate that the time is just before 11:00, John, in his words, is "filled with . . . a sense of imminent calamity." Looking carefully at the watch, the narrator notes a miniature painted on ivory in the inside case. John says that the portrait is of Bramwell. The narrator replies that it looks just like John. For a little experiment, the narrator sets the watch back to just before 11:00 and challenges John to look at it freely, and safely, since it is now almost midnight. John does so, curses the physician in a strange voice, then bravely tries to smile, but sways and falls dead. The narrator theorizes that at a person's death a feeling may survive "to seek expression in a kindred life . . . ," and that Bramwell must have been hanged by anti-Tory rebels just before 11:00 one evening. The narrator sees to it that John and the watch are buried together and hopes that the souls—or soul—of Bramwell and John are at peace. Bierce cleverly suggests the approach of Bramwell's spirit by describing gusts of rain causing tree branches to rattle against the narrator's window.

"JOHN BOLGER, HYPNOTIST." *See* "The Hypnotist."

"JOHN HARDSHAW: THE STORY OF A MAN WHO MAY BE SEEN COMING OUT OF THE NOSE." *See* "The Man Out of the Nose."

"JOHN MORTONSON'S FUNERAL" (1906). Short story. (Characters: John Mortonson, Miss Mortonson, Mrs. John Mortonson.) At two o'clock, family and friends gather at John Mortonson's funeral. The widow and her daughter come. The minister speaks. The widow approaches the glass-topped coffin, shrieks, and faints. Others rush up, look, and stumble in terror into the coffin, knocking it down. The glass breaks. Out walks Mortonson's cat, its muzzle crimson. In a note, Bierce says that this story, in note form, was found among the papers of Leigh Bierce* (his son) and is here printed with minor revisions. A model for Bierce's awful cat may have been the titular heroine of "The Black Cat" by Edgar Allan Poe.
Bibliography: Miller.

"JOHN SMITH, LIBERATOR (FROM A NEWSPAPER OF THE FAR FUTURE)" (1873, 1909). Essay. (Original title: "John Smith.") At Smithcester, often thought to be the site of ancient London, people are celebrating "the thirtieth centennial anniversary of the birthday" of John Smith. Only six centuries ago this "*fête* day" became popular. Smith started or developed "the Smithocratic form of government." Shakspar, a once voguish poet, called him "the noblest Roman of them all." According to a Siamese manuscript, Smith captured a Neapolitan general at "the water battle of Loo." Smith transformed every European country except Ecuador into a Smithocracy. The year Smith was born, Martin Farquhar Tupper, a uniquely fine writer, died of starvation in London. Tupper was once arrested for stealing deer, fought a duel while blind, and wrote a work which was long hidden in a hollow tree. Smith and Tupper are named in history books, as are others, notably Julia Caesar, often called the Serpent of the Nile. Such names conjure up half-lost moments of history, many of them gory when compared to the serenity of our Smithocratic times. In former epochs, people settled questions by voting and feared immortality, women were free, and "A.D.," which are now mysterious letters, "had perhaps a known signification." Today we live happily under our sovereign, John CLXXVIII. The narrator quotes Professor Mimble on Equador in Europe and thanks Bungoot for helping to eliminate "the old order of things."

"JOHN SMITH'S ANCESTORS" (1899, 1911). Essay. A man—let's call him John Smith—has or had two parents, four grandparents, eight great-grandparents, and so on. Allowing thirty-four years per generation, in the year 879 he had 1,073,741,824 ancestors. That was about the world's population in the year 879. One generation earlier the population would have been over two billion. Thus one proves that a proposition can be both "unquestionable and impossible." This essay is demonstrably silly on its face.

JOHNSON. In "The Man Out of the Nose," this was the name John Hardshaw used after his release from prison when he and his wife lived near Market Street in San Francisco. *See* Hardshaw, John.

JOHNSON. In "Mr. Masthead, Journalist," he recently bought the *Claybank Thundergust of Reform*, a weekly newspaper in Kansas, to use it to defeat Jefferson Scandril, his brother-in-law, who is running for the legislature. Johnson asks his friend Norton, of Warm Springs, Missouri, to recommend a suitable editor. Norton sends Masthead, whom Johnson asks to write political editorials. When Masthead writes that Broskin, Scandril's opponent, was once in an insane asylum, Broskin's friends challenge Johnson to a duel. Johnson recovers, only to learn that Broskin was earlier a physician in charge of the mental institution and that Masthead had a son who was one of Broskin's patients in the asylum.

"A JUG OF SIRUP" (1893). Short story. (Full title: "The Jug of Sirup: Some Fantastic Passages from the Chronicles of a Village.") (Characters: Creede, Alvan Creede, Eddy Creede, Jane Creede, Deemer, Mrs. Silas Deemer, Silas Deemer.) On 16 July 1863, Silas Deemer, a conscientious merchant in Hillbrook, dies and is soon buried. Another merchant buys his goods *en bloc*, and his widow and his two grown daughters leave town. The shop is vacant. Three weeks later, Alvan Creede, the town banker and its most respected citizen, comes home one moonlit evening, fatigued from attending a directors' meeting. He greets his wife and asks her where the half-gallon jug of maple syrup is, which he bought from Silas that evening and just now set by the door. Tardily realizing that Silas is dead, Creede grows fearful of his sanity. His wife tries to assuage his fears. But then their tiny daughter toddles in and asks whether her little brother can play with the jug when it is empty. By next evening many townspeople have heard about Creede's "adventure." They gather around Silas's empty store. Some throw stones at it to challenge his ghost. Suddenly its interior is suffused by an ever-growing yellow light, which reveals Silas standing behind his counter checking his salesbook. Three brave men enter the store and are soon seen gesticulating, shouting, and cursing. A line of spectators enters; while the store interior turns dark for them as they tumble about, the store for a brief while is still visibly illuminated for those remaining outside. Morning comes. The interior of the store appears littered with torn clothes and bits of hair. The last entry in Silas's salesbook is dated 16 July 1863. The local historian opines that since Silas Deemer alive was honorable, Silas Deemer dead should have been allowed to continue his business without being mobbed. In "A Jug of Sirup," Bierce handles lighting effects like a modern horror-movie director.

"JUPITER DOKE, BRIGADIER-GENERAL" (1885). Short story. (Original title: "Materials for History.") (Characters: Brigadier-General Schneddeker Baumschank, Major-General Dolliver Billows, Joe Briller, Esq., Major-General Gibeon J. Buxter, the Confederate Secretary of War, Jabez Leonidas Doke, Brigadier-General Jupiter Doke, Mrs. Jupiter Doke, Major-

General Simmons B. Flood, Hannibal Alcazar Peyton, the President, the Secretary of War, Major-General Blount Wardorg.) This story is in the form of a series of letters, diary entries, a newspaper editorial, a Congressional resolution, and an oral comment from 3 November 1861 through 15 February 1861. The Secretary of War in Washington writes Jupiter Doke that the President has appointed Doke a brigadier-general of Illinois volunteers. Doke writes the Secretary from Hardpan, Illinois, to express his delight at the honor. The Secretary writes Major-General Blount Wardorg that he has assigned Doke to Wardorg's department. Wardorg writes the Secretary of War from Louisville, Kentucky, that he will accept Doke but that Doke's route to him, from Covington to Distilleryville, is infested with Confederate guerrillas. The Secretary orders Doke to get to Wardorg by that route while dressed in full uniform. Doke writes the Secretary from Covington, Kentucky, that he has given his proxy to Joel Briller, Esq., his wife's cousin, now proceeding to Distilleryville, and adds that he is writing the President to ask that he appoint Jabez Leonidas Doke, his son, to be postmaster of Hardpan, their hometown. Jupiter Doke writes Wardorg from Distilleryville, Kentucky, that a flood has prevented Briller from getting there and that perhaps he is dead. In his diary, Doke discusses living quarters, politics, the enemy position and moves, Union Army desertions, maneuvers he ordered, his desire for a supply contract, and his petition to the President to be appointed governor of the Idaho Territory. An editorial in the *Maverick* of Posey, Illinois, praises Doke's clever retreat from Distilleryville, enabling the "perfidious enemy" to attack and adds that Doke should run for president in 1864. Wardorg in Louisville orders Doke to hold Distilleryville but to retreat if even slightly pressed by the Confederates. Wardorg writes the Secretary from Louisville that a big enemy force is advancing on Doke, whom he regards as "a fool." The Secretary's reply from Washington to Wardorg is that the President has faith in Doke, who, however, may be well sacrificed in light of Wardorg's plan. Doke writes Wardorg from Distilleryville about Doke's plan to retreat to Jayhawk, adding that in the event of suspicion of treason each man is to mount a mule and head for Louisville. Major-General Gibeon J. Buxter of the Confederate Army writes the Confederate Secretary of War from Bung Station, Kentucky, that his major-general, Simmons B. Flood, was about to attack Covington near Distilleryville, defended by undisciplined troops without a leader, when he felt "an earth-shaking rumble" and Flood's front was hit by a tornado, causing terrible casualties, including Flood's death and heavy losses of men under Major-General Dolliver Billows. Buxter also writes that he plans to "push southward" on the morrow. Billows writes his Secretary of War from Buhac, Kentucky, that 50,000 enemy cavalrymen destroyed Buxter's division in a moment but that Brigadier-General Schneddeker's artillery brigade may have escaped. Baumschank writes his Secretary of War from Iodine, Kentucky, that he escaped to Iodine "mit no men und goons," that "Scheneral Peelows is deadt," and that he wishes to resign. By a resolution of Congress, Doke is voted thanks for overwhelming a vastly more numerous Confederate force, a day of thanksgiving is designated, and Doke is promoted to major-general. Finally, Hannibal Alcazar Peyton, a slave owned by Doke, states that he heard a movement of Confederate forces across the river near Jayhawk and roused "Marse Doke," who jumped out of his bedroom window "in his shir' tail" and scared 2,300 mules by looking like "de debble hese'f." The mules charged "like a yarthquake" into rebel forces at "de upper ford road."

"Jupiter Doke, Brigadier-General," a seemingly silly story of military incompetence and windy political rhetoric, has a bitterly serious side. Bierce shows how each report writer, whether attached to the Union Army or the Confederate Army, colors his account to aggrandize himself. The Secretary of War wants to get Doke killed and when that fails would not mind the tactical loss of Doke's brigade for strategic betterment. Doke's hometown newspaper is concerned only for local praise. More specifically, because the name "Jupiter" would surely remind Bierce's first readers of "Ulysses," it follows that Jupiter Doke's failings are a recognizably Swiftean echo of those of Ulysses S. Grant, whose memoirs had been published in 1885–1886 and about whom Bierce wrote critically in the *Wasp*.

Bibliography: G. Thomas Couser, "Writing the Civil War: Ambrose Bierce's 'Jupiter Doke, Brigadier-General,' " *Studies in American Fiction* 18 (Spring 1990): 87–98; Davidson; Grenander; Morris; Schaefer.

"THE JURY IN ANCIENT AMERICA: AN HISTORICAL SKETCH WRITTEN IN THE YEAR OF GRACE 3687: TRANSLATED BY AMBROSE BIERCE." *See* "Ashes of the Beacon."

"A JUST DECISION" (1901, 1911). Essay. (Original title: "The Sentimental Bachelor.") The Sentimental Bachelor tells the Timorous Reporter that a judge in a certain state supreme court threw out, as "[h]earsay evidence," a woman's statement that a male defendant promised to marry her. The judge opines that males ever since Adam have paid too dearly for "the favor—and favors—of the unfair sex." It is best that a man should tell his sequence of lady friends his intentions are honorable. They like to believe him, and it would be inhuman to disabuse them later. Amusingly, Bierce has his persona name nineteen of his variously endowed lady loves, from Adèle to Theodora.

Bibliography: Neale.

K

KENT, GEORGE W. In "The Stranger," he committed suicide in the cavern when he was trapped by Apaches.

"KILLED AT RESACA" (1887). Short story. (Full title: "Killed at Resaca: An Incident of the Civil War.") (Characters: Lieutenant Herman Brayle, Marian Mendenhall, Colonel Ward, Winters.) The narrator, a topographical engineer, admires Lieutenant Herman Brayle, a recent addition, probably from Ohio, to his heterogeneous Union Army brigade. Tall and handsome, Brayle displays foolhardy courage at the Stones River battle. In later engagements, he behaves in the same manner—sitting on his horse like a statue, standing rock-like without cover, handing his horse to an orderly, and walking erect to the front with orders. The men conclude that "he was vain of his courage." To a captain's remonstrance, Brayle smiles and replies that if he were mortally wounded he hopes that the captain will whisper, "I told you so." At the battle of Resaca, 14–15 May 1864, Brayle's brigade, its line curving near some protecting trees, faces not only an open field but also Confederate earthworks just beyond. Brayle is ordered to proceed from one end of the Union arc to a colonel at the far end, with orders for him to get closer to the enemy. Instead of going through the woods afoot, Brayle gallops into the open, parallel to the Confederate line. A wondrous picture: He is erect in the saddle, with his long yellow hair streaming, and his hat blown off. When enemy rifles open fire, Union soldiers answer, and a deadly, inconclusive artillery duel ensues. Once his horse is killed, Brayle might take cover in a ravine at a right angle to the enemy line. Instead, he stands firm until he is shot to death, after which both sides cease firing, and his corpse is carried away while awestruck Confederates play a fife-and-drum dirge in his honor. Brayle's effects are distributed, and the narrator receives his pocketbook. A year after the war ends, the narrator, on his way to California, examines the pocketbook, finds a letter in it to Brayle from Marian Mendenhall of San Francisco, dated 9 July 1862, and signed "Darling." Informing Brayle that a soldier named Winters told her that Brayle hid behind a tree during a battle in Virginia, she adds that she could accept news of his death but not of his cowardice. The narrator visits Marian at her "handsome" home and gives her the letter. She takes it indifferently but blushes when she sees a stain on it. The narrator tells her it is a brave man's blood. Recoiling, she says that she cannot bear the sight of blood, throws the letter into the fire, and asks how Brayle died. Noting the beauty of "this detestable creature," he replies that Brayle was bitten by a snake.

"Killed at Resaca" has autobiographical touches. Bierce was a topographical engineer at Stones River, Resaca, and elsewhere; also, his discovery in 1888 of alleged love letters addressed to his wife Mollie Day Bierce* caused grievous trouble. Bierce goes out of his way in this story to point out that the dramatic bravery of Brayle, motivated by Marian Mendenhall's letter, causes the firing on both sides, which causes a hundred soldiers' deaths. He adds, with typical sarcasm, "Is woman weak?" Bierce casually mentions his being at Resaca in his bitter essay titled "The Crime at Pickett's Mill."

Bibliography: William Conlogue, "A Haunting Memory: Ambrose Bierce and the Ravine of the Dead," *Studies in Short Fiction* 28 (Winter 1991): 21–29; Richard McMurry, "Resaca: 'A Heap of Hard Fiten,' " *Civil War Times Illustrated* (December 1971): 20–28, 43–49; Morris.

KING. In "The Middle Toe of the Right Foot," he is a deputy serving under Sheriff Adams of Marshall. King, Rosser, and Sancher participate in an elaborate "trick" that ultimately lures Manton to his death. King says that he discontinued a friendship with Gertrude because her right foot lacked a middle toe. Gertrude married Manton, who later murdered her and their two small children.

" 'THE KREUTZER SONATA' " (1888, 1890, 1911). Review. In *The Kreutzer Sonata*, the purpose of Leo Tolstoi, who is pitilessly observant and has gigantic literary powers, is not to entertain but to instruct—to the effect that "marriage, like wealth, offers no hope of lasting happiness." Since marriage is a sin, celibacy is virtuous, even dutiful. Men are polygamous by nature, and young girls therefore suffer. Marital vows are violated. What to do? Practice polygamy? Free love? No remedy is possible. The young should try fortitude, not celibacy, and should not expect happiness in marriage. *War and Peace* is full of detestable characters; yet Tolstoi thinks his depictions are realistic, not cynical. Though personally a fine Christian, he wrongly believes that "Human events occur without human agency." In *The Cossacks*, Tolstoi displays an imagination that is ignorant of human nature. Yet at his worst he is an eagle compared to hen-like contemporary popular writers.

L

"LACKING FACTORS" (1888, 1912). Essay. Not all nouns have feminine or masculine forms. We lack alligatrix, spinstress, gartress, cypror, encountress, banhee, queenfisher, Shebrews, etc. It seems a shame that Bierce did not latch onto "herstory."

"A LADY FROM REDHORSE" (1891). Short story. (Original title: "An Heiress from Redhorse: Told in Letters from Coronado to San Francisco.") (Characters: Auntie, Mary Jane Dement, James, Calamity Jim, Jack Raynor.) In a series of five letters from Coronado, Mary Jane Dement tells Irene about her love affair. June 20: Mary is falling in love with a handsome, well-mannered, brainy man. July 2: Jack Raynor tells Mary that the attractive man, called Dr. Barritz, may be a magician connected with people in India. July 16: While Mary's Auntie is at a dance in the hotel, Barritz calls on her briefly. Mary writes that she is "an ugly duckling" from the Redhorse mining field who inherited a million dollars from her father, Calamity Jim. July 17: Raynor's calling on Mary yesterday reminds her that she, Raynor, and Dumps were together in the mining area. When her father struck it rich, Dumps went to San Juan Smith, became a stage driver, and was killed by road agents. Mary feels inferior to Barritz. July 25: Barritz asks Mary to walk along the beach. She swoons, rebukes him for being a thug from India, and weeps. He says that he has loved her for years; is, in fact, Dumps; and was persuaded by Raynor to return from Vienna to Coronado. In a postscript, Mary tells Irene that Dumps, really to be named James, is not a thug.

The main virtue of this silly story may be the skill with which Bierce handles its epistolary form. The story may have been inspired by and have acted as a quick, lighthearted response to "A Strange Adventure," an anecdote by Bierce's friend William Chambers Morrow* (*Wave*, 7 March 1891). In it, Morrow tells how a beautiful young woman flirts with him, thinking he is Bierce, the famous author whose works she admires. Bierce's story was published eight days later (*Examiner*, 15 March 1891).

Bibliography: Lawrence I. Berkove, " 'A Strange Adventure': The Story Behind a Bierce Tale," *American Literary Realism 1870–1910* 14 (Spring 1981): 70–76.

"THE LAND BEYOND THE BLOW" (1909). Short story. (Characters: None separately identified.) As he is leaving the scene of a dogfight, the narrator is knocked unconscious by a "burly blackguard." He wakes up in a strange land, oddly colored and with strange landscapes and curious birds. The place is called Mogon-Zwair. Inhabitants are called Golampis ("Sons of the Fair Star"). They wear few clothes, despise the wealthy, regard hard work as a luxury that some do violence to obtain and others pray to obtain when they die, relish being tortured for their religious beliefs, and believe truth and virtue will prevail. Therefore they misbehave with impunity. The narrator is banished to Lalugnan for praising Golampians' vicious consistency. A Lalugwump named Gnarmag-Zote, a polite and learned spitter, tells the narrator that he does not believe in immortality and says that death is comfortable oblivion, and then ends a widower's grief by killing him as a religious act authorized by King Skanhutch.

The narrator escapes to Tamtonia, whose courteous inhabitants follow the advice of a long-dead chief named Natas and seek the glory of political office. Innumerable positions are filled, often by successful bribers and liars, sometimes by venerated idiots. Tamtonians are proud of their mismanaged government. Americans, the narrator adds, would be shocked by politicians who bought their way into office. The narrator sails away but is put ashore by a mutinous crew on the island of Ug, ruled by Jogogle-Zadester, who herds a flock of nice tigers. Ug, in the Southern Hemisphere, is wider than it is long. Its people show their liking of one by shaking fists at him. In their parliament, called the *gabagab*, each bill is passed only by voters able to profit from it. This would strike incorruptible American legislators as "novel." Jogogle-Zadester genially tells the narrator about a war involving the islands of Ug, Wug, and Scamadumclitchclitch, and about a blockade preventing the shipment of garlic. Grumsquutzy, Ug's prime minister, tells the narrator that when Ug ends a war, its military leaders are blinded, given clubs, and beat each other to death; survivors, if any, are boiled or smothered to death. Then the common soldiers are executed, since it is feared that a standing army might support factory workers so discontent that they would strike. Few soldiers, however, survive unsanitary field-camp conditions anyway and often beg to be sent into combat to have a better chance of living. Incidentally, Wuggards got a singular revenge on their Uggard conquerors, by surrendering in droves to put the victors into heavy debt by having to feed them. Uggard writers of history and biography—which is to say, fiction— are assigned to work on roads and in cemeteries. Known as the author of *David Copperfield, Ben Hur*, and the like, the narrator sweeps streets until he disguises himself as a sailor, escapes, sails south for thirty-seven months, and goes ashore on Ganegwag with a small party for provisions. When they shoot a loathsome dog, the natives, who are dog-worshippers, capture them. The Ganegwagians wear copper clothes, live in liquid houses, and have such longevity that they must sail eventually to a distant isle to enjoy "the Happy Change," that is, death. Meanwhile, they utterly revere and abase themselves in making deities of hordes of ungrateful dogs.

After seven years, the narrator goes to the prosperous island of Ghargaroo to consult with Juptka-Getch, the wisest man on earth. About 250 years old, he lives in a cave and now lectures the querulous narrator. Juptka-Getch says that the poor are blessed and that the rich cannot easily enter heaven. Therefore the king of Ghargaroo benefits his nicest subjects by impoverishing them and suffering the burden of keeping their property himself. Since the pleasures of the wealthy are "vain and disappointing," they are punished by enduring "high living." Rich criminals are given "the life penalty," while the righteous poor are permitted to die when they wish. Juptka-Getch silences the narrator by getting him to admit that his country's scriptures also "teach the vanity of life, the blessedness of poverty and the wickedness of wealth."

A seven-weeks' sail ends in shipwreck, with the narrator the sole survivor. He strides to the capital of Batrugia, a part of the Hidden Continent. Tghagogu, a friendly Batrugian, whose compatriots are all gigantic but friendly, shows him a letter from Joquolk Wak Mgapy, his brother who visited America by "skyship" and describes the country. The city of Nyork contains "puny" people of "limited intelligence" and a "harsh language." Their buildings are so tall that they could never have built them; they must have invaded the island in such swarms that they drove out the giant builders once living there. Some of those giants built bridges from the mainland back to the island, returned, mounted the tall buildings, and now hide up there seeking heaven. Imagine if one such giant should fall to the earth. Within a year, the narrator marries the three daughters of a politician and learns the language, becomes a salaried interpreter, but converses with only two professors of rhetoric. Attending the execution of a murderer one day, he tries to interfere by claiming that the fellow is insane; this supposed defense is ridiculed, as is his outlandish comment that in America it is thought better to free ninety-nine guilty people than to punish one innocent person.

The narrator sails off to Gokeetle-guk, called Trustland. Its king is elected for ten years, then shot on the grounds that he must have committed sins and blunders by then. Jumjum, an affable official, tells him to ask questions, because they care not a whit about where he came from. The narrator learns that honest trusts manage every trade, industry, and profession in the country. Work is easy, and prices for necessities and even luxuries are moderate. Jumjum remembers a Chicagoan who came to Gokeetle-guk and started a factory to manufacture bells for donkey tails, to suppress their braying. He set up a sales force, middlemen, and a ruinous profit system based on sharp competition; prices inevitably soared, sales fell, and unemployment ensued.

After six years of travel over mountains and through a desert, the narrator builds a boat and heads for the island kingdom of Tortirra, where the people are divided into equally erroneous and mutually destructive "parties." For years the Tortirrans traded amiably with nearby islanders called Stronagus, until Pragam, a demagogue, said such buying and selling was "piracy" and ordered his army to drive would-be foreign merchants away with stink pots. When prosperity ended, the Tortirrans removed Pragam, but his "noxious" economic plan "had struck root too deeply to be altogether eradicated . . . [and] a majority of the people still hold a modified form of it." Stronagus trade now, but if they bring in more than a "lawful limit" of merchandise, stink pots are employed and restrictions are applied against them. Tortirra is composed of twenty-nine islands. They send elected representatives to a legislature in its capital, which has a changing executive leadership. Each island has a chief and a council. All the islands and the capital have controversial courts to interpret laws in contradictory ways, thus establishing *lantrags* (precedents), which are sometimes followed, sometimes ignored. Sometimes longstanding laws are found to be in violation of the *Trogodal* (constitution). Oddly, representatives are usually lawyers, who deliberately create "uncertain and perplexing" laws, since just and clear laws would force them out of office and "compel them to seek some honest employment." An especially onerous type of injustice is the convicting and imprisonment of men who after time-consuming appeal are found innocent, though without redress. The narrator wonders what an outcry would be heard if America suffered under such a governmental system. The narrator closes with a description of a noted Tortirran high judge celebrated by a gold statue. For thirty years no one addressed him directly but only through his clerk. One day an earthquake shattered the statue, found filled with sawdust; at home, the judge while writing a decision was simultaneously killed by a falling chandelier. And it was found that his clerk, dead twenty-five years, was being impersonated by his idiot twin brother ignorant of the law. While hearing about the judge's statue, the narrator falls asleep. Upon awakening, he finds himself in a hospital with a bandaged head.

As does Jonathan Swift's *Gulliver's Travels*, "The Land Beyond the Blow" touches on human foibles mainly political and rampantly evident in the United States of Bierce's time. They are easily identifiable. In places, his long and rambling satire seems to show the influence of Herman Melville's *Mardi*, although echoes and parallels are undoubtedly coincidental. One might more fruitfully compare "The Land Beyond the Blow" and *A Connecticut Yankee in King Arthur's Court*, the much-superior 1889 classic by Mark Twain.* Both "heroes" are launched into adventures resulting in political observations by blows to the head. Bierce's sour technique is to suggest that admirable practices seen by his narrator are to be contrasted with American villainy, whereas disgusting behavior he sees is presented as closely resembling American immorality and pusillanimity in various forms. In sum, however, Bierce has no faith in the notion of human perfectibility, hence no faith, more specifically, in either American customs or American republican government.

Bibliography: Anonymous review of volume 1 of *The Collected Works of Ambrose Bierce*, pp. 18–30, in Davidson, *Essays*; Lawrence I. Berkove, "Two Impossible Dreams: Ambrose Bierce on Utopia and America," *Huntington Library Quarterly* 44 (Autumn 1981); 282–292.

LARUE. In "The Death of Halpin Frayser," he is the second husband of Catherine Frayser, whom he murdered in San Francisco. Calling himself Branscom, he is pursued by authorities, including Holker of Napa and Jaralson of San Francisco, who find Catherine's grave near Mount St. Helena and beside it the body of Halpin Frayser, her son by a previous marriage. Larue remains at large. At one point, Holker thinks Larue's name was Pardee.

LARUE, CATHERINE ("KATY"). In "The Death of Halpin Frayser," she was a granddaughter of Myron Bayne, the colonial Tennessee poet. She married Frayser, a would-be Nashville politician. As Catherine Frayser, she became the excessively doting mother of Halpin Frayser, who called her Katy, whom she spoiled, and whom she wanted to accompany to California but did not. Later she married Larue, who cut her throat in San Francisco. She was buried in the White Church graveyard near Mount St. Helena. While in pursuit of Larue for murder, Holker and Jaralson find her rotting headboard and also Halpin's corpse. It seems that Halpin dreamed of her there and was strangled to death. Or perhaps he was the waking victim of a visitation.

LASSITER. In "Three and One Are One," he is Barr Lassiter's father. They live together near Carthage, Tennessee, with Barr's mother and older sister. The two men are estranged when in 1861 Barr announces his intention to join the Union Army. Two years later, Barr, now a seasoned cavalry trooper, returns to visit his home; but his father, mother, and sister—though he sees them—are all dead and buried. Bierce's depiction of Barr Lassiter's father echoes his memory of Marcus Aurelius Bierce,* his own father. Both were severe, uncompromising, but affectionate deep down.

Bibliography: Morris.

LASSITER. In "Three and One Are One," she is Barr Lassiter's older sister. When Barr, a fine cavalry trooper, returns to visit his home, he sees his family—although they are dead and gone.

LASSITER, BARR. In "Three and One Are One," he is the son, twenty-two, of a pro-Southern family near Carthage, Tennessee. When he decides to join the Union Army in 1861, he is estranged from his parents and older sister. Two years later, Barr Lassiter, now an experienced cavalry trooper in a Kentucky regiment, visits his old home one moonlit evening. He sees his father, who spurns him, his mother, who sits silent, and his sister, who stares at him and walks away. Next day he visits the place again, finds it a blackened ruin, and is told by Albro Bushrod, a friend, that the dwelling and its three occupants were destroyed by a Union shell a year before.

LASSITER, MRS. In "Three and One Are One," she is Barr Lassiter's mother. She is estranged from him when he goes against his family's pro-Southern sentiments and joins the Union Army in 1861. Two years later he revisits the home, imagines that he sees his parents and sister, but the next day observes that all is in ruins.

"THE LATE LAMENTED" (1889, 1911). Essay. After what length of time does a corpse cease to be a sacred relic and become a legitimate exhibition in a museum? It was regarded as improper to show a lock of hair from the head of Charles I of England but all right to dig up and show the body of Rameses the Great, a more glorious ruler than Charles. We indiscriminately disturb Roman funeral urns and Indian burial mounds, while the bones of old settlers must make way for new city halls.

LAWSON. In "The Major's Tale," he is the adjutant-general of a U.S. Army division. The general's staff is headquartered in a civilian home in Nashville. As a joke on Lieutenant Haberton, a ladies' man, his fellow officers dress Orderly Arman as a girl and put "her" in Lawson's office to fool Haberton.

"LEAN KINE." *sSee* "A Flourishing Industry."

"LET US EAT." *See* "The Religion of the Table."

LEVERING, COLONEL. In "The Other Lodgers," he is a U.S. Army veteran of the siege of Atlanta. As he explains to a listener while the two are sitting in the Waldorf-Astoria hotel in New York City, he was wounded during the siege of Atlanta and was taken by train in September 1864 to an Atlanta hospital, which he now calls the Breathitt House. He goes on to describe a nightmarish experience he endured there.

LEZINSKY, DAVID LESSER (1864–1894). Poet. Lezinsky was a member of the San Francisco literary group in the 1890s. In 1893 he attended a memorial program in honor of Richard Realf,* a colorful, unstable poet who

had committed suicide. Ina Coolbrith,* a respected California poet, attended the ceremony but asked Lezinsky to read her contributions for her. Bierce savagely ridiculed Lezinsky's poetry. Soon thereafter, the young poet also committed suicide, and Bierce was attacked by his numerous enemies for having been the cause. Undeterred, Bierce vigorously denied the charge, saying that he merely disliked the man's poor poetry; he is alleged to have said that Lezinsky's killing himself was "the only decent thing he ever did." Lezinksy's being Jewish contributed to the charge of anti-Semitism leveled against Bierce (*see* Anti-Semitism in Bierce, Alleged). In 1894 Lezinsky's *Daddy, Daddy, Ruth and Company* was issued by the Iris Publishing Company of San Francisco in twenty-two pages.
Bibliography: De Castro, Morris, O'Connor.

"LIEUTENANT BIERCE: TELLS HOW HE EARNED PROMOTION TO THAT RANK." *See* "Across the Plains."

LIGHTNIN'. In "A Providential Intimation," this is the name of Bob Scotty's horse.

LIGHTNING EXPRESS. In "The Race at Left Bower," this is the nickname the people of Left Bower assign to Colonel Jackhigh's slow-moving horse.

"A LIGHT SLEEPER" (1888). Short story. (Originally part of "Bodies of the Dead: Additional Incidents of Physical Activity after Death.") (Characters: John Hoskin, Mrs. John Hoskin, Martin L. Whitney.) John Hoskin, of San Francisco, learns by a telegram in the spring of 1871 that his beautiful, beloved wife has died of heart disease while visiting relatives, including her father, Martin L. Whitney, in Springfield, Illinois. Her body arrives in a metal case. It is lying on its right side, the right hand under cheek, the left hand on the breast. Hoskin thanks Whitney by letter for having the body placed in the position of a sleeping child. Whitney replies that the body was placed on its back with its arms at its sides. Hoskin suspects that "medical incompetency" caused his wife to be prematurely coffined and to have died of suffocation. He re-examines the body, but it is now on its left side. The presence of expensive rings on his wife's fingers rules out any foul play en route. Hoskin goes insane. Next, a California physician looks a final time at the body and notes that it was embalmed at Springfield. Hoskin dies years later in a Stockton asylum.

"THE LION'S DEN" (1901, 1911). Essay. (Original title: "The Sentimental Bachelor.") This is the first of two essays featuring the Sentimental Bachelor. He complains to his unidentified auditor that pretentious people show off their books, which are usually mere ugly blocks anyway, the way art collectors parade guests too quickly past one masterpiece after another. Instead, he places his revered books on the floor and treasures pictures mainly because he likes associating them with friends who drew them. He praises the Japanese, "the only civilized people in our modern world," and admires them for not cluttering a vase with too many flowers or a room with more than one painting. The Bachelor incidentally names seven former girlfriends.

LITTLE JOHNNY. He is the narrator of upwards of 340 sketches by Bierce, on a variety of subjects and cast in childishly misspelled prose. Bierce wrote the first Little Johnny piece when he was in London. It is "Essays in Natural History," written under the pseudonym of Little Johnny, and it appeared in *Fun* (3 October 1874), the magazine edited by his friend Tom Hood.* Bierce wrote twenty-eight or so more Little Johnny pieces for *Fun*, ending in August 1875, shortly before he left England. He resumed the Little Johnny series in the *Argonaut* with "Anecdotes of Animals" (4 August 1877) and continued it with about fifty more in that periodical, ending in October 1879. He favored the *Wasp* with about fifty more (April 1881–March 1886). Little Johnny intermittently resurfaced in the *San Francisco Examiner* (July 1887–November 1889; December 1890–December 1901), with a total of a little more than fifty more. Meanwhile, the *Oakland Daily Evening Tribune* (March–July 1890) published fifty-three or so more. The *New York Journal* (later renamed the *New York American*) steadily issued about 140 more (November 1901–June 1906), nine of which are stories that Little Johnny relays from his well-traveled "batchelor" Uncle Ned, who also figures in many other pieces, though not as the primary narrator. Finally, Bierce wrote three for *Cosmopolitan* (March–May 1909). Several Little Johnny sketches were quickly republished in other periodicals. Totals here are skewed because some items were recombined under new titles.

Bierce selected thirty-three Little Johnny items for inclusion, under the title "Kings of Beasts," as part of volume 12 of *The Collected Works of Ambrose Bierce*. It is difficult to say why, since most of them seem quite tedious. The first of these sketches, called "Rats," Bierce pieced together from parts of "Little Johnny on Rats" (*American*, 25 August 1902; *Examiner*, 29 August 1902) and "The High Noble Toby and Mush Rats" (*Cosmopolitan*, May 1909). "Rats" begins thus: "Rats is radiants [rodents] and the little ones is a mouse, and thats the feller which pursues the women folks up into a high tree and blankets [?] on her blood! But the old he rat eats bread and cheese like a thing of life [thing alive]." Misspellings and malapropisms abound, with "Dan Vouvers" (Vancouver), "caroar" (career), "evil tenor" (even tenor), "endowered" (endowed), "laps of time" (lapse of time), "stopipe" (stovepipe), "amfabulous" (amphibious), "a infaluble" (an infallible), and "Kangaroon" (Kangaroo). A sometimes tedious parade of other misspelled, and often misshapen, animals includes "buflo," "cracky dile," "dox hoond," "ephalent," "giraft," "gofurious," "gorilly," "high eany," "hi potamus," "hipporippus," "jackus," "munky," "ostridge," "pol patriot," "rhi nosey rose," "kioty," "snale," "tagger," "wale," and "you." It is a relief that Little Johnny fails to misspell horse, goose, rooster, and shark. The "buzard" deserves special mention here, because of its "carry on diet" (from "Buzards"). The names of the first creatures, Adam and Eve, are not misspelled but the loving couple gets parodied, as when Adam relieves Eve, who wonders whether he was ever in love before, by averring, "No darling, I swear it, never till I met you" ("The Crane"). Far better is Satan's rejoinder when Adam says that he, Eve, and Satan are supposed to "go 4th into all the waste places of the earth and multiply" ("The Snake"). The serpent says, "I cant multiply. Ime a adder." Bierce can wax sacrilegious, as when Billy, Johnny's brother, explains to Pitchel the preacher that Christ stayed alive "forty days . . . in the wildness" by imitating hibernating bears and sucking his feet ("Moles"). Gipple the "Methody" missionary, back out of Africa, is reported as having talked un-pleasantly about using rum and tobacco to convert "the natif niggers," who in gratitude offer him "all the wives that you can eat"; whereupon Gipple dreams of "conjuggle happiness" ("Domestical Hens"). Later Gip's "one leg-ger" friend, another "mitionary," escapes being invited to the king's dinner—the guest being the dinner—by offering his cork leg as an hors d'oeuvre, which "rattled" the king, whereupon Gip hops away to freedom ("The Hip-porippus"). History fares no better than religion; for example, we read that "Patrick Henry he said, 'Give me liberty or treat me mighty well in jail' but George Washington he waved the big sticker and shouted the bottle cry of freedom!" ("Kangaroons"). Faintly allied to cockeyed misspellings may be goofy redundancies, as "the spine of your back" and "and the stomach of your belly." Although Little Johnny's favorite euphemism is "gum dasted," he does record his father Robert's "bedam," in connection with that man's harsh disciplining of his sons—Missy, their sister, seems exempt—for "dizzy bedience" ("Jackusses"). Little Johnny says little about war, but he does listen to Gipple, who fought at "Gettyburg," saw "Mister Picket a comin," and then observed "memorble slotter" resulting in "the Confedit slane" ("Sol-jers"). More amusing is General Grant's calling "statutes" in Washington "gam doodled scare crows," and being warned by a nearby preacher thus: "General, you oughtnt to swear, cause the wicked shall be casted to Hell." To which, Grant replies: "I shouldn't mind that so very much, but I sure dont want to be casted in to bronze" ("Sheeps"). A better pun is Ned's explanation that "a polly wog is like the feller that writes short stories, cause his tail is not to be continued" ("Frogs"). Bierce rarely has Little Johnny refer to the West; a quite revealing exception occurs when he explains that a guide for soldiers out there wears a "big boy knife" ("The Bufflo"). Also more revealing of Bierce than of Little Johnny is the latter's comment that "[e]very boy ought to have a dog cause boys are masculine, but girls are efemeral" ("Dogs").

Taken in small doses, the Little Johnny pieces are often humorous. If read too conscientiously, however, they become tedious. Bierce preferred wit to the folksy, long-winded yarns of humorists such as Bill Nye, Mark Twain,* Artemus Ward (*see* "Wit and Humor"); yet his Little Johnny pieces are in the American humor, not wit, mode. One Little Johnny story, however, is worthy to challenge the artistry of Mister Magoo's best animators. Johnny's father, having forgotten "his spettacles," is walking down the street when ("bime by," as Johnny ought to have said, since he likes "bime by") he comes upon a dog chewing a short stick "in the corner of its mouth." So "he took the cigar that he was smoking his self, and knocked off the ashes with his little finger, and held it down to the dog and said: 'Have a light?' " ("Dogs"). *Bibliography:* Grenander, Joshi and Schultz, Neale.

"A LITTLE OF CHICKAMAUGA" (1898, 1909). Essay. (Original title: "Chickamauga.") Bierce, who fought at Chickamauga, Georgia, 19–20 September 1863, explains that he intends not to give a history of the battle but only to tell part of what he saw there. After sketching the background, he says his exhausted brigade fell back, but so did the infantry line. Confederate soldiers then advanced, a bombardment followed, and the brave Confederates were all knocked off their feet and covered with dust. The next morning the Union forces prepared intrenchments. A dogged enemy attacked and fell back, only to attack again—once with success. Ordered by General William B. Hazen* to get artillery ammunition, Bierce rode across a field, obtained the ammunition, but could not return with it because the enemy was suddenly on that very field. Bierce comments on an erroneous report by General William S. Rosencrans and on the insignificant "heroism" of General James A. Garfield. Bierce wrily says that he too "detour[ed]," the way Garfield did, but "never felt that it ought to make me President." After more galloping about, Bierce found Hazen's brigade again, at "memorable Snodgrass hill." The enemy might have charged advantageously but did not. Darkness fell. Hearing "the rebel yell" of Confederate General Braxton Bragg's men—"the ugliest sound that any mortal ever heard"—Bierce and his fellow soldiers "retired" safely, through a part of the rebel lines that was silent. Bierce closes this essay with a reverent tribute to "the heroes in blue and the heroes in gray, sleeping their last sleep in the woods of Chickamauga." Bierce made this region the scene of the story titled "Chickamauga," perhaps his most gruesome Civil War tale. *Bibliography:* Morris.

"THE LITTLE STORY" (1874). Short story. (Characters: none named.) In the form of a short, two-person play, a "probationary contributor" reads a story for possible publication to a "supernumerary editor," who occasionally interrupts him by saying that he has read a version the contributor submitted elsewhere. The story concerns a little orphan girl standing on a San Francisco street in a cold, windy rain on New Year's Eve. Adults walk by with presents of toys and candy for their children back home. The little girl turns envious and wishes that she were an uneaten tart, to be warmed over daily. Bells ring in the new year, a tart drops on her, then a sandwich, some bread, flour, bacon, and sausages. More food follows, and finally a quarter of beef lands smack on her head. She is buried under twenty feet of the accumulated stuff. At dawn the merchants come with shovels and wheelbarrows and take away their new provisions. As for the flattened girl, they take her to the coroner, who says that she resembles a map a fellow tried to sell him yesterday. Some dense readers may conclude that this tale is meaningless unless Bierce is trying to satirize charitable impulses that some ignorant citizens find themselves moved by.

LONDON, JACK (1876–1916). Author. He was born John Griffith Chaney, in San Francisco. His mother, Flora Wellman, was deserted by William Henry Chaney, who was her common-law husband and also allegedly Jack London's father, while she was pregnant. She married John London, a widower with two daughters. The family lived in uncertain circumstances (1876–1885), then moved to Oakland, where Jack London held odd jobs, read in the public library, finished grammar school, became an oyster pirate in San Francisco Bay, then worked for the Fish Patrol to catch such pirates (1892). He sailed on a sealer at age seventeen, returned to work in a jute mill, and won a *San Francisco Morning Call* prize for an essay about a typhoon. In 1894 he hoboed eastward and was jailed in Erie County, New York, for vagrancy. In 1895–1896 he attended Oakland High School and became a socialist. After taking classes at the University of California at Berkeley (1896–1897), he participated in the Klondike Gold Rush (1897–1898). In 1899, back in San Francisco, he published a short story in the *Overland Monthly*. In 1900 London married Bessie Mae Maddern; although they had two children, the marriage proved to be unhappy. His first book, *The Son of the Wolf* (1900), was a collection of Alaska stories. He ran unsuccessfully in a race for mayor of Oakland in 1901 and again in 1905.

London spent some months in 1902 in the slums of London, England, about which he wrote in *The People of the Abyss* (1903). *The Call of the Wild* (also 1903) proved far more popular. William Randolph Hearst,* the newspaper publisher, sent London to the Orient in 1904 to cover the Russo-Japanese War for his syndicate. London's *The Sea-Wolf* (1904) was an enormous popular success. In 1905 he bought what became his permanent home—ranch property near Glen Allen, California—and also obtained a divorce and immediately married Charmian Kittredge. *The Iron Heel* (1908) was his pessimistic fictional vision of sociopolitical urban chaos. In *Martin Eden* (1909), his most autobiographical novel, the poet Russ Brissenden may be based on London's friend the poet George Sterling,* whose art colony in Carmel, California, he visited occasionally in 1910. London became president of the Intercollegiate Socialist Society, lectured widely, and published

Revolution and Other Essays (1910). After he and Charmian took a twenty-seven-month voyage throughout the South Pacific, he published *The Cruise of the Snark* (1911) and also became an agronomist. He was briefly interested in supporting the Mexican Revolution (1911), but after a reporting stint in Vera Cruz (1914) he changed his opinions. He studied Jungian psychology in an effort to rejuvenate his body and spirit, but soon died of renal colic, causing uremia, and then a stroke and heart failure. Rumors of his committing suicide, despite wide circulation, are now doubted.

London was prolific; he wrote two hundred stories, twenty novels, four hundred nonfictional pieces, and three plays. Translated into more than eighty languages, London has proved influential both for his liberal content and for his plain, hard-boiled, impassioned style. Most of London's personal papers are now in the Huntington Library at San Marino, California, This is ironic because the Huntington Library was endowed by the nephew of Collis P. Huntington,* one of the most ruthless, antisocialistic, procapitalist robber barons ever to despoil the California that London loved.

When Bierce first heard of London, it was in connection with London's taking up the cause of socialism, which Bierce reviled, and London's finding a sympathetic ear in Sterling, who was supported by others. In 1904, Bierce warned Sterling about socialism; and when the public acclaimed London's *The Sea-Wolf*, Bierce in a letter to Sterling (18 February 1905) called it "a disagreeable book," found fault with its structure and style, expressed "contempt for both the sexless lovers" in it, but called Wolf Larsen, its hero, a "tremendous creation." In 1910, at a Bohemian Club summer outing, Sterling reluctantly introduced London to Bierce. Spectators feared bloodshed because of their opposing opinions, but the two were soon matching each other drink for drink at the bar. A mutual friend of the two at this time was the photographer Arnold Genthe.*

The subject of Bierce and London is complex. On a philosophical level, Bierce despised London's politics. On a professional level, he was simultaneously reviled by and jealous of London's success as an appealingly tough writer. And on a personal level, he fussed that Sterling, his protégé, could independently seek London's friendship and also his advice as a writer and a political liberal. On the other hand, London wrote a literary friend, Cloudesley Johns (30 March 1899), that Bierce's short stories show a "total lack of sympathy," "owe nothing to grace of style," and have "a metallic intellectual brilliancy." To Sterling, he wrote (25 July 1907) "What a pen he [Bierce] wields. Too bad he hasn't a better philosophic foundation." And to his wife Charmian, London wrote (29 July 1910), "Damn Ambrose Bierce. I won't look for trouble but if he jumps me, I'll go him a few at his own game." Like many readers during Bierce's forgotten period shortly after his death, London mistakenly critiqued Bierce's stories in a letter to Sterling (7 March 1916) as exposing "naked baldness that buys nothing."

Bibliography: Earle Labor and Jeanne Campbell Reesman, *Jack London*, rev. ed. (New York: Twayne Publishers, 1994); *The Letters of Jack London*, ed. Earle Labor et al., 3 vols. (Stanford, Calif: Stanford University Press, 1988); O'Connor.

"THE LONG AND SHORT OF IT." *See* "Revision Downward."

"THE LOVE OF COUNTY" (1892, 1911). Essay. Although love of country has been properly extolled, love of county is more praiseworthy, because such love is both stronger and more fervent. Patriotic love of "ninety million . . . Americans, Americanesses and Americanettes" gets spread too thin; loving the few in one's county, however, represents dignified parochialism.

M

MacGREGOR, JANET. In "The Secret of Macarger's Gulch," she was the wife of Thomas MacGregor, who murdered her in their cabin in Macarger's Gulch. Both were from Edinburgh.

MacGREGOR, THOMAS. In "The Secret of Macarger's Gulch," he and his wife, Janet MacGregor, moved from Edinburgh to Macarger's Gulch, where he killed her and then disappeared.

MADWELL, CAPTAIN DOWNING. In "The Coup de Grâce," he is a Union Army infantry company commander, serving under Major Creede Halcrow. The two mortally hate one another and trade sarcastic insults. Captain Madwell is a close friend of Sergeant Caffal Halcrow, Creede's brother. After a combat skirmish, Madwell finds Caffal hideously wounded and out of compassion stabs him to death. There will be dreadful trouble for Madwell, however, because Creede and two stretcher bearers happen to come forward and witness the mercy killing.

"A MAD WORLD" (1891, 1912). Essay. Bierce says that as our solar system whirls through "the unthinkable reaches of space," it is bombarded with objects from tiny to gigantic. Perhaps even by something that could craze us all? We may all, right now, be lunatics. Perhaps various persons, including John D. Rockefeller, "my laird of Skibo" Andrew Carnegie, and "Fatty [President William Howard] Taft" are all products of Bierce's diseased imagination here in Washington, D.C. Bierce's funniest creation is this: William Randolph Hearst,* now eyeing the White House "to defile it."

MAGONE, SARAH. In "That of Granny Magone," she is an old woman who lives alone in a cabin outside Whitesburg, Kentucky. She is reputed to be a witch with supernatural powers. When she dies, she is laid out before her hearth fire, readied for a funeral to be conducted the next morning by the Rev. Elias Atney. But that night he and three other watchers see a black cat leap on her body and bite her face. Her right arm hurls away the cat, which disappears. Efforts to revive Sarah fail, and four days later, obviously deceased, she is buried. She is also called Mary and Granny.

"THE MAJOR'S TALE" (1890). Short story. (Original title: "A Practical Joke: Major Broadwood Recalls the Heroic Past.") (Characters: Orderly Arman, Major Broadwood, Lieutenant Haberton, Lawson.) Major Broadwood, the narrator, is a U.S. Army officer on the staff of the general commanding a division that is part of forces driven out of Georgia and Alabama. They are now fortified in wintry Nashville, awaiting attack by Confederate units. The division headquarters are in a house abandoned by its civilian owners. Broadwood and his cohorts find some "lady-gear"—dresses, gloves, and the like—in a closet. To get even with Lieutenant Haberton, whose boasts of amorous conquests they are tired of hearing, they disguise their Orderly Arman, age seventeen and effeminate looking, as a coy girl. They put "her" in the office of Lawson, their adjutant general. When the general catches sight of her and grows eager to query her privately, Broadwood steers him off by saying that she is a nurse seeking supplies for her smallpox hospital. The jokesters bring Haberton to her and eavesdrop as she complains to him about her possessions being looted by "lawless [Union] soldiery." Holding her hands, Haberton is all "deferential and assenting nods," until an enemy shell hits the upstairs of the house and scatters plaster over everyone. Arman leaps up with a bit of masculine profanity and tears at his confining garb. Haberton, petrified at first, manages a sickly grin, and asserts that he was not fooled.

In "What Occurred at Franklin," Bierce describes the military events of November 1864 leading up to his advancing with General John Schofield to Nashville. At the beginning of "The Major's Tale," Bierce delightfully digresses even as he explains that he must not—indeed, does not, will not—digress. He livens the story by lamenting that in post–Civil War times young men are less experienced, younger looking, and less aware of humor in life than young soldiers of his time were. However, he darkens the tale by reporting to his readers that his befuddled general was killed a few days later and, further, that of his eight staff members five were also killed and now only he remains—"a harmless skeleton at your feast and peace-dance." *Bibliography:* Grenander.

"MALFEASANCE IN OFFICE" (1891, 1911). Essay. Since we now have societies to prevent "this and that," why not a society for the prevention of malfeasance in office? Half of all tax money is stolen, by everyone from janitor to governor. The press does not expose corruption because the press itself is corrupt, the public is passive, and courts, in which judges are "boss-made," would not convict. Change can easily come when money is available, investigators and attorneys become zealous and able, and journalists "spread the light" to educate the public. A tough reform leader can expect trouble but also distinction.

MALSON, DR. STILLING. In "A Resumed Identity," he is a physician living in Murfreesboro, Tennessee. Returning at dawn from calling on a patient, he encounters the U.S. Army veteran of the Stones River battle. The veteran is an amnesiac, and decades have passed.

MAMMON. In "Hades in Trouble," he is a greedy devil and is one of several trying to rescue Satan from the earth.

"THE MAN." *See* "A Resumed Identity."

"THE MAN AND THE SNAKE" (1890). Short story. (Characters: Harker Brayton, Druring, Dr. Druring, Mrs. Druring, Morryster.) An epigraph states that snakes can hypnotize, then bite and kill. Harker Brayton, back from foreign travel, has accepted the hospitality of Dr. Druring, who is a distinguished scientist in San Francisco and who has a large home with a wing called the Snakery and housing living specimens. They sometimes wander freely. One night, in a guest room, Brayton reads about the hypnotic power of snakes in Morryster's *Marvells of Science*. He laughs heartily but then sees two greenish points of light under his bed. He knows that he could ring for a servant or retreat, but doing so would be craven. Instead, he leans on a chair, steps forward, and knocks the chair down. The snake does not move. Its eyes are sparkling needles, approaching and receding. Brayton hears music, as though coming from the Nile. He sees sun, rain, and cities framed by a rainbow. The snake's eyes resemble those of his mother. The scene goes blank. Brayton falls, breaks his nose, and bruises his lips. Prone, on his elbows, he drags himself toward the snake. Meanwhile, Dr. Druring and his wife, while in the library discussing his latest acquisition, a snake-eating ophiophagus, hear a ringing scream. The doctor and his servants rush to its source and find Brayton dead and staring—of a fatal fit, the doctor quickly concludes. But then he sees under his guest's bed a stuffed snake, with shoe-button eyes. Bierce adds a tiny touch of incest when he has Brayton fancy the snake was gazing at him "with his dead mother's eyes."
Bibliography: Grenander; Russell Roth, "Ambrose Bierce's 'Detestable Creature,' " *Western American Literature* 9 (November 1974): 169–176; Woodruff.

MANCHER, DR. WILLIAM. In "A Watcher by the Dead," he is a physician in San Francisco. When his friend Dr. Helberson says that everyone is in awe in the presence of the dead, their young friend, Dr. Harper, replies that his friend, Jarette, a rich gambler from New York, is willing to bet that he can stay all night in a dark room with a corpse and emerge unaffected. Mancher agrees to be the corpse. That night Jarette soon grows uneasy. Mancher rises from the dead. The two fight, and Mancher kills Jarette, exchanges clothes with him, and escapes through a gathered crowd the next morning—grown all white-haired through shock. Seven years later, Harper and Helberson encounter Mancher by chance in New York. He explains matters and adds that, calling himself Jarette, he is now a physician at the Bloomingdale Asylum—or so he says. Mancher jokingly calls Dr. Harper "Dr. Sharper" and Dr. Helberson "Dr. Hell-born."

MANNERING, DR. In "A Diagnosis of Death," he lived in a house in Meridian, was considered an eccentric, and wrote a book about one's ability to foretell the death of an apparently healthy person by as much as eighteen months in advance. Attended by Dr. Frayley, he died three years before. When Hawver rented Mannering's vacant house, he saw Mannering's ghost but doubted that the man was dead when he saw Mannering on the street later. Frayley is aware that when Mannering raised his right finger to Hawver, it was a diagnosis that the man would soon die, which he did.

MANNING, GUNNER. In "One Kind of Officer," he is a soldier under Captain Ransome's command. He and Corporal Hassman tell Sergeant Morris that the enemy is approaching.

"A MAN OF LETTERS." *See* "Timothy H. Rearden."

"THE MAN OUT OF THE NOSE" (1887). Short story. (Original title: "John Hardshaw: The Story of a Man Who May Be Seen Coming out of the Nose.") (Characters: Barwell, Barwell, Elvira Barwell, John Hardshaw, Mrs. John Hardshaw, Officer No. 13.) In North Beach, a poor area of San Francisco, stands a humble house with windows like eyes, a nose-like door, and a mouth-like aperture made by a missing board below the door. Out of the nose at 2:00 P.M. every day comes a neatly dressed man, about fifty-five but pallid and looking older. He walks to a shabby factory that used to be a grand dwelling, stares up at a dingy window, and then returns home. His wife, who takes in laundry to support him, helps him inside. It seems that thirty years ago this man, Dr. John Hardshaw, and his wife lived well on Rincon Hill. Their friends included Barwell, a mining engineer in and out of Sacramento, his wife, Elvira Barwell, and their two children. Hardshaw got too friendly with Elvira, and was arrested sneaking out of her Sacramento residence one night with her miniature portrait, set in diamonds. Shortly before his trial, Mrs. Hardshaw visited him in jail but was so meanly treated that she disappeared—"gone back to the States." By deposition, Elvira avowed that she had put the portrait, intended as a gift to her husband, then on business in Europe, on a parlor table. Hardshaw served three years at San Quentin; his wife, back from the States, met him at the gate; and it is thought that they spent some years thereafter in Europe, perhaps Paris. Years later they returned to San Francisco, poor and spiritless, and obtained quarters south of Market Street. Mrs. Hardshaw ministered tenderly to Hardshaw, who was idle and dejected. One day something moved him to walk to North Beach and to a grand dwelling (later a shabby factory). When he looked up at a window, he saw Elvira. She leaned forward to see him, fell out, and on the pavement below was soon a bloody corpse, which he rushed to embrace and kiss. The Barwells that same day had returned home after spending two years in Peru. Hardshaw spent a year in the Stockton asylum, where his wife cared for him. He was released to her as harmless though still insane. They moved first to a poor place near Mission Hill and then to "the blank-faced shanty" on Goat Hill. Hardshaw's walk to the factory, once a house, is regularly pleasant; the return from it, tiring. One must wonder why Bierce gave this story the title he did. Was it his intention to reduce poor John Hardshaw to ambulatory mucus?

"THE MAN OVERBOARD" (1876?). Short story. (Original title: "Some Unusual Adventures.") (Characters: Captain Abersouth, Claude Reginald Gump, Samuel Martin, Captain Billy Troutbeck.) The narrator, named Claude Reginald Gump here, is drifting and reading aboard the *Nupple-duck*, with Captain Abersouth in command, when the ship strikes a coral reef and sinks. The narrator calls another ship, steps aboard, and gives orders to be taken to his aunt, who lives on Tottenham Court Road, London. The second ship is the *Bonnyclabber*, with Captain Billy Troutbeck in command. When passengers complain that she will smash into a cloud bank, the narrator twirls the wheel and returns toward Tottenham Court Road. Suddenly a lookout sounds off in unintelligible "vocal explosions." The ship's doctor works a sausage out of the lookout's blocked throat, and he shouts "Man overboard." After tossing life belts and other floatation devices, including an iron crowbar, into the water to aid the victim, they hold a roll call, which reveals that no one is missing. Troutbeck wants to record all procedures in his logbook, which, however, the narrator says he threw overboard also. He suggests that, in case the shipowners hold an inquiry, they should indeed throw a man overboard. So they chuck Troutbeck. In truth, the narrator kept the logbook and now records entries from June 22 through June 27, including the fact that Troutbeck fell into the sea by accident while fishing. Samuel Martin, first officer of the *Bonnyclabber*, interferes, takes the book, and goes on deck. The narrator follows, and the two part noisily. Some years later, the book is found, with some shreds of clothing, in the stomach of a whale. The last entry, in "straggling handwriting," concerns "svivors rescude by wale wether stuffy" and is signed by Martin. But now for the facts. Abersouth was the man spotted as overboard. He made a raft out of the stuff thrown toward him. The narrator, on leaving the *Bonnyclabber*, is saved by Abersouth and his raft. He tells the narrator that he saw the old friend Troutbeck floating by, drowned. Abersouth reproaches the narrator for writing sea stories, including the one that ended by leaving the *Camel*, captained by Abersouth, frozen in the South Polar Sea with his crew (*see* "The Captain of the 'Camel' "). The narrator admits it when Abersouth adds that he was told that the narrator had him also lost at sea while commanding the *Mudlark* (*see* "A Shipwreckollection"). This, even though Abersouth was harmlessly reading George Eliot at that time. In conclusion, the narrator says that he must escape to tell his stories and that Abersouth should have a brave end. He hints by a gesture that Abersouth should drown himself, which, looking reproachfully at the narrator, he does.

MANRICH. In "The Realm of the Unreal," he is the narrator, a resident of San Francisco. Dr. Valentine Dorrimore hypnotized him on a San Francisco street into believing that Dorrimore was stabbed to death, recovered on the spot, and disappeared. Five years later, while Manrich is driving from Newcastle to Auburn, Dorrimore suddenly appears on the road. At this point, Dorrimore hypnotizes Manrich into believing that he went to Auburn with him, wooed Manrich's fiancée Margaret Corray away from him, and fought him in a cemetery, and also that Manrich wound up back in his Auburn hotel room delirious. Later, now married to Margaret, Manrich reads in the Baltimore *Sun* about Dorrimore's feats of hypnotism the night before.

MANRICH, MRS. MARGARET. In "The Realm of the Unreal." *See* Corray, Margaret.

MANTON. In "The Middle Toe of the Right Foot," he or she is either of the two children of Manton and his wife, Gertrude. Manton murdered all three members of his family.

MANTON. In "The Middle Toe of the Right Foot," he is a big, burly man. He murders his wife, Gertrude Manton, and their two small children in their home near Marshall, and then disappears. Ten years later he returns to Marshall, clean shaven, with shorter hair, and calling himself Robert Grossmith. Because he eavesdropped on the conversation of King, Rosser, and Sancher, he is insulted by Rosser and challenges him. He dies of fright at the outset of the "trick" duel that King requires him to fight in the abandoned Manton house. He was evidently scared to death when Gertrude's ghost and those of their children approached him.

MANTON, GERTRUDE. In "The Middle Toe of the Right Foot," she is rejected by King because she is lacking a toe, marries Manton, and has two children with him. Manton murders her and their children. Ten years later, Manton is frightened to death at the outset of a duel in their abandoned, dusty house. Investigators find her footprints, including that of her right foot with the missing middle toe, leading to Manton's body but not leaving it. Brewer, one of the investigators, identifies the print as that of Gertrude, his sister.

"A MAN WITH TWO LIVES" (1905). Short story. (Originally part of "Some Uncanny Tales.") (Characters: Sergeant William Briscoe, Private David William Duck.) David William Duck, living in Aurora, Illinois, and known as "Dead Duck," tells the following story. In the autumn of 1861, he was a private stationed at Fort Phil Kearney. After the Fetterman Massacre of American soldiers by Sioux Indians, 21 December 1866, Duck was ordered to carry dispatches to Fort C. F. Smith, went on foot with his Henry rifle and three days' rations, and traveled only at night. He was stalked by Indians anyway, was driven into a cul-de-sac, and on the third morning rushed out delirious and firing wildly. At this point his memory went blank. The next event he could recall was getting out of a river at night and making his way to Fort C. F. Smith, but without his dispatches. Once there, he met Sergeant William Briscoe, who stared at him and calmly told Duck that he had buried him. Briscoe explains that Duck had been shot, scalped, and "somewhat mutilated otherwise, also," and that the men in the burial party all identified him. Called an impostor, Duck was jailed but soon escaped. He tried twice to find his grave but could not do so.
Bibliography: John Stands In Timber and Margot Liberty, *Cheyenne Memories* (New Haven: Yale University Press, 1967).

MAREN, ROBERT MOSELY. In "The Isle of Pines," he is a witty lawyer from Columbus, Ohio, known as a *litterateur* for having written the *Mellowcraft Papers*. He doubts the Rev. Henry Galbraith's account of having seen Herman Deluse, who is known to be dead. Maren accompanies Galbraith and his son to Deluse's house. Their investigation results in young Galbraith's mysterious death.

MARGOVAN. In "One of Twins," he is John Stevens's friendly coworker in a San Francisco office. By mistake he invites John's twin brother, Henry Stevens, to dinner. Henry accepts; but John goes, falls in love with Margovan's daughter, Julia Margovan, and eventually proposes to her.

MARGOVAN, JULIA. In "One of Twins," she is the beautiful daughter of Margovan and his wife. She meets John Stevens when he goes to dinner at the Margovan home. She soon accepts his proposal of marriage but is then seen by Henry Stevens, his twin brother, consorting with a dissipated stranger. Henry apprises her of this fact but says he will oppose her marriage "on other grounds." Later, John evidently learns of Julia's behavior, poisons her, and shoots himself to death.

MARGOVAN, MRS. In "One of Twins," she is the mother of lovely Julia Margovan. At Mrs. Margovan's dinner party, John Stevens meets Julia.

"MARIE BASHKIRTSEFF" (1890, 1911). Review. The diary of Marie Bashkirtseff (Marya Konstantinovna Bashkirtseva [1860–1884]) contains a dozen years of "undigested thoughts, fancies and feelings." Her honesty is to be doubted. She probably revised it for publication. She should have revised much entirely out. She mistook love of art for ability to paint; and rich, ignorant Americans have foolishly bought some of her paintings. Her art and drama criticism is crude and senseless. The account of her mortal illness (tuberculosis) is pathetic but should not have been written. Her journal is "morbid, hysterical and unpleasant."

MARKHAM, EDWIN (1852–1940). (Original name: Charles Edward Anson Markham.) Poet. He was born in Oregon City, Oregon. His father was a hunter and farmer; his mother, a bright, greedy, religious fanatic. After his parents got divorced, his mother took her children to California, where young Markham tended sheep and did farm work even before he was a teenager. He graduated from Christian College in Santa Rosa (1873), taught school, entered politics, became a school official, read socialist Christian books, and in the 1880s began publishing prolabor poetry. In 1890, Markham became a school principal in Oakland, California, where he made friends with a number of California writers, including Mary Austin, Joaquin Miller,* and Bierce. In 1895 or so, Markham began to use Edwin as his first name. He was inspired by Jean-François Millet's painting, *The Man with the Hoe* to write a poem titled "The Man with the Hoe," which was published in 1899 in the *San Francisco Examiner*, owned by William Randolph Hearst.* The poem so pleased Hearst that he hired Markham to be literary editor of the *Examiner*. The Hoe Poem, as it was called, was a national success and ultimately earned Markham a reputed $250,000 in the following three decades. Its message was so prolabor that the antilabor California railroad tycoon, Collis P. Huntington,* offered a $750 prize for the best poem refuting Markham's.

Bierce helped Markham when he was a neophyte poet. In return, Markham admired Bierce, calling him "our literary Atlas" and regarding him as "a blending of Hafiz, the Persian, Swift, Poe, Thoreau, with sometimes the gleam of the Galilean." Markham must have felt that Bierce would be pleased by his Hoe Poem, published while Bierce was reporting Huntington's efforts to influence Congressmen in Washington, D.C., to give his railroads more financial concessions. Bierce, however, attacked the poem in three *Examiner* columns (22 and 29 January 1899, 12 February 1899), as "stiff, inelastic, monotonous," containing "seepage from the barnyard," lacking "the vitality of a sick fish," and displaying "sand-lotism." Nevertheless, when Markham was accused of plagiarizing his Hoe Poem, Bierce defended both the poet and the originality of his poem. (*See also* "Edwin Markham's Poems.")

Markham was unhappily married to Annie Cox from 1875 to 1884 and unhappily married in 1887 to Caroline E. Bailey, who soon left him. He was happily married to Anna Catherine Murphy in 1898 and had a child with her. They moved to New York City, where he wrote "Lincoln, the Man of the People" (1900), another success. Markham's last years were notable for his continuing to espouse liberal causes but were marred by insignificant writing and disastrous investments. Widowered in 1938, Markham died soon after.

Bibliography: George Truman Carl, *Edwin Markham: The Poet for Preachers* (New York: Vantage Press, 1977; Morris; Joseph A. Slade, " 'Putting You in the Papers': Ambrose Bierce's Letters to Edwin Markham," *Prospects* 1 (1975): 335–368; W. A. Swanberg, *Citizen Hearst: A Biography of William Randolph Hearst* (New York: Charles Scribner's Sons, 1961).

MARLOWE, BABY. In "The Eyes of the Panther," she was the baby daughter of Thomas Marlowe and his wife, who clutched Baby to death when she saw the eyes of a panther at their cabin window.

MARLOWE, CHARLES ("OLD MAN MARLOWE"). In "The Eyes of the Panther," he was a hunter. He and his family lived at the fringe of the forest. Returning one night after shooting a deer for meat, he found Baby Marlowe dead in the arms of his suddenly demented wife. Three months later, she gave birth to their second daughter, Irene Marlowe, and died. He and Irene have lived for years in his cabin. Only after her death is the old man able to grieve in the local graveyard, at peace at last.

MARLOWE, IRENE. In "The Eyes of the Panther," she is the quietly demented daughter of Charles Marlowe and his long-deceased wife. She declines to marry Jenner Brading on grounds of her insanity. He doubts her explanation that the sight of the eyes of a panther at her parents' cabin window was the cause of her dementia—that is, until he sees a panther near her, later sees the eyes of a panther at his own cottage window, fires at it, and kills Irene.

MARLOWE, MRS. CHARLES. In "The Eyes of the Panther," she was the wife of Charles Marlowe, a hunter. Despite her pleas not to leave her one fatal night, he goes hunting, returns with game, and finds her having clutched their daughter, Baby Marlowe, to death. Three months later she gives birth to Irene Marlowe and dies.

MARSH, WILLARD. In "The Suitable Surroundings," he is a Cincinnati businessman. When James R. Colston, a ghost-story writer, sees Marsh reading one of his stories while on the streetcar, he says that if Marsh were to read one of his stories in an eerie setting, doing so would kill him. Marsh takes up the challenge, follows Colston's suggestion and goes with a story by Colston in manuscript to the supposedly haunted house once owned by Charles Breede, now deceased. While reading it by candlelight near the front window, he sees a farm boy looking in at him, hears a screech owl, and dies. In the story, Colston wrote Marsh that he was going to kill himself and then haunt Marsh. The next day Marsh's body is discovered when the farm boy leads three adults to the scene. One of the three men was Breede's son-in-law.

MARSHALL. In "That of Granny Magone," this family name is mentioned as belonging to distinguished people who know the Rev. Elias Atney.

MARTIN, SAMUEL. In "The Man Overboard," he is the first officer of the *Bonnyclabber*. When he argues with Claude Reginald Gump, the narrator, the two go overboard. Martin is swallowed by a whale and while inside writes down a final entry in the ship's logbook.

MASTERSON, GENERAL. In "An Affair of Outposts," he is the officer in command of Union Army troops that include Captain Armisted and his infantry company. He permits the Governor to go forward in search of Armisted. After the skirmish in which Armisted is killed, General Masterson happily calls it "the beautifulest fight ever made." Bierce notes that its beauty is proved "by a row of dead . . . and another of wounded." In "One Kind of Officer," General Masterson is the Union Army officer in command of General Hart and also of General Cameron, who is Captain Ransome's superior officer. Obeying Cameron's offensively delivered orders, Ransome has his artillery men fire on all troops in front of him, even Hart's men, whom Masterson has ordered Hart to bring up in support of Cameron's flank. When no one can justify Ransome's behavior, Masterson will undoubtedly order his execution by firing squad.

MASTHEAD. In "Mr. Masthead, Journalist," he is the man from Warm Springs, Missouri, whom Norton recommends to Johnson as the editor of Johnson's *Claybank Thundergust of Reform*, a weekly published in Claybank, Kansas. Johnson wants Masthead to write editorials to defeat Johnson's brother-in-law, Jefferson Scandril, who is running for the legislature. Masthead first attacks Scandril's family and then writes that Scandril's opponent, Broskin, spent time in the insane asylum at Warm Springs, Missouri. It develops that Broskin was earlier the physician in charge of the asylum, that

Masthead's son was one of his patients, and that Masthead said he would care for the lad if he were released.

MASTHEAD. In "Mr. Masthead, Journalist," he is the demented son of Masthead, who becomes the editor of Johnson's *Claybank Thundergust of Reform.* The lad's father promised to care for him if he were released from the asylum in Warm Springs, Missouri.

"MATERIALS FOR HISTORY." *See* "Jupiter Doke, Brigadier-General."

"THE MATTER OF MANNER" (1889, 1906, 1911). Essays. Words are supremely important, because they dominate thought and master character. Those with rich, obedient vocabularies are "the wisest thinkers" (for example, Charles Darwin).

MATTHEWS, MARY. In "A Holy Terror." *See* Porfer, Mary Matthews.

MAY. In "The Thing at Nolan," he is Charles May's brother. He lives nearby and is said to have a temperament like Charles's sullen son, John May.

MAY. In "The Thing at Nolan," she is either of the young daughters of Charles May and his wife.

MAY, CHARLES. In "The Thing at Nolan," he, his wife, their son John May, and their two young daughters live between Leesville and Hardy, Missouri. Charles has a quick temper but one that easily returns to amiable. He hits his son during a misunderstanding one day, quickly apologizes, but is quietly threatened. Charles goes to dig at the family spring, is followed there by John, and is soon reported missing. John is tried for murder; but since Henry O'Dell, Charles's cousin, saw Charles eight miles away at the time he was supposedly murdered, John is acquitted. Later Charles's body is found by the spring where his footprints and those of his son had been seen by authorities earlier.

MAY, JOHN. In "The Thing at Nolan," he is the sullen son of Charles May and his wife. When Charles hits him in the face during a dispute, John calmly says he will die "for that" even though the father has already immediately apologized. John follows his father to their spring a mile away, returns home alone, gets sick and delirious, and mutters something about murder. He is tried for murder but is acquitted on the grounds that Charles's cousin, Henry O'Dell, and others, saw Charles eight miles from the spring where he was supposedly killed. John leaves the country. Later Charles's body is found by the spring.

MAY, MRS. CHARLES. In "The Thing at Nolan," she is the wife of Charles May and the mother of John May and two young daughters. After Charles's disappearance and John's acquittal on the charge of murdering Charles, she and her daughters move to St. Louis.

MAYNARD. In "An Adventure at Brownville," he was the father, now deceased, of Eva Maynard and Pauline Maynard. They evidently lived in San Francisco. Richard Benning knew him and became the girls' evil guardian.

MAYNARD, EVA. In "An Adventure at Brownville," she is the young sister of Pauline Maynard. Eva may be suffering from consumption. She and Pauline, who are wards of Richard Benning, are vacationing with him in Brownville when Moran, the narrator, mostly watches as Benning evidently exerts a hypnotic influence first over Pauline, causing her death, and then over Eva, causing her suicide.

MAYNARD, PAULINE. In "An Adventure at Brownville," she is the sister of Eva Maynard and is older than Eva. Moran, the narrator, hears Pauline ask Benning whether he intends to kill both sisters. A month later Pauline is dead, evidently the victim of Benning's hypnotic influence.

McARDLE, COL. J. C. In "The Spook House," he is a lawyer living in Frankfort, Kentucky. In June 1859, he takes refuge from a storm in the Spook House with his friend Judge Myron Veigh. They enter a mysterious room full of corpses. When Veigh boldly pushes past him to examine one corpse, McArdle backs out, closes the door by chance, and faints. He comes to his senses in Manchester. When Veigh is never heard from again, his family doubts McArdle's story and turns hostile. McArdle, cleared of a charge of insanity, publishes his account of the "adventure" in the Frankfort *Advocate* of 6 August 1876.

McKINLEY, WILLIAM (1843–1901). The twenty-fifth president of the United States (1897–1901). He was born in Niles, Ohio, attended Allegheny College in Meadville, Pennsylvania, but withdrew after one term because of illness and financial problems. He served in the Union Army during the Civil War (1861–1865), attaining the rank of brevet major. He practiced law in Canton, Ohio, and in 1871 married Ida Saxon. They had two daughters; but both soon died, and Mrs. McKinley grew permanently ill and despondent. McKinley was a Republican member of the U.S. House of Representatives (1877–1883, 1885–1891) and was influential in passing the McKinley Tariff Act (1890), which was unpopular with most citizens but pleased wealthy and grateful Ohio industrialists. He was the Republican governor of Ohio (1892–1896). Early in his second term as president, he was assassinated in Buffalo by Leon Czolgosz, an anarchist.

Bierce, who had worked in San Francisco for newspaper-owner William Randolph Hearst* since 1887, as the chief editorial writer for his *San Francisco Examiner*, wrote as early as 1895 in opposition to war with Spain over Cuba. In 1896 Hearst assigned him to Washington, D.C., to lobby against a funding bill favoring railroad-mogul Collis P. Huntington.* When Hearst bought the New York *Journal* and began whipping up a pro-war frenzy, Bierce turned curiously silent on the subject of war. Hearst may have ordered him to avoid the subject. In addition, Bierce hated war, even though it fascinated him and became the focus of much of his writing. He also despised hypocritical patriots, who were in reality motivated by political ambition; moreover, he figured that the Cuban populace, being for the most part black in his view, were not worth fighting to free. When the Spanish-American War began, Bierce alternately boasted that the American navy (not the army) could easily defeat the Spanish in Cuba. He also ridiculed not only American political leadership but also American war correspondents assigned to Cuba. In addition, he presciently warned of long-term complications in the Philippine Islands and regarded American ambitions there as a form of colonial expansionism.

On 31 January 1904, Kentucky governor-elect William Goebel was shot in a political quarrel and died three days later. Bierce naturally heard about it and wrote the following poem for Hearst's *Journal*:

> The bullet that pierced Goebel's breast
> Can not be found in all the West;
> Good reason, it is speeding here
> To stretch McKinley on the bier.

Because Hearst's vociferous newspapers were reviling McKinley's protrust position, he and especially Bierce were in hot water immediately over the ditty. In "A Thumb-Nail Sketch," Bierce details the events surrounding the quatrain. Bierce, long preoccupied with violence and death, had written an 1881 *Wasp* column on President James A. Garfield's assassination. Bierce also wrote a number of silly little dramas in which McKinley figures as stupid and inept. The plays are "Aspirants Three," "A Baffled Ambition," "For Intervention," "Frosting a Bud," "An Indemnity," and "A Provisional Settlement."

Bibliography: Berkove; John M. Dobson, *Reticent Expansionism: The Foreign Policy of William McKinley* (Pittsburgh: Duquesne University Press, 1988); Lewis S. Gould, *The Presidency of William McKinley* (Lawrence: Regents Press of Kansas, 1980); Joshi and Schultz; Morris.

MENCKEN, H. L. (1880–1956). (Full name: Henry Louis Mencken.) Editor and author. He was born in Baltimore, was educated at the Baltimore Polytechnic Institute, and was employed by the *Baltimore Evening Herald* beginning in 1899. After becoming its city editor (1903) and managing editor

(1905–1906), he worked for the *Baltimore Sunpapers* (1906–1917, 1920–1938, 1948). Mencken was on the editorial staff of *The Smart Set* (1908–1923), wrote a daily *Evening Sun* column titled "Free Lance" (1911–1915), and visited Europe (1912, 1916, 1917). In 1924 he cofounded the *American Mercury* and edited it until 1934. He married Sara Powell Haardt (1930), was widowed (1935), suffered a career-ending stroke (1948), and died childless. All his life, Mencken criticized America's so-called "booboisie" democracy, with its political corruption and philistine "culture." Mencken wrote books on George Bernard Shaw (1905) and Friedrich Nietzsche (1908), an enormous linguistic study titled *The American Language* (1919, with revisions and supplements [1921–1948]), many savage essays collected in six series of *Prejudices* (1919–1927), and four autobiographical volumes (1940, 1941, 1943, and 1993).

When Bierce went to Baltimore to attend the funeral of the critic Percival Pollard* in 1911, he met Mencken, who had been Pollard's friend and disciple. After the ceremony, attended by only five people, Mencken was impressed by Bierce's witty but gruesome comments on death and on how to dispose of Pollard's cremated remains. Mencken delighted in Bierce's *The Devil's Dictionary*, labeling its witticisms "gorgeous." He would have especially relished Bierce's string of twenty-five synonyms for "Drunk, *adj.*," the best including "top-heavy" and "pious." Though published in the *Wasp* (12 August 1882), this list did not appear in any edition of *The Devil's Dictionary* at Mencken's disposal then. Nor were Bierce's thirty-six synonyms for alcohol published earlier—the best surely being "liverpickle" and "screwmouth" (*Wasp*, 5 March 1881)—probably available for Mencken's pleasure. In *The American Language*, Mencken lists dozens and dozens of synonyms for the challenging words "drunk" and "alcohol" himself. In many ways, Bierce and Mencken were kindred spirits: Both wielded ferocious pens, both commanded extensive vocabularies, and both despised sham of all sorts in American politics and culture. Mencken composed one of the most incisive and accurate comments on Bierce ever written: "What delighted him [Bierce] most in this life was the spectacle of human cowardice and folly. He put man, intellectually, somewhere between the sheep and the horned cattle, and as a hero somewhere below the rats. . . . So far in this life, . . . I have encountered no more thorough-going cynic than Bierce was. . . . Out of the spectacle of life about him he got an unflagging and Gargantuan joy. He was an almost amorous connoisseur of theology and theologians. He howled with mirth whenever he thought of a professor, a doctor or a husband." And you too, H. L.?

Bibliography: "Ambrose Bierce to H. L. Mencken," *Book Club of California Quarterly News Letter* 26 (Fall 1961): 27–33; Fred Hobson, *Mencken: A Life* (New York: Random House, 1994); "H. L. Mencken to Ambrose Bierce," *Book Club of California Quarterly News Letter* 22 (Winter 1956): 5–10; H. L. Mencken, "Ambrose Bierce," pp. 259–265 in *Prejudices: Sixth Series* (New York: Alfred A. Knopf, 1927); Morris.

MENDENHALL, MARIAN. In "Killed at Resaca," she lives well in San Francisco. When she is informed by a soldier named Winters that Union Army Lieutenant Herman Brayle behaved in a cowardly manner during a battle in Virginia, she writes Brayle a letter in which she says she could stand news of his death but not of his cowardice. This letter, signed "Darling," motivates Brayle to display bravery so suicidally foolhardy that he is killed by Confederate rifle fire at Resaca. The narrator retrieves the letter from Brayle and takes it after the war to Marian, who is indifferent to it but when she sees blood on it recoils and tosses it into the fire. Finding her "beautiful" but "detestable," he tells her Brayle was killed by a snake bite. Bierce, a confirmed misogynist, occasionally equates snakes and women. In this instance, he may have been comparing Marian Mendenhall with Bernice Wright, his wartime sweetheart in Warsaw, Indiana, who jilted him.
Bibliography: Carey McWilliams, "Ambrose Bierce and His First Love," *Bookman* 35 (June 1932): 254–259; Russell Roth, "Ambrose Bierce's 'Detestable Creature,' " *Western American Literature* 9 (November 1974): 169–176.

MERLE, WILSON. In "At Old Man's Eckert's," he is a lawyer who, with John Holcomb and Andrus C. Palmer, investigates the haunted house of Philip Eckert. He and Holcomb see Palmer walk past them and simply disappear.

"THE MIDDLE TOE OF THE RIGHT FOOT" (1890). Short story. (Characters: Sheriff Adams, Brewer, King, Manton, Manton, Gertrude Manton, Rosser, Sancher.) In their house a mile from the town of Marshall, Manton kills his wife, Gertrude Manton, and their two young children, by slitting their throats. Then he disappears, and ten years pass. King, who is the deputy serving under Sheriff Adams of Marshall, and King's friends Rosser and Sancher are chatting on the porch of a Marshall hotel. A fourth man, registered as Robert Grossmith, is listening. King says that he regards deformity of any kind in a woman as a symbol of her moral deficiency. He says he "threw over" a girl once on learning that she had had a toe amputated. Sancher jokes by saying that the woman married another man, who was liberal about a missing toe but cut her throat. King says that he sees Sancher is referring to Manton and his wife. Rosser accuses the man calling himself Grossmith of eavesdropping and orders him away. The fellow turns offensive. Sancher tries to break up the argument. But Rosser remains belligerent. Grossmith demands a duel, says that he is a stranger in these parts, and persuades Sancher to be his second. King, who has been staring at Grossmith, will be Rosser's second and says that the duel will take place at the abandoned Manton house. When the four men arrive in a wagon driven by King, Grossmith is terrified but proceeds. The antagonists are required to remove all outer clothing, are furnished with bowie knives, and are placed in opposite corners of the room, which is then darkened. Grossmith drops his knife and dies of fright. Distraught, Rosser, clad only in his underwear, rushes out, and King and Sancher drive him away. Sheriff Adams, his deputy, King, and a man named Brewer go to the Manton house together and find Grossmith rigid in death. Brewer identifies him as Manton. King calmly agrees, adding that he knew Manton but that the man then had long hair and a beard, whereas "Grossmith" was clean shaven. King might have added but did not that when the man calling himself Grossmith challenged Rosser he recognized him as Manton. King then alerted Rosser and Sancher as to his identity, and they agreed to play the trick on him of staging the duel at his old home—a trick proving fatal to him. Adams, King, and Brewer then see on the dusty floor three sets of footprints leading to the dead Manton but not away from him. Two sets are of children. The right foot of the third set is that of an adult, with a missing middle toe. Brewer, who is Gertrude's brother, recognizes her footprint.

Bierce narrates "The Middle Toe of the Right Foot" awkwardly out of chronological order. First he locates the empty Manton house and says that witnesses call it haunted. Then he tells how four unnamed men approach and enter it, one reluctantly. Then he sets the stage for the knife duel. He backtracks to describe the discussion of King, Rosser, and Sancher, and Grossmith's interruption of it, leading to the duel. Then he has Adams, King, and Brewer go to the house and find Manton. Next he awkwardly enters King's mind for an explanation withheld from the others. Finally comes the mystery of the footprints and the identification of one set as belonging to Gertrude, tardily called Brewer's sister.

MILLER, JOAQUIN (c. 1839–1913). (Real name: Cincinnatus Hiner Miller). Author and poseur. Born near Liberty, Indiana, he went with his family to Oregon when he was young. He had many adventures as a miner, schoolteacher, Indian fighter, horse thief, pony-express rider, editor, lawyer, and judge. He published two small books of poetry, *Specimens* (1868) and *Joaquin et al.* (1869) and was shown by Ina Coolbrith,* his San Francisco friend, how to read his verse in public. She also claimed she suggested that he change his first name to Joaquin. Miller left San Francisco, where he had known Charles Warren Stoddard,* Bret Harte,* and several other writers, and went to London (1870–1871, 1872–1783). Already sporting long hair, Miller dressed in Western garb—cowboy boots, spurs, buckskin shirt, red-belted Bowie knife, cape, sombrero, and the like—to the disgust of more competent Western expatriate writers then living in London; but the British welcomed him as an authentic curiosity. Once established, Miller published *Pacific Poems* and *Songs of the Sierras* (both 1871) and was dubbed "The Poet of the Sierras" and "The Byron of Oregon." His *Life Amongst the Modocs* (1873) is allegedly autobiographical. After more traveling and publishing, Miller settled in the United States (1876) and ultimately in California (1886). His later writings are now mostly forgotten. He went to Alaska and the Yukon as a reporter for the *New York Journal*, published by William Randolph Hearst* (1897–1898), then returned to San Francisco, where he died. He is now known for sentimentalizing, romanticizing, and mythologizing the West. His best poem, "Columbus," is from his *Songs of the Soul* (1896).

Shortly after Miller returned from London to California in 1871, Bierce invited him to San Rafael, where he and his bride Mary Ellen Day Bierce* were living. Miller's warm reception in England may have helped persuade Bierce to emigrate, which he and Mollie did in March 1872. He and other California writers, including Stoddard and Mark Twain,* greeted Miller in London when he returned later in 1872. They were disgusted by his pretentious Western garb, which Bierce's British friend Tom Hood* may have encouraged him to show off in. When Miller was in London once more, early in 1873, he, Bierce, and Twain were guests at a banquet held at the White Friars Club in Fleet Street, London. During the festivities, Miller swallowed a fish whole to amuse the British.

Naturally Bierce soon had a dispute with Miller. A freelance journalist calling herself Olive Harper (really Helen Burrell) tried but failed to interview Bierce in London in 1873; so she retaliated by writing that he was a snob living in London on money provided by his wife Mollie (in truth it had come from Mollie's father). Concluding that only Miller could have given "Olive" this information, Bierce published an open letter in several London journals (16 November 1973) lambasting both "Mrs. Harper" and Miller. Miller missed the invective, however, having just escaped two love affairs in London and being in Rome embroiled in another. Bierce, ever the discreet lover, could not have liked Miller's publicized amours. In the 1850s Miller and an Indian woman named Paquita had a child, Calli Shasta, whom Coolbrith informally adopted. In 1862 Miller married Theresa Dyer, an Oregon poet writing as Minnie Myrtle. They were divorced in 1869. He married Abigail Leland in 1879 and lived in the East with her; but they were separated by 1883. Once back in California, Miller and Bierce resumed a cool friendship. In 1892 Gustav Danzinger* persuaded Miller and a couple of other writers to form the Western Authors Publishing Company with him and issue a collection of Bierce's poems. The result was *Black Beetles in Amber*, which lost money. Next, Bierce in the *San Francisco Examiner* (30 January 1898) wrote thus: "In impugning Mr. Miller's veracity, or rather, in plainly declaring that he has none, I should be sorry to be understood as attributing a graver moral delinquency than he really has. He cannot, or will not, tell the truth, but he never tells a malicious or thrifty falsehood." When an expansion of *Black Beetles in Amber* was published as volume 5 of Bierce's *Collected Works*, Bierce added "The Mormon Question By J-qu-n M-ll-r," in which an oversexed Miller is spoofed by being made to say that he "will go to the place of the Mormon: the place / Where the jackass rabbit is first in the race."

Bibliography: Roger Austen, *Genteel Pagan: The Double Life of Charles Warren Stoddard*

(Amherst: University of Massachusetts Press, 1991); O. W. Frost, *Joaquin Miller* (New York: Twayne Publishers, 1967); M. E. Grenander, "A London Letter of Joaquin Miller to Ambrose Bierce," *Yale University Library Gazette* 46 (October 1971): 109–116; Benjamin S. Lawson, *Joaquin Miller* (Boise, Idaho: Boise State University Press, 1980); M. M. Marberry, *Splendid Poseur: Joaquin Miller—American Poet* (New York: Thomas Y. Crowell, 1953); McWilliams; Morris; O'Connor; Starr.

"A MINERAL PORCUPINE." *See* "Pectolite."

"THE MIRAGE" (1887, 1909). Essay. (Full title: "The Mirage: Strange Optical Illusions on the High Plains.") Bierce says that ever since people have been able to travel by rail across the Western plains, there has been much talk about mirages—"magicians of the air." He wants to note a few such sightings himself. One morning, while he was the surveyor on a post-inspecting tour, he sought water for "my ablutions" and noted a line of willows three hundred yards distant. With a kettle in hand, he marched toward them, but they constantly receded. The sun grew hot; he returned to camp and was asked if he wished to plead temporary insanity. Later his chief (General William B. Hazen*) stalked a dead coyote, thinking it was a buffalo he might bag. One noon Bierce sighted a cool spot near the Big Horn Mountains for their night camp, but three days passed before they got there. One clear morning after a thunderstorm, the whole party thought they saw several monsters a quarter of a mile ahead. They might, on the other hand, have been houses or machines. Then "this pageant" appeared to move. Once, while at the upper Missouri River, Bierce saw an ocean shore, complete with bays and boats and hills, islands with trees and houses, and a city far beyond. He was aware that all was a mirage, but what an "enchanting," even "precious" show it was. Bierce ends with a final example. One day while steaming along the sultry-calm Hudson River, he dozed, awoke, and across the water seemed to see a city. Asking what the vision was, he was told it was Poughkeepsie. Bierce waxes literary in "The Mirage," quoting and paraphrasing Shakespeare's *Macbeth* and *The Tempest*, Percy Bysshe Shelley's "Ozymandias," and John Keats's "On First Looking into Chapman's Homer."

MITCHELL-HEDGES, FREDERICK ALBERT (1882–1959). Explorer and author. He was born in Stewkley, Buckinghamshire, England, and was educated at the University College School in London. He became a daring and distinguished explorer, mainly in South and Central America. He penetrated previously unknown regions of Panama (1922–1923) and returned with hitherto unrecorded ichthyological specimens to present to several British museums. He explored the interior of British Honduras (now Belize) and codiscovered and helped clear ruins of the Mayan city of Lubaantun (1924, 1925). He led an expedition from the United States into Mosquitia, Republic of Honduras (1930), found some fine pottery there, and donated it to the Museum of the American Indian (Heye Foundation). He explored the Islas Bahia off Honduras and gave his finds to the Museum of the American Indian, the British Museum, and other museums (1932, 1934). He explored the Seychelles (1950) and Tanganyika (1951). Mitchell-Hedges's books include *Battles with Giant Fish* (1923), *Land of Wonder and Fear* (1931, about Central America), *Battles with Monsters of the Sea* (1937), and his autobiography *Danger My Ally* (1954). This adventuresome and mysterious man died in Haldon, England.

It has been theorized, somewhat extravagantly, that in the summer of 1913 Bierce met Mitchell-Hedges in Mexico. It is known that Mitchell-Hedges was in Mexico during that time and that both he and Bierce joined Pancho Villa's army that November. It is further speculated that the two men were commissioned to act together as secret agents to gather intelligence concerning Japanese and German activities in Mexico shortly before World War I began.

Bibliography: Sibley S. Merrill, *Ambrose Bierce, F. A. Mitchell-Hedges and the Crystal Skull* (San Francisco: Cadleon Press, 1972); Morris.

"THE MOCKING-BIRD" (1891). Short story. (Full title: "A Mocking-Bird: The Story of a Soldier Who Had a Dream.") (Characters: John Grayrock, Private William Grayrock.) In the autumn of 1861, Private William Grayrock of the Union Army is on lonely picket duty one Saturday night in southwestern Virginia. With his imagination working overtime, he grows disoriented, hears a sound, shouts "Halt!" and "[W]ho goes there?" and fires with accustomed precision at the supposed enemy. Other pickets fire and then retreat. Not doing so himself because he does not know where his main forces are, he is soon labeled a hero for holding his position. On Sunday, he obtains a pass and wanders forward to find what he shot at, is unsuccessful, and sits by a tree to rest. He falls asleep and has a dream. He dreams of his childhood with his twin brother, John Grayrock. They shared a pleasant life together, but when their mother died, kinsmen who were enemies adopted the boys and William went to a big city in "the Realm of Conjecture" while John went with "wicked" people to "the Enchanted Land." The boys wrote each other but soon lost touch. Through this dream—and in reality, when William awakens—is heard the song of a mocking-bird. William sees the bird and weeps, then wanders and finds John's body, shot through the chest. William then kills himself.

In calling John's country wicked, Bierce is implicitly calling the Southern political position wicked. In "What I Saw of Shiloh," Bierce eloquently tells how "in the Southern midnights . . . the mocking-bird poured out his heart in the moon-gilded magnolia."*Bibliography:* Grenander, Woodruff.

MOCUMP, PETER WODEL. In "My Credentials," he is a deceased person who, though lauded by society members, feels unworthy to enter heaven.

"MODERN WARFARE" (1888, 1892, 1896, 1899, 1900, 1911). Essay. (Original title of part: "Superior Killing: A Strolling Comment on a Certain Amiable Error.") Those who dream of universal peace think that war will become too dreadful and too expensive to be tolerated any longer. On the contrary, the more costly the military machine is, the more inevitable is its eventual use. Defensive devices become aggressive. It is erroneous to believe that better weapons mean more widespread killings. Old naval battles were gorier than recent ones. In the 1863 attack on Fort Sumter, during the Civil War, a total of 2,360 shots were fired and three men were killed. Hand-to-hand combat involving ancient Greeks and Romans caused more "proportionate mortality" than occurred in "the later and more scientific Franco-German and Turko-Russian wars." Bellicose materiel is virtually perfect, including small arms; so peace should reign for only a short time. A Union Army general recently wrote that weapons have grown so terrifying that "a partial cessation of war" ought to follow. The more damaging the weaponry, however, the more likely will be fewer casualties, because men will not rush to be killed. Long-range weapons, and defensive measures attending them, tend to make "cowards" of their users. Future wars will demonstrate a fine balance of attacking and defensive measures. Armor-piercing missiles mainly penetrate the U.S. Treasury. Nowadays, patriots volunteer for service but plan to do their killing of the enemy at long range; still, they can expect some injury. This essay is wrong-headed so persistently that one wonders if it was intended to be at least partly satirical.

MOLOCH. In "Hades in Trouble," he is a strong devil and is one of the host trying to rescue Satan from the earth.

THE MONK AND THE HANGMAN'S DAUGHTER (1891). Novel. (Characters: Aegidius, Nathan Alfinger, Amula, Father Andreas, Ambrosius, Benedicta, Rochus, Romanus.) On 1 May 1680, three Franciscan monks—Aegidius, Romanus, and young Ambrosius, the narrator, twenty-one—are ordered by their superior to go from Passau to the monastery at Berchtesgaden, near Salzburg. During their five-day journey, the pious and God-fearing Ambrosius delights in the beauty of nature, is frightened by birds of prey, and hopes he will not be led astray by the pretty girls demonstrating their eagerness to kiss his hand along the wayside. In a craggy region they see a gallows with a hanged man. A beautiful maiden is there, routinely driving away the vultures. She tells Ambrosius that she is Benedicta, the widowed hangman's daughter. In a dispute with his companions, Ambrosius pities, defends, and praises her. They come to a clearing and find their monastery.

A few weeks pass. Ambrosius thinks of his deceased parents and his beloved stepmother, anticipates being ordained, and might actually like being tempted to err and to sin so that by resisting he can become stronger. The food and malt drink are fine in the monastery. Nearby are men who work the salt mines in the mountains. They are bossed by the so-called Saltmaster, who has a handsome, wild son named Rochus. The men often vie for girl-friends, as stags do for their does. When Ambrosius sees Benedicta spurned by the villagers, he leads her to mass and watches her pray in her assigned corner. His superior, Father Andreas, rebukes him for this and puts him "under hard penance" in his cell. Benedicta tosses him a bunch of edelweiss, which she plucked after a dangerous climb up a sheer cliff. The flowers grow above a lake said to be haunted by specters. Ambrosius, the youngest and strongest brother, is told that he must soon visit the sick among those high places.

One day the monastery celebrates a festival, which begins with a holy procession. The wise Saltmaster rides a fine horse nears the mine entrance. Benedicta is absent—both from sneers and from solace. The feast is sump-tuous, with beef, fish, and bitter beer, followed by music, wrestling matches, and fights with fists and knives. Handsome but fiendish Rochus, prominent at these events, warns Ambrosius to stay away from Benedicta. When the dancing starts, Rochus spurns Amula, his attractive girlfriend, and leads a group of rioters with torches through the dark forest to go get Benedicta. Warned and led by Amula, Ambrosius takes a shortcut to Benedicta's hut. She reluctantly leaves her sick old father and escapes. But, returning to the crowd, Ambrosius finds her dancing with Rochus. He wants to protect her not only from seductive Rochus but also from jealous Amula. When Amula gossips about Benedicta, Ambrosius tries to defend her reputation, but the Superior calls him a false witness and confines him to his cell once more. Benedicta, calumniated by Amula and others as a "fallen" woman, is tied to a pillory in the town square. Amula reviles the patient victim, while Ambro-sius wonders why Rochus does not defend her. Ambrosius concludes that he loves Benedicta but without any feeling of guilt, now reasoning that "spiri-tual and . . . carnal love are not so widely different as I have been taught to think them." He hopes to become a priest soon and watch over Benedicta better.

Father Andreas orders him to go into the mountains to collect gentiana roots, from which the monastery distills a spicy, sin-curing liquor sent to Munich for sale. A young guide takes Ambrosius through wild woods and over a misty lake near Saint Bartholomae, the Superior's garden-like summer residence, and on to the stone hut where he is to live while gathering roots. Dairy women will bring him a little food daily. He soon feels at peace. Benedicta comes by, says that her father has died, and bitterly reveals that, as was the fate of her mother, the man was denied Christian rites of burial. At this, Ambrosius feels rebellious against the Church, and even God. Later, when Ambrosius spoils some cooking, Benedicta comes by and bakes a cake for him.

More time passes. Ambrosius responds positively to the grandeur of his awesome locale. He reprimands the women when they tell lies about Benedicta. He also warns the lovely girl that Rochus will mislead her. Ambrosius feels totally in love with her himself now, and he thinks of asking for a dispensation so that he can become a hunter, live nearby, and possibly marry her one day. Sending for Ambrosius, the Superior tells him that the Bishop of Salzburg will give him holy orders three days hence. Ambrosius is sad at the prospect, because now Benedicta will surely become a lost soul. Failing to get her to vow that she will avoid Rochus, he bids her a sad farewell.

Now behold Ambrosius in prison, to be hanged tomorrow for murder. He wonders where God has left him. His final journal entry follows. It seems that when he left Benedicta, he returned to his cabin, suddenly heard Benedicta's voice, and rushed to save her. But he encountered Rochus, who derided him and pulled a knife. Ambrosius grabbed and threw it aside, challenged him to a fair fight, but was quickly pinioned at the cliff's edge. Rochus contemptuously spared him and left, saying, "[Y]ou shall leave her to me." Dawn broke. Ambrosius fasted for three days and two nights, felt free again, and looked forward to becoming a priest. Suddenly he saw God, who told him the means of Benedicta's salvation was given to his hand. He found Rochus's knife, took it, felt he was God's emissary, and rushed to Benedicta's hut. She was smiling sensuously. When she naively said that Rochus promised to introduce her to his father and also to get the Superior to lift the church "curse" from her, Ambrosius seized her, made her kneel, and stabbed her to death. The Lord then guided his steps down to the monastery, where he informed the Superior that he was an ordained priest and how he had saved Benedicta. Only Amula, Rochus's lover, came to Ambrosius—to thank him.

Ambrosius's old manuscript has a few final lines in another hand: On 15 October 1680, Ambrosius was hanged and buried under the gallows with Benedicta, whom Rochus identified as the "bastard" daughter of the hangman's wife and Rochus's father. Rochus added that she secretly loved the monk, who killed her, in ignorance of that love. In other respects, the entry ends, the monk was God's loyal servant and should be prayed for.

In a brief preface, Bierce explains that Dr. Gustav Adolf Danziger (*see* Danziger, Gustav) showed him his translation of *Der Mönch von Berchtesgaden* (1891), a German novel by Richard Voss (1851–1918), and asked him to rewrite it in better English for American publication in serial form. Bierce agreed, provided that both Voss and Danziger would give him a free hand. Danziger said that Voss agreed. It was published by a Chicago firm that, Bierce believed, failed without ever marketing it. On title pages of later books he wrote, Danziger claimed he was the author of *The Monk and the Hangman's Daughter*. Bierce concludes his preface by praising Voss, demeaning his own contribution, and saying that he and others deserve so little credit that he even agreed to put Danziger's name on his title page as collaborator. It has since been determined that the publisher printed 6,000 copies of *The Monk and the Hangman's Daughter* before failing financially, and never paid anything to either Danziger or Bierce. Bierce, obsessed with death, including modes of execution, has this morbid "definition" of hangman in *The Devil's Dictionary*: "An officer of the law who produces suspended animation."

The book has been generally ridiculed, and Bierce has been laughed at for ever having had anything to do with it. However, Ambrosius's worry over the condition of his soul, his gradually being deeply enamored of Benedicta, and descriptions of what may be called Gothic mountain scenery are all commendable. Furthermore, Bierce here seems to anticipate Freudian theory by equating religious fervor and sexual ferment.

Bibliography: Grenander; Frank Monaghan, "Ambrose Bierce and the Authorship of *The Monk and the Hangman's Daughter*," *American Literature* 2 (January 1931): 337–338; Morris; Chris Powell, "The Revised Adolphe Danziger de Castro," *Lovecraft Studies*, no. 36 (Spring 1997): 18–25.

"MONSTERS AND EGGS" (1892, 1911). Essay. Since it has been discovered that Gila monsters relish gulls' eggs, we can domesticate the "calumniated reptile" and eat him when grown. Indians like to roast Gila monsters; since we have followed the Indian lead with respect to potatoes and tobacco, why not in this? Is the Gila monster poisonous? Let Theodore Roosevelt,* the publishing zoologist, be bitten and we will see.

"MONTAGUES AND CAPULETS" (1905, 1911). Essay. George Bernard Shaw says that he has written a better play than *As You Like It* and that William Shakespeare wrote poor blank verse. Now, in truth, Shakespeare's blank verse is mostly "dramatic blank"; *As You Like It* depicts "decency," but *Romeo and Juliet* is morally "detestable," and modern audiences are beguiled into accepting it only because of Shakespeare's handling of "wit, pathos and poetry."

"A MONUMENT TO ADAM" (1880, 1912). Essay. Americans will glow with pleasure: Adam is to have a monument here. It will be inscribed in American English. Adam was "first" in more things than George Washington was. The Adam monument will be fancier than a mere Cleopatra's needle. If subscribers for the Adam monument keep their names off it, it is possible that viewers may believe that Adam reposes underneath. But let no statue be erected to the Missing Link. One subscriber to the Adam monument is Mark Twain,* who memorably sobbed "at the paternal tomb."

"THE MOON IN LETTERS" (1887, 1889, 1903). Essay. (Original title of part: "Concerning Terrestrial Lunarians.") Many authors write incorrectly about the moon. In *King Solomon's Mines*, H. Rider Haggard (1856–1925) has the new moon rise in the east, the full moon come up, and the moon eclipse the sun—all in two and a half days. In *A Princess of Thule* by William Black (1841–1898), the moon rises in the south. Other inaccurate authors are noted. Poetic license may be tolerated, but ignorance is not admirable. If we had no moon but then one appeared and revolved steadily around the earth, we would study astronomy fervently. Meanwhile, few know the difference between a star and a planet. The average foolish man, alone under a starlit sky, would find himself bored and hurry home to his wife and their bed—"unfailing expedient of intellectual vacuity."

"THE MOONLIT ROAD" (1907). Short story. (Characters: Bayrolles, Joel Hetman, Joel Hetman Jr., Julia Hetman.) Joel Hetman Jr., a student at Yale, writes the following account. He was called back to the family home just outside Nashville, where his beloved mother, Julia Hetman, had just been found strangled. It seems that his father had returned home from a business trip in town, saw a man disappear from the rear of the house, entered it himself, and found his wife dead. The father turned fitfully apprehensive. One summer night a few months later, as the father and his son were walking home, the father stopped and stared at something in the moonlit road ahead. The son saw nothing there but did feel "an icy wind." A servant turned on the light in an upstairs room. The father disappeared. A man calling himself Caspar Grattan writes the following. He is soon to die. He writes that he remembered nothing of his life until twenty years ago. He gave himself his present name. He had visions of suspecting his wife's fidelity and trying to trap her. He deliberately returned home early by the back door, saw someone leave hastily, rushed into his dark bedroom, and encountered and strangled his cowering wife. Later he saw her infinitely grave eyes trying to comfort him in a shadowy road. Today his punishing penance will end. The late Julia Hetman offers the following statement through Bayrolles, a medium. While her husband was away on business overnight, she went to bed but soon fancied that "a monster of the night" was approaching her door. She heard it go back down the stairs but then return. She crouched in darkness, tried in vain to call her dear husband's name, but was choked fiercely into the "stammering" ghost she now finds herself to be. During safe nights she tried to communicate her sense of love and pity to her husband and dear son, but they only glared back in terror at her. Once she tried to reach out to them in the moonlight, but her husband showed fear and fled—whither, it is not permitted for her to know. Her son too is "lost to me forever." Bierce handles the structure of this complex story excellently. Notable too is the harrowing sense in Julia Hetman's message that the dead know that they know too little of events following their death.

MORAN. In "An Adventure at Brownville," he is the narrator, teaches at a school just outside Brownville, and lives in a hotel there. He mostly eavesdrops and observes Pauline Maynard and her young sister, Eva Maynard, while Richard Benning exerts a fatally hypnotic influence over his wards. When Pauline dies mysteriously, Moran beseeches Eva, with whom he has quickly fallen in love, to let him help. But, though briefly coquettish, she expresses hopelessness and declines his offer. Moran sees Eva commit suicide and accuses Benning, who, however, will get away with it.

MORGAN. In "The Secret of Macarger's Gulch," he is the narrator Elderson's host at a dinner party in Sacramento. While he, his wife, and Elderson are dining, Morgan relates the circumstances of his discovery of Janet MacGregor's murdered body in the shanty at Macarger's Gulch and of his finding the photograph of Thomas MacGregor, her missing husband.

MORGAN, HUGH. In "The Damned Thing," he is a hunter in a region of farmers and woodsmen. He writes in his diary of his belief that creatures can be opaque but invisible because they are of a color outside the spectrum of colors seen by humans, and further that "the Damned Thing" is an invisible marauding creature that briefly blots out stars on the night horizon and may one day destroy him. When Morgan and his friend William Harker are out hunting, they see a field being trampled, but by something invisible to them. Morgan fires, approaches the scene, and is mauled to death.

MORGAN, MRS. In "The Secret of Macarger's Gulch," she is the wife of the narrator Elderson's host at dinner.

MORRIS, SERGEANT. In "One Kind of Officer," he is Captain Ransome's sergeant, who reports that, according to Corporal Hassman and Gunner Manning, the enemy is approaching their position.

MORRISON. In "The Affair at Coulter's Notch," he is the adjutant general serving on the staff of Captain Coulter's colonel. Morrison reveals to the colonel the rumors that their newly arrived general had, or tried to have, an affair with Coulter's wife.

MORRITZ, SAMUEL. In "Present at a Hanging," he is the itinerant peddler evidently murdered by Daniel Baker in 1853, after Baker lured him to his farm house to rob him. Seven years later, Morritz's ghost points to the bridge where Baker has hanged himself and under which Morritz's bones may be found. Clearly, his ghost was present at a hanging.

MORROW, WILLIAM CHAMBERS (1853–1923). California author. His novels include *Blood-Money* (1882), *A Man: His Mark: A Romance* (1900), and *Lentala of the South Seas: The Romantic Tale of a Lost Colony* (1908). He also wrote *Bohemian Paris of To-day* (1900), on Parisian social life and customs. Two of his books were published posthumously: *The Logic of Punctu-*

ation, for All Who Have to Do with Written English and six California stories collected in *The Ape and the Idiot* (1939). He also wrote minor pieces.

When Morrow was still a neophyte publishing in the *Argonaut* in the late 1870s, Bierce on occasion praised him in print. He also advised him then and later. According to Gustav Danziger,* he, Morrow, and Joaquin Miller* formed the Western Authors Publishing Company in 1892 to publish Bierce's *Black Beetles in Amber*, which was a financial failure although its contents proved sensational at once. After Morrow moved to Washington, D.C., in 1896, Bierce corresponded with him and in a "Prattle" column (*Argonaut*, 13 June 1897) praised his "taste for the shadow side of life," as evidenced in his short fiction. Morrow wrote an introduction to *A Son of the Gods and A Horseman in the Sky*, a 1907 book reprint of Bierce's two stories. Bierce wrote Morrow (9 October 1907) to reminisce about California, to recommend Carmel, and to suggest that Morrow make the aquaintance of the poet George Sterling* there.

Bibliography: Fatout; William Chambers Morrow, *The Monster Maker and Other Stories*, S. T. Joshi, ed. (Seattle: Midnight House, 2000).

MORRYSTER. In "The Man and the Snake," he is the reputed author of a book titled *Marvells of Science*, in which the hypnotizing powers of snakes are reported.

"MORTALITY IN THE FOOT-HILLS" (1873, 1912). Essays. (Original title: " 'Items' from the Press of Interior California.") Bierce presents paragraphs on high death rates in mining towns and sundry other topics. A girl kept her promise to wed whoever horsewhipped some editors who had killed her brother. A miner killed a hymn-book peddler. A wild fellow entered town, was met by the sheriff, and shot him. Persons not attending a public hanging are deemed to be the condemned's accomplices. A revenge-seeking lover fell down while drunk, broke his leg, and was killed by the doctor to relieve his pain. The girls left a certain dance hall when an editor got "his cock-eyed sister" a job there. Miners have stopped dropping "Chinamen and Injins" down shafts and are using a well instead. People should deny hospitality to a liar who claims he shot the sheriff. Some men had fun with a stovepipe-hatted stranger whose funeral is now being arranged. The hanging of the stranger who upset the newspaper office caused the following-day's paper to be canceled. A nefarious Methodist flirted, was shot, then was axed to death by the editor's wife. A certain judge has no right to object to a news item saying that he killed his father, beat his wife, and stole some mules, when the facts are only slightly otherwise. When a man would not give a friend his watch, that friend should not, as a practical joke, have killed the watch-owner's half-breed children. The editors will not name John Lowry as the man who stole the Frisco stranger's gold dust. The murder of Chinese railroad workers is delaying construction of the line northwest. A wounded man ought to die soon, because the attending doctor wants to go visit his mother-in-law out of town. Hanging the judge will prevent suits started by widows hoping to settle disputes over land titles.

MORTONSON, JOHN. In "John Mortonson's Funeral," his is the corpse gnawed in his coffin by his cat.

MORTONSON, MISS. In "John Mortonson's Funeral," she is John Mortonson's grieving daughter.

MORTONSON, MRS. JOHN. In "John Mortonson's Funeral," she is John Morton's grieving widow. She is shocked when she peers through the glass top of his coffin. His cat has been busy inside.

"MORTUARY ELECTROPLATING" (1887, 1911). Essay. The objection that electroplating a corpse does not get rid of it may be countered. A dying husband would like to stand nickel-plated at his "conjugal fireside" and be contemplated by his successor. Plated corpses of distinguished men could do duty as statues, in representative postures, around public buildings, in parks, and in art galleries. Soon, however, the statues would overcrowd our living space. Yet polishing the surface of a beautiful female "electroplatee" would be pleasant labor. But no, it would be selfish to metalize countless corpses, eventually only to have to cord them up and disfigure the landscape with them.

MOXON. In "Moxon's Master," he is a philosophically inclined inventor. He tells the narrator that he believes machines think. He may be the inventor of a chess-playing automaton. In his workshop, he plays chess with an adversary that loses and kills him. The adversary may be a machine; or Haley, Moxon's machinist assistant, may be the killer.

"MOXON'S MASTER" (1899). Short story. (Original title: "A Night at Moxon's.") (Characters: Haley, Moxon.) The callow narrator gets his friend Moxon to say that he indeed believes a machine thinks about what it is doing. He explains that plants, for example, those with water-seeking roots, and minerals, for example, beautiful crystals, surely think. In another room is Moxon's workshop, where Haley, his machinist assistant, toils. Suddenly a machine inside the workshop makes a noise. Moxon goes in alone, seemingly scuffles with something, and emerges with scratches on his face. He lectures the narrator on the sentience of all things, from atoms upward, and theorizes that rhythm causes consciousness. The narrator departs but quickly returns in a sudden rainstorm, lets himself into Moxon's house, and quietly enters the workshop. Moxon is intently playing chess there, with his adversary's back toward the narrator. The creature is short, broad, and dressed in crimson. He seems to be the "automaton chess-player" that Moxon once said he had invented. It seems irritated. Moxon makes a move, shouts "checkmate!" and stands up. Amid whirring sounds, the creature leaps at Moxon and throttles him. The table overturns, the candle goes out, and the room is plunged into darkness. A sudden flash of light reveals Moxon in dying agony and the assassin looking tranquil and thoughtful. Three days later, Haley visits the narrator in the hospital and explains that he rescued him from Moxon's burning home. When the narrator asks if Haley also rescued the chess-playing machine, Haley enigmatically says only, "Do you know that?" Although the narrator immediately says that he was sure, years pass and now he is less confident.

It is regrettable that Bierce did not live into the era of "artificial intelligence" in computers, about which he would have had a word or two. An obvious influence on Bierce's story here is "Maelzel's Chess-Player" by Edgar Allan Poe.

Bibliography: Edna Kenton, "Ambrose Bierce and 'Moxon's Master,' " *Bookman* 62 (1925): 71–75; Miller.

"MR. MASTHEAD, JOURNALIST" (1874). Short story. (Characters: Broskin, Johnson, Masthead, Masthead, Norton, Jefferson Scandril.) The narrator, who calls himself Johnson, has bought a weekly newspaper in Kansas, called the *Claybank Thundergust of Reform*, in order to publish articles that will assure the defeat of his brother-in-law, Jefferson Scandril, of Weedhaven, who is running for the legislature. Johnson writes Norton, a friend in Warm Springs, Missouri, to recommend an outsider as editor. Norton sends Masthead, a seedy little fellow in big cast-off clothes. Masthead writes some withering editorials, attacks Scandril's family verbosely until asked not to, and then, when Johnson suggests his doing so, turns to praising Scandril's opponent. That man is Broskin, whose background, as Masthead sketches it in his next issue, includes a stay of some years in the Warm Springs "lunatic asylum"; he adds that Broskin's "detractors" could not be treated effectively by residing there because they are "rottenly incurable." Johnson fights a few duels with Broskin's advocates and, while recovering, has to let Masthead handle the weekly alone. When he publishes only news of Broskin's time in the asylum and advertising revenue ceases, Johnson orders Masthead to write stories praising Scandril. Suddenly Broskin appears. Masthead quails. Broskin explains that, yes, he spent three years in the asylum some time ago, was its physician in charge, and recently heard that Norton had persuaded authorities to release Masthead's son because Masthead, to whom Broskin now turns and speaks, promised to take care of the lad in the future. Norton, Johnson concludes, "was ever an obliging fellow." Bierce's purpose in writing this story was evidently to satirize the absence of any kind of editorial honesty in Midwestern newspapers, and, by extension, perhaps most American newspapers. Note the names Claybank, *Thundergust*, *Reform*, and Weed-haven.

"MR. SWIDDLER'S FLIP-FLAP" (1874). Short story. (Characters: Jerome Bowles, Jim Peasley, Swiddler.) Swiddler, the narrator, learns that his friend Jerome Bowles is to be hanged at 5:00 P.M., November 9, in the town of Flatbroke, simply for shooting an Indian to death "without direct provocation." He repeatedly importunes the governor, is finally sent for, and is given pardon papers in Swan Creek, the state capital, fifteen miles from Flatbroke. Swiddler cannot send a telegram to the sheriff at Flatbroke, catch a train there, or even rent a horse. The entire town is emptied of people, all on their way to see the hanging. It being 10:00 A.M., Swiddler has a seven-hour, cloudy-day walk to Flatbroke. He starts along the monotonously straight railroad tracks, on each side of which are endless rows of telegraph poles pointing to the flat horizon ahead. Jim Peasley, a practical joker known as "That Jim," joins him, will now walk ahead or behind, teases him, and finally, remembering that Swiddler was once a circus acrobat, asks him to do a somersault. While Swiddler is proudly doing so, Peasley gives him "a twirl that almost sent me off the track." About half way to Swan Creek and Jerome, Swiddler walks on, with Peasley well behind now. But Swiddler suddenly finds himself amid familiar sights. Turned halfway around in his somersault by Peasley, he is back in Flatbroke. Passengers returning in the evening by train from the sad hanging are cheered by being told that Swiddler's flip-flop broke Jerome's neck seven miles away.

MUNNIGLUT. In "Why I Am Not Editing 'The Stinger,'" he is the proprietor of *The Stinger*. When Muskler demands to know who wrote an article about him, Munniglut asks Peter Pitchin, his editor, to explain and then absents himself from the office.

MURLOCK. In "The Boarded Window," he is an Ohio pioneer who in 1830 incorrectly believes that his wife has died of fever. Grieving terribly, he prepares her body for burial the next day, places it on a table, and falls asleep. He seems to hear a cry, senses a fall and a scuffle, fires his rifle, and by its glare sees a big panther dragging the body toward the window of their cabin. In his wife's teeth is a piece of the animal's ear. Murlock boards up the window and lives in the cabin for the rest of his wretched life.

MURLOCK, MRS. In "The Boarded Window," she is an Ohio pioneer's loving wife. Believing that she has died of fever, he prepares her for burial. A panther comes through the window of their cabin and tries to return with the body to the woods. Murlock scares it away with his rifle and finds a piece of the panther's ear in his wife's teeth.

MURPHY, MANUELITA. In "A Holy Terror," she was an evidently disreputable camp follower, known as Scarry because of a disfigured face and called "a holy terror." She was born at Mission San Pedro, died at forty-seven in Hurdy-Gurdy, California, and was buried by Barney Bree in the deserted cemetery there. Lured to her grave by a letter from Bree promising gold nearby, Jefferson Doman digs up her coffin, confuses her decomposed face with that of Mary Matthews, and dies.

"MUSIC" (1889, 1911). Essay. Be glad you have a tin ear and therefore are not tempted to write musical criticism. Henry Edward Krehbiel (1854–1923) stupidly wrote that Richard Wagner composed "artistic truths" and therefore his music will survive, whereas Italian opera merely "tickle[s] the ear" and hence must die. Music is supposed to stimulate emotionally. Primitive men and woman sang to each other, like birds, to be attractive. Then followed songs of war, hunting, death, and so on, and then musical instruments. If couples were ever "born happily married," the need for music would cease.

MUSKLER. In "Why I Am Not Editing 'The Stinger,' " he was the subject of an article written by Peter Pitchin and published in *The Stinger*. In an effort to learn who wrote it, Muskler brings a bulldog and a revolver to the *Stinger* office. Munniglut, the proprietor of the newspaper, will not identify the author but decamps, whereupon Muskler positions himself across the street with a shotgun.

"MY CREDENTIALS" (1888). Short story. (Characters: Peter Wodel Mocump, St. Peter.) Peter Wodel Mocump, the narrator, dies on 17 June 1879, enjoys watching his funeral attended by gaudily attired friends from many official societies, and while in "the Other World" collects eulogies printed about him and binds them in a book. When St. Peter greets him at heaven's gate, Mocump presents the book but is rejected. St. Peter shows him a secret letter reporting that several persons recommended by societies and admitted to heaven have been committing acts of theft and vandalism there. The letter suggests admitting in the future only those who have led "godly" lives and have accepted "the Christian religion." Seeing "the Name" at the bottom of the letter, Mocumb humbly "came Here." This little parable says much about Bierce's idealistic faith, which his reputed cynicism cannot quite cancel out.

"MY FAVORITE MURDER" (1888). Short story. (Full title: "My Favorite Murder: How I Disposed of an Objectionable Relative.") (Characters: Professor Davidson, Ridley, Ridley, Mary Ridley, Mrs. Ridley, Samuel Ridley, William Ridley.) Samuel Ridley, the narrator, murdered his mother in 1877 under what he calls "circumstances of singular atrocity." His trial has lasted seven years, until 1884. In charging the jury, the judge says that the crime was "one of the most ghastly. . . . he had ever been called upon to explain away." The narrator's attorney jumps in and tells the judge that the narrator killed his uncle in a far more ferocious manner and was acquitted only because the judge in that case was associated with a life insurance company that would have had to pay if the narrator were found guilty and executed. The narrator will describe how he killed his uncle if doing so will persuade the judge to reconsider his opinion regarding the relative severity of the present case. Samuel now tells his story.

He was born in 1856 in Kalamakee, Michigan. In 1867 he moved to California with his parents. His father established a prosperous road agency near Nigger Head. Four years later an itinerant preacher, while staying with them, converted them to religious beliefs. Father sent for his brother, William Ridley of Stockton, gave him the agency business—and its weapons and flour-sack masks—and opened a dance house at Ghost Rock. In the fall of 1875, the narrator was on the stagecoach out of Ghost Rock when it was held up by Uncle William and his two sons, disguised but recognized by him. To protect them, the narrator let them take $40 and a gold watch from him. When his uncle professed innocence, refused to return the loot, and even threatened to set up a rival dance house, the narrator decided to kill him. The narrator went to Uncle William's house near Nigger Head, found him, cut his hamstrings, and put him in a wheat sack. He hoisted him by the rope of a children's oak-tree swing. He then enticed his uncle's titanically militant goat to charge the sack repeatedly and butt its moaning occupant to a pulpy death. The narrator tellingly concludes that "in point of artistic atrocity" that murder "has seldom been excelled."

"My Favorite Murder" is much more complex than the bare summary of its plot would lead one to believe. This savage satire concerning total depravity is more than overflowing with details of criminal ambition, the goat's epic power, and the victim's suffering. "Jo Dornan and the Ram," an unsigned item (*Fun*, 15 November 1873), provided the plot base for "My Favorite Murder." Bierce's poem "The Challenge" (*Argonaut*, 2 November 1878) describes a bull enraged by a woman's red skirt washed and drying on a clothes line. In this case, it is the animal that loses the engagement. The woman's tongue-like sock, hanging nearby, tells the bull, "I know your sex—you're all alike. / Some small experience I've had—You're not the first I've driven mad."

"MY SHIPWRECK." *See* "A Psychological Shipwreck."

"THE MYSTERY OF CHARLES FARQUHARSON" (1888). Short story. (Originally titled "The Mystery of John Farquharson," part of "Bodies of the Dead: Some Authentic Accounts of Seeming Caprices.") (Characters: Charles Farquharson, William Hayner Gordon, Henri Granier, Charles Richter.) In the summer of 1843, William Hayner Gordon of Philadelphia puts aside a book he has been reading in bed, extinguishes his candle, and prepares for sleep. Realizing that he does not have his watch nearby, he gets up in the dark to fetch it from his waistcoat pocket across the room, but stumbles on something. Striking a match, he observes a corpse. His shriek arouses Henri Granier in an adjoining room. Granier breaks through the bolted door to help Gordon, who is too agitated to move. An inquest indicates that the corpse was that of a healthy, uninjured man. Months later Gordon receives a letter from Bombay. In it Charles Richter, whom Gordon knew as a boy, reports the death in Bombay of Charles Farquharson, whom both knew when all three were boys together. With the letter Richter sends a daguerreotype of the adult Farquharson, whose features are exactly those of the dead man in Gordon's room. Furthermore, both had died at the same hour. Gordon writes to ask how Farquharson's body was disposed of. Richter replies that since Farquharson had became a Parsee, it was properly placed naked at the Tower of Silence and was consumed by buzzards. When Gordon gets permission to open the grave of the man in his room, he finds the undisturbed coffin empty but for a moldy shroud. "The Mystery of Charles Farquharson" slightly resembles "A Tale of the Ragged Mountains," a much more detailed 1844 story by Edgar Allan Poe.

"THE MYSTERY OF JOHN FARQUHARSON." *See* "The Mystery of Charles Farquharson."

N

"NATURA BENIGNA" (1888, 1900, 1912). Essay. Disasters can kill more than pagans on faraway islands. If the hot core of the Earth should blast an ocean's bottom, the march of evolution would have to recommence. We constantly repopulate regions devastated by earthquakes, tornadoes, floods, and volcanoes, because we cannot avoid exposing ourselves to danger. Death challenges all. Did God really give us such an excellent Earth to live in? It has a fiery center, oceans we cannot breathe in, many uninhabitable lands. We neither enjoy it much nor miss it when we lose it. Despair makes us have faith in a better world, "but Hell is an inference by analogy." If alive today, Bierce would nod in an "I told you so" manner at disclosures of el Niño, la Niña, and tsunami threats.

"THE NATURE OF WAR" (1902, 1911). Essay. (Original title: "The Bald Campaigner.") The Timorous Reporter asks the Bald Campaigner whether he approves of General Jacob Smith's dismissal for acts of barbarism. The Campaigner explains that General Smith, of the U.S. Army, made the mistake of orally ordering his troops on the island of Samar to take no prisoners, but to kill and burn everyone and everything. He would have been a national hero if, instead, he had written these identical orders in euphemistic language. The purpose of war is to devastate a people's "means of subsistence," and to kill their soldiers only if they are protecting their food supply, their clothing factories, and their arsenals. A "humane" way to kill enemies is to render them naked and starve them. During the Civil War, generals William Tecumseh Sherman and Philip Henry Sheridan won victory by devastating the region between Atlanta and Goldsborough and the Shenandoah Valley area, at which time Confederate hopes "went up in smoke." This is the first of three little essays featuring the one-armed Bald Campaigner.

"A NAUTICAL NOVELTY." *See* "The Captain of the 'Camel.' "

NEALE, WALTER (1873–1933). Publisher and author. Neale was born in Eastville, Virginia, the scion of a long line of Virginia colonial and military leaders. He was always pro-Southern in his comfortable post–Civil War life. After attending the College of William and Mary, he founded in 1894 and was thereafter president of the Neale Publishing Company. In 1897 he married and had five children, including a son whom he named Robert E. Lee Neale. In 1898 Neale established the *Conservative Review*, published in Washington, D.C., where he then lived. He founded in 1911 and managed the Cosmopolitan Press. Thereafter, he established *Neale's Monthly* in 1912, founded in 1919 and was president of the Authors and Publishers Corporation, and founded in 1921 and was president of the Scenario Supply Corporation. Neale wrote a novel, *The Betrayal* (1910), and *Life of Ambrose Bierce* (1929), and compiled *Masterpieces of Southern Poets* (1912). From 1903 on, he made his home in New York City.

Bierce called on Neale at his office in Washington, D.C., in 1901. Thereafter they often met, talked, walked, and traveled together. Neale's company published *Can Such Things Be?*, Bierce's 1903 collection of short stories. Neale easily persuaded Bierce to let him publish an edition of his writings. The result, after much labor and many frustrations, was *The Collected Works of Ambrose Bierce* (12 vols., 1909–1912). At one point, Neale wanted to add several volumes, perhaps as many as five, to the set, which, however, did not do well financially. While the multivolume edition was still in production, Neale delivered a speech, published as "The Sovereignty of the States, an Oration: Address to the Survivors of the Eighth Virginia Regiment, While They Were Gathered about the Graves of Their Fallen Comrades, on the Battle-ground of Manassas, July 21, 1910." Bierce attended the ceremony. The two men often discussed the Civil War, and Neale alleges that Bierce evolved the opinion that he had quite possibly fought on the wrong side. It is often noted by scholars that Neale played the Boswell to a willingly Johnsonian Bierce, drew him out on sundry subjects, and was thus able to swell his biography.
Bibliography: Fatout, McWilliams, Morris, Neale.

NECROMANTIUS, PARAPELIUS. In "Beyond the Wall," he is the author of a theory that Mohun Dampier quotes to the narrator. It concerns "the 'fatal triad,' " and Dampier applies it to the three series of tappings by which he and his beautiful female neighbor communicate.

"NEW 'IMAGINARY CONVERSATIONS.' " *See* "At Santiago," "The Ordeal," and "A Provisional Settlement."

"THE NEW PENOLOGY" (1902, 1911). Essay. (Original title: "The Curmudgeon Philosopher.") Francis Bacon's *Novum Organum* overthrew Aristotle's belief that reason, unaided by observation and experience, could find truth. A vicious deduction is the notion that criminals can be reformed. Habitual criminals descend from criminals. The Philosopher's new method of reforming criminals would be to destroy two generations of them. Ah! No more misery, no police, no judicial system, lighter taxes. Criminals, lacking all respect and hunted cruelly, ought to prefer death. Mass executions now would lessen the sum of human misery later. If criminals sought to escape to soft nations still believing in reform, the Philosopher would favor holding them here by writs. (The Timorous Reporter is not identified as present.)

"NEWSPAPERS" (1878, 1882, 1892, 1893, 1911). Essay. When good, newspapers foster good republican government; but most are bad, combine toadying and bullying, and could lead to anarchy and then despotism all in the name of freedom of the press. Bad papers control elected judiciaries. Editors are foolish if they make predictions, especially as to outcomes of political campaigns. Papers often "snout out" dirt about candidates. A clean, honest paper could thrive if managed cleverly. It need not make huge profits.

NICK. In "Hades in Trouble," he is Satan's son. He leaves the earth and visits Hades with a message from Satan appealing for Beelzebub, Belial, Mammon, Moloch, and other devils to come and rescue him from the earth. Nick entertains the devils with stories about Adam, Aggie, Cain, and Eve, and would also tell them about Zel'y except that he grows too drunk and falls asleep.

"A NIGHT AT MOXON'S." *See* "Moxon's Master."

"THE NIGHT-DOINGS AT 'DEADMAN'S' " (1877). Short story. (Full title: "The Night-Doings at 'Deadman's: A Story That Is Untrue.") (Characters: Hiram Beeson, Signorina Festorazzi, Ben Hike, Baldy Peterson.) For two lonely years, Hiram Beeson, who looks perhaps seventy-four but is really a scrawny twenty-eight, has been living alone in his log shanty in Deadman's Gulch, a played-out mining area in the mountains near the Pacific, some fourteen miles from Bentley's Flat. One sharp, clear winter night, while the moon is shining on the snowy slopes, a muffled, green-goggled old creature arrives. Beeson greets him effusively, and with surprising courtesy. He reveals the following to the unresponding person, as a coyote barks in the distance and the wind howls in the pines: He lived in the shanty with two companions two years back. They had a Chinese servant who died. Since the ground was frozen, they buried him under a trap door in the shanty. Beeson cut off the fellow's pigtail and nailed it to an overhead beam. News

of a gold rush emptied the Gulch. Beeson and his friends left, but he returned for his forgotten revolver and never left the shanty again. The "Chinaman" keeps returning for his pigtail, since it is a requirement for going to heaven. When the silent stranger would appear to be wondering why Beeson does not return the pigtail, he boasts of his courage in retaining it, invites the stranger to spend the night with him, and watches him retire to another bunk. Beeson gets up and tugs at the hanging pigtail. The wind rushes down the chimney and scatters ashes and smoke all about. A swarthy, well-dressed little man appears—from San Francisco, Beeson figures. Then "another actor." He is "the departed Chinaman," clad in a quilted blue tunic and "covered with grave mold." He leaps out of the trapdoor at his pigtail, grabs it with his yellow teeth, and holds on, swinging around. When the swarthy man consults his watch, the muffled stranger stands up and takes hold of Beeson's revolver. A shot rings out. The "Chinaman" drops with his pigtail through the trapdoor, which closes. The swarthy man makes flourishes with his hat and vanishes up the chimney. The following spring, some miners stray into Beeson's shanty. He lies there dead, with a bullet hole through his heart. Upon careful inspection, they conclude that the bullet, fired from across the room, glanced off a blue-scarred knot in the beam, cut through a braided horsehair rope attached to it, and plunged down through Beeson. Also noted are some clothes, moldy like the cerements in which citizens of Deadman's had been buried years ago. How could this be? It seems unlikely that "Death himself" had worn them in disguise. This early California mining story reflects the influence of Bret Harte,* soon outgrown, on Bierce. Although Bierce regularly displays the power of his imagination, he rarely uses figures of speech; he peppers this story, however, with several effective similes and metaphors.
Bibliography: Morris.

NORTON. In "Mr. Masthead, Journalist," he is Johnson's friend in Warm Springs, Kansas. When asked, he sends Masthead to be employed as an editor by Johnson, the owner of the *Claybank Thundergust of Reform*, a Kansas weekly newspaper. Norton persuaded the authorities at the Warm Springs mental hospital to release Masthead's son by assuring them that Masthead's father had promised to care for him.

"A NOVEL." *See* "Evolution of a Story."

"THE NOVEL" (1907, 1911). Essay. Bierce says that only a half-dozen recent novels are of value. Novels are panoramas not paintings, stories padded with inessentials. The art of novel writing is dead in England and the United States. Samuel Richardson and Henry Fielding started a grievous tradition. Only Russians among Europeans produce admirable novels now.

Romances, for example, Sir Walter Scott's and Nathaniel Hawthorne's, are more appealing than realistic novels.

NUGGETS AND DUST (1873). (Full title: *Nuggets and Dust Panned Out in California*.) Bierce's second book, written under the pseudonym of Dod Grile but collected and arranged by the pseudonymous J. Milton Sloluck. John Camden Hotten,* the disreputable London publisher, contracted with Bierce to publish it but died before he could complete the arrangements. His successor, the London publishers Chatto & Windus, issued it. The contents were mainly taken, and often revised, from Bierce's *San Francisco News Letter and California Advertiser* columns, often about violent acts and some denigrating women; but Bierce added some new stories and little essays about travel in England under the title "Notes Written with Invisible Ink by a Phantom American." Bierce offered to add new copy of this sort at first, but when Andrew Chatto, of Chatto & Windus, asked for it, he grew offended.
Bibliography: Fatout, Grenander, Morris.

NUPPER, PROF. In "For the Ahkoond," he identified an area of the Ultimate Hills (once called the Rocky Mountains) as "the ancient Nevraska, the capital of Kikago."

O

"OBJECTIVE IDEAS" (1887, 1912). Essay. We mix sensations. Thus, a trumpet sounds scarlet. Hearing nice music makes one wish to paint it. Eating pineapple can make one relish the memory of being witness to a hanging. Imagine numbers from one to a hundred ascending in angles along a blue streak. A remarkably foolish essay.

"AN OCCURRENCE AT BROWNVILLE." *See* "An Adventure at Brownville."

"AN OCCURRENCE AT OWL CREEK BRIDGE" (1890). Short story. (Characters: Farquhar, Mrs. Peyton Farquhar, Peyton Farquhar.) Peyton Farquhar, an Alabama planter, slaveowner, and politician is about to be hanged by Union Army soldiers from a beam over ties along a railroad bridge at Owl Creek. A Federal scout, posing as a Confederate soldier, stopped at the Farquhars's farm, thirty miles away, and Mrs. Farquhar gave him a drink of water. The scout said that the bridge, with a Union Army fort at its northern end, could be set afire to halt the Union Army advance after the battle at Corinth. Farquhar, a pro-Secession civilian with romantic notions about war, took the bait. Standing on a plank end, he now awaits his fate. His watch sounds preternaturally loud. A captain nods to his sergeant, who steps off his end of the plank, and down goes Farquhar. But suddenly "he knew that the rope had broken and he had fallen into the stream." He sees a light. His hands get free, wrench the strangling rope loose, beat his gasping way up to air. With incredible distinctness he sees the forest at the southern bank, leaves of trees, insects, dew drops in prismatic colors. His enemies fire at him with pistols, rifles, and the big brass cannon. They miss. Spun around in the water sickeningly, Farquhar makes his way to the shore and the woods, eludes grapeshot from the cannon, walks all day, partly along an untraveled road. The golden stars form new constellations. His neck and tongue feel swollen. He must have fallen asleep as he walked. He is at the gate of his home. His wife, "looking fresh and cool and sweet," steps forward to embrace him. Suddenly, a blinding light, a shocking sound, darkness, silence. Farquhar is dead, swinging slowly beneath the bridge timbers.

"An Occurrence at Owl Creek Bridge" is in three numbered parts, each showing a different side of Farquhar's psychological makeup. First, Farquhar realistically sees that he is about to be executed. Second, the reader learns that he entertained foolishly romantic notions about war. Third, he falls victim to hallucinatory misperceptions. The varied styles of the story brilliantly match these alternative aspects of the nonhero. The real Owl Creek is in Tennessee. Bierce changed its locale to northern Alabama, presumably because during the Civil War there was no railroad near Owl Creek, Tennessee. Bierce assisted at three military executions. Soon after he was promoted to first lieutenant, in April 1863; he served briefly as provost marshal under General William Nelson. A duty of persons in such a position was to assist at executions. Two Union soldiers killed Southern civilians and were accordingly tried, convicted, sentenced, and hanged. In addition, a cavalry officer had deserted in a combat situation, was tried, convicted, and shot standing astride his own coffin. Bierce wrote about the executions in the San Francisco *Argonaut* (21 December 1878). It has been suggested that "The Snows of Kilimanjaro" by Ernest Hemingway and "Pincher Martin" by William Golding owe much to "An Occurrence at Owl Creek Bridge."

Bibliography: John Kenny Crane, "Crossing the Bar Twice: Post-Mortem Consciousness in Bierce, Hemingway, and Golding," *Studies in Short Fiction* 6 (Summer 1969): 351–376; Davidson; Davidson, *Essays*; Grenander; F. J. Logan, "The Wry Seriousness of 'Owl Creek Bridge,' " *American Literary Realism* 10 (Spring 1977): 101–113; F. H. Marcus, "Film and Fiction: 'An Occurrence at Owl Creek Bridge,' " *California English Journal* 7 (1971): 14–23; Morris; David M. Owens, "Bierce and Biography: The Location of Owl Creek Bridge," *American Literary Realism* 26 (Spring 1994): 82–89; James G. Powers, "Freud and Farquhar: An Occurrence at Owl Creek Bridge?" *Studies in Short Fiction* 19 (Summer 1982): 278–281; Peter Stoicheff, " " 'Something Uncanny': The Dream Structure in Ambrose Bierce's " 'An Occurrence at Owl Creek Bridge,' " *Studies in Short Fiction* 30 (Summer 1993): 355–365; Edmund Wilson, "Ambrose Bierce on the Owl Creek Bridge," *New York* 27 (8 December 1951): 144, 147–148, 150, 152, 154.

O'DELL, HENRY. In "The Thing at Nolan," he is Charles May's cousin and is a storekeeper at Nolan, a town eight miles from the May family's home. O'Dell and four friends see Charles walk into his store and out the back. Since he has a cut on his brow, they assume that he is planning to wash up at the brook behind the store. But Charles is never seen again. When Charles's son John May is tried for murdering his father, the Nolan men's testimony acquits him, because they saw Charles at the very hour it was (rightly) thought that John killed him.

OFFICER NO. 13. In "The Man Out of the Nose," he is the policeman who arrested John Hardshaw when he left Elvira Barwell's house with her diamond-encased miniature portrait.

"OIL OF DOG" (1890). Short story. (Full title: "The Oil of Dog: A Tragic Episode in the Life of an Eminent Educator.") (Characters: Bings, Boffer Bings, Mrs. Bings.) The narrator is Boffer Bings. His father manufactures dog oil. His mother kills and disposes of unwanted babies. Boffer helps his father by bringing dogs to his vats and helps his mother by carrying away "the debris of her work." His father is in cahoots with local physicians, who habitually prescribe *"ol. can."* Boffer has to be nimble to avoid the police. Once, while carrying away a dead foundling from his mother's "studio," he sees a constable, ducks into his father's oilery, and, to get rid of the evidence, tosses the baby into the cauldron of boiling dog oil. The next morning his father notes the improved quality of his oil. Boffer feels duty-bound to explain. So his mother and father combine their industries, wrongly kept separate in the past. His mother moves her studio to a wing of the father's factory. Boffer stops supplying dogs, falls idle, and might have become dissolute but for his mother's piety and for his father's being a church deacon. His mother not only accepts "superfluous . . . babes" but begins gathering children and enticing adults to the oilery. The authorities warn the Boffers to stop their raids. Boffer spies on his father, who is preparing a noose and approaching his mother's apartment. He obviously wants to boil her. But she enters, aflame with the same plan for the father. They fight, she with the dagger she has used on babies, he with his bare hands. Mortally wounded, the father grabs the mother and leaps with her into the boiling pot, where a committee of citizens, who visited the day before with a summons, are helping to produce oil. Aware that his career here is at an end, Boffer moves to Otumwee and writes this autobiography. Bierce must have liked the concept of "oil of dog." In "The Broom of the Temple," one of his *Fantastic Fables*, someone suggests that "the columns of the capitol be rubbed with oil of dog by a person having a moustache on the calf of his leg."

"OLD IBIDEM." In "A Jug of Sirup." *See* Deemer, Silas.

OLD SAWS WITH NEW TEETH (1899, 1911). Fables, added to *The Collected Works of Ambrose Bierce* (vol. 6, 1911). In various fables, sometimes involving animals, Bierce inserts cynical morals. A rich man's lie sticks in his crane-like throat. A mouse-like thief becomes a judge. Thieving legislators are about to kill themselves, until thieves steal their prepared shrouds. When workers stage a strike at a shoe factory and the owner burns the place down, the workers boycott a tanner. An editor improves sales when he stops boasting of his newspaper's honesty. Wealthy legislators deride a successful gold miner for not being industrious. While a ghost tells a would-be thief that he cannot "throw up [i.e., vomit (sorry)]" his hands because he has not eaten them, another thief steals from the first. When two thieves cannot divvy up a piano, an honest fellow buys it for his daughter to practice boxing on. A white settler, having stolen an Indian's land, asks the Indian how he got it anyway. A rough militia man scares some civilians until he falls on his sword; then they sing. Laborers tell a statesman to be honest, but then he starves. A man believed praise of him, got appointed as an asylum commissioner, but was then put in a glass case. Voters discontented with dishonest Democrats elect Republicans who steal even more. A senator muses so dreamily on how to develop a crooked career that he loses out, remains honest, and hence is tortured by a clean conscience. One writer, brilliant but indolent, wrote only a couple of fine books, whereas a dull but busy writer tabulated sixteen books about "the domestic hog." A city asks for more and still more money to build "a public Deformatory" until the government gives nothing and is damned. Some newspaper editors enlighten their readers so well that a statesman warns them that doing so is bad for "the business of others." Each "saw" has a title leading to an ironic twist of the text that follows. Thus, the title about the writers, one bright, the other dull, is "Hare and Tortoise."

"ON A MOUNTAIN" (1909). Essay. In this work Bierce tells of being part of a group of Ohio soldiers in the Union Army in the autumn and early winter of 1861 and of his delight at first seeing the beautiful Cheat Mountain country of western Virginia, full of sweet spruce and pine. Some of the young fellows had already fought at Philippi. During a reconnaissance, a friend named Abbott was killed by a cannon shot with the word "Abbott" imprinted on it in sunken letters. They cut trees and built a fort. They hunted bears and deer, idled, and occasionally scouted the enemy. One bright day they heard shots, advanced forward, and saw bloody, pale corpses. Returning the next day, they noticed that the faces of the dead had been eaten off by a herd of swine.

"ONE KIND OF OFFICER" (1893). Short story. (Characters: General Cameron, Hamilton, General Hart, Corporal Hassman, Gunner Manning, General Masterson, Sergeant Morris, Lieutenant Price, Captain Ransome.) General Cameron of the Union Army curtly tells Captain Ransome that he is not permitted to know anything but instead simply to obey orders, which are to fire his artillery guns at any troops in front of him. Ransome asks Lieutenant Price, his subordinate, if the order is clear. Price agrees that it is. In the ensuing fog, Ransome at a rampart learns that he lacks support and that the enemy is approaching. He orders immediate fire. Meanwhile Cameron's superior, General Masterson, corrects Cameron's fear that his flank is exposed by informing him that he has ordered General Hart to hook up with Cameron. Ransome's firing continues. When Price rides up to try to tell Ransome something, Ransome curtly tells him that he is not permitted to know anything but instead simply to obey orders. Soon Masterson rides in to commend Ransome but looks over the dead in front of Ransome's position and accuses Ransome of killing Union soldiers. Ransome says he knows that. When Masterson demands to know why, Ransome replies that his orders contained no explanatory information and refers Masterson to Cameron. Masterson says that Cameron is dead; in the opinion of Ransome's men, Masterson seems to be conducting an informal, preliminary court mar-tial. Ransome calls for clarification from Price, who says only that when he apprised Ransome of the situation he was insulted and ordered back to his post. When Ransome asks Price if he knew details of Cameron's orders to him, Price denies knowing anything. Ransome hands his sabre to an arrest-ing officer and seems even now to be hearing "Ready, aim, fire!" and feeling bullets in his heart.

Bierce, in showing the nihilistic rigidity of the military mindset, here dramatizes the utter stupidity of a soldier literally obeying a superior's orders even when they become manifestly hideous. But ordinary readers, whether or not they ever had to receive and act on orders while serving in any branch of the armed services, must question the reflexive superciliousness of Ran-some's conduct toward Price and, more important, his spiteful mass murder of members of his own army. "One Kind of Officer" should be taken as a parable and not as realistic fiction.

Bibliography: Morris.

"ONE OFFICER, ONE MAN" (1889). Short story. (Original title: "A Coward.") (Character: Captain Anderton Graffenreid.) Captain Anderton Graffenreid of the Union Army knew the governor of his state and therefore was held back, although he had had a military education, and was assigned to "hateful duties" during the first two years of the war. Now he is happily at the front, and finds himself one summer morning in command of a com-pany of rather scoffing veterans. He is eager to prove himself to be a brave, heroic officer, and thereby impress someone back home with "a pair of dark eyes." The sudden whish of an enemy artillery shell surprises him. He puts his hands over his eyes, and his men snicker. He fears that he feels fear. Enemy rifle fire from the right kills a man next to him. The enemy moves toward the front. On orders, the battalion Graffenreid is in springs to at-tention. Then comes a delay. Suddenly his sergeant sees him deliberately fall on his sword and die. Later the major general in command of the Union left corps reports that the enemy withdrew and that his casualties amounted to one officer and one man. Bierce, who was much interested in suicide, would obviously regard Graffenreid's behavior as an example of a bad sui-cide. The moral is that imagined combat can unstring one more than combat itself.

Bibliography: Morris.

"ONE OF THE MISSING" (1889). Short story. (Characters: Lieutenant Adrian Searing, Mrs. Jerome Searing, Private Jerome Searing, General [William Tecumseh] Sherman.) One sunny morning, the general commanding a Union Army division under General Sherman outside Kennesaw Mountain, Georgia, sends Private Jerome Searing, his brave loner of an orderly, forward to scout the enemy position. He proceeds through his picket lines to an abandoned farm, sees the retreating Confederates, positions himself under a shaky little barn on four teetering posts, cocks his trusty Springfield rifle, and sets the trigger. As he is about to kill an enemy, fate intervenes. A certain man from the Carpathian Mountains fled his army after a breach of discipline, happened to get to New Orleans rather than New York, joined the Confederate Army, became an artillery officer, and now is opposite Searing's position. Before Searing can fire, an enemy artillery shell blasts Searing's position and tumbles the barn timbers all over him. He finds himself tightly pinioned and staring at his rifle muzzle, inches away and pointed at the center of his forehead. He cannot free himself. He reminisces, fantasizes, and agonizes. After useless movements, he pushes a loose board at the trigger to end the uncertainty. No explosion follows. The rifle fired when it was dropped. "But it did its work." Meanwhile, Lieutenant Adrian Searing, Jerome's brother, is the commander of the pickets through whose line Jerome recently passed. He hears a distant sound like the collapse of a building. His watch says 6:18 P.M. Advancing with skirmishers, he finds Jerome's body, unrecognizable through apparent decay. His watch says 6:40 P.M. Adrian judges the stranger to be dead a week. "One of the Missing" is notable for Bierce's suspenseful description of brave Jerome's spiral into terror.
Bibliography: Davidson; M. E. Grenander, "Bierce's Turn of the Screw: Ironic Tales of Terror," pp. 209–216 in Davidson, *Essays.*

"ONE OF TWINS" (1888). Short story. (Full title: "One of Twins: A Story Found Among the Notes of a Scientist.") (Characters: Mortimer Barr, Mrs. Mortimer Barr, Margovan, Julia Margovan, Mrs. Margovan, Henry Stevens, John Stevens.) Henry Stevens, the narrator, and John Stevens are identical twins, whose parents could not tell them apart, except for their obscure little "H" and "J" tattoos. The family goes to San José, California, where the insolent parents die in one week. The twins move to San Francisco, obtain jobs, and live separately. One afternoon a pleasant man, unknown to Henry, calls him Stevens on the street and invites him to dinner, *en famille*, the following evening. Henry asks the man to thank Mrs. Margovan, his hostess-to-be, and accepts. Then he silently wonders how he knew the name Margovan. The next morning Henry goes to John's office. John says that on an impulse he asked Margovan, his friendly coworker, his address. When Henry explains the dinner invitation, John says *he* will go, does so, falls in love with the Margovans's beautiful daughter, Julia Margovan, and soon successfully proposes to her. Weeks later, not having met his prospective sister-in-law,

Henry sees a dissipated stranger on the street, is prompted to follow him, and sees him meet a beautiful young woman in Union Square and go with her to a disreputable house. A week later, invited with John to the Margovans's home, Henry meets Julia, recognizes her as the woman with the stranger, and delicately says that like himself she has "a double," for he saw her in Union Square. Turning pale, she says that she will do what he thinks best. He replies that he will oppose her marriage "on other grounds." The next evening, feeling irrationally apprehensive, Henry takes a walk in a cold fog, returns home, and sits shuddering before his fireplace. He hears John scream, looks outside, but sees only a quiet policeman; a second scream, near him, sends him rushing to the Margovan house, where he finds Julia dead by poison and John dying of a self-inflicted gunshot wound. Six weeks later, Henry comes back to life, nursed to consciousness by Mrs. Mortimer Barr, his dear friend's "saintly wife." Years pass, and one night Henry is again in Union Square, with sad memories. The same dissipated man, absorbed in thought and gray and haggard, approaches, sees Henry, shouts "Damn you, John Stevens!" and tries to strike him, but falls dead. This entire narrative is in the form of a letter by Henry Stevens to Mortimer Barr, his psychologist.

"ONE SUMMER NIGHT" (1906). Short story. (Characters: Henry Armstrong, Jess.) Henry Armstrong has been buried alive but is apathetic about his situation through being very ill. He hears something overhead. Jess, "a gigantic Negro," digs up the coffin and unscrews the lid. Lightning shoots into the dark clouds. Two medical students from a nearby college wait. When Armstrong suddenly sits up, they dash to town. In the morning, the pair, in pain and still terrified, go rather mechanically to the dissecting room. Awaiting them there is Jess. He has laid out Armstrong's head-bashed corpse on a table and asks for his money.
Bibliography: St. Pierre.

"ON KNOWING ONE'S BUSINESS—AN INSTANCE" (1895, 1912). Essay. (Original title: "The Prevailing Corsican.") Military scholars analyze Napoleon Bonaparte's first Italian campaign with unique assiduity. They conclude that more than courage, God's will, and luck produce military victory. In one year (April 1796–April 1797), Napoleon, at first age twenty-six, led some 40,000 soldiers in fifteen battles against seven armies totaling 60,000 soldiers, and drove them all out. He said that victory results from calculating details thoroughly and conducting movements systematically. To his "natural aptitude" Napoleon added "minute knowledge of the business at hand." Recent philosophers may say that individuals are of little moment in the sweep of events; but military history and Napoleon, who lauded Caesar, Hannibal, Alexander, and Frederick, say otherwise. Tolstoi's military novels display "the splendid irresponsibility of the fictionist." Can anyone believe that European history would be no different if Napoleon had been killed at Montenotte (April 1796)? To be recommended is *Napoleon Bonaparte's First Campaign* (1895) by Herbert H. Sergent (1858–1921), who writes so clearly, says Bierce, that even "the self-taught strategist of the press" can follow it.

"ON LITERARY CRITICISM" (1888, 1893, 1894, 1897, 1903, 1911). Essay. Critics reveal more about themselves than about the works they criticize. When discussing great or popular writers, critics such as William Dean Howells* and Richard Rogers Bowker are sycophantic. Critics are esteemed when asserting, often foolishly, an author's hidden purpose. Critics idiotically compare inferior writers to Edgar Allan Poe. Bierce ridicules Hamlin Garland for overpraising non-Eastern writers and writers (for example, local colorists) vainly seeking originality. He also ridicules critics for complaining that writers in California were not born there.

"ON POSTHUMOUS RENOWN" (1903, 1911). Short story. The Melancholy Author tells the Timorous Reporter that he plans to have no posthumous fame because the dead can own nothing. Since it is nothing, desiring it is comic. The earth itself will die.

"ON PUTTING ONE'S HEAD INTO ONE'S BELLY" (1906, 1911). Essay. The publisher Henry Holt (1840–1926) has griped that literature is being commercialized. True, books are promoted like patent medicine, and popular authors are fawned over. It was not that way, however, back in our nineteenth century. At present, literature is both commercialized and in "decay." But Holt's complaint is caused by his now having to pay too much for advertising in order to compete. Formerly, publishers were happy "to drink wine out of the author's skull"; now, authors' agents hawk their wares, and authors demand "some of the wine" for themselves. Holt even laments the fact that authors do not have outside incomes. Do publishers?

"ON READING NEW BOOKS" (1901, 1911). Essay. (Original title: "Beware of Reading the Very Newest Books.") So few new books are "great" that it is better to stick with established masterpieces.

"ON THE RIGHT TO KILL THE SICK." *See* "On the Uses of Euthanasia."

"ON THE USES OF EUTHANASIA" (1899, 1906, 1911). Essay. "Pain is cruel, death is merciful." Physicians, nurses, and combat soldiers know about pain and grow compassionate, not hard. Lawyers opposed to euthanasia should not argue that judgment in such cases is fallible. Much is fallible, from courts and jurors to compasses. If one says that death is "a penalty for crime," say also it is "a boon to hopeless pain." Some doctors say that their duty is to cure illness and minimize pain, and fear that they would be labeled executioners if they ended hopeless suffering. But the distinguished Dr. Nehemiah Nickerson has said frankly that he has killed incurably ill patients. We put down badly injured horses and dogs and feel comfortable about doing so. We reply that animals lack souls whereas humans have them? All the more reason, if so, to send human sufferers to "the shining altitudes of Paradise." Why say euthanasia frustrates God's plan for us to endure all? If God is omnipotent, no one can frustrate His plan. No one has asked for his or her existence; if God does not offer an explanation of its advantages, why not feel free to end a life riddled with suffering? If life is God's nice gift, an illness coming into it may intimate "God's altered mind." If so, then wanting death may signal a "cheerful submission to the divine will." Advocates of the right to commit suicide ought logically to advocate mercy killing as well.

" 'ON WITH THE DANCE!' A REVIEW" (1880, 1911). Essay. (Original title: "On with the Dance!") Prudery in America has resulted in "expurgated editions, emasculated art, and [timid] social customs." Literary prudes include "Miss Nancy Howells [William Dean Howells*], and Miss Nancy James, Jr. [Henry James]." Prudes have attacked fun-loving dancers, calling dances lascivious in *The Dance of Death*. Yet everything—heartbeats, breathing, work, music, poetry—has rhythm, vibrates, iterates. In Egypt, the source of much of our civilization, dancing was a religious ceremony. Dancing is also for amusement and pleasure. In olden times, Jewish dances were ritualistic and social—and not always discreet, either. Cuneiform inscriptions, Plato, Anacreon, Horace, and other ancients laud dancing. Cicero, who did not, was "a wall-flower." The modern Almé Egyptian dance became so indelicate that "numbers of the softer sex" acquired and practiced it as a siren song of seduction. The Japanese have two types of dances, one a beastly lewd striptease, the other cool and decent as snow. In China, there is no dancing, either profligate or seemly; upper-class women mutilate their feet too much, whereas the lower classes lack the good sense to dance. Siamese woman are dominated and spiritless. In India, women live in deplorable conditions. Wealthy men in Persia and Asia Minor buy female Circassian and Georgian dancers for their entertainment. Persia also sports boys dressed like women and dancing.

In regions where men are lazy, women are depraved and dances are indelicate. Some racy dances are immoral, but the girls performing them are chaste because fatigued. Many old-time authors esteemed dancing, notably Geoffrey Chaucer, John Milton, Lord Herbert of Cherbury, and Oliver Goldsmith. Why not dance, since it is "natural, . . . innocent, wholesome, enjoyable"? Prudes say dances provide opportunities for immorality. But decent girls and wholesome lads dance and still hew to a righteous path. Life provides countless opportunities for indecency, for example, in schools,

churches, libraries, galleries, picnics, fairs, theaters, and Bible classes. Is it immoral to waltz? Well, we smoke and drink wine because doing so is pleasant. Remember your first waltz? It decently gratified your "passion for rhythm." It would be nice if we knew more about our ancestors' dancing habits. What about their coranto, cinque-pace, rigadoon, gavot, contra, and so on? Our grandmothers danced admirably when they were "giddy girls." Lord Byron, with a bad foot, could only poetize about the dances of others. William Makepeace Thackeray wrote from personal experience. Let the "witching strain" of the *Blue Danube* present the finish here.
Bibliography: Fatout, Grenander.

OOPSIE. In "A Story at the Club," she is the person who signed a note on a card, which Will Brady says is the card of the man whom he saved from being crushed by a railroad train. When Brady's friend Dr. Dutton repeats the name "Oopsie," Brady is nonplussed.

"THE OPPOSING SEX" (1890, 1891, 1894, 1895, 1909, 1912). Essay. The emancipation of woman began in Europe, not America, and has changed more laws, customs, and traditions there than here. Subjection of British women now is social, not legal. British men are in legal subjugation, husbands being responsible, for example, for their wives' wrongdoings and debts. Women's suffrage will coarsen women. Giving women political equality will eliminate their social superiority. When women, high or low, flock to the polls, they will participate in the continued election of tyrants, whose tempers and morals will show no improvement. Women in the home elevate; elsewhere, they debase. Are any female workers, anywhere, more moral, more scrupulous, more honest than men at work? Although women workers elevate the tone of "table talk" at business dinners, their "chastity" is disappearing, to a degree. If women enter politics, they will resemble men more, as they compete with men—all to women's detriment. Men want women to be different, unlike them "in knowledge, character, accomplishments, manners." Men don't have to revolt against the emancipation movement; if reason prevails, it will subside. It makes obvious sense for men, naturally promiscuous, to value virtuous women. Cities, ships, and inventions are all the products of men. Women by themselves could hardly have invented even the bicycle. Women observe, think, judge, and understand by processes unlike those of men. Women have not written great poetry or composed great music. Men praise women for beauty, allure, grace, virtues. Women who develop exceptional brain power lose their beauty and become masculine. Bierce fires this conclusion at "mesdames": "I hate woman and love women—have an acute animosity to your sex, adoring each individual member of it. . . . I am in bondage to your charms . . . I esteem you eminently fit—to be mothers of men." For this function, women have "utility and dignity."

"THE ORDEAL" (1898). Short drama. (Originally part of "New 'Imaginary Conversations.' ") The historian asks Clio, the muse of history, who commanded American forces during "the Yanko-Spanko [Spanish-American] war." She does not know.

"THE OTHER LODGERS" (1907). Short story. (Character: Colonel Levering.) Colonel Levering is at the Waldorf-Astoria hotel, in New York City. Levering tells a friend that when he is between trains and waiting down in Atlanta, he should not stay in the Breathitt House. He explains that it is in poor shape, with big holes in the walls, and bedrooms with no door locks and insufficient bedding and furniture. One night Levering, when wounded and arriving in Atlanta after a long train ride, was obliged to stay there. The night clerk gave him a candle. Worn out, he fell asleep, fully clothed, on the mattress. Toward dawn a bluish, "spooky" moonlight woke him up and suffused the room. Lying on the floor were a dozen dead men, some with "clouted faces." He tried but could not cry out. He rushed out to find the night clerk. The pale, blank-eyed fellow stood, bowed, and vanished. A kind, portly gentleman, tapping Levering on the shoulder, explained that the building used to be a hotel but was converted to a hospital. The room in which Levering passed the night was a room reserved for numerous corpses. The so-called night clerk, responsible for booking patients brought to the hospital, has been dead for some weeks now. When the kind man said that he was now looking after the place and offered to go check the room in question, Levering cursed him and ran out to the street. Again, he advises his listener not to stop at the Breathitt House. His friend says that he will not and asks when the described incident occurred. Levering says it was in September 1864, soon after the siege of Atlanta. "The Other Lodgers" has autobiographical echoes: Bierce was wounded (at the Kennesaw Mountain battle, 27 June 1864), endured a train trip partly in the moonlight to the hospital, and must have felt between two worlds at that time and even later. *Bibliography:* Morris.

"OUR AUDIBLE SISTERS" (1901, 1911). Essay. (Original title: "The Curmudgeon Philosopher.") Women do not elevate men. It was better before women erupted into public affairs. Now they play both the fool and the devil. Women prefer ideas to practical improvements. Audible women have given up real advantages for illusory ones. The Philosopher used to observe women; now neither does he observe nor is he observed. Men love only the helpless and the dependent. Now demanding equality, women forfeit tenderness. Romantic love flourished only when men were chivalrous and women were worshipped, fought for, placed on pedestals, and serenaded. When the Philosopher threatens to read a love poem, the Timorous Reporter tries to leave, only to be cursed. This is the first of eleven little essays featuring the Timorous Reporter, who is often insufficiently attentive to the lectures he endures.

"OUR DEBT TO WILLIAM THE CONQUEROR." *See* "The War Everlasting."

"OUR SACROSANCT ORTHOGRAPHY" (1907, 1911). Essay. The Melancholy Author gripes to the Timorous Reporter about British criticism of American efforts to reform English spelling. Americans have a right to revise the English language; if it does not change, it will die. *Beowulf* is not written in modern English. Should would-be reformers try to change current English back to earlier times? The words "music" and "public" were formerly spelled with a final "k." It does not help to suggest retaining old spellings of words to display their etymology. To do so, one would have to use Greek letters to spell "phthisis." When the Reporter timidly suggests that modernized spellings look "uncouth," the Author squelches him by saying all reforms seem uncouth at first.

"OUR SMART SET" (1883, 1887, 1888, 1889, 1890, 1892, 1912). Essays, divided into "Urban" and "Rural." (Original title of parts: "Society Notes.") "Urban" society columns concern church noises, marriages, parties, a kidnapping abroad, engagements, travels, receptions, art purchases, a graduation party, a "post-mortem reception," jewelry displays, a funeral, misfortunes, and a scandalous burial. "Rural" notes involve parties, picnics, a church service, a reception, a villa, a club party, and a wedding announcement. Bierce tries to enliven this collection of tediously forced pieces by introducing comical names, for example, Emmeline Cartilagina Cmythe, Dreffeldude P. Milquesoppe, and Moriarty Fitz Flaherty O'Blairney. Bierce undoubtedly gave his "Society Notes" the new title "Our Smart Set," some time after he learned that his friend H. L. Mencken* had started a new magazine titled *The Smart Set* in 1908. Bierce may have been inspired to string out O'Blairney's whole name here because the full name of Oscar Wilde, whom Bierce saw in San Francisco in 1882 and was revolted by, was Oscar Fingal O'Flahertie Wills Wilde.

P

PALMER, ANDRUS C. In "At Old Man Eckert's," he is a teacher. He agrees to go with John Holcomb and Wilson Merle to investigate the haunted house of Philip Eckert. Palmer evidently goes on ahead. When Holcomb and Merle are seated in Eckert's front room, they see Palmer enter from an inner door, walk past them, and disappear out the front door—leaving no footprints in the snow. Palmer is never heard from again.

PARDEE. In "The Death of Halpin Frayser," Holker incorrectly thinks the murderer Larue's name was Pardee.

"THE PARENTICIDE CLUB." Volume 8 of *The Collected Works of Ambrose Bierce*, 1911, placed under this rubric the following ugly stories: "The Hypnotist," "An Imperfect Conflagration," "My Favorite Murder," and "Oil of Dog."

"PARKER ADDERSON, PHILOSOPHER" (1891). Short story. (Original title: "James Adderson, Philosopher and Wit.") (Characters: Sergeant Parker Adderson, General Clavering, Captain Hasterlick, Private Tassman.) Sergeant Parker Adderson, a spy for the Union Army, has just been brought to the small tent, lighted by a candle, of General Clavering, a Confederate officer. Feeling certain that he will be executed in the morning, he reveals his name and rank, declines to identify his regiment, and provides morbidly witty answers to Clavering. When Clavering sends Private Tassman with orders to the provost-marshal, Adderson says that he hopes the execution ceremony will be nicely arranged, since he plans to attend. He even philosophizes on death as a deprivation of pain, and pain as disagreeable but only until one dies. Shocked, Clavering upbraids his prisoner, begins to muse, and concludes by exclaiming that "Death is horrible!" and that he would not like to die this night. When captain Hasterlick, the provost-marshal, enters, Clavering orders him to take Adderson out and have him shot immediately. Adderson is aghast, says that he must not die until by hanging at dawn, but is coldly rebuked. Hasterlick draws his sword and points to the tent exit. Adderson grabs the bowie knife from Clavering's sword belt, hanging from the tent pole, and leaps on the general. Hasterlick springs forward to aid Clavering. In the melee, the tent collapses, plunging all in darkness. Tassman tries to pull the tent canvas free. A sentinel fires his rifle. Soldiers, half dressed, rush into line. When order is restored, it appears that Hasterlick is dead with the bowie knife in his neck, his sword has badly wounded Clavering in the shoulder and thigh, and Adderson, cowering, has a broken right arm and facial bruises. While a surgeon aids the injured, Clavering, lying on the ground, orders Adderson shot at once. The adjutant general confirms the written order that Hasterlick received. Blubbering and begging for mercy, Adderson is killed by twenty riflemen. Clavering looks amiably about him, smiles sweetly, and, saying, "I suppose this must be death," dies.

Bierce mocks the horror of this story, which is a classic example of chiasma (or reversal), by his usual stylistic quirks. Thus, when Tassman has a chance to explain matters to the surgeon, it is "the opportunity of his life"; so when he finishes, he recounts everything over again, although "nobody gave him any attention." And when Clavering is about to die, he "opened his big blue eyes" and looks around him "pleasantly." Parker's initial behavior has been rightly compared to that of a Shakespearean jester.

Bibliography: Davidson; Arno Heller, "Ambrose Bierce: 'Parker Addison, Philosopher,' " pp. 89–99 in Klaus Lubbers, ed., Die englische und amerikanische Kurzgeschichte (Darmstadt: Wissenschaftiche Buchgesellschaft, 1991); Alfred Kazin, "On Ambrose Bierce and 'Parker Adderson, Philosopher,' " pp. 31–34 in Calvin Skaggs, ed. The American Short Story (New York: Dell, 1977).

PARLOW. In "A Baby Tramp," he is "a young spacegrace" living in Boston. He marries Hetty Brownon there. She takes him to Blackburg, her hometown. They have a child, whom they name Joseph. Parlow becomes a town councilman. He and Hetty die when Joseph is one year old.

PARLOW, HETTY BROWNON. In "A Baby Tramp," she is a beautiful, sweet, and pure Blackburg resident. She marries Parlow in Boston and returns with him to Blackburg, where they have a child, named Joseph, and then die when he is one. Her ghost is seen in the cemetery reaching out and calling for Joseph.

PARLOW, JOSEPH ("JO," "JOEY"). In "A Baby Tramp," he is orphaned at age one in Blackburg, when his father and his mother, Hetty Brownon Parlow, die, along with other relatives. Jo wanders about, is adopted in Nevada, is sold by Piute Indians to Mrs. Darnell, and goes with her to Cleveland. He finally wanders back to Blackburg, where he dies on his mother's grave.

PARTINGTON, JOHN HERBERT EVELYN (1843–1899). British-born painter living in San Francisco. Bierce enjoyed socializing with him and with his children, Blanche Partington, Gertrude Partington, and Richard Partington. Beginning about 1892, in person and also in numerous letters, Bierce commented on Blanche's juvenile literary efforts while more positively encouraging her to develop her mind through reading authors whom he carefully recommended. Bierce's son, Leigh Bierce,* studied art under Partington for a brief time. When Leigh was ambitious to become a reporter and began in 1893 to room with the poet George Sterling* in San Francisco, Bierce wrote Partington asking him to keep an eye on the young fellow. Partington painted a portrait of Bierce in 1893. It shows Bierce standing beside his writing table, which has a skull perched on it. The dark work was awarded a gold medal when it was exhibited at the 1893 World's Colombian Exposition in Chicago. It was quickly the subject of a caricature, of Bierce contemplating a skull on a stick. Ina Coolbrith,* the respected California poet, memorialized Partington in "The Dead Artist, J. H. E. Partington" (*San Francisco Examiner*, 31 January 1899). Bierce cautioned Sterling in a sharp letter (16 December 1901) that Blanche, if she could, would make a murderous anarchist out of him. Soon recanting, Bierce wrote Sterling that Blanche was a mere "child" and "will never be other than lovable" (25 March 1902).
Bibliography: De Castro, Fatout, McWilliams.

"PASSAGES FROM THE 'BEST-SELLING' BOOKS." *See* "The Sample Counter."

"THE PASSING OF SATIRE" (1909, 1911). Essay. The Melancholy Author is surprised when the Timorous Reporter tells him that his journal publishes works by a certain satirist. The Melancholy Author doubts the satirist's existence on the grounds that satire would not be tolerated in our sentimental age. Today we talk of the brotherhood of man, tolerance, and socialism, and theorize that crime is a disease not curable by punishment. Satire is punishment of rascals, and today punishment is out of favor. Satire used to be "a glory to literature" which the unworthy feared. If alive today, Jonathan Swift would be comfortably jailed, coddled, and prayed for, and women would propose marriage to him.

"THE PASSING OF THE HORSE" (1903, 1911). Essay. (Original title: "The Future of the Horse and the Horse of the Future.") Some have said that "the automobile is going to make of this bad world a horse elysium," in which horses will be free and easy and even have "opportunities for mental culture." But this is doubtful. We already have dogs as freeloaders. We eat "inutile" pigs but not dogs or horses. When horses disappear in our auto-loaded culture, stories and statues featuring them will strike us as astonishing. Vegetarians will probably argue that if horses become extinct, other "meat-bearing animals" ought to be allowed to do so as well. Some species, however, should be kept alive though not all eaten. English pheasants are nicely preserved for gaming. If men did not enslave horses and oxen, they too would disappear. Further, where would "the American negro" be but for slavery? Perhaps we should now pass a "bill pensioning the entire negro race!"

"PASTORAL JOURNALISM." *See* "The Rural Press."

PEASLEY, JIM ("THAT JIM"). In "Mr. Swiddler's Flip-Flap," he is a practical joker who encourages Swiddler to execute a somersault while walking with papers to save his friend Jerome Bowles from being hanged for murder. Peasley disorients Swiddler, who walks back home and thus fails to save his friend. Some joke.

"PECTOLITE" (1888, 1911). Essay. (Original title: "A Mineral Porcupine.") In 1828, a German scientist discovered a rare mineral having splinters which if touched cause pain like that occasioned by handling nettles. It resembles unpleasant briars, cacti, and poison ivy so much that one wonders why nature has not distributed it more widely. As it is, manufacturers of arsenic and importers of rattlesnakes favor its use. It would also make a fine military weapon. Scientists will mine this stone and thereby further nature's mysterious purposes.

PEN NAMES AND PSEUDONYMS. Bierce used the following pseudonyms, some only once: Agb, H. B., Bashi Basouk, Hamin Benjarrison, A Brute, Choggins, Clementina, Clericus, D., Etcetera, Almira Faircheek, D. G., Dod Grile, Gwinnett, A Gwinnett, Gwinnette, William Herman, Hestiba, Jamrach Holobom, Ignotus, Infallible, An Insulted Giant, W. J., Jax, Jex, Dr. K*n**ly, Q. K., J. D. L., Lex, Little Johnny, Little Johnnie [sic], The Man from Milpitas, A Mandarin of the Order of the Golden Teapot, Michael Mugg, Pylades Nupkins, Our Special Philosopher, Eli Perkins, Phrytz, Doddington Pry, Rutland, Agapius Samaritanus, DD., Samboles, Dr. John Satan, Satanella, Shellback, J. Milton Sloluck, Theophilus Smallbeer, John Smith, Thersites, Ursus, and X. He also signed many of his columns "A. B.," "A.G.B.," and "B."

PERIODICALS. Bierce published thousands of columns, full of definitions, dramas, essays, fables, poems, squibs, and stories, in many periodicals, journals, newspapers, and magazines. The most frequent such outlets were the

Argonaut (beginning 25 March 1877, ending 11 October 1879), *Cosmopolitan* (August 1905–May 1909), *Figaro* (London, 8 June 1872–29 September 1875), *Fun* (6 July 1872–18 September 1875), the *New York American* (12 March 1902–11 July 1906), the *New York Journal* (10 February 1896–7 March 1902), the *Oakland Daily Evening Tribune* (22 March–22 November 1890), the *San Francisco Examiner* (13 February 1887–28 June 1906), the *San Francisco News Letter* (7 March 1868–25 December 1886), and the *Wasp* (5 March 1881–23 October 1886). He published most frequently under the following rubrics: "The Town Crier" (2 December 1868–16 August 1873, in *San Francisco News Letter, Figaro*), "The Passing Show" (20 August 1873–June 1906, *Figaro, New York Journal, San Francisco Examiner, Cosmopolitan*), "The Prattler" (25 March–2 June 1877), "Prattle" (9 June 1877–19 March 1899, *Argonaut, Lantern, Wasp, San Francisco Examiner, New York Journal, New York American*), "Views of One" and "The Views of One" (14 January 1905–15 June 1906, *New York American*), and "Small Contributions" (February 1907–May 1909, *Cosmopolitan*).

Bierce's most celebrated such writings were his relentless attacks on Charles Crocker,* Mark Hopkins,* Collis P. Huntington,* and Leland Stanford,* who were The Big Four,* managers of the Central Pacific Railroad monopoly. When he became editor in 1877 of the *Argonaut*, Bierce did not especially oppose Frank Morrison Pixley,* its prorailroad owner. But when Bierce returned from his failed search for gold in the Black Hills of Dakota Territory and Pixley refused to rehire him in 1881, Bierce began editing the *Wasp*, which favored satire and cartoons. Bierce transferred his "Prattle" columns from the *Argonaut* to the *Wasp* and began lashing out at what he called the "railrogues." In 1885 a railroad supporter named Colonel J. P. Jackson acquired the *Wasp*; Bierce could not stomach subsequent praise of the Big Four therein and therefore quit. In 1887 Bierce joined forces with William Randolph Hearst,* owner of the *San Francisco Examiner*, which immediately ran more virulent "Prattle" attacks, thus satisfying Bierce's love of battle and Hearst's desire for increased circulation. In 1896 Hearst dispatched Bierce to Washington, D.C., to use his pen to thwart Huntington's efforts to bribe and lobby congressmen. Bierce was ultimately successful, although the final settlement, in 1897, did not fully satisfy his blood lust.
Bibliography: David Lindley, "When Ambrose Bierce Took On the Railrogues," *Wild West: Chronicling the American Frontier* (October 1997): 44–48, 91–92; Frank Luther Mott, *A History of American Magazines 1885–1905* (Cambridge, Mass.: Harvard University Press, 1957); Mott, *A History of American Magazines 1865–1885* (Cambridge, Mass: Harvard University Press, 1967).

"PERRY CHUMLY'S ECLIPSE" (1874). Short story. (Characters: Ben, Perry Chumly, Thomas, William.) Thomas, the narrator, helps his friend Ben set up his spectroscope to analyze the composition of a comet now flaming in the heavens. William tediously interrupts them by telling about

Perry Chumly's love of solar eclipses. Ben lets down a blind to block out light above his instrument poking through his observatory window. While he is identifying elements in the comet—carbon, iron, but then meat, and even whisky, soap, and hair—William busily explains how Perry, to see his eclipse better, went down a well, gazed up, and fancied that the round aperture above was the sun—until, that is, the moon-like face of a "hideous Negro," seeking some water, appeared with flashing eyes and teeth. Perry screamed, fainted, and drowned. The black man also grew deranged and died in some weeds. The two were buried together. Having concluded his story, William tells Ben that he may as well stop spectroscopically analyzing the red-haired maid up in the dormer window, because she pulled her blinds when William pouted at her.

PETE, CARPENTER. In "The Famous Gilson Bequest," he is the carpenter in Mammon Hill. Between drinks, he constructs the pine coffin in which Milton Gilson, hanged for horse stealing, is placed by Pete's "not ungentle hands" and is buried. Not long thereafter, Pete dies.

PETER, ST. In "My Credentials," he guards the gates of heaven. When he shows Peter Wodel Mocump a letter from "the Name," Mocump feels unworthy to enter.

PETERSON, BALDY. In "The Night-Doings at 'Deadman's,'" Hiram Beeson tells the muffled stranger that Baldy Peterson shot Ben Hike. A quick nod from the stranger hints that he is Death.

PEYTON, HANNIBAL ALCAZAR. In "Jupiter Doke, Brigadier-General," he is Brigadier-General Jupiter Doke's black slave, who, though illiterate and partially blind, gives an accurate statement of Doke's mysterious mule attack.

PHOEBE. In "Curried Cow," she is the unnamed narrator's Aunt Patience's pet cow, which gives neither milk nor veal but likes to be curried. Phoebe has perfected a lightning kick, which scatters all in her path. Phoebe makes the mistake of assuming that a tall, cast-iron pump is Patience's brand-new husband, the Rev. Berosus Huggins, who has disguised it in his clothes to resemble a scarecrow. Phoebe gives it a monstrous kick, is maimed for a long time, and when feeling better gets even with Patience by fatally kicking her into a stone wall—spreading her upon its surface, in fact, as though by a trowel.

PICKERING, LORING (1812–1892). Journalist. He was born in Cheshire County, New Hampshire, was educated locally, and at the age of twenty went to the Mississippi Valley, where he had jobs in Illinois, Louisville, New

Orleans, and St. Louis. He bought two newspapers in St. Louis (1846), merged them as the St. Louis *Union*, and soon made it a voice for the Democratic party. He became a director of the Bank of Missouri (1848). When it failed, he went to California, where, after doing some prospecting, he and George K. Fitch bought into the *Placerville Times* and combined it with the *Sacramento Transcript* as the *Times Transcript*. After they moved it to San Francisco (1852), it became the leading Democratic paper of California. He and Fitch sold it (1855) and bought the *Alta California*. Pickering vacationed in Paris (1857–1860), returned home, and with Fitch sold the *Alta California* and in partnership with James A. Simonton bought the *San Francisco Bulletin*. The two bought the *Call* (1868). It and the *Bulletin* were leading Pacific coast newspapers.

During his long career, Pickering was a force for reform and tolerance, as, for example, when he editorialized in 1877 against the persecution of Chinese immigrant laborers. Still, Bierce, who freelanced with contributions to the *Call*, felt that Pickering was only paying lip service to liberalism and, in an *Argonaut* piece (9 March 1878), verbosely accused him of arming those conservatives who opposed unrestricted Chinese immigration with weapons that would help their adversaries. Elsewhere Bierce called Pickering "a magniloquent idiot" for his circumlocutions and disputed his hypocritical policy of paying his employees in silver while editorializing in favor of currency payments instead. In a short verse drama, "The Two Cavees" (28 April 1887), Bierce satirized Pickering, and Fitch too, as ineffective would-be saboteurs of railroads under construction. In "The Grin without the Cat" (*San Francisco Examiner*, 22 February 1889), Bierce spoofs Pickering's theological opinions.
Bibliography: Joshi and Schultz, McWilliams, O'Connor.

PITCHIN, PETER. In "Why I Am Not Editing 'The Stinger,' " he is the author of an article in *The Stinger* about Muskler. When Muskler goes to the office of the newspaper to find out who wrote it, Munniglut, the proprietor, Henry Inxling, Pitchin's bookkeeper, and William Quoin, the foreman, all write Pitchin, who, however, changes addresses, resigns, and leaves town, allegedly to go to his mother's funeral.

PIXLEY, FRANK MORRISON (1825–1895). Attorney and journalist. He was born in New York City, graduated from Hamilton College, practiced law in Michigan, and moved to California in 1849. Pixley was state attorney general (1862–1863) when Leland Stanford* was governor of California, and Pixley was U.S. attorney general (1869) in the cabinet of Ulysses S. Grant. Then Pixley did extensive editorial work and writing back in California. He, along with Frederic Maxwell Somers,* cofounded the weekly *Argonaut* in 1877, hired Bierce as associate editor (until 1879), and was associated with the periodical until 1893. Pixley used it to influence political events both in the city and in the state. He inveighed against the Irish as in "bondage to papal authority," favored removing the Chinese from San Francisco, defended suppliers of water to the city when they sought to profiteer, opposed the Workingman's Party, and favored the prohibition of liquor. Several of Pixley's celebrated orations were published.

From the outset Bierce was at odds with Pixley, who did, to his credit, support Western writers, albeit with editorials that were too romantic in tone. He published works by, among others, Gertrude Atherton,* Ina Coolbrith,* Bret Harte,* and Joaquin Miller*—all of whom Bierce knew. Pixley hoped that Bierce would write columns advancing Pixley's ambition to become state governor or federal senator. But in vain—so when Bierce returned to San Francisco in 1881, both Pixley and Somers declined to rehire him. Thereafter, Bierce excoriated Pixley in and out of print for years, calling him "Mr. Pigsley of the Hogonaut" and "Crank F. Fixley." In his poem "For President, Leland Stanford" (1885), Bierce has Pixley play "Pixley Pasha" to "Mahomet Stanford." Pixley once sought a cowardly revenge. When Bierce's son Day Bierce* died in a duel in July 1889, Pixley wrote in the *Argonaut*, "May not the death of the younger Bierce teach the older man, his father, how sinister have been the bitter, heartless, and unprovoked assaults which he has spent his life in cultivating that he might the more cruelly wound his fellow-man?" (5 August 1889). Bierce was hurt but replied mildly, using understatement thus: ". . . [A]ssuredly I love you as little as ever," and allowing himself merely to define Pixley as a "sycophant and slanderer for hire" (*Examiner*, 25 August 1889). After both Pixley and Somers died, Bierce lamented the fact that the two had received too much credit for the excellence of the *Argonaut*, while he was not sufficiently recognized for his own valuable writings in it. In addition, he offered this epitaph: "Here Lies Frank Pixley— As Usual."

Bibliography: Joshi, Lindley, McWilliams, Morris, O'Connor.

"A POET AND HIS POEM" (1907, 1911). Review. An example of poetic genius is "A Wine of Wizardry" by George Sterling,* who is "incomparably the greatest [poet] that we have on this side of the Atlantic." The poem is as good as anything published during Alfred, Lord Tennyson's time and better than anything in Rudyard Kipling's era. It is pure poetry, as the skylark emits pure song. Not one of its lines is prosaic. Descriptions in it are vivid, ghastly, chilling; epithets in it, memorable. Sterling bears comparison to John Milton, Edmund Spenser, Leigh Hunt, Samuel Taylor Coleridge, and John Keats. It is difficult, now, to understand why Bierce was so favorably disposed toward Sterling's orotund, vapid, ultraconservative "Wine of Wizardry."

"POETRY AND VERSE" (1878, 1911). Essay. Most popular so-called "poetry" is merely rubbishy verse. True poetry, though it may be highly varied, is best when "severely simple in diction." A poem must concern an important idea to be great, regardless of how fine its style may be. Well-managed meters, which are often nothing but sound, and rhymes alone cannot convert mere verse to poetry. Most literate adults cannot recognize poetry. Poets without faults lack readers. It is of no importance that great poets write badly on occasion. Nor should their private lives and correspondence have any bearing on interpreting their finest works. The imagination lacks many new ideas to be inspired by. For the modern poet, nature's secrets are revealed and dull. The ancients were ignorant of telescopes, microscopes, photographs, and the like, which have combined to deglamorize nature. The greatest poets lived in more barbarous epochs. Today the versifier's style hides "the poverty of [the poet's] matter."

POETRY BY BIERCE. Bierce wanted to be a poet and believed that supremely fine poets were the best possible type of author. This high regard is indicated in "To a Dejected Poet," an 1897 poem in which he says "Who haggles o'er his hire with Fate / Is better bargainer than bard," and closes thus: "The sacred ministry of song / Is rapture!—'twere a grievous wrong / To fix a wages-rate for play." In his mind his savage satirical poems, his vicious epigrams and aphorisms, and also the old-fashioned sentimental verse that he composed all fell short. Still, much of his poetic output deserves serious consideration. A few of his earliest verses are little love poems inspired by his courtship of and marriage to Mary Ellen Day (*see* Bierce, Mary Ellen Day). The addressee in "Rosalie" (1869, signed only "B"), though called the persona's "blithesome daughter," is invited to let her "primrose spring" rejuvenate autumnal being. In "To Thee, My Darling" (1870, unsigned but attributed to Bierce), the poet calls himself "The God of Day" as he kisses her "lovely face." In "Oneiromancy" (1886) his persona awakens and sadly sees his "love / Conceal a letter in her glove"; tragically, two years later Bierce found love letters from another man in his wife's possession and irrationally walked out on her forever.

Over a period of forty years or so, Bierce wrote streams of poems, some of them excellent, many of them good, but more of them dreary and trivial. He assembled two main collections of his poetry, *Black Beetles in Amber* (1892) and *Shapes of Clay* (1903). He incorporated *Black Beetles in Amber*, along with some other poems, when he put together what became volume 5 (1911) of *The Collected Works of Ambrose Bierce*, published in twelve volumes by his friend and biographer Walter Neale* (1909–1912). Volume 5 contains 239 poems and five verse plays. Bierce included *Shapes of Clay* in volume 4 (1910) of *The Collected Works*, along with more poems under what he called "The Scrap Heap." Volume 4 contains a total of 284 poems. Although Bierce wrote and published hundreds of poems, he was too honest—and hence modest, quite rightly—to regard himself as a uniformly successful poet. Instead, he defined himself as mostly a versifier and remained in awe of poets

whom he esteemed as the finest—and therefore the most exalted of all authors.

In his preface to the 1910 reprint of *Shapes of Clay*, Bierce says that if his
writings have "intrinsic interest," they will all eventually be published; so,
he added, he ought to have the right to put his fugitive items in more permanent shape now. Since he disagrees with the notion of criticizing the sin
but not the sinner, he is herewith republishing items critical of persons
whom he deems unworthy, whether they are dead yet or not.

In his preface to the 1911 reprint of *Black Beetles in Amber*, Bierce again
replies to the complaint that many poems in it are about obscure people and
events of the Pacific coast. He boldly expresses the hope that he is raising
his subjects to some distinction and adds that the great satirists, notably
Aristophanes, Horace, Jonathan Swift, and Alexander Pope, have preserved
and exhibited otherwise unknown victims in poetic amber.

In both volumes 4 and 5, Bierce included several poems not previously
published. Here are snatches from several examples, from both reprinted
volumes, of Bierce's frequent excoriations and necessarily fewer lines in
praise of individuals; some subjects are still famous in their own right, but
others would now be unsung save for Bierce. Several of his most vicious
poems, first collected in *Shapes of Clay*, he called "ante-mortem epitaphs."
Since he liked James F. Bowman (?–1884), the gentle editor of the *Californian* and the *Golden Era*, his sonnet "J. F. B." (1882) expresses muted joy that
the man's honestly expressed philosophical doubts might well provide others
with "highways leading to the light." Bierce professes concern that "[An-
drew] Carnegie . . . [must] evermore explain / . . . Why . . . / you and God are
identically right" ("An Impostor," 1888). Bierce begins his poem "A Vice-
President" (1885), thus: "Here the remains of Schuyler Colfax [1823–1885;
he served with President Ulysses S. Grant] lie; solidus / Born, all the world
knows when, and God knows why"; the poem ends thus: "He came to life
just long enough to die." In "A Trencher-Knight" (1889), Bierce ridicules
Chauncey Mitchell Depew (1834–1928), railroad attorney-executive and
after-dinner speaker, as "Eater and orator, the whole world round / In feats
of tongue and tooth alike renowned." In "In Warning" (1911), Bierce warns
Rudyard Kipling to stay away from San Francisco, where he once accepted
hospitality at its "Jollidog Club," but then "when of your hunger you were
well rid / (And your manners too) like a cub / You snarled at the speeches
and grub." In "An Attorney-General" (1903), he demeans a member of the
cabinets of presidents William McKinley* and Theodore Roosevelt* by beginning with "Philander Knox [1853–1921]!—I know him by the sound; /
His sleep, unlike his learning, is profound," and concluding that ". . . no
important crisis he ignores, / But sleeps upon it, and for action—snores."
Bierce says that Leland Stanford,* supreme egotist, "Thought it odd / That
he should go to meet his God" instead of God doing the advancing (in "On
Stone," 1887). Thomas Arundel Harcourt, Bierce's collaborator in *The Dance*

of Death (1877), their successful literary hoax, is praised in "T. A. H." (1884) for accepting a "ghastly stroke" (his wife's infidelity) by silently overdrinking "like a devil" and becoming "grandly dead" (he jumped out a window). San Francisco broker-poet William Greer Harrison would be long forgotten but for Bierce's saying that the fellow "loved to loll on the Parnassian Mount / His pen to suck and all his thumbs to count" (in "On Stone"). In "A Literary Method" (1884), Bierce says that reading poetry by James Whitcomb Riley, which Riley says he writes on an empty stomach, "empties ours!" John D. Rockefeller is punningly described in "Compliance" (1911) as "pra[e]y[ing] / ... Upon his knees and neighbors." An otherwise-forgotten officer in the California National Guard is attacked in "To E. S. Salomon" (1911) for his Memorial Day oration against the propriety of decorating Confederate soldiers' graves. Bierce says in part: "The brave / Respect the dead; but ... you draw ... / ... the ass's jaw, / And shake it o'er a hero's grave." Bierce put other targets in his crosshairs, but they are too numerous even to list here. On the other hand, his most tender elegy is for otherwise unknown "William F. Smith" (1911):

> Light lie the earth upon his dear dead heart,
>   And dreams disturb him never.
> Be deeper peace than Paradise his part
>   Forever and forever.

Bierce especially disliked judges and lawyers. The former he comprehensively castigates in "Judex Judicatus" (1891) thus: "Judges, of judgment destitute and heart." As for the latter, he ends "To an Insolent Attorney" (1887) thus: "Who serves however clean a plan / By doing dirty work, he is a dirty man!" having just said that lawyers have "ambidextrous consciences."

Several of Bierce's poems concern historically significant figures. His straightforward elegy titled "The Death of Grant" (1885) proved popular. In it he praises the fallen general and president for "Disputing not ... / Nor questioning ... / ... anything but duty's deed." In an 1888 poem, Bierce also praises Dom Pedro II, Brazil's sovereign who, the poet says, freed slaves as Abraham Lincoln and Czar Alexander II did, and therefore might expect to be assassinated as they were. When Pedro survived the military coup of 1889, Bierce called the poem "A False Prophecy" for the 1910 volume. Less halcyon was the untitled poem Bierce wrote in 1900 following the assassination of William Goebel (1854–1900), governor of Kentucky. Bierce rashly wrote that the bullet that killed Goebel was speeding toward President William McKinley,* who was also shot to death, twenty short months later. This did not stop Bierce from reviling McKinley's successor, Theodore Roosevelt,* whom he met in the White House, felt patronized by, and regarded as a poseur and a dangerous chauvinist. In "After Portsmouth" (1910), Bierce has the Russian "Tsar, bewildered," lament the consequences of the Russo-

Japanese peace treaty that Roosevelt famously arranged at Portsmouth, New Hampshire (August 1905).

Many of Bierce's poems, especially short, pithy ones, made their first appearance in his *Devil's Dictionary*. Examples include his poetic definitions of "Inauspiciously," "Infralapsarian," and "Right," all of which illustrate his occasional poetic turn toward philosophical ideas, in these instances to determinism, a concept often driving the action in his short fiction as well. In "Inauspiciously," a Roman augur accepts a bribe from a slave and only then tells him that his plan is fated to fail—the plan being to "seize / On Juno's poultry" which the augur is guarding. In "Infralaparsian," Bierce waxes sarcastic about "poor Adam and what made him fall." Opposing theologians, fighting verbally and with fists over "foreordinational freedom of will," are interrupted by a professor of Latin who says that the infralapsarian should say "Adam slipped down" and the supralapsarian should say "Adam slipped up." Bierce, who wrote a poor poem titled "The Pun" (1878), ends "Infralapsarian" with a pun so bad that it deserves to be quoted: ". . . Adam analyzed not his blunder, / But thought he had slipped on a peal of thunder!" In "Right," Bierce accuses God of "contributory negligence" if it is true that kings really rule by "Right Divine."

Most of Bierce's poems, which often take the form of exempla, diatribes, fables, and mini-dramas and mini-narratives, show considerable verbal ingenuity, which is often capricious or viciously humorous as well. They are often best read aloud, in a wry, dry voice. Even when the subject might be regarded as trivial or no longer relevant, Bierce spices them up in his unique way. He should be regarded as a first-rate American poetic voice of the second rank.

Bibliography: M. E. Grenander, "Introduction," *Poems of Ambrose Bierce* (Lincoln and London: University of Nebraska Press, 1995); McWilliams; Morris; Ambrose Bierce, *A Vision of Doom: Poems*, ed. Donald Sidney-Fryer (Kingston, R. I.: Donald M. Grant, 1980).

POLLARD, PERCIVAL (1869–1911). Author and critic. He was born in Greifswald, Germany. Migrating to the United States in 1885, Pollard lived in Iowa as a teenager and in Baltimore; Saybrook, Connecticut; and Sag Harbor, Long Island, later in life. Pollard was the literary critic for New York's *Town Topics* from 1897 to 1911. During these years, he wrote three novels, several short stories, a successful play, travel essays, and a book favoring Germany and opposing England, which pleased H. L. Mencken,* his close friend. Pollard had a brain tumor and suffered a horrible death after surgery in Baltimore.

On his way from San Francisco to Washington, D.C., in January 1896, Bierce stopped to see Pollard. He had delighted Bierce by writing in the *New York Journal* (22 May 1896) that Bierce's description of the wounded in "Chickamauga" was better than anything in *The Red Badge of Courage* by

Stephen Crane. In the *San Francisco Examiner* (26 July 1896), Bierce returned the compliment by praising Pollard as a "hard and ingenious" critic. He was Pollard's guest at his summer home at Sag Harbor. Bierce reviewed Pollard's novel *Lingo Dan* (in the *New York American*, 7 September 1903). The two traveled together in 1907 from Washington, D.C., to Chattanooga, Tennessee, where Bierce showed Pollard some battlefields; then they went on together to Galveston, Texas, in order, among other activities, to visit their mutual friend Silas Orrin Howes.* Bierce wrote several fine letters to Pollard and through him met Mencken, with whom he attended Pollard's funeral and cremation in Baltimore. Mencken later recalled many macabre remarks Bierce made at the time. Bierce wrote his friend George Sterling* the poet an unusual letter (27 December 1911) in which he describes Pollard's final suffering and expresses sorrow at losing his friendship. Bierce wrote Howes in the same vein. Bierce's friend and publisher, Walter Neale,* knew Polland well, wrote about Pollard's friendship with Bierce, and published two of Pollard's books of criticism, *Their Day in Court: The Case of American Letters and Its Causes* (1909) and *Vagabond Journeys* (1911).

Bibliography: Grenander; Fred Hobson, *Mencken: A Life* (New York: Random House, 1994); George N. Kummer, "Percival Pollard: Precursor of the 'Twenties' " (Ph.D. dissertation, New York University, 1947); McWilliams; Morris; Neale; O'Connor.

PONDRONUMMUS. In "The Captain of the 'Camel,' " he is mentioned by Captain Abersouth as a character in a novel by Mary Elizabeth Braddon that he is reading.

PORFER. In "A Holy Terror," he is a prominent San Franciscan. He was a successful faro dealer in Hurdy-Gurdy and escaped a step ahead of vigilantes, undoubtedly because he was a wily cheat. He married Mary Matthews of Elizabethtown, New Jersey. He was probably the New York gambler, Jo. Seeman, who knifed Mary.

PORFER, MARY MATTHEWS. In "A Holy Terror," she is from Elizabethtown, New Jersey, and had a love affair with Jefferson Doman. She declined to wait for him to return rich from the California gold fields, took up with Jo. Seeman instead, was knifed in the face by him, and sent Doman a photograph showing her disfigurement to break off their engagement. Called Split-faced Moll, she made her way to California and married Porfer. When she and Porfer locate Manuelita Murphy's disturbed grave and she finds Doman's body with her letters and photographs in his jacket, she falls dead. Porfer is probably the former Seeman.

"PORTRAITS OF ELDERLY AUTHORS" (1907, 1911). Essay. A youthful picture of an aged writer is false. But why should an aged picture be used to represent a writer whose best works were done decades ago?

"A POSSIBLE BENEFACTOR" (1902, 1912). Essay. (Original title: "The Crime of 1902.") A Frenchman named Verneuil has invented artificial rubies identical to real ones, in "composition, hardness and color." It is to be hoped that he will be able to produce other, cheaper gems. People who wear "pebbles" falsely allege that they are beautiful, whereas they wear them because they are costly and do not wear paste gems that look real. Similarly, Indians wear eagle feathers and wildcats' tails because they are hard to acquire. Women abandon "barbaric modes" tardily; this is proved by the fact that men no longer daub their faces to show their tribes, whereas women still use makeup and pretend that doing so improves the complexion. Let's pray for an extension of Verneuil's success.

"POST MORTEM" (1902, 1905, 1912). Short drama. (Original title of parts: "An Un-dolly Dialogue" and "The View of One.") President Theodore Roosevelt* enters army headquarters and pummels late-rising General Nelson Miles (1839–1925), commander of the army. Later, when his secretary tells Roosevelt that Miles is dead, he dispatches a colonel to make sure that Miles, reported to be still moving, is finished off. This dated ditty is written in heroic couplets, some of which are not bad, for example, "What? six o'clock!—and day's already broke? / I'm too late to escape him. Holy smoke!"

"POVERTY, CRIME AND VICE" (1900, 1904, 1908, 1911). Essay. (Original title: "If Reform Reformed.") The comment that Andrew Carnegie once made to a Bible class that all great men "come from the ranks of the poor" is not completely true. Rich men are sometimes great. Carnegie was right in implying that a world without poverty would be replete with "incapables." Bierce goes on: "Poverty . . . is [often] Nature's punishment for incapacity and improvidence." It often weeds out the unfit. Crime also helps improve humanity's "moral and material welfare." We should not, however, encourage either poverty or crime. An experiment in Chicago to relocate slum dwellers from the city to farms failed. They were called back by their very genes to the slums. The poor distrust, envy, and hate the wealthy; but they should not do so. These feelings are wrongly fostered and exploited by demagogues, who criticize acts of philanthropy as paltry. The wealthy do not hate the less lucky, the able, thrifty, and ambitious, even while holding themselves aloof. The super-rich enjoy money only by spending it. Getting rid of it helps laborers, directly or indirectly. If poverty were abolished, the following would die: generosity, gratitude, foresight, the fighting spirit. Small numbers of Mexicans and Japanese could then invade and enslave us. Virtues and vices grow from one seed in one soil, ripen and perish together. Our soft citizens will give way to barbarians. Let us pray that we can keep fighting and yet not prevail.

"A PRACTICAL JOKE: MAJOR BROADWOOD RECALLS THE HEROIC PAST." *See* "The Major's Tale."

"PRESENT AT A HANGING" (1888). Short story. (Characters: Daniel Baker, John White Corwell, the Rev. Mr. Cummings, Samuel Morritz, Abner Raiser.) In 1853, Daniel Baker of Lebanon, Iowa, is suspected by neighbors of welcoming an itinerant peddler (later identified as Samuel Morritz) to his farm home, only to rob and kill him. One misty night seven years later, the Rev. Mr. Cummings is driving his horse and buggy past Baker's place when a ghostly figure, with pack and stick, points down at the far edge of the bridge nearby and then disappears. Cummings gets home fast. The next morning he and two neighbors go to the bridge, find Baker hanging from a beam, and while getting the body down disturb "the loose, friable earth" on the slope beneath. They discover Morritz's bones. A jury decides that Baker went insane and hanged himself, and that Morritz was murdered by "some person or persons . . . unknown." Bierce takes delight in hinting at the stupidity of some people, in this case, members of a rural jury.

PRESIDENT, THE. In "Jupiter Doke, Brigadier-General," he is the President of the United States and appoints Brigadier-General Jupiter Doke to his present rank in the Union Army.

"A PRESIDENTIAL PROGRESS" (1901, 1912). Short drama. (Originally part of "Apocryphal Conversations.") Two citizens argue as the president is speaking from the rear platform of his train. One man is delighted, while the other criticizes the president's toadying to the people. But when the president shakes their hands, both are pleased. The unnamed president is William McKinley.*

PRETZEL, COUNT VON. In "A Shipwreckollection," he is, according to the narrator, the New York coachman who ran away with the narrator's sister.

"THE PREVAILING CORSICAN." *See* "On Knowing One's Business—An Instance."

PRICE, LIEUTENANT. In "One Kind of Officer," he is Captain Ransome's subordinate officer. When General Cameron treats Ransome curtly, Ransome fatally treats Price with similar discourtesy. After confusing fire, Ransome asks Price to clarify his orders from Cameron, who has been killed by enemy fire, so that their commanding officer, General Masterson, may understand. To get even, Price coldly says that he knows nothing about the orders and was insultingly treated by Ransome when he questioned the orders earlier. Price's silence will result in Ransome's being executed by firing squad on orders from Masterson.

"THE PROBLEM OF SUCCESS FOR OLD MEN—A SCAMPOSIUM." *See* "Advice to Old Men."

"A PROVIDENTIAL INTIMATION" (1874). Short story. (Original title: "The Tale of a Coat.") (Characters: the Rev. Mr. Boltright, Clipper, Budd Doble, Lightnin', Algernon Jarvis, Sally Meeker, Sim Salper, Bob Scotty, Stenner, Staley Tupper, Upandust.) Algernon Jarvis of San Francisco gets up in a bad mood, goes to a hotel billiards room, and is placing and knocking "the indocile globes" about when a stranger named Stenner bets that Jarvis cannot make a certain shot. While he is trying to do so, Stenner sneaks away with Jarvis's fashionable coat and takes it to his room in North Beach. In a pocket he finds a telegram reading "Buy Sally Meeker." Remembering that Sally Meeker is a race horse, Stenner buys a sporting paper and reads about upcoming races of horses of various names and with various owners. He concludes that the man sending the wire knew that Sally was to win and that her owner did not and must want to sell her. Stenner rushes to Vallejo, wins $100 at poker from a victim he knows, and sends the sum by check, with the terse message "Bi Saly Meker," to the Rev. Mr. Boltright, the only clergyman he knows in San Francisco. Being a man of religion, he must be honest, Stenner thinks. (The narrator disagrees.) After a week of revelry, Stenner goes to a friend, asks about Sally, and is told that Sally the horse broke her neck during the first heat but that her owner Sim Salper does not care since he has just struck it rich in a mine he named after his horse. Sally Meeker Mine stock is sky-high. Wondering if Boltright by any chance bought stock not mare, Stenner rushes to him and asks if he bought any Sally. The clergyman first advises Stenner to think of spiritual not material things, but then adds that he received and acted on "a Providential intimation," which was "accompanied with the secular means of obedience," and did indeed buy "largely" of the stock mentioned, on margin. Boltright has the $25,000 to this day.

"A PROVISIONAL SETTLEMENT" (1898, 1912). Short drama. (Originally part of "New 'Imaginary Conversations.'") President William McKinley,* Práxedes Mateo Sagasta (1827–1903, premier of Spain), and Emilio Aguinaldo (1869–1964, Filipino leader) are discussing American demands with respect to the Philippines. Sagasta is critical, calls the president "Porco" in asides, but is powerless. Aguinaldo, though ultimately fooled, makes an eloquent comment on what McKinley calls America's "manifest destiny" concerning Manila, Luzon, and Spanish interests. Aguinaldo says, "It is as if the French, having assisted your forefathers to independence, had kept

Boston and all New England for themselves and restored the other colonies to Great Britain."
Bibliography: Berkove.

"A PSYCHOLOGICAL SHIPWRECK" (1879). Short story. (Original title: "My Shipwreck.") (Characters: Zenas Bronson, Denneker, Gordon Doyle, Harford, Janette Harford, Mrs. Harford, Mrs. William Jarrett, William Jarrett, William Jarrett.) The New York mercantile firm of Bronson & Jarrett failed in 1873. Zenas Bronson, a partner, died. In the summer of 1874 the narrator, William Jarrett, the surviving partner, is in Liverpool and has just finished some business. Feeling lazy and tired, he decides to return to New York slowly by the *Morrow*, a sailing vessel, instead of by a passenger steamer. The *Morrow*, sailing on 15 June, has only three passengers—Jarrett, Janette Harford, and her servant, who is "a middle-aged negress." Miss Harford says that the servant was left with her father by William Jarrett and his wife, a South Carolinian couple who both died on the same day in her parents' home. Another William Jarrett, the narrator, puzzled by the coincidence of names, recalls that a branch of his family settled in South Carolina. He knows nothing "of them and their history." Dining together on board the ship during weeks of pleasant weather, Jarrett and Janette become "well acquainted." He feels powerfully attracted to her, though without feeling "love." However, wanting "to seek her," he asks on 3 July for her assistance in resolving his "psychological doubt." She stares at him fixedly, and on returning her strange gaze he senses familiar faces straining to see him behind her eyes. The scene about him vanishes, darkness falls, then his physical sight returns. Janette is sitting with her eyes closed, a finger on a passage of her book, which is Denneker's *Meditations*. Jarrett carefully reads in it about souls leaving bodies, how the stronger soul washes over the weaker, and how certain both souls are of "kin whose paths intersect." Janette rises and shudders. The captain and his first officer look at the barometer in sudden shock. Next, Jarrett finds himself floating in the dark sea, and the sinking vessel's vortex tears Janette from his grasp. He comes to in a stateroom of the steamer *City of Prague*. Gordon Doyle, a friendly man he met in Liverpool the day he boarded the *Morrow*, is reading beside him. Jarrett asks if they "save[d] *her*." Doyle asks who and turns in wordless amazement when Jarrett names Janette Harford. Jarrett says that he can hardly believe he was not aboard the *Morrow*. On being requested to do so, Doyle first explains that he and Jarrett embarked together on the *City of Prague*, that Jarrett has behaved like a "lunatic," and that the vessel broke a shaft and is powerless up to now, 3 July. Assured that he has been aboard all that time, Jarrett asks about Janette Harford. Doyle explains that he met her in London a year ago, they fell in love, her rich family objected, and they decided to elope—on separate vessels to avoid detection. She took the *Morrow*, and they plan to meet and marry in New York. He is worried about the delay of his vessel. He adds that Janette, who believes the Harfords are her real parents, was really adopted. Her mother died in a fall from a horse, and her grief-stricken father committed suicide the same day. Jarrett asks what Doyle has been reading and learns that it was the identical passage from Denneker that Janette was reading aboard ship. When Doyle, saying that Janette gave him the book, asks Jarrett how he could know her name and that of the ship she sailed on, Jarrett contents himself by explaining that Doyle talked in his sleep. A week later the *City of Prague* is towed to a New York port. The *Morrow* is never heard from.

Q

"A QUEER STORY; TRANSCRIBED FROM THE NOTES OF AN INVESTIGATOR." *See* "The Thing at Nolan."

QUOIN, WILLIAM. In "Why I Am Not Editing 'The Stinger,' " he is the foreman of *The Stinger*, who writes Peter Pitchin, the editor, reports Muskler's presence there with his dog, asks for copy to publish, and says that he and his fellow workers will leave without copy.

R

"RABID TRANSIT." *See* "The Wizard of Bumbassa."

"THE RACE AT LEFT BOWER" (1874). Short story. (Characters: Colonel Jackhigh, Lightning Express.) Colonel Jackhigh, sitting at a bar with an Englishman, offers to bet that his "pisen little beast" of a horse can defeat anything around. The Englishman smiles, remarks that his horse is in good condition, and proposes a $100 wager next afternoon. Done. Everyone in Left Bower attends. The Englishman, puffing a cigar, waits "atop his magnificent animal." The colonel ambles up on a tall, skeletal, crooked-legged, earless, wrinkle-lipped mount. Spectators call it the Lightning Express. The two-mile circular race starts. The Englishman is immediately way ahead, returns as though to view the bony rear of his rival, then toward the finish line tries to canter ahead. But he cannot, because the colonel's creature has turned and "let[s] fall a smile," and its opponent stops as though shot, and cannot be urged forward. At the end, the colonel's steed drops accurate grins left and right, then turns, and stares at the thoroughbred, which screams and gallops to the rear. The colonel's winning time is 20 minutes, 10 seconds. This weird tale has ghastly religious overtones. The colonel is called "the fiend"; his beast, "the unthinkable quadruped" and "the incarnate nightmare." The pride of the Britisher certainly is followed by a kind of destruction. Bierce lightens the narrative with tall-tale language; for example, he says that the colonel's horse cannot be called "a perfect skeleton," because certain bones are missing which one would think could not be spared. Bierce's description of the winning horse echoes some of the animal depictions in *Roughing It* by Mark Twain,* which appeared in 1872, two years before "The Race at Left Bower."

RAISER, ABNER. In "Present at a Hanging," he and John White Corwell accompany the Rev. Mr. Cummings to the bridge and find Daniel Baker hanged there and the murdered Samuel Morritz's bones buried beneath it.

RANSOME, CAPTAIN. In "One Kind of Officer," he is a cool Union Army artillery officer. His superior, General Cameron, orders him to fire on any troops in front of him and adds that he needs to know nothing but simply to obey. But, in callous obedience, Ransome fires on the troops of his comrades, under the command of General Hart, whose forces General Masterson has ordered up in support of Cameron. Meanwhile, Cameron is killed in action. Since Ransome treated his subordinate officer, Lieutenant Price, with insulting discourtesy, similar to his treatment by Cameron, Price truthfully denies any knowledge of the orders under which Ransome acted. Therefore, Masterson will order Ransome's execution by firing squad.

"THE RAVAGES OF SHAKESPEARITIS" (1903, 1911). Essay. (Original title: "The Ravages of Shakespeariosis.") Bierce curiously opines that Shakespeare lacks restraint, spends his "conceptions, images and descriptions" too prodigally, and dazzles us blind. We Teutons, unlike the ancient Greeks and the modern French, love "savage profusion."

RAYNOR, JACK ("GIG," "GIGGLES"). In "A Lady from Redhorse," he is a friend of both Mary Jane Dement and James. She would marry Raynor, except for his being too short. Raynor encourages James, evidently long in love with Mary, to return from Vienna to Coronado, where he and Mary are staying. At first Mary thinks James is Dr. Barritz, a handsome, well-mannered magician from India. She falls in love with him. He turns out to be a man from the mining fields called Dumps and thought to be dead. Truth prevails, and all is well.

REALF, RICHARD (1834–1878). British-born poet, who migrated to the United States at the age of twenty as a newspaperman. He published his *Guesses at the Beautiful: Poems by Richard Realf* (1852). Realf was so impressed by John Brown (1800–1859), the militant abolitionist, that he became the secretary of state in Brown's provisional government in Canada. Although Realf was arrested after Brown's unsuccessful attack at Harpers Ferry, he was released and served in the U.S. Army as an officer during the Civil War. He was unstable, hypocritically lectured on temperance but drank excessively, married but deserted his wife, married again while drunk, and then deserted his second wife. He moved to California evidently in 1878, partly for reasons of deteriorating health but also to avoid his second wife, who pursued him to San Francisco and had their marriage annulled. Realf submitted poetry to the *Argonaut*, which Bierce as editor accepted, only to learn to his annoyance that Realf had sold it elsewhere earlier. In trouble with yet another woman, Realf committed suicide in Oakland. Ina Coolbrith* wrote a memorial piece which David Lesser Lezinsky,* another poet, read at a program commemorating Realf in 1893. Posthumously published were *Poems by Richard Realf, Poet, Soldier, Workman* (1898) and *Richard Realf's Free-state Poems; with Personal Lyrics Written in Kansas* (1900). In a "Prattle" column (*San Francisco Examiner*, 23 September 1894), Bierce mentions Realf's suicide.

Bibliography: Fatout, Grenander.

"THE REALM OF THE UNREAL" (1890). Short story. (Characters: Margaret Corray, Mrs. Corray, Dr. Valentine Dorrimore, Manrich.) Five years before, the narrator, Manrich, was with friends at the Bohemian Club in San Francisco discussing the feats of *prestidigitateurs* when swarthy Dr. Valentine Dorrimore, a disagreeable but captivating hypnotist from Calcutta, entered. Soon he and Manrich walked out together. On the street, Dorrimore hypnotized Manrich into seeing Dorrimore stabbed to death, withdraw a gem-studded sword, fling it aside, rise, and disappear. Five years pass. Manrich is driving a horse and buggy from Newcastle toward Auburn. Suddenly Dorrimore appears in the dark road and evidently hypnotizes Manrich. The two travel on to Auburn. Once there, they check into the Putnam Hotel. Manrich is surprised when his fiancée, Margaret Corray, and her mother, both from Oakland, arrive. They are all happy for two weeks. Then, one moonlit night in an abandoned cemetery outside of town, Manrich sees Dorrimore arm in arm with Margaret. Manrich attacks Dorrimore but is found the next morning bruised and bloodied, wakes up in delirium in his hotel room, and is told that Mrs. Corray and her daughter never checked into the hotel. Married now to Margaret, who never saw Auburn, Manrich reads in the Baltimore *Sun* about Professor Valentine Dorrimore's feats of hypnotism and his lectures about the art just the night before.

REID. In "Dead and 'Gone,' " he is George J. Reid's father. He and his wife see their son fall lifeless, but later George disappears.

REID, GEORGE J. In "Dead and 'Gone,' " he falls lifeless at the age of twenty-one in his parents' home in Xenia, Ohio, on 14 August 1872. Attempts to revive him fail, and he is covered with a sheet. When a physician enters the room with his parents, George has disappeared from the bedroom, which has one door and a locked window. His clothes are on the floor, and the outline of his body is distinctly visible under the sheet.

REID, MRS. In "Dead and 'Gone,' " she is George J. Reid's mother. She and her husband cannot revive their son's lifeless body; nor can anyone account for his disappearance from the secure bedroom in which they placed him.

"THE REIGN OF THE KING" (1892, 1911). Essay. In Europe, wearing finger rings is going out of fashion. The fashion will return. Wearing nose rings will probably be in style again. Wearing rings predates history. Ancient Egyptian priests wore rings of mystical design. Rings of ancient Jews indicated authority. Old stories tell of rings that could make one invisible, indicate directions, cure the ill, detect poison, curse the wearer. Wedding rings make half of our population happy. Time was that divorce was once easy. He could pull off her ring, untroubled by matters of legal fees, alimony, and custody. If alive now, Bierce would point to evidence of current body piercing and say, "See?"

"RELIGION" (1888, 1891, 1898, 1900, 1909, 1912). Essay. (A section was originally part of "Ambrose Bierce Says: Missionaries Cause the Chief Trouble in China.") What is right? What would Jesus Christ have done under the circumstances? Charles Monroe Sheldon (1857–1946), who wrote *In His Steps: What Would Jesus Do?* (1896), has been criticized by those who do not know the basis of Sheldon's thought or his motives. Instead of asking how Christ "would . . . do this," we should wonder whether Christ would do "this" at all. Defenders of Sheldon wrongly equivocate about Christ's anti-materialism. Make no mistake: Christ "not only lived in poverty and taught poverty as a blessing, but commanded it as a duty and a means to salvation." Hypocrites abound. Richard Jordan Gatling (1818–1903) foolishly rationalized that his Gatling machine gun was so potent that it would make war obsolete. Nations that are falsely called "Christian" arm themselves ever more expensively, for offense and defense, despite Christ's teaching "not only abstention from aggression but non-resistance." Burdensome weaponry costs "are obviously judgments of Heaven for disobedience to the Prince of Peace." "Missionaries . . . [are] a perpetual menace to peace." Governments admit foreign missionaries only under compulsion. A given country is ruled wisely when it adheres to its people's religion. Only Christian "truth" emboldens Christians to proselytize abroad. Caucasians are disliked in China not because of race or religion but because they meddle in other people's business. The Chinese don't come and bother adherents of our religions. American ministers rarely admit that people en masse avoid Sunday services because they are dreary and because preachers offer nonsensical, tiresome talk. By contrast, Satan "is . . . a good entertainer." Like physicians of the body, ministers are physicians of the soul; both should offer their visitors what is efficacious, not nasty, or leave them alone. Prayers during a week set aside for such probably do not influence God, who is probably not a nose counter. Why expect credit for praying for a solar eclipse when astronomers have already published its date? Prayers are not always answered. Two chaplains prayed hard that congressmen would become good and wise—to no avail. Humankind prays to become blessed—to no avail. Christ admonished all to help the poor. We circumvent that wisdom to "find . . . imaginary warrant for all our pranks and fads."

"THE RELIGION OF THE TABLE" (1869, 1873, 1911). Essay. (Original title: "Let Us Eat"; later title: "A Call to Dinner.") By dining well, Philip of Orleans, "skilled in the mysteries of the cuisine," set a fine example to the starving French peasantry. Items of a fine dinner are "redolent of religion." Skinny, hungry folks rightly avoid churches. Religion is for the fat, who could not swallow and digest the parson's wisdom unless they had first dined well. Worship is best managed by knife and fork. The fat dead will be credentialed and passported to heaven fastest. When Shakespeare wrote of Falstaff's dying, Fat Jack must really have been babbling about "green turtle," not green fields. Eat well and you are a good Christian. Eat nothing and you are not godly.

"A RESUMED IDENTITY" (1908). Short story. (Original title: "The Man.") (Character: Dr. Stilling Malson.) One summer evening, a man is looking at a forest and a field, while the full moon hangs low in the west. A column of cavalrymen, infantry men, and artillerymen marches past him. He attributes their total silence to "acoustical shadows," that is, gaps in which nothing is heard. He thinks their presence means that his side has lost a battle and that the defeated soldiers are proceeding to Nashville. Feeling a chill, he notes that the moonlit road ahead is empty. He sees a black man with some mules, hears a dog barking, and feels his head. Now behold an old man. He encounters Dr. Stilling Malson, returning on horseback to his home in Murfreesboro, Tennessee, and explains that he is a lieutenant serving under General William B. Hazen.* He asks which army won the battle, gets no answer, and says he was wounded slightly in the head. Dr. Malson says that the fellow is not in uniform. He agrees, says he cannot understand why, and, when asked, says he is twenty-three. He says he saw troops. Outraged when Malson says he saw none, the fellow trudges on, observes that his own hand looks ancient, and wonders how it can be summer when the battle was fought in winter. He gets tired and stops by a weather-stained stone marker placed in memory of the men of Hazen's brigade killed at "Stones River, Dec. 31, 1862." He sees his face reflected in a pool of water nearby, shrieks, and surrenders "the life that had spanned another life." There are obvious autobiographical touches in "A Resumed Identity": Bierce fought in the Stones River battle, was later wounded in the head, and often felt that he lost part of his identity as a soldier in combat. It has been pointed out that this story exemplifies the mimetic tale, in which a series of events reproduces in the reader emotions duplicating those of the hero.
Bibliography: Grenander, Morris.

"REVISION DOWNWARD" (1903, 1911). Essay. (Original title: "Is the Human Race Decreasing in Stature?"; later title: "The Long and Short of It.") Nations wrongly continue to prefer tall soldiers. In modern combat, personal contacts are rare, and big men tire first and are often shot first. Apart from horses used to haul artillery pieces, wiry little horses are best. Various literatures tell of giants bigger and stronger than later generations. In truth, people are getting smaller, and this represents an improvement. Where have the dinosaurs gone? Elephants are on their way out. Huge birds can no longer even fly, whereas tiny fleas can really leap, and little ants can shoulder large burdens. Animalcula may well have attained excellent civilizations. We cannot boast of mastering the world until we rid it of fleas and flies. Bierce should also have added cockroaches and rats to his list of unendangered species.

"A REVOLT OF THE GODS" (1886). Short story. (Original title: "The Ancient City of Grimaulquin: A Record of Industrial Discontent.") (Characters: none named.) The narrator lives with his parents in the ancient city of Sardasa. His father deodorizes dead dogs. His mother sells cat meat. Cats are sacred in Sardasa; so they multiply, and their owners secretly supply the mother. After arguing with the mother, the father thrashes the clergyman who married them. This act causes an outraged populace to stop using the father's services. The mother retaliates by refusing to sell cat meat. Cats are everywhere. Old maids in a federated union demand arbitration, are refused, and go on strike. Next, cats, feeling doomed to starve, stage an insurrection—a veritable "revolt of the gods." Dead dogs, by smelling worse and worse, also go on a kind of strike. Seeing dogs' teeth everywhere, the cats attack their corpses. What carnage! Springing into the fray are the old maids, the narrator's parents, city leaders, and finally the people. The dead, after a meeting in the cemetery, strike and destroy headstones and much else. When night comes, the dead and the living are "alike exterminated." Sardasa becomes an excavation, littered with dead flesh, then a stagnant pool in the desert. Two questions: Why would not another enterprising Sardasan begin to receive and slaughter cats and market their meat? And what could have been Bierce's purpose in writing this silly story? Perhaps Bierce is satirizing people in overpopulated India who venerate sacred cows at the expense of health and nutrition.

"RHETORICAL MONKE-SHINES." *See* "The Game of Politics."

RICHTER, CHARLES. In "The Mystery of Charles Farquharson," he was a boyhood friend of Charles Farquharson and William Hayner Gordon. One night in Philadelphia in the summer of 1843, Gordon stumbles over a body in his dark room but is soon cleared of any wrongdoing. Months later, Richter, then living in Bombay, sends Gordon word that Farquharson, also a resident of Bombay and by then a Parsee, died at what proves to have been exactly the time Gordon found the corpse. To Gordon's inquiry about particulars, Richter sends a daguerreotype of Farquharson and explains that his body was consumed by buzzards. When Gordon gets permission to inspect the coffin of the man found in his room, it proves to be empty but for a moldy shroud.

RIDLEY. In "My Favorite Murder," he is the narrator Samuel Ridley's father. He moved with his family from Michigan to California in 1867, became a prosperous road agent, but then got religion, and turned over his agency to his brother, William Ridley. The Ridley family moved to Ghost Rock and opened a dance house. It has been suggested that in describing Samuel's father as "a reticent, saturnine man," though with "the austerity of his disposition" somewhat "relaxed" with the passage of time, Bierce was thinking of his own father, Marcus Aurelius Bierce.*
Bibliography: Morris.

RIDLEY. In "My Favorite Murder," he is either of the two sons of William Ridley, the narrator Samuel Ridley's uncle. When the uncle and his sons robbed Samuel in 1875 and refused to return the loot, Samuel determined to murder his uncle.

RIDLEY, MARY. In "My Favorite Murder," she is the wife of William Ridley and hence the narrator Samuel Ridley's aunt. When Samuel told her that he planned to kill William, she calmly expressed doubts as to his ability to do so.

RIDLEY, MRS. ("THE BUCKING WALRUS"). In "My Favorite Murder," she was the narrator Samuel Ridley's mother. She moved with her husband and son from Michigan to California in 1867. When the family got religion, they gave their road agency to William Ridley, Samuel's uncle, and moved to Ghost Rock, where Mrs. Ridley opened a dance house, which they called "The Saints' Rest Hurdy-Gurdy." Her dancing "grace" earned her the nickname of "The Bucking Walrus." Samuel murdered his mother in 1877.

RIDLEY, SAMUEL. In "My Favorite Murder," he is the conscienceless narrator. He was born in Kalamakee, Michigan, in 1856, moved with his parents to California in 1867, and settled with them near Nigger Head. His father was a road agent there until the family got religion and moved to Ghost Rock, where they opened a dance house. Samuel murdered his mother in 1877. At the end of the seven-year trial, the judge says that details of the killing are atrocious in the extreme, whereupon the narrator seeks to be acquitted by explaining that his murder of William Ridley, his father's brother, was manifestly more atrocious. Uncle William, who took over Samuel's father's road-agency business, sought to cheat Samuel in 1875; so Samuel cut his victim's hamstrings, put him in a sack, swung him from a tall tree, and enticed his uncle's goat to butt him to death.

RIDLEY, WILLIAM ("BILL"). In "My Favorite Murder," he was the brother of the narrator Samuel Ridley's father. When Samuel and his parents got religion near Nigger Head, California, they sent for William, living in Stockton, to come and take over their road-agency business. Uncle William and his two sons robbed Samuel and refused to return the loot. Samuel decided to kill William and did so by putting him in a sack and having his goat butt him to death.

"THE RIGHT TO TAKE ONESELF OFF." *See* "Taking Oneself Off."

"THE RIGHT TO WORK" (1893, 1895, 1897, 1909, 1912). Essay. We should support an able-bodied man unemployed through no fault of his own. We have almshouses and asylums to care for people who are weak in body and mind. They all feel hunger, cold, and exposure. Those who choose to be shiftless tramps "are irreclaimable degenerates"; but unemployed men who want to work are another matter, are both "unfortunate and dangerous," and should be provided with work "by law." Employing them at lower than competitive wages would not hurt private industry but would lower the crime rate.

ROBARDIN, HOSEIB ALAR. In "An Inhabitant of Carcosa," this is the spirit source of the story, which was "imparted" to Bayrolles, the medium.

ROCHUS. In *The Monk and the Hangman's Daughter*, he is the handsome, conceited, and sinful son of the Saltmaster at Berchtesgaden. He drops Amula, his girlfriend, in order to dance with Benedicta, whom he wants to seduce. When Ambrosius, the monk-narrator, tries to stop Rochus, Rochus defeats the monk in a fight but does not throw him off a cliff. Benedicta believes Rochus's false promise of marriage; so Ambrosius, to protect her from sin, kills her. Rochus then lies that Benedicta harbored a forbidden passion for the monk.

"A ROLLING CONTINENT" (1912). Essay. Everyone likes to predict coming events. But why bother? Our continent is turning over like a person in bed. The bottom of San Francisco harbor is rising, while the Atlantic coast is being eaten away by waves. Should Easterners head west or stay and become fish? For millennia this rolling will probably continue. The Pacific slope will continue to Hawaii. Inhabitants there will have to pay heavily to ride the "San Francisco and Honolulu Pacific Railroad," construction of which will cost our government $50 million a mile.

ROMANUS. In *The Monk and the Hangman's Daughter*, he is a Franciscan monk who accompanies Ambrosius and Aegidius from Passau to Berchtesgaden.

ROOSEVELT, THEODORE (1858–1919). Author, outdoorsman, conservationist, and twenty-sixth president of the United States. Roosevelt was born in New York City, graduated from Harvard University (1880), studied law at Columbia University (1880–1881), entered New York politics (1881), and was a rancher-hunter in the Dakota Badlands (to 1886). Returning to politics, he rose to the position of assistant secretary of the navy (1887–1898). The Spanish-American War thrust him into international prominence. He served with the Rough Riders in Cuba (1898) and returned a hero—to become governor of New York (1899–1900), vice president under President William McKinley* (1901), and, upon that man's assassination, president (1901–1909). During his tenure as a staunch Republican, Roosevelt authorized the Open Door Policy, fostered by his secretary of state John Hay,* recognized Panama's independence from Columbia (1903), thus starting the Panama Canal, and helped end the Russo-Japanese War (in 1905). In a speech on 17 March 1906, Roosevelt criticized liberal journalists, bent on exposing political and commercial corruption, as wrongly wielding "the muckrake" and looking "no way but downward." Thus the term "muckrakers" was initiated. Also a prolific writer, Roosevelt published numerous books on hunting, politics, history, and military matters.

Walter Neale,* Bierce's friend, publisher, and biographer, wrote that Roosevelt regarded Bierce as the greatest short-story writer who ever lived. Neale also described a White House meeting between Bierce and Roosevelt (probably in 1903); Bierce allegedly judged the president to be insincere. According to Neale, Bierce later regarded Roosevelt as "a dangerous man, because unsteady, prone to emotional decisions." Roosevelt figures in eight short dramas by Bierce, who presents him as blustering, too ready to issue rash orders to cabinet officials (notably Hay and Elihu Root, secretary of war and later of state) and other subordinates, enamored of big-stick diplomacy, and toothy. Bierce's short dramas in which Roosevelt appears are "A Baffled Ambition," "Diplomatic Triumph," "The Post Mortem," "A Strained Relation," "A Sucked Orange," "A Twisted Tale," "A White House Idyl," and "A Wireless Penultimatum." Bierce's satirical little plays are funny but superficial and insignificant.

Bibliography: Oscar M. Alfonso, *Theodore Roosevelt and the Philippines 1897–1909* (Quezon: University of the Philippines Press, 1970); Howard K. Beale, *Theodore Roosevelt and the Rise of America to World Power* (Baltimore: Johns Hopkins Press, 1956); Richard H. Collin, *Theodore Roosevelt's Caribbean: The Panama Canal, the Monroe Doctrine, and the Latin American Context* (Baton Rouge and London: Louisiana State University Press, 1990); Neale; St. Pierre.

ROSCOE. In "A Fruitless Assignment," this is the name of the family who lived in the Roscoe house on Vine Street in Cincinnati. It is now deserted and presumed to be haunted.

ROSSER. In "The Middle Toe of the Right Foot," he is a friend of King and Sancher. When Rosser sees Manton, who calls himself Robert Grossmith, eavesdropping on their conversation at the hotel in Marshall, he insults him and is challenged to a duel. Manton dies of fright at the outset of the duel, which King has required to occur at the old Manton house. Rosser, whose second is King, is so scared that he rushes out clad only in his underwear and is driven away by King and Sancher.

"THE RURAL PRESS" (1868, 1873, 1911). Essay. (Original title: "The Country Paper"; later title: "Pastoral Journalism.") Rural editors will be glad when they can quit writing about types of vegetables and turn for subject matter to farm animals. Country newspapers are full of "the deep void of . . . nothingness." No startling, hurtful news. As one holds such a paper, one hears soothing country sounds and begins to drowse, seemingly far from the noisy city.

S

SALA, GEORGE AUGUSTUS (1828–1896). (Full name: George Augustus Henry Sala.) Journalist and author. He was born in London. His father died the year of the boy's birth. His mother became a self-supporting singer and actress, taught her precocious son French, and encouraged his ability to write and draw. He painted theater scenes (1845–1848), illustrated books, taught himself to etch, and published his own comic-picture guidebook for tourists (1850). More artistic work, including lithographs, followed. Sala wrote articles for a variety of periodicals (1848–1858), including *Household Words* and *All the Year Round*, both of which were published by Charles Dickens, who dispatched him to Russia to cover the Crimean War (1856). Sala republished some of his essays as books; wrote huge, serialized novels and republished them in book form (1859–1863); and did editorial work. He sent weekly contributions to the *Illustrated London News* (1858–1886) and the *Sunday Times* (1886–1894). Some of these pieces, called "Echoes of the Week," reappeared as books. Sala was a foreign correspondent in the United States during part of the Civil War (1863–1864) and later on (1879–1880, 1884–1885), and also in Algiers (1865), often on the continent (between 1865 and 1883), and in Australia and around the world (1885). In 1892 he founded *Sala's Journal*, a weekly that lost money. Although he estimated his annual income at £2,000 from 1863 to 1883, his lavish lifestyle occasionally caused him financial embarrassment. In addition to books on specific travels, he wrote three comprehensive autobiographies—*Things I Have and People I Have Known* (1892), *Life and Adventures* (1892), *The Life and Adventures of George Augustus Sala* (2 vols., 1895)—and a good cookbook (1895). Sala was married twice. His first wife, who married him in 1859, died while she was with him in Australia. He remarried in 1891.

Soon after arriving in London in 1872, Bierce met Sala and through him Tom Hood,* the London humorist. They soon comprised the core of a

hard-drinking group often meeting at the Ludgate railway station bar. After John Camden Hotten,* the disreputable London publisher, died in 1873, Bierce, Sala, and other cronies met at their bar, drank, and concocted epitaphs for the disliked deceased. Sala's "Hotten/Rotten/Forgotten" was considered the best. Bierce greatly admired Sala's polylingual scholarship, versatility, conversational sparkle, and drinking prowess. On the other hand, Sala with amiable candor told Bierce that he was essentially "a colonial" which no posturing as a clubbable man in London could change. An anecdote has it that Sala met President Abraham Lincoln and his wife at a White House function and criticized his hostess in print. Bierce warned Sala, in a jest taken seriously at first, that Robert Todd Lincoln, then minister to England, was looking for Sala with a bowie knife. Much later, Bierce generously profiled Sala in a *Wasp* column (14 February 1885).
Bibliography: De Castro, Fatout, Morris, O'Connor.

SALLY MEEKER. In "A Providential Intimation," this is the name of a race horse. She is owned by Sim Salper, who also owns a mine he has named after her. Thinking that Sally Meeker is a valuable horse, Stenner encourages the Rev. Mr. Boltright to buy her. Instead, Boltright invests in stock in Salper's mine, which rises in value when a strike is made there. In a race, Sally Meeker the horse breaks her neck.

SALPER, SIM. In "A Providential Intimation," he is the owner of a race horse named Sally Meeker and also a mine he has named after her. His horse breaks her neck, but he strikes it rich in his mine.

SAM. In "The Difficulty of Crossing a Field," he is Armour Wren's servant, described as "a little black boy." Sam's significance in the story is inexplicable. He takes charge of the team of carriage horses when Wren discovers his neighbor Williamson's disappearance, which the boy also notices.

"THE SAMPLE COUNTER" (1890, 1903, 1904, 1905, 1907, 1912). Essay. (Originally parts of "Extracts from the Best-Selling Novels of This Afternoon," "Passages from the 'Best-Selling' Books," and "Small Contributions.") Bierce satirizes inaccurate historical novels and foolish sentimental novels. Bits from nine historical novels concern Caesar and Scipio Africanus sweeping past Horatius and entering Rome; Napolean killing himself in Russia; a crusader killing seven Saracens and thus delivering Jerusalem; Bismarck letting an amorous traitor escape; Madame de Maintenon flirting with Wellington, after Blenheim; Henry of Navarre agreeing to let God wreak vengeance, only to be shot in the head; Richelieu eavesdropping as the king plots his assassination; Pompey excoriating Cicero, the defeated warrior, who is then killed in the Forum by Marcus Aurelius and other senators; and Cromwell ending the War of the Roses by besieging Worcester and beheading King Charles.

Twenty-one snippets are from sentimental tales. Nobleman averts his gaze as lady weeps, hugs him. Frenchman apologizes, lets lady leap into river, rescues her. Lady repents spurning "Invisible Knight" when his heel crunches gravel path. Duke ponders whether he would be wise to give up ancestral lands and flee to Rome with queen. When heroine hears bad news and swoons, lover follows etiquette, steals away. At Alpine sunset, lover walking along Riviera agrees to tell beautiful woman something later, when they are not alone. Man recovers female suicide's body from watery grave, tenderly throws it at feet of current beloved, and both pray. When baron withdraws declaration of love and woman friend leaps to death on rocks below, physician says she is dead, whereupon baron strides off. When timid man kneels, tells wordless lady of his love, she cannot reply because she is dead. Man and woman discuss her ideals; she looks at painting; he mentions golf; insect is on nearby screen. Man analyzes his heart in conscience's laboratory, thinks of countess and her count, hears her footstep. After lady stares, gentleman averts eye, stammers. Couple ponder whether they knew one another in a previous life; bird sings. Lady reports her father just back from India; duke, who has asked her about her money, says he attended her father's funeral in India. As lady dies, she asks Paul's uncle to tell Paul she loves him, will await him in heaven, whereupon uncle says, "Hay?" Nice girl spurns proposals from noblemen because she would prefer member of labor union. After seeing Wroth shoot Miss Mercer and her lover Harold dodge next bullet, let's flash back to when Miss Mercer rejected Wroth. One man sees another galloping toward battle scene, and withdraws his objection to the marriage. Demure lady answers earl's expression of love by nodding her head, watches him walk away, and goes to ballroom for ecstatic waltz. Wondering what she ever saw in fellow whose corpse reveals "impulchritude," lady tosses her knife into lake. Lady says man's statement of his love overcomes her doubts.

Bierce may have been inspired to write these spoofs by *Condensed Novels and Other Papers* (1867) by his friend Bret Harte,* who started his popular parody series with one on Victor Hugo's *Fantine* in an 1862 *Golden Era* issue and continued it in the *Californian*. Bierce, however, needed no spur, since he despised current popular fiction for romantically distorting history and for gushing over feelings better left under control. He rejoiced in creating such stylistic doozies as the following: Napoleon's "last die had been cast to the winds"; a "dreadful sound . . . was growing fainter and fainter, like herself"; "neither [lover] inaugurated a conversation"; "The full moon was rising in the east, for the hour was midnight . . . [and] the sky . . . [was] so blue"; "the lattice of the piazza"; "the hand of death had stepped in"; "the cricket droned among the glow-worms underfoot"; and Wroth was "embarking for Europe in another tongue." Bierce makes up fine titles, for example, *Lance* *and Lute* and *La Bella Damn*. His characters' names are also challenging: thus, Sir Guy de Chassac de Carcassonne; Hertha, Henry, and Minetta; Mrs. Rorqual and D'Anchovi; and Captain Gerard (with "the bar-semester in his crest").

SANCHER. In "The Middle Toe of the Right Foot," he is a friend of King and Rosser. While the three are talking at the hotel in Marshall, Rosser sees a stranger calling himself Robert Grossmith eavesdropping. Rosser insults the man and is challenged. When Sancher cannot prevent a duel, he agrees to act as the stranger's second. But at the duel site, which King arranges to be at the old Manton house, the stranger dies of fright, whereupon King and Sancher drive Rosser away quickly. (Grossmith is really Manton, the murderer.)

SATAN. In "Hades in Trouble," he is the majestic ruler of Hades. He and his fellow devils, including Beelzebub, Belial, Mammon, and Moloch, are bored in peaceful Pandemonium. But when Satan goes to the earth and tempts Eve, he becomes so troubled by her wiles that he sends his son, Nick, with a message back to Hades to beseech his cohorts to come to the earth and rescue him. To date, they have not succeeded.

SAYLOR, HENRY. In "A Fruitless Assignment," he is a reporter for the Cincinnati *Commercial*. His city editor tells him to go spend a night in the Roscoe house on Vine Street, which is deserted and presumed to be haunted. Saylor proceeds there and sees—or imagines he sees—a crowd outside, a woman's decapitated head upstairs, and a jeering crowd upstairs, which kicks the head about and disappears. In the morning, however, he tells his inquiring editor that nothing happened.

SCANDRIL, JEFFERSON. In "Mr. Masthead, Journalist," he lives in Weedhaven, Kansas, and is the brother-in-law of Johnson, the owner of the *Claybank Thundergust of Reform*. Johnson bought the Kansas weekly newspaper to publish attacks on Scandril and defeat him in his bid for the legislature. Johnson hires Masthead as his editor, to assist in this endeavor.

SCARRY. In "A Holy Terror." *See* Murphy, Manuelita.

SCHEFFAUER, HERMAN GEORGE (1878–1927). San Francisco author. An immigrant from Bavaria, Scheffauer regarded Bierce as a mentor, and Bierce got Scheffauer's first poem published in the *San Francisco Examiner*. Scheffauer called Bierce "Thor" and "Magister" but once enraged Bierce by comparing him to Jonathan Swift. Bierce preferred to think of himself as incomparable. Scheffauer, whom Bierce referred to as "Scheff" when they were on friendly terms, wrote a poem titled "The Sea of Serenity," which so pleased Bierce that he reported in a "Prattle" column—as a hoax—that the poem was a recently discovered work by Edgar Allan Poe. When the joke backfired through public indifference, Bierce wrote a follow-up column blaming Scheffauer for the idea. Still, Bierce continued to try to advance Scheffauer's publishing career. In 1903, Scheffauer and George Sterling,* another poet friend of Bierce's, planned the publication of Bierce's *Shapes of Clay*. Sterling provided money, while Scheffauer designed the cover. In 1904 Bierce and Scheffauer went to New York and also Saybrook, Connecticut, to see Percival Pollard,* a critic who had praised Bierce's fiction. Scheffauer journeyed on to Europe and North Africa, and sent Bierce postcards and also long letters telling about his affairs with women. This offended Bierce, as did his correspondent's conceit. In 1906 the relationship between the two became frosty. A year later, Scheffauer promised to behave himself and Bierce promised to forgive him. But in 1908, Scheffauer made negative pronouncements about Bierce's worth as an uneducated critic both to New York publisher Walter Neale* and to Sterling, with whom Scheffauer associated at Sterling's colony for writers and artists in Carmel, California. When Bierce learned about Scheffauer's remarks, some of which were relayed to him by Neale, he put an end to their friendship (by a letter on 10 January 1909) but did continue to praise the man's writing, especially two of his gloomy poems about death, "The Sleepers" and "Miserere." (*See* Bierce's "Writers of Dialect.") One of the last essays Bierce read was Scheffauer's "The Death of Satire" (*Fortnightly Review*, June 1913), in which Bierce is lauded; from Washington, D.C., he wearily wrote a friend named Amy Wells (5 August 1913) that he did not care how dead satire was.

Scheffauer's two books of verse are *Of Both Worlds: Poems* (1903) and *Looms of Life: Poems* (1908, published by Neale). He continued his writing career in Europe. He translated works by several German authors, including Heinrich Heine and Thomas Mann. His *Debates and Differences* (Amsterdam, 1919) reprints his essays on G. K. Chesterton, John Galsworthy, and H. G. Wells, among other items. He issued postwar diatribes against America, including *The German Prison-House: How to Convert It into a Torture-chamber: Suggestions to President Wilson* (Berlin, 1919) and *Blood Money: Woodrow Wilson and the Nobel Peace Prize* (Hamburg, 1921), and wrote *The New Vision in the German Arts* (London, 1924) and much else. He sometimes used R. L. Orchelle and Sagittarius as pseudonyms. In a hotel in Berlin in 1927 he murdered his woman companion—she was his wife, according to one account—and then committed suicide (either by poison or by jumping out the window, depending on the account).

Bibliography: Grenander, McWilliams, Morris, Neale, Joshi and Schultz, Starr.

SCOTTY, BOB. In "A Providential Intimation," he is the owner of Lightnin', a horse.

"THE SCOURGE OF LAUGHTER" (1911). Essay. Since laughter causes wrinkles, we should watch out. We often laugh without cause. Often, however, there are causes that provoke proper laughter, for example, a politician saying that he works for the public good, or a pig standing on its head. But by vigilance we can subdue chuckles at such events by avoiding them. Read the comics and shun editorials rebuking current commercialism, and you will stop laughing and your face will retain its "pristine smoothness."

SEARING, LIEUTENANT ADRIAN. In "One of the Missing," he is Private Jerome's brother. Both are in the Union Army. Adrian commands the picket line through which Jerome passed one morning on a scouting mission. On the evening of the same day, Adrian finds Jerome's body, cannot recognize it as that of his brother, and concludes that the stranger has been dead a week.

SEARING, MRS. JEROME. In "One of the Missing," she is the wife of Private Jerome Searing, who fantasizes about her and their children when he is trapped in the collapsed barn.

SEARING, PRIVATE JEROME. In "One of the Missing," he is a brave orderly and scout in the Union Army. Ordered to probe the enemy position near Kennesaw Mountain, Georgia, and report his findings, he makes his way to a position near a delapidated barn and is about to fire on the retreating Confederate forces when an artillery shell collapses the barn on top of him. Almost totally pinioned and unable to extricate himself, he is frightened when he sees the muzzle of his cocked Springfield rifle pointed right at him, fantasizes about his wife and their children, and is plunged into agony. He manages to press a loose board against the trigger to end his uncertainty. No explosion follows, since the rifle discharged when it fell. But Jerome, dead of shock, is so altered in appearance by absolute terror that when his brother, Lieutenant Adrian Searing, finds him, he cannot recognize Jerome, and says he must be dead a week. Earlier, Adrian checked his watch twice: the artillery shell hit the barn at 6:18 p.m., and he found the corpse twenty-two minutes later. It has been ingeniously suggested that Bierce puns on "Searing," since "sear" is a gunlock catch, while Searing is a "seer," prophetic at one point about his own fate.
Bibliography: Davidson.

"THE SECRET OF MACARGER'S GULCH" (1891). Short story. (Characters: Elderson, Janet MacGregor, Thomas MacGregor, Morgan, Mrs. Morgan.) One summer day in 1874, Elderson, who is the narrator, is hunting quail in the Sierra Nevada foothills. In Macarger's Gulch he finds a one-room cabin, deserted and in ruins. Fond of solitude and the night, he builds a fire inside, roasts a quail, has a little red wine, and prepares to sleep.

He soon feels uneasy, points his loaded shotgun at the empty doorway, rests only fitfully, and has a dream. In his dream, he is seeking someone unknown but a person he will recognize, in a foreign city. In a stone house, he sees a stout, fine-eyed young woman and a dark man with an evil, diagonally scarred face. He is certain that the two are married. Awakening, he is aware that the city he dreamed of is Edinburgh, which he has never visited, and says involuntarily that the MacGregors must have come here from Edinburgh. The fire emits a final flame, and he hears a thud like that of a body falling, then hears a woman's dying scream and gasp. By the light of his stirred-up fire he notes that the cabin is undisturbed.

Years later Elderson meets a man named Morgan in Sacramento, through a mutual friend from San Francisco. Dining at the Morgans's home one night, he observes trophies mounted on the walls and asks whether Morgan ever hunted near Macarger's Gulch. Morgan, saying yes, tells him how a year ago he and a companion found a shawl-wrapped skeleton there under the floor boards of a blown-down shanty. They told reporters about it. Elderson says that he was away and hence missed reading about the discovery. Morgan terrifies Elderson by adding that the name Macarger is a corruption of the name MacGregor. Authorities determined that the deceased was Janet MacGregor, killed by blows from a person unknown but thought to be her husband, Thomas MacGregor, of Edinburgh. They found his photograph in the shanty, revealing a man with an evil, diagonally scarred face.

This macabre tale, with many hints as to the nature of dreams, is livened by comic touches. For example, unnerved by Morgan's revelations, Elderson drops his wine glass, deposits a chicken bone in his finger bowl, and puts pepper in his coffee—all of which Morgan tactfully comments on.

SECRETARY OF WAR, THE. In "Jupiter Doke, Brigadier-General," he receives in Washington mostly incorrect reports from the battlefield.

SEEMAN, JO. In "A Holy Terror." *See* Porfer. ("Jo." is the form of Seeman's first name.)

SEIDEL, MAJOR. In "A Baffled Ambuscade," he is a Union Army cavalry officer. One night soon after the Stones River battle, Major Seidel is leading a small group of soldiers toward the Confederate lines when he alone sees Trooper Dunning, one of his sentinels, in a road near a forest of cedars. Dunning is standing over his dead horse and what appears to be a dead enemy soldier. Dunning silently warns Seidel back and points toward a forest of cedars. In the morning, Seidel and his men find Dunning, long dead and lying on his horse. There is evidence that Confederate soldiers were hidden among the cedars to ambush Seidel's forces. Seidel is based on Major Charles

B. Seidel, with whom Bierce served on an abortive ambuscade in the spring of 1863 outside Murfreesboro.
Bibliography: Morris.

"THE SENTIMENTAL BACHELOR." *See* "A Just Decision" and "The Lion's Den."

767. In "The Moonlit Road." *See* Hetman, Joel.

"SEX IN PUNISHMENT." *See* "Some Features of the Law."

"THE SHADOW ON THE DIAL" (1879, 1888, 1893, 1894, 1895, 1900, 1901, 1903, 1909, 1912). Essay. Brutes dissatisfied with politics turn either to socialism (total government management) or anarchy (abolition of all law). We now live somewhere between these two forms. Authority is now under attack, the end being lawless chaos. Anarchists, if they mutilate, incite to kill, or kill, should be mutilated in response and then executed. Why not? Should those who would destroy law enjoy legal protection? Two persons living together, a family living together, a state of citizens living together—all need laws. Laws are, however, "faultily administered." Some forms of "socialism" are needed, for example, the postal system and public ownership of certain utilities. Jean Paul Pierre Casimir-Périer (1847–1907) was "manly," and exemplary as well, to resign as president of France (1894) in the face of slander and insults. American leaders are not slandered much; they are usually "so bad that calumniation is a compliment." The world is drifting toward socialism, because no government has been good. The only "real government[s are] . . . absolute Monarchy and absolute Democracy"; either, when "limited," is "futile." Governments not protecting life are "flat failure[s]." In America, lives are insecure and murderers are treated indifferently, all because the masses, with "dark understanding and criminal instincts," are inimical to the civilizing processes that a good despot would insist on. Our successful American Revolution prevented us from valuing aristocratic leadership rightly. Our government fails to repress disintegrating forces within. Mobs become too powerful, and their success invites foreign anarchists and their decivilizing actions. Our government will devolve from rioting to discontent with military authority, killings, divisive popular parliaments, ruin, the emergence of a "man on horseback," and warfare. These predictions are like those the gods told Cassandra—also not believed.

THE SHADOW ON THE DIAL AND OTHER ESSAYS (1909). Essays. This book was assembled by Bierce's friend Silas Orrin Howes,* with whom Bierce entrusted his files of newspaper items. It is thought that Howes provided titles for some of the essays. Counting "The Shadow on the Dial," the collection contains nineteen essays of varying merit. The book sold poorly.

Nevertheless, all but one of these essays, together with twenty-two other essays, were reprinted as *Antepenultimata*, volume 11 (1912) of *The Collected Works of Ambrose Bierce* (1909–1912).

SHAPES OF CLAY (1903). The second collection of poems by Bierce in book form. It was surreptitiously financed (for $600) by the poet George Sterling,* Bierce's friend at the time. Another temporary friend, the poet Herman George Scheffauer,* designed the cover of the book. Largely culled from Bierce's newspaper and magazine files, the poems are divided here into "Shapes of Clay" and "Some Ante-Mortem Epitaphs." The title of the book, inspired by the image in "Once more within the Potter's house alone / I stood, surrounded by the shapes of Clay," from *The Rubaiyat* of Omar Khayyam, was suggested to Bierce by his friend Gertrude Atherton.* Bierce, who dedicated the book to Scheffauer and Sterling, was annoyed when in 1904 he learned of Sterling's generosity. The collection earned no money, and it took Bierce years to reimburse Sterling. It would have fared better if Bierce had not insisted on including much of his second-rate poetry, on the grounds that he wanted to be fully represented—not by his good verse alone but by his average stuff as well. The San Francisco fire of 1906 destroyed the plates and most of the unsold copies of *Shapes of Clay*. A few years later, *Shapes of Clay* provided most of volume 4, published in 1910, of *The Collected Works of Ambrose Bierce*, issued by Bierce's friend and publisher Walter Neale.* Many of the poems assembled in *Black Beetles in Amber* (1892) are better than most of the verse in *Shapes of Clay*. When Neale wanted to reissue *Shapes of Clay* in 1910, Bierce reorganized the contents, omitted some of the poems, including some from *Black Beetles in Amber*, and altered the last part, which he titled "The Scrap Heap." *See also* Poetry of Bierce.
Bibliography: Fatout, McWilliams.

SHARPER, DR. In "A Watcher by the Dead." *See* Harper, Dr.

SHAW, WILLIAM. In "The Stranger," he committed suicide in the cavern when trapped by Apaches.

SHERMAN, GENERAL WILLIAM TECUMSEH (1820–1891). U.S. military officer. Sherman was born in Lancaster, Ohio, graduated from the U.S. Military Academy at West Point in 1840, and in 1861 became a brigadier general of volunteers during the Civil War. After taking part in many crucial battles, he marched eastward through Georgia and from Atlanta to the Atlantic Ocean in 1864. Sherman replaced Ulysses S. Grant in 1869 as commander-in-chief of the army, until his retirement in 1884. Bierce would agree with Sherman's famous 1880 pronouncement that "War is hell." In "One of the Missing," Sherman is identified as the general in command of Union forces outside Kennesaw Mountain, Georgia. A general under Sherman orders Private Jerome Searing to scout out the Confederate forces beyond the Union picket lines and report back to him.

"A SHIPWRECKOLLECTION" (1874). (Original title: "Cruise of the 'Mudlark.' ") Short story. (Characters: Captain Abersouth, Madame Fahertini, Count von Pretzel.) When the narrator leaves home, a certain woman says she hopes he will not return. He sets sail with Captain Abersouth of the *Mudlark*. Because Abersouth will not state his destination and loads the ship with novels he wants to read, the ship has few passengers and less cargo. Some passengers get seasick, which amuses the healthy narrator. The rather idle crew plays cards, the prize being a pair of leather-bottomed pants. A storm interrupts Abersouth's reading. To lighten the *Mudlark*, he lets the narrator throw heavy passengers overboard. When a pretty girl wants her lover, Henry, to be spared and suggests throwing her mother overboard instead, the narrator tosses both the old woman and Henry over the side. He says he could add that he stole a lifeboat, spirited the girl away, married her in Fiji, and then ate her—but he did not. Instead, Abersouth heaves the narrator over. Visions of his past flash by—his cradle, schoolmaster, nurse, brother, sister, parents. Suddenly his feet hit bottom, and he is saved.

"THE SHORT STORY" (1892, 1897, 1911). Essay. (Original title: "Short Story versus Novels.") Edgar Fawcett (1847–1904) wrongly says that short stories cannot present interactions of characters and implies their inferiority to novels. But every novel is too long for its unity to be grasped. The novel is a faulty art form, with "no permanent place in literature." It often merely reports. Novelists can write well, surely, just as epic poets have done; but novelists and epic poets alike should have shortened their works. Stories in contemporary magazines provoke neither thought nor emotion, but instead are exclusively sentimental. The master of this school is William Dean Howells.* Lacking imagination, he takes notes and writes them up. He is too busy as a critic and a novelist. His vocabulary is unruly. When he looks at a given subject, he reports on it wrongly. Magazine fiction is vacuous, as proved by Christmas stories, which are always dull. Why should uninteresting real-life events be interesting if written up? Followers of "Cato Howells" write exclusively of the probable, unaware that truth can be stranger than their fiction. Suppose a novelist writes that a disappointed lover commits suicide not by drowning in the bay but by finding a tug there and throwing himself into its fire-hold furnace. Critics would say that the event defied probability. But just such a suicide happened in San Francisco. If a writer relates "the impossible," he has simply moved from realism to romance, and into the company of Daniel Defoe, Nathaniel Hawthorne, and those who wrote the *Arabian Nights*—and also into the company of historians.

"SHORT STORY VERSUS NOVELS." *See* "The Short Story."

"A SINFUL FREAK." *See* "The Baptism of Dobsho."

"SLEEP" (1892, 1911). Essay. (Original title: "Will the Coming Man Sleep?") Sleep is not "a natural function." Our remote ancestors, before the invention of light-producing devices, slept a lot simply because it was dark a lot and there was nothing else to do. It was hard for them to pursue and brain each other in the dark. With much more light now, we sleep less; city folks, having a good deal of light, sleep less than people in rural areas. Since we often perform certain actions out of habit rather than necessity, we sleep too much of the time not only out of habit but also despite having plenty of light to illuminate "malign activity." City citizens are now addicted to insomnia's joys. However, the city's drinking water is now hurt by "solution of dog and hydrate of husband." If lighting systems invade farm regions, plants, which do not sleep, will flourish and force farmers to include night shifts in their regimen.

"SMALL CONTRIBUTIONS." *See* "The Sample Counter," "A Strained Relation," and "A White House Idyl."

SMITH, JOHN K. In "The Man Out of the Nose," this was the name John Hardshaw used when he was arrested in Sacramento, charged with stealing Elvira Barwell's miniature portrait, and sentenced to a three-year prison term in San Quentin. *See* Hardshaw, John.

"THE SOCIALIST—WHAT HE IS, AND WHY" (1910, 1911). Essay. Many a man, born rebellious against almost everything, turns singlemindedly to socialism. He is unreasonable, incurable. After the anarchist demands the end of laws, the socialist follows to opt that law is all we have. The socialist fears that luxuries are perilous. In truth, a clean and healthy rich man can outfight and outprogeny a hulking worker and his underfed wife. But the rich are envied. Most youths start out equally poor. The poor used to be proud of our few millionaires, but now there are too many millionaires. The socialist wrongly believes that the world's wealth is a fixed number, that the rich live off the poor. But, truly, the poor live off the rich. The socialist reviles both the wealthy man who spends lavishly and the wealthy man who is stingy. The United States is so attractive that millions migrate here, aware of opportunities to become rich men—only to be reviled for their success. Moreover, the socialist approves of the policy of "sentimentaliters and ef-femininnies" to "coddle . . . the felon," and also argues that punishment does not deter crime. A few socialists have minimal brain power, but most of them are motivated by envy and revenge. Perhaps we should cap private fortunes at a certain figure.

"SOCIETY NOTES." *See* "Our Smart Set."

"SOLDIERS AND GHOSTS." *See* "A Baffled Ambuscade" and "Two Military Executions."

"A SOLE SURVIVOR" (1890, 1909). Essay. (Full title: "A Sole Survivor: A Lonesome Sort of Business in Which to Engage.") Bierce says that the art of surviving is of interest. Some survive by avoiding accidents; others, by having good health. Many old people are thought to have barely escaped a sequence of disasters, but not so. Bierce never experienced a close call in a railroad crash, a flood, a plague of widespread disease, a fire, or the like. True, he "once followed the perilous trade of a soldier." He remembers that of three men, one of whom wanted to be rich, another to be president, only he, the third, is now alive. He remembers that of six men on horseback at the onset of a well-remembered military engagement, only he survived. Of a sequence of women he knew, all are "chill under the daisies"; he names four, then discreetly stops, since "one would [should] not survive and tell." He remembers being with three companions, General William B. Hazen,* the famed black mountain-man Jim [James Pierson] Beckwourth (1800?–1866?), and one other, out West, surrounded by wolves, including some "of the variety known as Sioux." Only Bierce has survived. He reminisces about writers he knew in London. All were "agreeable, hospitable, intelligent, amusing." He could now serve dinner to all of them on his desk. Bierce refers to John Camden Hotten,* a London publisher who pirated non-British writers and who also owed Bierce a hundred pounds. Hotten's partner finally gave Bierce a check signed and postdated by Hotten, who died before Bierce could rush to the bank and cash it ahead of news of Hotten's death. On the way, Bierce paused to drink at a taproom. Present were several men of letters. The mellow fellowship included Tom Hood,* writer, illustrator, and editor of *Fun*; Thomas Mayne Reid (1818–1883), Irish-American novelist; Henry Sampson (1841–1891), owner of *Fun* (1874–1878); and George Augustus Sala,* journalist and author. The roisterers attended Hotten's funeral, and all except Bierce are now dead, he notes. He recalls transporting $30,000 in Black Hills mining funds by wagon in 1880, from Deadwood to Sidney, Nebraska. His armed guard, Boone May, was a marksman both renowned and indicted for murder (but later acquitted). When a road agent tried to rob them, May reacted speedily. Bierce adds that May later died of fever in Brazil, and Bierce is the sole survivor. When Bierce escorted a lovely *prima donna* across the Atlantic Ocean to New York, he and other would-be lovers were losing out to a handsome, attentive Italian until, once in her New York hotel with her, Bierce discovered that the Italian was merely her servant. Bierce is aware that she now has "a permanent engagement Above" and hopes that her "servile wretch" is dead too. Bierce recalls a glorious dinner at a London tavern, replete with soup, white-bait, roast beef, sherry, port, Stilton cheese, walnuts, coffee, and cigars. One wine drinker sang a poem Bierce scribbled during the dinner. It was in praise of

Satan, "the greatest of gods" and of the seventy roads leading to Hell, which place he defined as "the best of abodes." Only Bierce of the seven diners has survived.

Bibliography: Joshi and Schultz; Morris.

"SOME ASPECTS OF EDUCATION" (1897, 1899, 1911). Essay. Ouida [Marie Louise de la Ramée (1839–1908)] favored allowing illiterates to migrate, because they make good servants. Although illiteracy does not aid one in voting or becoming a politician, neither does the ability to read and write make one intelligent. Often the literate read degrading stuff, which fans their conceit. After they rise, they either get shot or lead ignorant followers to revolt. In turn, those masses are resubjugated by small, intelligent minorities. This cycle is called "Progress," and America is now tripping toward it. Popular education is helpful in some ways, but it also "produces 'industrial discontent.' " The poor are lured into getting educated by being told they can thereby avoid labor, which is always tough but necessary and always impossible to make dignified despite sentimentalists' efforts. Those working with their heads may tell the others that head-work is harder than hand-work, but they do not renounce head- for hand-work. Tax-supported higher education results in overcrowding the professions. Industrial discontent is not caused alone by too much education, but rather in part also by female competition in the work force and by labor-saving machines that increase efficiency and hence unemployment. The well-educated fellow who finds it hard to get into his preferred line of work will not opt for manual labor but instead wedge himself into a profession and become unethical to survive. An American dictator ought to come along; he would abolish all institutions of learning except one or two universities. They would train scholars in original research and make them the best in the world. Enrollment numbers would be limited by rigorous entrance examinations.

"SOME DISADVANTAGES OF GENIUS" (1909, 1911). Essay. (Original title: "The Handicap of Genius.") The Melancholy Author tells the Timorous Reporter that a literary genius is sharply handicapped by his very genius, because no one understands him. Since his work impresses people as disagreeable, it is hard to get it published. Geniuses are ill-paid, for example, Edgar Allan Poe and Lafcadio Hearn (1850–1904); but after such writers die, there is a scramble for their leavings. A genius who gains prosperity does so through publicity and despite his genius. He "know[s] . . . things without having to learn them." He channels general ability to a specific end; but once acclaimed, he will be rebuked if he tries to exercise his indubitable versatility. Yet if he sticks with what the public likes, he will be called "written out." If a genius achieves popularity, he will be asked to repeat and not vary. For fear of being called a trespasser, a genius must not use aspects of a previous classic to create a new work. Jonathan Swift's masterpiece (*Gulliver's Travels*) prevents followers from writing about other travelers to other fictitious lands; also, after Bret Harte,* fiction about California mining camps was branded as plagiarism. Yet Poe is so splendid that his erring adorers would have us believe that he was the first to write about terrors and the supernatural. Originality, which is merely "a matter of manner," is wrongly demanded too often of fine writers and is mainly attempted by inferior writers. Bierce livens this ramble about genius by having the Reporter fall asleep, hear the liquored-up Author depart, and be glad he himself was called a genius by a fool.

"SOME FEATURES OF THE LAW" (1883, 1884, 1887, 1892, 1894, 1895, 1899, 1904, 1909, 1912). Essay. (Original titles of parts: "I Decline to Answer," "Sex in Punishment," and "To an Insolent Attorney.") Many little laws circumvent the intent of law. The right to appeal provides a chance of acquittal to those unjustly sentenced. Preliminary examinations allow defense attorneys to behave maddeningly. Refusal to testify surely implies a degree of guilt; yet it is right to permit a person to avoid self-incriminating admissions. Lawyers wrongly impute other vices to men who are nothing more than "loose . . . with . . . women." Disinterested liars can make fairly good witnesses. Attorneys ought to be cross-examined in court. Some lawyers "slander . . . the dead to defeat justice" and to line their own pockets. If prosecutors profess total belief in a defendant's guilt, his lawyer can pretend to be as certain of his innocence. Judges have no right to punish people in their courts for disrespectful statements. Decent, intelligent judges need no outmoded defenses; sadly, however, some judges are "chosen in the backrooms to tipple-shops." A law preventing only the "unsuccessful" person in a divorce case from remarrying is "unrighteous." Guilty women have historically been punished less severely than men convicted of the same crime; women, however, have often been punished dreadfully in the past—by being burned, drowned, smothered in mud, and even impaled. Recently, women have been subject to sentences identical to those of men for the same crime; juries, however, are reluctant to commit convicted women to punishment of any kind. It should not be legal for testators, "snug[ly in] . . . the grave," to threaten heirs with disinheritance. In truth, the dead no longer have any wishes. Judges and juries cannot always properly evaluate the testimony of witnesses, who sometimes lie or are coached by "conscienceless attorneys licensed to deceive." Permitting hearsay evidence may lead by chance to truthful revelations. It would be nice if jurors were "neither friendly nor hostile," and if judges were not "ignoramus[es]." The press can best serve the cause of justice, not by inuring the public to crime through overexposure, but by arguing in favor of "non-elective judges, well paid, powerful to command respect, and holding office for life or good behavior." What we have instead are "boss-made, press-ridden and mob-fearing judges."

"SOME PRIVATIONS OF THE COMING MAN" (1892, 1893, 1905, 1911). Essay. (Original titles of parts: "Concerning Noses," "The Decay of the Nose," "The Head of the Future," "Some Trivial Privations of the Coming Man.") We are losing our sense of smell. If we lose our noses, cartoonists will have less to caricature and will be distressed. Noses figure in history and literature. But they will disappear, and so will human hair. Organs have consciences and therefore allow themselves to disappear when they are of no further use. Bald men live longer and are more prosperous than nonbald men. Stone-Age savages had better teeth than moderns do; Celts, than old Romans; Romans, than moderns. People in the future will subsist on spooned food and long memories. This essay ranks close to Bierce's silliest.

SOMERS, FREDERIC MAXWELL (1850–1894). Journalist. He was born in Portland, Maine, graduated from the Massachusetts Agricultural College with a B.S. in 1872, taught school in Fairmount, Kansas, and then became a journalist in Leavenworth, Kansas. He moved to San Francisco in 1875, wrote for the *Chronicle* there, and in 1877 cofounded and began with Frank Morrison Pixley* to edit the *Argonaut*, soon to become a popular and influential weekly. Somers kept only a proprietary interest in the periodical in 1879, began to publish the monthly *California* in 1880, sold it quickly, started the *Epigram*, an afternoon daily, in 1880, but discontinued it when he fell ill. He traveled, was a successful stock broker in New York City and Chicago, and founded *Current Literature* in 1888 and *Short Stories* in 1890; he sold both of these successful periodicals in 1891. After extensive travel, he went to England to found yet another magazine but suddenly died there.

When Somers became editor of the *Argonaut*, Bierce signed on as assistant editor, serving until 1879. When Bierce returned to San Francisco in 1881, both Somers and Pixley were happy that the magazine had done well without the acerbic fellow and did not rehire him. Much later, when both cofounders of the *Argonaut* were dead and too effusively eulogized, Bierce said that they had received too much credit for its success and he too little.
Bibliography: De Castro, McWilliams, Morris.

"SOME TRIVIAL PRIVATIONS OF THE COMING MAN." *See* "Some Privations of the Coming Man."

"SOME UNCANNY TALES." *See* "An Arrest," "The Man with Two Lives," "A Vine on a House," and "A Wireless Message."

"SOME UNUSUAL ADVENTURES." *See* "The Man Overboard."

"A SON OF THE GODS: A STUDY IN THE PRESENT TENSE" (1888). Short story. (Character: General X.) One sunny day, a line of troops by some woods is facing the enemy, whose position and strength must be learned. To save the lives of skirmishers about to be ordered forward to see, a young officer on a white horse with a scarlet saddle blanket volunteers to ride on ahead. In silence the men watch as he approaches the forest ahead, goes toward a break in a wall and hedge, then turns to ride parallel to the unseen line. He leaps the hedge, observes, and returns to report. Sudden overwhelming enemy fire fells his horse. He stands erect, salutes with his sabre, and is killed. His comrades answer the enemy fire but soon withdraw. The soldier-narrator pronounces the hero a "militant Christ!" and "great soul"; but he also calls his sacrifice "a vain devotion." Then he asks, with a poignancy rare in Bierce, could not the self-sacrificial man's life have been spared as a "one exception" to "the pitiless perfection of the divine, eternal plan?"

Bibliography: Morris, Woodruff.

SPITTLEWORTH, LONGBO. In " 'The Bubble Reputation,' " he is a reporter, known by his editor only as 216, for the San Francisco *Daily Malefactor*. To gain fame, he maligns Inhumio, the superintendent of the Sorrel Hill cemetery, in grotesque reports about goings-on at his cemetery. By the name "Longbo Spittleworth," Bierce suggests both that some reporters bend the long bow and that their spewings are worthless.

SPLIT-FACED MOLL. In "A Holy Terror." *See* Porfer, Mary Matthews.

"THE SPOOK HOUSE" (1889). Short story. (Characters: Colonel J. C. McArdle, Judge Myron Veigh.) In 1858 or early 1859, a wooden plantation house on the road between Manchester and Booneville, Kentucky, is abandoned; the fields, fences, and outhouses, including "negro quarters," are all in ruins. In June 1859, a noisy lightning storm forces two men from Frankfort—Colonel J. C. McArdle, a lawyer, and Judge Myron Veigh, a state militiaman—to seek shelter in the old house. As soon as they enter, the place turns dark and silent. McArdle tries to retreat out the front door, but when opened it discloses an inner room, suffused in green light and containing eight or ten corpses. Veigh resolutely pushes in ahead of McArdle and examines one shriveled body. McArdle reels against the door, which clicks shut. Taken unconscious by strangers to Manchester, he comes to his senses six weeks later. Two months after that, he returns to Frankfort, and learns that Veigh has not been heard from since that fateful night in June. When the house is examined, the room McArdle says he entered is not found. Veigh's family disbelieves him and turns hostile toward him. McArdle is examined for insanity but is cleared of the charge. In 1862, the house, by then called the "Spook House," is still vacant. A year later, stragglers among Union Army soldiers under General George W. Morgan, retreating from an attack by General Kirby Smith's Confederate forces, burn the empty house to the ground. In the Frankfort *Advocate* on 6 August 1876, McArdle publishes his description of the "adventure." Bierce tries to heighten suspense by narrating events out of chronological order. He begins his account in 1862, moves ahead a year, backtracks "four or five years," then dates McArdle's actions as June 1859, and concludes by quoting his *Advocate* article of 6 August 1876. An unresolved question concerns the identity of the corpse that Veigh concentrated on.

SPOONY GLUM. In "The Man Out of the Nose," this was the cruel nickname that little boys used in talking about John Hardshaw when he and his wife were living in the Market Street area in San Francisco. *See* Hardshaw, John.

"THE S.P.W." (1911). Essay. Someone should organize the Society for the Protection of Writers. Too many people ask tiresome, discourteous, and costly favors of writers, including Bierce and Rudyard Kipling. Descriptions by Charles Dickens show how rude Americans can be.

"STAGE ILLUSION" (1878, 1911). Essay. Scenery painters and carpenters provide effects that the playgoer's imagination ought, as in the past, to supply.

"STALEY FLEMING'S HALLUCINATION" (1906). Short story. (Characters: Atwell Barton, Denneker, Staley Fleming, Dr. Halderman.) Staley Fleming summons Dr. Halderman to his house and tells him that every night now he is awakened and sees a black Newfoundland dog with a white forefoot looking at him "earnestly." He wonders if the physician can recommend "a specialist in psychopathy." Instead, Dr. Halderman says that the event is probably hallucinatory but adds that the dog would seem to resemble the late Atwell Barton's dog. Professing to remember Barton vaguely, Fleming recalls that the man's death was suspicious. Dr. Halderman sturdily reminds Fleming that Barton was Fleming's enemy and was found stabbed to death three years ago near Fleming's and Barton's adjacent houses. He adds that although no one was arrested, he has a theory and wonders if Fleming also has one. Fleming counters by saying that he went to Europe soon thereafter and has been back only a few weeks. When he asks about the dog, Dr. Halderman says that it found Barton's body and later starved to death on his grave. A distant dog howls. Fleming, after pacing about, says that Dr. Halderman must be forgetting why he was called here. So Dr. Halderman tells his patient to go to bed, leave the door unlocked, and ring for him if necessary. He will be reading downstairs. After dozing, he chances to be reading a passage in Denneker's *Meditations* about the interpenetrations of spirit and flesh in beasts as well as in humans, when a thud shakes the house. He rushes upstairs, breaks down Fleming's locked door, and finds the man dying of a throat wound. He believes it to be suicide until an examination discloses fang marks in the jugular but no animal.

STANFORD, LELAND (1824–1893). (Full name: Amasa Leland Stanford.) Railroad builder, politician, and philanthropist. He was born in Watervliet, New York, and attended the nearby Clinton Liberal Institute (1841–1844) and Cazenovia Seminary (1844–1845). He practiced law in Port Washington, Wisconsin (1848–1852), married Jane Lathrop in Albany, New York (1850), and became a successful businessman there and then in Sacramento, beginning in 1852. He helped organize the Republican party in Sacramento (1856). Although he worked successfully for the party, his efforts in politics failed until he was elected governor (1861–1863). In 1861, he also became president of the Central Pacific Railroad, in the days when conflicts of interest went unchallenged. Together with Charles Crocker,* Mark Hopkins,* and Collis P. Huntington* Stanford formed The Big Four,* which began controlling the railroads in and out of California. Leland Stanford Jr. was born in 1868. Stanford was part of the celebration party at Promontory Point, Utah, in 1869, when the Central Pacific and the Union Pacific linked. The Stanfords moved to San Francisco in 1874. In the course of the 1870s and 1880s, Stanford grew immensely, and ostentatiously, wealthy, aspired unavailingly for national political success, and collected horses on his Palo Alto ranch and art objects in his lavish San Francisco mansion. He served as president of the Occidental and Oriental Steamship Company (1878–1893). The Stanfords's son died of typhoid fever in Florence, Italy, in 1884, while touring Europe. His distraught parents began that year to found a university in his name. Stanford was president of Southern Pacific of Kentucky (1885–1890) and an undistinguished member of the U.S. Senate (1885–1893). He vainly sought the presidency in 1888 and again in 1892. In 1891 Leland Stanford Jr. University, in Palo Alto, opened. When Stanford died, the university was in financial jeopardy, because his many railroad company obligations were rendered tangled after his falling out with Huntington, who called the university "Stanford's circus."

As editor of the *Wasp* beginning in 1881, Bierce branded as "railrogues" the big three who remained after Hopkins's death, and went on bravely to label them indictable criminals, public enemies, freebooters, rascals, and thieves. In "The Birth of the Rail" (1881), a satirical verse drama, Bierce features Stanford as Leland the Kid, who leads fellow road agents Cowboy Chakey (Crocker) and Happy Hunty (Huntington). In Bierce's subsequent editorials, Stanford became "£eland $tanford" and "$tealand £andford." Other writers called him "Stealand Standfirm." The May 1880 fight at Mussel Slough, caused by the railrogues' demand that farmers leave or pay $35 an acre, not $5 as agreed, culminated in the killing of five settlers and two railroad thugs. Bierce penned the following quatrain: "Our fallen brave sleep

well; each keeps / This ground, where none besets him. / And well the fallen Stanford sleeps—/ When conscience lets him" (*Wasp*, 2 April 1881).
Bibliography: Hopkins; Lindley; Morris; Starr; St. Pierre, Norman E. Tutorow, *Leland Stanford: Man of Many Careers* (Menlo Park, Calif.: Pacific Coast Publishers, 1971).

STENNER. In "A Providential Intimation," he is a San Franciscan ne'er-do-well. He steals Algernon Jarvis's coat and finds a copy of a telegram in it. He misunderstands its message, "Buy Sally Meeker," as Jarvis's suggestion to a friend to buy a race horse named Sally Meeker. Stenner wins $100 at poker in Vallejo and sends it to the Rev. Mr. Boltright with the suggestion that he buy the horse. Instead, Boltright buys stock in a mine owned by Sim Salper and named after Sally Meeker, a horse Salper also owns. Boltright makes $25,000 when the stock rises but does not share his windfall with Stenner.

STERLING, GEORGE (1869–1926). (Full name: George Ansel Sterling II.) Poet. Sterling was born in Sag Harbor, on Long Island, New York. His family converted to Roman Catholicism in 1886, and Sterling enrolled in St. Charles College, in Ellicott City, Maryland, where he met John Bannister Tabb, a priest and teacher, whose love of poetry impressed him. Ignoring his parents' hope that he would be a priest, Sterling left college in 1889 and a year later moved to Oakland, California, to work for Frank C. Havens, his rich and generous uncle. Sterling met Joaquin Miller* in 1891 and through him joined the San Francisco Bohemians. In 1896 Sterling married Caroline Rand and began to write poetry in earnest. After he published *The Testimony of the Suns and Other Poems* (1903), he became a leading figure among the Bohemians. It began his tradition of writing verse with romantic imagery and content. He was friendly with a number of writers in the San Francisco area, including Ina Coolbrith,* Jack London,* Edwin Markham,* and Charles Warren Stoddard.* In 1903, Sterling and Herman George Scheffauer,* another friend of Bierce's, arranged for the publication of his *Shapes of Clay*. Sterling, aided with money from his uncle, built a home in Carmel, California, in 1905, and helped substantially in founding an art colony there. It soon flourished, especially after the San Francisco earthquake of 1906. Sterling, dubbed "the King of Bohemia" and then "the King of Carmel," published "A Wine of Wizardry" in *Cosmopolitan* (1907), which publishing magnate William Randolph Hearst* had recently purchased and for which Bierce was writing. With this poem Sterling gained national renown. Although his work was too indebted to the Victorian tradition in form, style, love of archaic diction, and emphasis on exalted topics—including weary awareness of evil and despair—he remained popular, especially among younger Bohemians. In 1907 Nora May French,* a beautiful but unstable poet and the Sterlings's friend, committed suicide in their home. She and

Sterling were probably not romantically linked, but gossipers were happy to hint otherwise. *A Wine of Wizardry and Other Poems* (1909) was followed by *The House of Orchids and Other Poems* (1911); the latter was the last collection in which he ignored modern verse trends. He sought more popular recognition with later occasional poems, for example, on the Panama Canal and on World War I; but it was too late. In 1914, Carrie Sterling divorced Sterling, who was long an unfaithful alcoholic. He left Carmel, moved to New York, failed to establish himself as a poet there, and returned to San Francisco in 1915. In 1918 Carrie committed suicide by taking cyanide. In his final tedious poetry, and in versified dramas as well, Sterling continued to express his personal pessimism, now aggravated by excessive drinking. He surprised few of his friends when he took his own life, dramatically—by cyanide in the room kept for him from about 1915 by an anonymous donor (now identified as Barbour Lathrop, a businessman) in San Francisco's Bohemian Club. Sterling's *Robinson Jeffers, the Man and the Artist*, published posthumously in 1926, championed the poet from Carmel, the beauty of which region Sterling had popularized earlier. Much of Jeffers's poetry was of the sort Bierce would have esteemed.

In 1892, Sterling met Bierce at Lake Temescal, near Oakland, at the camp of Bierce's brother Albert Bierce. Impressed by Sterling, Bierce invited him to lunch in San Francisco, and the two became friends. Bierce valued Sterling sufficiently to write him poignantly in 1901 about the death of Leigh Bierce,* Bierce's younger son. When Sterling began to produce serious poetry, he became Bierce's protégé, addressing him in their correspondence as "Magister" and "Master" and welcoming his advice—and compliments. Having arranged for "A Wine of Wizardry" to be published in *Cosmopolitan*, Bierce reviewed it there favorably, with unaccustomed irrationality. He called Sterling the greatest American poet "we have." Joaquin Miller, even more impressed, called Sterling the greatest poet since Dante. Soon Sterling was distancing himself from Bierce, who began to find the young man's personality offputting: Sterling could be narcissistic, tactless, affected, and too dependent emotionally. Oddly, Bierce not only was distressed by his inability to dominate Sterling any more but also despised Sterling's conduct toward his wife Carrie, not to mention his flirting with socialism. Bierce evidently also resented Sterling's preference for the friendship of Jack London. Russ Brissenden, the poet in London's *Martin Eden* (1909), is partly based on Sterling. In 1910, Sterling introduced London to Bierce. In the summer of 1911, Bierce, ailing and sad, visited Sterling in Sag Harbor but evidently was not treated hospitably. It seems safe to say that Bierce liked Sterling until the young man gained fame and grew independent. Very likely, Bierce's semisuicidal disappearance into Mexico may have had a part in Sterling's decision to kill himself. London's apparent suicide was certainly an influence. (*See also* "An Insurrection of the Peasantry" and "A Poet and His Poem.")

Bibliography: Thomas E. Bendiktsson, *George Sterling* (Boston: Twayne Publishers, 1980); J. R. Dunbar, "Letters of George Sterling to Carey McWilliams," *California*

Historical Society Quarterly 46 (Summer 1967): 235–252; Horace Gregory and Marya Zaturenska, *A History of American Poetry 1900–1940* (New York: Harcourt, Brace and Company, 1946); Grenander; Dalton Gross, "George Sterling: King of Carmel," *American Book Collector* (October 1970): 8–15; McWilliams; Harriet Monroe, *A Poet's Life: Seventy Years in a Changing World* (New York: Macmillan Company, 1938); O'Connor; Starr; George Sterling, "The Shadow Maker," *American Mercury* 6 (September 1925): 10–19.

STEVENS, HENRY. In "One of Twins," he and John Stevens are identical twins. After their insolvent parents' death in San José, the twins move to San Francisco and obtain separate employment there. Henry is invited by mistake to dinner by Margovan, John's friendly office coworker. John goes, falls in love with Julia Margovan, the Margovans's beautiful daughter, and soon successfully proposes marriage to her. Henry sees Julia secretly meeting a dissipated stranger, lets her know about it, but says only that he will oppose her marriage "on other grounds." Somehow John learns about it, poisons Julia fatally, and kills himself. Much later, Henry sees the dissipated stranger, who dies trying to hit him. Henry writes a letter to Mortimer Barr, his psychologist, all about these events.

STEVENS, JOHN. In "One of Twins," he and Henry Stevens are identical twins. After their parents' death in San José, they get jobs in San Francisco. John goes to dinner at the home of Margovan, his friendly office coworker, meets Margovan's beautiful daughter, Julia Margovan, there, and soon proposes to her. Trouble ensues when Henry Stevens discovers Julia's apparent infidelity. John learns of this somehow, poisons Julia, and shoots himself to death.

STODDARD, CHARLES WARREN (1843–1909). Author. Stoddard was born in Rochester, New York. His father failed in business in 1851 and relocated to San Francisco. In 1859 young Stoddard began to work in a bookstore and publish poetry in the *Golden Era*. After developing a few literary friendships, including a lifelong relationship with fellow poet Joaquin Miller,* he made the first of many joyous visits to the Hawaiian Islands in 1864. In 1867 he published *Poems*, edited by Bret Harte.* Also in that year Stoddard became a Roman Catholic, returned to Maui, and sent various newspapers early examples of fine travel writing. For the next twenty years he was a curious combination of devout Catholic and quasi-pagan homosexual, traveling to Tahiti, Europe, and the Middle East, Honolulu again, and Europe again. The best of his travel books are *South-Sea Idyls* (1873), *Marsallah!: A Flight into Egypt* (1881), *Hawaiian Life: Being Lazy Letters from Low Latitudes* (1894), and *A Cruise Under the Crescent: From Suez to San Marco* (1898).

In between, while in London in 1873–1874 Stoddard associated with Joaquin Miller, Mark Twain*—as his secretary-companion—and other literary folk, including Bierce, whom he had already met in San Francisco in 1868. The two soon became drinking companions. When Bierce was courting Mary Ellen Day (*see* Bierce, Mary Ellen Day) in 1871, Stoddard played cards with the couple and the poet Ina Coolbrith,* their mutual friend. Bierce was familiar enough with Stoddard, and his sexual inclinations, to query him crudely by letter (29 December 1872) about loving " 'nigger' boy[s]" in Hawaii. When Stoddard first arrived in London, Bierce warned him by letter to "avoid any appearance of eccentricity" (28 September 1873). Stoddard naturally ignored the advice. During his stay in England, Bierce wrote Stoddard, often absent, a few letters in which he commented about his wife—this, contrary to his reticence about her in letters. Stoddard returned to San Francisco in 1878, and he and his "Biercy" had a permanent falling out, doubtlessly owing to Bierce's dislike of Stoddard's homosexuality.

After 1878, Stoddard continued to be unsettled. He taught at the University of Notre Dame (1885–1886), revisited Europe (1888–1889), taught at the Catholic University of America (1889–1902), freelanced, accepted the charity of friends, suffered worsening health, returned permanently to California (1905), and settled in Monterey. He met George Sterling,* the poet and Bierce's whilom protégé. Stoddard died before writing a planned autobiography, which might well have been a valuable social and literary document.

Bibliography: Roger Austen, *Genteel Pagan: The Double Life of Charles Warren Stoddard* (Amherst: University of Massachusetts Press, 1991); Robert L. Gale, *Charles Warren Stoddard* (Boise, Idaho: Boise State University Press, 1977); M. E. Grenander, "Ambrose Bierce and Charles Warren Stoddard: Some Unpublished Correspondence," *Huntington Library Quarterly* 23 (May 1960): 261–292.

"A STORY AT THE CLUB" (1886). Short story. (Original title: "Told at the Bohemian Club.") (Characters: Will Brady, John Doane, Dr. Dutton, Oopsie.) Dr. Dutton shows his friend Will Brady a newspaper report that John Doane of Peequeegan, Maine, has inherited $750,000 from the estate of a man he rescued from rowdies fifteen years earlier. Brady replies that back in 1892 in Peoria, Illinois, he rescued a man whose foot was perilously stuck in some railroad tracks when a train was approaching. In gratitude, the man promised to work hard, get rich, and leave his rescuer a fortune. Brady shows Dutton the card that he says the rescued man gave him. But the card is a love note signed Oopsie. Brady is about to name the rescued man, whom he describes as honorable, when Dutton pronounces the name Oopsie. Brady, nonplussed, adds that the rescued man died in 1901 and willed him $900,000. But Brady could not inherit, since, he explains, he died first. (Was Brady the other man in the life of Oopsie, the rescued man's wife? Did the man on the tracks plan to let himself be killed? Did Brady fake his death, making himself unable to inherit? The "Story at the Club" is a puzzling story.)

"THE STORY OF A CONSCIENCE" (1890). Short story. (Original title: "Dramer Brune, Deserter: A War Memory of the Cumberland Mountains.") (Characters: Dramer Brune, Captain Graham, Captain Parrol Hartnoy.) Captain Parrol Hartnoy of the Union Army is at a forward post of his pickets with a sergeant. Hartnoy is in charge of guarding a significant military column in Tennessee's Cumberland Mountains. Suddenly a man in "butternut" homestuff approaches, is halted, speaks with a Southern accent, and presents a pass of the sort Hartnoy has signed for friendly civilians in the nearby village. The stranger leaves; but Hartnoy, tardily recognizing him, rushes after him revolver in hand, calls him by name—Dramer Brune—and arrests him. Brune admits that he is a Confederate spy, adds that has detailed written intelligence about Hartnoy's forces on his person, and promises to accompany him quietly back to camp for "whatever penalty may be imposed." The next morning, the two men converse. Hartnoy reveals that he knew Brune had been a private from Ohio who deserted and joined the Confederates, was caught and sentenced to death, but escaped from his sleepy guard out of a railroad car at Grafton, Virginia. Brune then informs Hartnoy that he knows the guard who slept on duty was Hartnoy. This surprises Hartnoy. Brune says that he may be a traitor and is surely a spy, but he would never think of begging for his life. Hartnoy replies that Brune could have escaped from that railroad car and thus caused Hartnoy to be executed for dereliction of duty. Hartnoy weeps. The bugle calls assembly. Brune hastily reveals that he had a change of political thought and requested a discharge from the Federal forces but was punished instead. When Hartnoy expresses sorrow that events have put Brune "in the shadow and imminence of death," Brune is startled. Hartnoy orders Brune to be shot, and he is; then Hartnoy shoots himself to death. The two are buried without any military ceremony and now "sleep well."

Bierce, who was intrigued by the concept of suicide, would regard Hartnoy's as an example of an acceptable suicide. Bierce seems to undercut the seriousness of this parable by having Hartnoy begin a phase of his reminiscing to Brune with the shopworn cliché: "One dark and stormy night . . . a soldier was put on guard over you."
Bibliography: Morris.

"A STRAINED RELATION" (1907, 1912). Short drama. At the White House in October 1906, the president, upset by a report that Japanese children are being denied admittance to public schools in California, sends an official to investigate. In August 1907, the president grows terrified at news that some Japanese battleships are taking on coal in Tokyo. Several associates

of President Theodore Roosevelt,* including George Dewey, are involved in this silly skit.
Bibliography: St. Pierre.

"THE STRANGER" (1909). Short story. (Characters: The Captain, Berry Davis, Ramon Gallegos, George W. Kent, William Shaw, Sam Yountsey.) A half-dozen gentlemen adventurers, led by the Captain and including Sam Yountsey, are camping near the Gila River when a stranger walks in and offers to tell his story. Thirty years ago Ramon Gallegos, William Shaw, George W. Kent, and Berry Davis, all of Tucson, were seeking gold between Santa Clara and the Gila when attacking Apaches chased them into a dry little cavern. After three days, they decide to commit suicide to avoid capture and torture. First Gallego shoots himself, then Shaw, and then Kent. As the stranger concludes by explaining how he carefully laid out their bodies, Yountsey springs at him, outraged that he escaped, and would shoot him except that the Captain restrains him. The Captain explains that he himself saw the mutilated bodies of four white men at the cavern mouth, and that all four are now buried. One of the gentlemen campers, on guard, reports that three harmless men are standing outside. The stranger leaves. When Yountsey says that he ought to have shot the stranger, the Captain replies that the fellow is already as dead as possible.

"THE STRIKE OF 1899." *See* "The Great Strike of 1895."

"A SUCKED ORANGE" (1905, 1912). Short drama. (Originally part of "The Views of One.") President Theodore Roosevelt* and Elihu Root, his secretary of state, discuss the fact that, during discussions regarding the Open Door Policy, English and Japanese rulers made no mention of Roosevelt. The entire dialogue is in irregular anapestic hexameters. Roosevelt fulminates thus: "My sorrow / Has better foundation. King Edward of England has joined the Mikado / In making a shameless alliance to tighten their grip upon Asia!"

"THE SUITABLE SURROUNDINGS" (1889). Short story. (Characters: Charles Breede, James R. Colston, Willard Marsh.) A farmer's boy, living ten miles outside Cincinnati, has been chasing lost cows and is now returning home late through the dark Copeton forest. He comes upon Breede house, deserted and hence thought haunted. Looking through a blank front window, he sees a dead-looking man sitting motionless at a table, illuminated by a candle and with papers before him. When the boy bravely peers in and a screech owl cries out, the man springs up, knocks the table over, and blows out the light. Thinking he has seen a ghost, the boy runs home.

The day before, Willard Marsh, a businessman, was on a streetcar reading a ghost story by James R. Colston, just published in the *Messenger*. Colston, also aboard the streetcar, said that the only proper way to read his stories would be by candlelight, alone, at night. Sensing a dare, Marsh agreed to read something by Colston in a lonely place and with a candle for illumination. Colston said that he had the manuscript of a ghost story in his pocket; if thus read, it would actually kill Marsh. Marsh challenged Colston to put him in such a spot and call for him later. He would recite the plot and kick Colston out of the place.

The next day the farm lad, having told what he saw at the Breede house, leads three skeptical men back there. They find a dead man sprawled near a manuscript. One of the three men reads the first part of the manuscript aloud. In it Colston writes that he will kill himself at midnight on 15 July, since Charles Breede killed himself on that date four years earlier at his Copeton woods house and Colston pledged to commit suicide also. The man holding the manuscript reads the next part to himself. In the last part, which he reads aloud, Colston explains that he has a week to arrange his affairs and will leave this manuscript on his person at his death. But then in a postscript, addressed to Willard Marsh, he says that he will instead give Marsh the manuscript. It will explain the manner of Marsh's death. Colston concludes by saying that he will call on Marsh after Colston has killed himself. The man holding the manuscript then burns it—this despite the immediate objections by his auditors and a later rebuke by the coroner. The man who burned the manuscript was Breede's son-in-law.

The *Times* reports that Colston, the well-known local writer, was seen by a fellow lodger on the evening of 15 July stropping his razor and evidently about to slit his throat. He was immediately taken into custody and is now straitjacketed in the asylum.

In this curious story, the farm boy thinks that he has seen a ghost but has not. Marsh thinks that he has seen and heard dead Colston's ghost but has not. Colston figured that his story would kill Marsh, but the story was not the cause of his death. Colston plans to kill himself but does not. Readers ought to expect to learn what Breede's son-in-law kept to himself that was in Colston's manuscript, but they do not. Did Colston bother Breede's wife? Or Breede's daughter? Did Bierce himself believe in the transmigration of souls and therefore suggest that dead Colston became a live owl? Assuredly, Bierce through Colston is rebuking readers who do not take authors with a proper degree of seriousness.

Bibliography: Howard W. Bahr, "Ambrose Bierce and Realism," pp. 150–168 in Davidson, *Essays*; Davidson; Grenander.

"SUPERIOR KILLING: A STROLLING COMMENT ON A CERTAIN AMIABLE ERROR." *See* "Modern Warfare."

SUTRO, ADOLF (1830–1898). Developer and mining engineer. Sutro was born Adolph Heinrich Joseph Sutro in Aachen, Prussia. His father's death

in 1849 forced the family's lucrative wool-cloth factory to close. Political upheavals at the same time prompted the family to move to Baltimore in 1850. Proceeding alone, Sutro became a commission merchant and tobacconist in California. In 1855 he was slashed in the face by a bully who wrongly felt insulted. Sutro then alternately enjoyed and suffered a string of successes and disasters. He developed mine-engineering capabilities in Nevada's silver fields. His reduction mill, built in 1861, burned down two years later. Succeeding in mining-stock ventures, he planned what became the Sutro Tunnel to drain Virginia City mines of water seepage and to ventilate harmful gases from them. Beginning in 1865, he received financial help from the Nevada legislature, but California bankers soon blocked further advances. A disastrous mine fire in 1869 made Sutro's idea seem worthwhile; and elaborate financing, including a federal loan, enabled the six-mile tunnel to be completed in 1878. Sutro sold his shares in 1880, shortly before mining in the region began to play out. With immense wealth, he amassed a 200,000-volume library, built a lavish mansion on the San Francisco coast, bought the popular Cliff House restaurant and resort, and built the saltwater Sutro Baths. In 1894 he was elected mayor of San Francisco on a Populist ticket, but numerous squabbles made it seem a relief to avoid serving more than a single two-year term. Widowered in 1893 after thirty-seven years of marriage, Sutro died in 1898. What he bequeathed to his six children eventually proved valueless. Cliff House had burned down in 1894, and the Gothic palace he erected in its place burned down in 1907. His baths closed, burned, and were leveled. Fire after the 1906 San Francisco earthquake destroyed more than half of his library. The gardens and statuary of his estate, which had become a city park, were vandalized, and the mansion was ordered razed.

Bierce must have been gratified when in 1894 Mayor Sutro opposed Collis P. Huntington* and other Southern Pacific Railroad executives in their effort to have their massive debt to the federal government refunded to their dishonest advantage. Sutro called for Huntington's arrest, even as Bierce was calling for his conviction and suggesting that the "rogue" should be hanged. Sutro wrote President Grover Cleveland recommending foreclosure of the railroad's mortgages. Oddly, Gustav Danziger* asserted that Bierce was so jealous of anyone who also attacked Huntington, whom he regarded as his private quarry, that he actually disliked Sutro. The worst Bierce could manage to say about Sutro appears in a "Prattle" column (*San Francisco Examiner*, 4 October 1891), in which he criticizes members of the Women's Press Association in San Francisco who "kiss [up to] Adolph Sutro."

Bibliography: De Castro; Fatout; Joshi and Schultz; O'Connor; Robert E. Stewart, Jr., and Mary Frances Stewart, *Adolph Sutro: A Biography* (Berkeley, Calif.: Howell-North, 1962).

SWIDDLER. In "Mr. Swiddler's Flip-Flap," he is the narrator, a former circus acrobat. When he learns that his friend Jerome Bowles is to be executed in Flatbroke for shooting an Indian, Swiddler is able to obtain pardon papers from the governor in Swan Creek, the capital. With no means of transportation available, Swiddler starts to walk the fifteen miles to Flatbroke along the railroad tracks. When halfway there, Jim Peasley, a practical joker who is walking with him, challenges him to do one of his somersaults. Landing after doing so and with his head spinning, he is twisted halfway around by Peasley. Disoriented, he walks back to Swan Creek; Bowles, without Swiddler's intervention, is hanged.

SWIN, THE REV. MR. In "The Baptism of Dobsho," he is the leading revivalist of a religious movement in Harding, Illinois. Thomas Dobsho gets religion. His friend, Henry Barber, the narrator, gently hints to the Rev. Mr. Swin that Thomas has been a believer in total immersion and that a basin of water, or, better still, simply a mere sprinkling, should suffice at his baptism. But Swin takes no chances and pours an earthenware bowl full of water over Tom's head. The narrator, however, has put an effervescent powder in Tom's hair, which causes dramatic results. Reluctant to judge the narrator, Swin contents himself with breaking the bowl over the joker's head and telling him to sin no more.

"SYMBOLS AND FETISHES" (1892, 1898, 1911). Essay. (Original title of part: "War Topics.") Before the ancients could write, they distinguished their groups by heraldic pictures. Though unnecessary now, such images grow ever more complicated and costly. Our state seals are also ridiculous. The eagle, our national symbol, is really a bloody-beaked creature. Our flag is venerated unduly, and to it are attributed virtues belonging only to us. Civilians kneel to it; but soldiers in combat are indifferent to it, unless they are inspired by it—stupidly. William Jennings Bryan once bought a chair on which a renowned Japanese admiral had sat. Such a "sycophantic souvenir hunter" is as barbarous and superstitious—and rampant—as primitive fetish worshippers.

T

"TAKING ONESELF OFF" ((1893, 1894, 1900, 1912). Essay. (Original title of part: "The Right to Take Oneself Off.") Life is like a game of chance, which we can briefly win but in the end are always defeated by. "The time to quit is when you have lost a big stake, your foolish hope of success, your fortitude and your love of the game." Why wait until "summoned"? The summons may be disease, a murderer's club, a cow's kick. Asserting that we have no right to kill ourselves in an egotistical coward's excuse. Enduring life beyond pleasure is not virtuous. Romans who killed themselves were not cowards. The "pursuit of happiness" implies avoiding pains as well. Suicide is justified by specific circumstances. A person who kills himself is courageous, because he knows that he thus "incurs . . . reproach." One whose suicide leaves his family in trouble is cruelly selfish. One should pay little attention to differing racial and religious predilections. Not only is suicide justifiable; it is also a duty, under these circumstances: If one is horribly diseased, is a permanent burden to friends, is likely to become permanently insane, is hopelessly addicted to drunkenness or another destructive or offensive habit, is without friends or property or work or hope, or has disgraced oneself. We honor soldiers, sailors, and firemen brave in facing "the danger of death"; therefore, we should more greatly honor "the suicide [who] braves death itself!"

All of his adult life, Bierce was fascinated by the subject of suicide and by those who committed it ingeniously and dramatically. Several of his columns in the *News Letter* in the late 1860s and the *News Letter* and the *Argonaut* in the 1870s concern suicide. Several of his Civil War stories involve suicide, notably "George Thurston," "Killed at Resaca," "A Son of the Gods," and "A Tough Tussle." The following friends of Bierce committed suicide: Nora May French,* Thomas Arundel Harcourt, David Lesser Lezinsky,* Richard Realf,* William Herman Rulofson, Herman George Scheffauer,* and

George Sterling* and his wife Caroline Rand Sterling. In addition, Bierce probably thought that his friend Jack London* had killed himself. Bierce wrote his daughter Helen Bierce* (27 January 1913) for the purpose of transferring ownership to her of a family cemetery lot; he said that he did not wish to be buried there and that she would not be "bothered about the mortal part" of her father. His disappearance into Mexico in 1914, if that was the location and year of his death, must have been motivated by a long-smouldering desire for self-destruction. (*See also* "On the Uses of Euthanasia.")
Bibliography: Morris, Neale, St. Pierre.

"THE TALE OF A COAT." *See* "A Providential Intimation."

TASSMAN, PRIVATE. In "Parker Adderson, Philosopher," he is a Confederate soldier under General Clavering's command. He delivers Clavering's written order, to Captain Hasterlick, to execute Sergeant Parker Adderson, a Union Army spy. When Tassman returns, he finds the three entangled in a mortal struggle in Clavering's tent and rather glories in describing matters.

"THANKSGIVING DAY" (1869, 1911). Essay. (Original title: "The Annual Gobble.") Is it grateful to stuff oneself with turkey and drink too much wine? If God grants us favors to be grateful for, He also afflicts us with evils. No, Thanksgiving Day provides the gluttonous with an excuse to extend their waistcoats. All the same, stomach and soul are one entity. Gratitude is an "imponderable ether" produced by the action of gastric juices on "rich provend and comforting tope." That gas ascends and is emitted as a belch, sometimes in the form of an audible "Praise God."

"THAT OF GRANNY MAGONE" (1888). Short story. (Originally part of "Bodies of the Dead: Some Authentic Accounts of Their Seeming Caprices.") (Characters: The Rev. Elias Atney, Catharine Doub, John Hershaw, Sarah Magone, Marshall, William C. Wrightman.) In a deserted area of a cove in the Cumberland mountains, about ten miles southeast of Whitesburg, Kentucky, Sarah Magone lives alone in a log cabin beside her vegetable garden. She is reputed to be a miserly witch with supernatural powers. In November 1881 her corpse, still warm, is found by a hunter. He locks the cabin and reports the news to people nearby. The Rev. Elias Atney, a respected Methodist, arrives that evening to conduct the funeral the next day. Several neighbors also appear. That night the watchers are startled to see a black cat leap onto Sarah's body, laid on a plank before the bright hearth fire. Her right arm grabs the cat, tears it from her face, and throws it against a wall. The cat disappears out a window. Repeated efforts to revive Sarah fail, and four days later she is obviously in need of burial. Witnesses confirm the story; and when Atney recounts these events to a friend and is doubted, he adds that Sarah's long-nailed right hand had black fur in it.

"THEFT VERSUS BLACKMAIL." *See* "Certain Areas of Our Seamy Side."

"THE THING AT NOLAN" (1891). Short story. (Original title: "A Queer Story: Transcribed from the Notes of an Investigator.") (Characters: Jackson, May, May, Charles May, John May, Mrs. Charles May, Henry O'Dell.) Charles May lives with his wife, their grown son John, and their two young daughters in a house by the road between Leesville and Mardy, Missouri. Charles has a quick temper, but it quickly dissipates. On the other hand, John has a sullen, slow-burning temper. One day a misunderstanding causes Charles to hit John in the face, drawing blood. He quickly apologizes, but John calmly tells his father he will die "for that." Two brothers named Jackson overhear the threat. All seems well. One Sunday two weeks later, Charles takes a spade and goes out to dig at his spring a mile away. At 2:00 P.M. John leaves the house, returns at 5:00 P.M. with wet clothes, and soon falls ill. Charles does not return home, and a search around the spring reveals nothing but footprints of father and son. John rambles vaguely about a murder. After the Jacksons mention the threat, a deputy is posted on Tuesday to watch John. On Wednesday, Charles's cousin, Henry O'Dell, who is a storekeeper in Nolan some eight miles from the Mays's house, reports that he and four neighbors were sitting in the store when Charles walked through it and out the back door. He had a gash above his left eyebrow and blood on his gray shirt. The witnesses assumed that he had been in a fight and was heading for the brook behind the store to wash up. When Charles disappears, investigators look for him in and around Nolan—to no avail. John, once he recovers, is tried for murdering Charles but is acquitted on O'Dell's testimony that he saw Charles that Sunday afternoon. John leaves the country and is never heard from again. His mother and sisters move to St. Louis. An adjacent farmer buys the May land. The May house stands vacant and is called haunted. One day some boys find Charles's spade by the spring, after which investigators find his body buried nearby, with a wound over his left eyebrow and blood on his gray shirt. What thing passed through the store at Nolan?

THOMAS. In "Perry Chumly's Eclipse," he is the narrator. He watches as his friend Ben tries to analyze the composition of a comet with his spectroscope. Ben, however, points his instrument awry and instead analyzes the composition of a red-haired chambermaid in a dormer window.

"THOUGHT AND FEELING" (1903, 1911). Essay. (Original title: "Thought and Feeling in Poetry.") Philosophers make us think. But poets aim to make us feel. Shakespeare's songs have little or no thought, but do have much feeling. Thought can accompany poetry, which is a butterfly not to be caught in any critic's net. Great art defies definition. Certain lines in Samuel Taylor Coleridge's "Kubla Khan" are adorable while without thought and hence inexplicable.

"THOUGHT AND FEELING IN POETRY." *See* "Thought and Feeling."

"THREE AND ONE ARE ONE" (1908). Short story. (Characters: Bushrod Albro, Lassiter, Lassiter, Barr Lassiter, Mrs. Lassiter.) Barr Lassiter, twenty-two, lives with his parents and older sister near Carthage, Tennessee. They are poor, respectable, but low on the social scale because they own no slaves. When in 1861 Barr tells his austere father that he is going to Nashville to enlist in the Union Army, bitter silence and estrangement follow. Barr becomes a fine trooper in a Kentucky cavalry regiment. Two years pass, and his unit happens to be near the war-ravaged region of his home. He obtains a leave of absence and approaches the old dwelling. He thinks that it must now be in ruins, but "apparently" nothing is changed. He sees his father, outside in the moonlight, but the old man sullenly enters the house. Barr follows and sees his mother sitting by a blackened fireplace, silent. His sister walks in, stares, and goes past him and out the front door. Barr weeps and heads back to camp. The next day, he starts to return to his family, meets a former schoolmate named Bushrod Albro, and tells him his intentions. Albro looks at him sharply, saying nothing, and accompanies him. They find the smashed ruins of the place; and Albro explains that it was destroyed, along with Barr's parents and sister, by a Union Army shell a year ago.

"A THUMB-NAIL SKETCH" (1912). Essay. Bierce describes meeting William Randolph Hearst* and being hired by him to write for his *Examiner*; the damage done to *Examiner* circulation and Hearst's political ambitions by Bierce's poem that some interpreted as responsible for the assassination of President William McKinley;* Bierce's countering Hearst's pro-union policy; and Hearst's irrationally generous treatment of inadequate employees, recently modified because of financial and political considerations. Bierce concludes by saying that the United States is so "daft with democracy and sick with sin" that it deserves to have Hearst as president.

Bierce is said to have told friends that this sketch was part of a longer work on Hearst. Since Bierce greatly admired Hearst's mother, Phoebe Apperson Hearst, he said that he would not publish it during her lifetime. Dying in 1919, she outlived Bierce, whose alleged book on Hearst, if it ever existed, has never been found.
Bibliography: Joshi and Schultz, McWilliams.

THUNDERMUZZLE, ANGELICA. In "The Captain of the 'Camel,' " she is mentioned by Captain Abersouth as a character in a novel by Mary Elizabeth Braddon that he is reading.

THURSTON, FIRST LIEUTENANT GEORGE. In "George Thurston," he is Colonel Brough's aide-de-camp and accompanies him when he takes temporary command of the brigade that the narrator serves as a topographical engineer. Lieutenant Thurston exposes himself to danger with his arms folded on his chest. He is wounded, recovers, and finally dies—arms folded—when he falls from a makeshift swing he deliberately "cannonade[es]" too far. A quartermaster in the brigade theorizes that Thurston was trying to overcome a tendency to run away by suicidal chance-taking.

TILBODY. In "The Applicant," he or she is any of the children of Silas Tilbody and his wife.

TILBODY, MRS. SILAS. In "The Applicant," she is the wife of the superintendent of the Abersush Home for Old Men in Grayville.

TILBODY, SILAS. In "The Applicant," he is the fat superintendent of the Abersush Home for Old Men in Grayville. He selfishly wants to convert the Home into a kind of Spanish castle with paying residents. When he goes shopping on Christmas Eve for presents for his family, he encounters Amasa Abersush himself, the philanthropist who gave Grayville the Home. Impoverished now, Abersush has applied for admission to the Home. Tilbody tells him that he and Deacon Byram, chairman of the board of trustees of the Home, have concluded that Abersush's application "disagrees with them." The next day Byram's son finds Abersush frozen to death in the snow.

TIME. In "Hades in Trouble," he is a friend of Satan and the other devils in Hades. He foresees the results of Satan's visit to the earth and tells his cohorts about Eve's being tempted by Satan and turning fierce.

"TIMOTHY H. REARDEN" (1892, 1911). Essay. (Original title: "A Man of Letters.") Judge Timothy Henry Rearden (1839–1892) has died. When a judge dies, another is appointed or elected, and the court continues to function. When a man of letters dies, the vacancy is permanent. Rearden was without equal in scholarship in the western part of the United States. He knew Greek, Latin, several modern European languages, and their literatures. He associated with Bret Harte,* and contributed prose and poetry to the *Overland Monthly* and the *Californian.* He was working on a book on Sappho when he died, and it would have reflected on his character gloriously. (Rearden's letters, papers, and legal decisions are in the Bancroft Library of the University of California at Berkeley.)

"TO AN INSOLENT ATTORNEY." *See* "Some Features of the Law."

" 'TO ELEVATE THE STAGE' " (1892, 1911). Essay. (Original title: "The Dawn of a New Era.") A theatrical troupe composed of formerly jailed Harvard alumni is popular. Lily Langtry and John L. Sullivan are stage stars simply for who they are rather than for their acting ability. So why not improve the stage by composing troupes for former assassins turned preachers? Deaf-mute grandsons of hanged men? Senators with warty noses? Best would be actors who are dead. They could outdo even Langtry and Sullivan. Other arts and industries might be inspired, and a new era of total inaction might dawn.

"TOLD AT THE BOHEMIAN CLUB." *See* "A Story at the Club."

"A TOUGH TUSSLE" (1888). Short story. (Character: Second-Lieutenant Brainard Byring.) One night in the autumn of 1861 in the wild Cheat Mountain country of western Virginia, brave Second-Lieutenant Brainard Byring of the Union Army deploys his pickets and two sergeants nearby and takes a position behind them at a fork in a road. They are to report to him if they learn of enemy movements. Byring sees a corpse, which he hates to do. He lectures himself on superstitions from olden times about "the malevolence of the dead body." In the changing moonlight, the dead man's limbs seem to move. Byring wants to move away but knows that his men expect him to be there. He grasps his sword so hard that his hand hurts. He laughs aloud but then wonders at the source of the sound. He sweats. He thinks he hears "a stealthy tread." The body has moved, he feels. One shot, then others, ring out. His pickets retreat, as ordered. Cavalrymen gallop past. The line is firm again. In the morning, a fatigue detail headed by a captain and a surgeon, checking on the dead and the wounded, comes upon Byring and a Confederate private. Byring is dead, his sword thrust through his own body. The enemy private shows repeated gashes but no blood, was lying on maggots, and emits the odor of decomposition. "A Tough Tussle" is nicely structured to show changes in Byring's thought processes and emotions, from fear of a living enemy, to disgust in the presence of a corpse, to annoyance, and finally to "a sense of the supernatural." In "Taking Oneself Off," Bierce wrote that under certain circumstances suicide is justifiable.
Bibliography: Davidson, Grenander, Morris, Woodruff.

"A TRADE OF REFUGE" (1901, 1912). Essay. (Original title: "Ambrose Bierce Says: Alas! We Cannot All Be Steeple Climbers.") Steeplejacks are occasionally in danger. One ventured down among ordinary folk and was killed by a trolley car. Sailors surviving storms pray for safety when ashore. Townspeople and farmers face civilization's "deadly devices," unknown to sailors and steeple climbers. The latter should be fed by kites.

"TO TRAIN A WRITER" (1899), 1911). Essay. Although great writers are gifted, ordinary people can be taught to write. Bierce recalls having some good "pupils." If allowed, he would take a promising person, have him read Greek and Roman classics for two years, experience joys, sorrows, and mistakes, and only then begin—by writing a monosyllabic pig story. Bierce regards "art and love as the only means to happiness."

TROUTBECK, CAPTAIN BILLY. In "The Man Overboard," he is the captain of the *Bonnyclabber*, which saves Claude Reginald Gump, the narrator, after the wreck of the *Nupple-duck*, run by Captain Abersouth, Troutbeck's friend. Troutbeck's lookout spots a man overboard. When the crew finds none, Gump says that someone really should be thrown over to make the ship's record correct. So Troutbeck is tossed overboard. His drowned body is spotted by Abersouth, who survived by making a raft of stuff thrown overboard from Troutbeck's *Bonnyclabber*.

TUCKER, SIMEON. In "For the Ahkoond," he is a wise archaeologist who, according to the narrator, contends that the Ultimate Hills were called the Rocky Mountains by "the ancients."

TUPPER, STALEY. In "A Providential Intimation," he is the owner of Upandust, a horse.

"THE TURKO-GRECIAN WAR" (1897, 1911). Essay. Contrary to popular opinion, Bierce avows that the Turks are not savage butchers. They are good-natured, a bit lazy, and no more corrupt than we are. Thousands of Americans are murdered each year. Accounts of massacres by Turks come from bigoted Christian missionaries whose accounts cannot be trusted. Armenian Christians are "scamps." Turkish soldiers are fierce fighters, as the Greeks well know. We owe a debt to a Greek civilization that is long dead. Nor are modern Greeks Christians in the best sense. Feeble and badly led, Greece was foolish to make war on Turkey and villainous to call it a religious conflict. Turkish counterattacks displayed courage, not fanaticism. Journalistic accounts of Turkish atrocities have followed the usual pattern of nonsensical exaggeration. Since Turks worship God in a manner unlike ours, they are called hateful and unspeakable, and "we lie about them," most uncharitably.

TURMORE, ELIZABETH MARY JOHNIN. In "The Widower Turmore," she is the wealthy wife of Joram Turmore. She foils his plan to immure her in his basement by escaping through an aperture made of loosened masonry. In addition, she steals his family treasures, converts them "into coin of the realm," and lives well in distant parts.

TURMORE, JORAM. In "The Widower Turmore," he is the smug, amoral narrator. He is proud of his criminal ancestors, whose annals go way back to the seventh century and who include Sir Aldebaran Turmore de Peters-Turmore, a master burglar. Joram Turmore teaches without salary, and almost without students, in the University of Graymaulkin. Marrying Elizabeth Mary Johnin for money, he attempts to kill her by walling her up in his basement. She not only escapes through an aperture she makes of loose bricks but has already stolen his family treasures, even before he tries to kill her. He can obtain no justice because he has declared her to be deceased. It is hardly a satisfaction that his inheritance from her estate is small, though enough to raise him "from poverty to affluence and . . . [bring] me to the respect of the great and good."

TURMORE, SIR ALDEBARAN TURMORE DE PETERS-TURMORE. In "The Widower Turmore," he was an ancestor of Joram Turmore, who esteemed Sir Aldebaran as a master burglar back in the seventeenth century. Joram was sad to learn that Sir Aldebaran actually assisted in one "operation" instead of merely planning it and not soiling his hands by work.

"THE TURN OF THE TIDE" (1890, 1900, 1912). Essay. (A section was originally part of "Ambrose Bierce Says: Missionaries Cause the Chief Trouble in China.") In 1890, we could have cured the problem of Chinese immigration by killing off the Chinese, the way we did the Indians. But it is too late now. The Chinese government would demand an indemnity. Beware. Multitudes of Asians "are learning war and navigation"—taught to them by Caucasians. China is becoming aggressive and dominant. Moreover, "Japan has made the impossible possible," and partitioning China is worth considering. Lawmakers try to exclude Asians, but fail and then smile. The westward movement of "empire" is turning backward like a tide. Our courts give immigrants rights they never had at home. American cities have "Chinatowns"; Japanese own industries and land along the Pacific coast, and hire their former employers. For four centuries, "the European has been wresting it [the New World] from the Indian"; "eminent domain" now enables the Asian to become our masters. In the process, our civilization will be destroyed.

TWAIN, MARK (1835–1910). Author. Mark Twain was born Samuel Langhorne Clemens in Florida, Missouri, grew up in nearby Hannibal, and left school when his father died (1847). He was in turn a journeyman printer, a Mississippi River steamboat pilot, a miner in Nevada, and then a journalist there (1862–1864) and in San Francisco (1864–1866). His "The Celebrated Jumping Frog of Calaveras County" (1865) gained him international renown. He lectured in the East, wrote *The Innocents Abroad* (1869) about a sensational tour he enjoyed in the area of the Mediterranean Sea and the Holy Land, married Olivia Langdon (1870), and settled in Hartford, Connecticut, with her and ultimately their three daughters. Was Twain turned into a vicious satirist by Eastern gentility, or did he remain essentially a frontier writer? Critics are still divided on this question. After *Roughing It* (1872), Twain and Charles Dudley Warner coauthored *The Gilded Age* (1873). A succession of classics by Twain quickly followed, including *The Adventures of Tom Sawyer* (1876), *The Prince and the Pauper* (1882), *Life on the Mississippi* (1883), *Adventures of Huckleberry Finn* (1884), *A Connecticut Yankee in King Arthur's Court* (1889), and *The Tragedy of Pudd'nhead Wilson* (1894). Twain had been advantageously involved in financing the publication of *Personal Memoirs of U.S. Grant* (1885) but was financially ruined by investing in a faulty typesetting machine (1894). To recoup, he lectured around the world and wrote *Following the Equator* (1897) about his adventures while doing so. Next came uneven work but also representative items such as "The Man That Corrupted Hadleyburg" (1899), *Christian Science* (1907), and the posthumous *The Mysterious Stranger* (1916). Twain's wife and two of his daughters predeceased him, all of which deepened the bitterness of his final years.

While in San Francisco, Twain published pieces in the *Californian*, the *Golden Era*, and the *Morning Call*. He associated with Bierce, Ina Coolbrith,* Bret Harte,* Charles Warren Stoddard,* and other writers in the general area. Bierce hardly knew Twain, who returned to San Francisco only briefly in 1868 to give a few lectures; even so, Bierce ridiculed him in several *San Francisco News Letter* pieces (summer 1870) for drinking too much, marrying money, and being lazy thereafter. When Bierce went to London in 1872, he met the unscrupulous publisher John Camden Hotten* and learned, among much else, that Hotten had made considerable money pirating *The Innocents Abroad* and that Twain, its author, was on his way to England in order to confront "Hottentot," as he called him, and also—as it turned out—to lecture and be lionized by the British. Early in 1873, Twain cold-shouldered and upstaged Bierce at a literary meeting of the White Friars' Club in London, for which, it is alleged, Bierce never forgave him. A few years later, Twain made the biggest social mistake of his life, by reading his spoof of Ralph Waldo Emerson, Oliver Wendell Holmes, and Henry Wadsworth Longfellow at the banquet celebrating John Greenleaf Whittier's seventieth birthday (Boston, 17 December 1877). When the proper Bostonians professed not to be amused, Bierce expressed the hope in an *Argonaut* column (5 January 1878) that Twain would be spared a deserved lynching. Bierce's "The Famous Gilson Case" (1878) is often said to have anticipated Twain's more famous "Hadleyburg" parable of avarice. *Mark Twain's Library of Humor*, edited anonymously by William Dean Howells* (1888), triggered Bierce's humorously expressed annoyance. The popular *Library* contained, in addition to six items from "The Fables of Zambri, the Parsee" by Bierce, a biographical sketch of Bierce including nine factual errors, all of which Bierce pointed out (*San Francisco Examiner*, 26 August 1888). In a short column in which he carefully distinguished wit from humor, Bierce expressed his preference for deep wit rather than the sort of shallow humor he professed to find in Twain (*San Francisco Examiner*, 23 March 1903). Gustav Danziger,* Bierce's unreliable friend and early biographer, records, perhaps inaccurately, Bierce's opinion of Twain as "a clown, clever enough to assume at time[s] the dignity of a blunderer in letters."

Bibliography: De Castro; Fatout; Grenander; Justin Kaplan, *Mr. Clemens and Mark Twain: A Biography* (New York: Simon & Schuster, 1966); McWilliams; Morris; O'Connor; St. Pierre; Edward Wagenknecht, *Mark Twain: The Man and His Work*, 3rd ed. (Norman: University of Oklahoma Press, 1967).

"A TWISTED TALE" (1903, 1912). Short drama. (Originally part of "Unauthenticated Dialogues—II.) John Hay,* secretary of state under President Theodore Roosevelt,* after a wink warns Count Arturo Paulovitch Cassini (1835–c.1916), the Russian ambassador, that Roosevelt is worried about the Jewish vote and therefore wants Russia to avoid oppressing Russian Jews. When Roosevelt enters, Hay says that he has just threatened Russia with gory military action. The title of this play, which is written in heroic couplets, puns on "twist[ing] the tail of the fierce Russian bear." In real life, Roosevelt disliked Cassini, and called him tricky and unreliable.

Bibliography: Norman E. Saul, *Concord and Conflict: The United States and Russia 1867–1914* (n.p.: University Press of Kansas, 1996).

"TWO CONVERSATIONS" (1905, 1912). Essay. (Original title: "Imaginary Conversations.") A publisher candidly tells a sensible author that he regularly publishes novels without merit, in order to make money, and that he must reject the author's work, beautiful though it is. Next, the editor of a journal called *The Waste Basket* tells the wealthy owner of a prosperous magazine that he accepts material only if it has been rejected by the wealthy man.

"TWO FAVORITES" (1903, 1912). Short drama. (Originally part of "Unauthenticated Dialogues.") Bellicose General Nelson Miles (1839–1925) sarcastically praises General Leonard Wood (1860–1927) of the army medical commission. Wood comments on his lifesaving work. Meanwhile, a citizens' chorus repeats some of Miles's utterances in a Gilbert-and-Sullivan manner; and Satan says that recent administrations have favored and supported him. This silly work is written in heroic couplets. It draws its title from the fact that Satan enters at the end of the play and says that the two recent presidential administrations (those of William McKinley* and Theodore Roosevelt*) are among his favorites.

"TWO KINDS OF HYDROPHOBIA." *See* "Dog."

"TWO MILITARY EXECUTIONS" (1906). Short story. (Originally part of "Soldiers and Ghosts," the other story in which was "A Baffled Ambuscade.") (Characters: Lieutenant Will Dudley, Gorham, Grayrock, Private Bennett Story Greene.) In the spring of 1862, a still somewhat untrained U.S. Army unit under General Don Carlos Buell is soon to do battle at Shiloh. Two soldiers are now in trouble. Private Bennett Story Greene struck Lieutenant Will Dudley. Later, when experienced, he would not have done so. Reported by Dudley, Greene is arrested, court-martialed, convicted, and sentenced to be shot. Greene tells Dudley that he might simply have beaten him up, as he used to do when the two were schoolmates together, instead of reporting the incident, which no one else had observed. Now Dudley feels apologetic. Greene is executed. A few weeks later, Buell's forward division crosses the Tennessee River to aid General Ulysses S. Grant. At dawn during roll call, the first sergeant in Dudley's company sings out "Greene" after "Gorham" and "Grayrock" through force of habit. A voice answers, "Here!" The captain orders Greene's name to be called again and yet again—with the same result. The instant the captain wonders aloud what all this means, a shot rings out from far away, and Dudley, stepping forward, says "It means this," shows a bleeding wound in his chest, and falls dead. Bierce goes out of his way in "Two Military Executions" to criticize Grant, as he often does, this time commenting on "Grant's beaten army."

216. In "The Bubble Reputation." *See* Spittleworth, Longbo.

"THE TYRANNY OF FASHION" (1881, 1888, 1894, 1895, 1896, 1911). Essay. (Original title of part: "Beauty and the Bird.") Men tactlessly criticize women's dress fashions. Their "rich, bright bravery" is attractive because it is natural. Those who object to killing birds for feathers, which women sport to appeal to men, should be consistent by not eating mutton, wearing furs, and so on. Women are foolish to gripe that "[f]ashion" is a tyrant (probably male), when they are free to avoid following one hideous, "fashionable" change after another. They complain that traditions compel them. Why personify women as "woman"? Does "woman" have to wear long, unhealthy skirts? "Can we reasonably expect large intellectual strides in those who voluntarily hamper their legs?" Bloomers and bathing suits are not immodest, nor is nudity. Nor is there "infamy" in sex. Instead of blaming "Man the Monster," woman should emancipate herself "by overthrowing the actual despotism maintained by herself." Bierce must have been chronically bothered by women's fashions to assemble this essay in 1911 into one of his longest.

U

"AN ULTIMATUMMYTUMMY." *See* "A Wireless Penultimatum."

"UNAUTHENTICATED DIALOGUES." *See* "Genesis of a Nation" and "Two Favorites."

"UNAUTHENTICATED DIALOGUES—II." *See* "A Twisted Tale."

"AN UN-DOLLY DIALOGUE." *See* "Post Mortem."

"AN UNFINISHED RACE" (1888). Short story. (Originally part of "Whither? Some Strange Instances of Mysterious Disappearance.") (Characters: Hamerson Burns, Barham Wise, James Burne Worson.) James Burne Worson is a shoemaker in Leamington, Warwickshire, England. He drinks too much. On 3 September 1873, he bets a man "whose name is not remembered" that for the amount of one sovereign he can run to Coventry and back, a distance of forty miles. The unnamed man, with Barham Wise and Hamerson Burns, closely follows Worson by cart or wagon. He does well for a while but then pitches forward and disappears without touching the ground. After remaining a while, the three witnesses return to Leamington, tell their story, and are taken into custody. But, being "of good standing," they are soon released, though not totally believed. Were they concealing something? If so, their methods were "amazing." Readers may wonder why Bierce omitted the name of the man who accepted Worson's wager.

UPANDUST. In "A Providential Intimation," this is the name of Staley Tupper's horse.

V

"THE VALUE OF COMPULSORY MILITARY SERVICE." *See* "Warlike America."

"THE VALUE OF TRUTH" (1899, 1903, 1911). Essay. Strangely, several state legislatures have passed laws against calling a person a liar; yet they do not legislate against being a liar. One maddened by the word "liar" is not maddened by the awareness of being one. Truth is valued as a virtue because it is expedient and promotes humankind's welfare. If happiness were advanced by falsehoods, falsehoods would become virtuous. Some erroneously rationalize that in business you must tell lies. Prince Otto von Bismarck found early on that the world of diplomacy was so full of liars that he could deceive only by telling the truth. Truth telling does not always result in success because some honest men are stupid, unenergetic, and unlucky. Nor does everyone especially want to succeed. What is success? One may feel prosperous when happy, but is anyone happy when prosperous? Be content, even though all are not yet so. Contentment now "seems . . . confined mainly to the wise and the infamous."

VEIGH, JUDGE MYRON. In "The Spook House," he is a state militiaman from Frankfort, Kentucky. In June 1859, he and his friend Colonel J. C. McArdle take refuge from a storm in the Spook House. Veigh pushes past McArdle to enter a ghastly room filled with corpses, and kneels to look at the blackened head of one body. McArdle faints. Veigh is never heard from again. Veigh's family doubts McArdle's account and turns hostile toward him.

"THE VIEWS OF ONE." *See* "A Diplomatic Triumph," "Post Mortem," and "A Sucked Orange."

"A VINE ON A HOUSE" (1905). Short story. (Characters: The Rev. J. Gruber, Harding, Matilda Harding, Robert Harding, Hyatt, Julia Went.) The Harding house, just outside Norton, Missouri, was last occupied in 1886 and is now regarded as haunted. Its signs of disrepair, now regarded as evidence of "the supernatural," are concealed by a huge vine covering the whole house. The place was occupied by Robert Harding, about forty years old, a stern, taciturn farmer; his wife Matilda, who lacked a left foot; her unmarried sister, Julia Went; and the Hardings's two young children. Gossip had it that Harding and Julia, his sister-in-law, were intimate. In 1884, Harding said that his wife went to visit her mother in Iowa. She never returned. Two years later, Harding, his children, and Julia left. Four or five years pass. The Rev. J. Gruber and a Maysville attorney named Hyatt chance to meet on horseback in front of the Harding house. They stop and talk shop, and in the warm, humid evening suddenly see that the huge vine is trembling while adjacent foliage is not. The two men hasten to Norton, tell what they saw, and return the next evening with two other men. They all see the vine wriggling. Neighbors day and night gather to "seek . . . a sign." Someone suggests that they dig up the vine. Its elaborate root system is in the form of a human body with a missing left foot. The county sheriff orders the roots replaced and the site smoothed over. Inquiries reveal that Matilda Harding never visited Iowa, and that Harding, his children, and Julia are in parts unknown. The replanted vine is "orderly and well-behaved." Bierce's tone here is notable for sarcastic little digs at the stupidity of the rural populace. In his earlier poem, "A Nightmare" (1903), Bierce dreams that "Out of my grave a giant beech upgrew. / Its roots transpierced my body, through and through, / My substance fed its growth."

"VISIONS OF THE NIGHT" (1887, 1911). Essay. (Full title: "Visions of the Night: The Stuff That Dreams Are Made Of, and How They Are Made.") Dreams are disordered memories rising like corpses from broken tombs. If they were domesticated like animals, dreams could, while we are asleep, help us use our imaginations and then write better. One cannot describe a dream well any more than one can summarize a story well. Nevertheless, Bierce describes three dreams of his. In the first dream, he walked through a dark forest to a bloody brook and a tank of blood around which were twenty naked bodies of men whose throats were cut; somehow, he felt responsible, and then he sensed that God was dead. In the second dream, which Bierce dreamed when he was sixteen, he walked at night over a blasted plain into a building towering overhead; consciously seeking something, he found the flickering-out fire of eternity and a corpse grinning and looking up at him; he was horrified that the corpse was living, whereas God and the angels had died. The scene of the third dream, which has been a recurring one, was a predawn moonlit glade, with a white horse chomping the dewy grass; the horse looked at Bierce and spoke terrifyingly in human words he could never understand. After death, he says, he may understand.

W

WANDEL, PIKE ("PIKEY," "WANNIE"). In "The Failure of Hope & Wandel," he is the partner of Jabez Hope in an idiotic scheme to ship ice from Lake Michigan to New Orleans, for sale there.

WARD, COLONEL. In "Killed at Resaca," he is the Union Army officer that the general orders Lieutenant Herman Brayle to tell to get as close to the Confederate Army lines as he safely can. This order leads to the suicidally inclined Brayle's death.

WARDORG, MAJOR-GENERAL BLOUNT. In "Jupiter Doke, Brigadier-General," he is a Union Army officer, who is ordered to welcome and make use of Brigadier-General Jupiter Doke. Wardorg calls Doke "a fool."

"THE WAR EVERLASTING" (1903, 1906, 1907, 1911). Essay. (Original title: "Our Debt to William the Conqueror.") For thousands of years, even in times of peace, a civil war has been raging between law breakers and law-abiding citizens. The latter gain victories but do not follow through. All crimes are defiant offenses against the state; hence, they are logically degreeless. Life and property could be best saved if nearly all criminals were executed, and certainly all habitual ones. Why accord mercy to the merciless? Such few crimes would then be committed that a tiny constabulary, few courts, and a small national prison would suffice. Punishment would not merely deter; it would permanently reform. At present, we moddycoddle criminals and homicide totals are high. Given "the new penology," prisons are too comfortable, and inmates are clothed, fed, exercised, and cleaned better than when they were before their incarceration. So-called reform elevates them to higher sorts of crime. A stupid thief emerges a clever forger and returns ambitious to murder the warden. France has that "dissuader," the guillotine, but it is currently not in use. Writers, who use their heads, understandably oppose the guillotine. Distrust of capital punishment represents a softening of head, not heart. Conquered people hate their oppressors' laws as well as their oppressors. The Anglo-Saxon people were a brutish, slovenly lot until William the Conqueror defeated them. He brought strict laws, which the subjected people hated. Americans have inherited this animosity to the death penalty, unfortunately.

"A WAR IN THE ORIENT" (1905, 1911). Essay. (Original title: "Have We a Navy?") The Bald Campaigner tells the Timorous Reporter that he is sorry the Japanese navy let two or three Russian ships escape in the recent Russo-Japanese War (1904–1905). The Japanese admiral responsible should be dismissed. A commander's duty is to overlook nothing. The Russians were defeated because they are an inland people without a seagoing tradition. You cannot teach seamanship to farmers. When the Campaigner offers the opinion that Americans are no longer good sailors, the Reporter mentions our victories at Manila Bay (1898) and Santiago de Cuba (1898). The Campaigner defines those victories instead as slaughters. When the Reporter with a shudder calls slaughter horrible, the Campaigner says it is better to die in battle than by disease. War is costly, but it profits some and a country is prosperous after a great war. The Russian army did well in the past, but Japanese soldiers—"these cantankerous little devils"—overwhelmed it. They are proud of their history, proud of their fascinating modern civilization erected on an artistic old one, proud of their honest government, proud of their deified ruler. All of this makes the Japanese a danger to America and "their overthrow . . . a military necessity." When asked the outcome of an evenly matched U.S.-Japanese naval battle, the Campaigner predicts a total American victory. At one point, the Timorous Reporter is also called the Inquiring Mind.

"WARLIKE AMERICA" (1900, 1901, 1912). Essay. (Originally part of "Compulsory Military Service" [retitled "The Value of Compulsory Military Service"] and "Ambrose Bierce Says: America Is Warlike, but Not Military.") President William McKinley* once declared that Americans are "not a military people," declare war only for peace, and fought Spain only to free Cuba. He meant that we aren't "warlike," meaning "to be fond of war," whereas being "military" means "to cultivate the arts and sciences of war." Germany is military; American Indians are warlike. McKinley was incorrect. We fought the British beginning in 1812, the Mexicans (1846–1848), "ourselves" (i.e., the Civil War [1861–1865]), and Spain (1898)—for peace, to be sure, but "peace on our terms." Wars are always like that. McKinley added that we do not seek land by conquest. But we gained territory from Mexico and "dependencies" from Spain. History reveals that "powerful republics are . . . warlike and unscrupulous." America would grab more but for a clumsy army and a navy unable to reach faraway targets. We should confess outright that we are warlike, and go ahead and become military. A standing army would preserve our republic and not endanger our liberty. Volunteer armies are a patriotic sight, to be sure, but are no match for a trained standing army. Men conscripted into a professional army enter it stupid and brutal, but emerge from it healthier, more moral, and brighter.

"WAR TOPICS." *See* "Symbols and Fetishes."

"A WATCHER BY THE DEAD" (1889). Short story. (Original title: "The Watcher by the Dead.") (Characters: Dr. Harper, Dr. Helberson, Jarette, Dr. William Mancher.) In San Francisco three physicians are discussing the superstitious fear people have about being alone with the dead. They are Dr. Helberson, the host, and his guests, Dr. William Mancher and young Dr. Harper. Harper says that Jarette, a dark-haired, rich, gambling friend of his has bet a big sum, held by Harper, that he can spend the night in a dark room with a corpse and emerge unharmed the next morning. Mancher, who happens to resemble Jarette, will play the corpse, stretched out and covered, in an upstairs room in an empty house owned by Helberson. At the appointed hour, Jarette—ignorant of the joke—enters the room, looks idly at the corpse, tries to read and then rest, but soon grows apprehensive, paces about, and talks to himself. Shortly before dawn, Helberson and Harper drive to the house but find a crowd of people there. Rushing upstairs, they meet Jarette, white-haired and frantic. He tears through the spectators and eludes pursuit. Inside the room a police lantern reveals a repulsive-looking body, dead about six hours according to a tall doctor. Helberson suggests that he and Harper decamp for Europe. Seven years later, the two are sitting in Madison Square, New York, when a white-haired man approaches, says that killing a man by coming to life in front of him makes it advisable to change clothes with him, and then reveals himself to be Dr. Mancher. Adding that he calls himself Jarette, he boasts that he is now a physician at the Bloomingdale Asylum. Helberson and Harper have become gamblers, evidently having started with the wager winnings Harper paid Helberson.

Bierce increases suspense by beginning "A Watcher by the Dead," which is divided into five parts, with Jarette entering the dark room with the supposed corpse, then turns to the earlier scene in which the physicians discuss awe in the presence of death, then returns to the dark room and Jarette's mounting unease. The last sections concern, respectively, the crowd at the fatal scene, and then the climax and denouement seven years later. Remarkable here is Bierce's handling of two subjects, time and physical resemblances, in ways which modern thinkers may find challenging.
Bibliography: Grenander.

"THE WATCHER BY THE DEAD." *See* "A Watcher by the Dead."

" 'WAY DOWN IN ALABAM' " (1909). Essay. After the Civil War, Bierce served as an aide in Selma, Alabama, to a Treasury Department special agent whose assignment was to collect and control captured and abandoned property once belonging to defeated Southerners. Such property was mostly cotton. If it had been sold but not delivered to the Confederate government, officials in Washington, D.C., decreed that it belonged to the United States. Southern farmers sought by ingenious devices to retain possession of their cotton, ship it by river to Mobile, and sell it abroad. One complication was the fact that private cotton was exempt from U.S. seizure; another, that Southerners hated Northern officials. Since "the carcass invites the vulture," many Treasury agents, paid one-fourth the value of all seized property for their work, were masters of fraud and objects of bribery. The result was "violence and crime." Two U.S. marshals were found with their throats cut. Bierce offers a few anecdotes. He says that he once offered two well-mannered Southern men he repeatedly dined and drank with a quarter the value of 700 bales of cotton (at $500 a bale) to disclose their hiding place; they offered him an identical quarter if he would register the cotton as private property. A permanent deadlock followed. A wild man named Jack Harris told Bierce that he knew the whereabouts of a thousand bales of cotton, hidden at several points along the Alabama River. He offered a bribe for Bierce to sign some blank shipping permits. Harris planned to steal the cotton, load it on his boat, slip "through Mobile Bay in the black of the night," and sail to Havana. Bierce declined. (Harris was later executed for supporting insurrectionists in Cuba.) Bierce met, soon revered, and was protected by Charles and Frank, two fiery ex-Confederate officers. Returning home one night after "an adventure" (dining, drinking, serenading "a local divinity"), they were followed. Frank filched Bierce's pistol and shot the man in the leg, which was amputated the following day. When tried by a prewar judge with no continuing authority, Frank was fined $5 plus costs, for disorderly conduct. One day, Bierce was conveying six hundred bales of "government cotton" by steamboat down the Tombigbee River, accompanied by a dozen or so soldiers, when the detachment was fired on. The soldiers hid belowdecks. Bierce shot one of the attackers. The ship veered about, was hit fifty times by gunfire, and lost several bales of cotton overboard before reaching safety past a convenient bayou.

As he often does, Bierce seasons with humor what might have been a somber essay on corruption and treachery. He says that after nocturnal roistering his "youth and temperance (in drink) pulled me through without serious inroads on my health." Jack Harris's last words, to a Cuban priest, were, "I am an atheist, by God!" Charles and Frank "would rather fight a duel than eat—nay, drink." When the pilot-house of the cotton-laden boat is fired on, "The jingle of broken glass made a very rude arousing from the tranquil indolence of a warm afternoon on the Tombigbee."
Bibliography: Joshi and Schultz.

WELCKER, ADRIAN (1858–1926). Author. Born in Troy, New York, he flourished in Oakland, California, where he published poetry and fiction from the 1870s, and where he died. His most popular work was probably a dramatic poem titled *A Dream of Realms beyond Us* (1902; 8th ed., 1904). Bierce frequently criticized him in print, once labeling him "Adair Welcker, of Berkeley, formerly known as the Sacramento Shakespeare" (*San Francisco Examiner*, 22 August 1891).

Bibliography: Edgar Joseph Hinkel, ed., *Biographies of California Authors . . .* , 2 vols. (Oakland, Calif.: Alameda County Library, 1942); Joshi.

WENT, JULIA. In "A Vine on a House," she is the sister of Matilda Harding, who is the wife of Robert Harding and the mother of their two young children. They all live together in a house near Norton, Missouri. Rumor has it that Julia and Robert are intimate. After Matilda's disappearance, Harding takes his two young children and Julia and disappears from record.

"WHAT I SAW OF SHILOH" (1881, 1898, 1909). Essay. Bierce says that this essay is a revision of an account "published several years ago in a local weekly." It starts with the date of 6 April 1962 and a description of the bivouac of fatigued soldiers in his Union Army division. Heavy, distant firing suddenly galvanized everyone to attention and scurrying action. Assembly was bugled. After the costly loss of Nashville, Tennessee, Confederate Army units moved to Corinth, Mississippi. Union forces under General Ulysses S. Grant established forces at Pittsburg Landing (Shiloh, in Mississippi), where their advanced brigades were partly destroyed by Confederate forces under General Albert Sidney Johnston. Union General Don Carlos Buell's reinforcements arrived by steamers across the Tennessee River. Bierce's unit came under artillery fire. Suddenly a woman with a little pistol was seen on one boat. On a beach were thousands of men, some wounded, others dead, still others numbed by cowardice. Bierce and his regiment advanced to a plateau and camped in darkness. Wounded and dead were to be seen both in and out of tents. Bierce's group crowded forward in the rain. Morning found them in open country. He saw Shiloh Chapel, a line of advancing skirmishers, trees in splinters, but no comforting Union artillery pieces. Among the dead Bierce saw a suffering Union sergeant, his head partly blown off. When one of Bierce's men wondered about bayoneting him mercifully, Bierce said not to—too many people were watching. When the enemy turned in retreat, Union forces were ordered to run forward. Sudden crashing fire mowed down many of Bierce's fellows. His position, described in detail, offered no protection and was especially exposed to grape shot. Many wounded burned to death in the leaf-littered forests. At midafternoon (7 April) Bierce noted three lines of enemy infantrymen, each half a mile long. Suddenly hideous fire erupted on both sides. The din was so great that nothing specific could be heard. Bierce was then part of a successful bayonet charge and watched fresh Union infantry complete the advance. Once he could say that the battle had ended, Bierce reflected on the wine of youth and the contrasting ugliness of later civilian times.

This summary does not do justice to Bierce's magnificent prose here. He is not candid when in his opening paragraph he says this account is by "a soldier who is no writer to a reader who is no soldier." He was a superb writer glorying in the precision of his prose, and many of his most admiring readers have been members of the armed forces themselves. Bierce describes the sight and sound of rifle and artillery fire, which is a combination of flashes, smoke, metallic ringing, musical humming, rattle, whisper and hurtle, and rush. He points out the part that accidents "play in the game of war." He sarcastically comments that midnight lightning, which could expose their position, "might have been inconvenient." The excitement of combat is so intense, he says, that a hand put on a rushing soldier's beard "would have crackled and shot sparks." When a Union artillery piece is brought forward, seeming—but only seeming—to offer protection, it appears to say "I've come to stay" and to insult the enemy by putting "its nose in the air." It is odd to label an area "neutral ground" when on it are "riddled bodies of my poor skirmishers." It was no comfort that, when fire comes unseen, "the enemy's grape shot was sharper than his eyes." Bierce harshly concludes that when part of an Illinois regiment refused to surrender, it "well deserved" to be destroyed. And he is bitter when, observing certain corpses in grotesque disfigurement, he says that they "had got what they enlisted for." Thrilling is his image of the rushing Union infantry "grandly and confidently . . . sweeping on like long blue waves of ocean chasing one another to the cruel rocks!" His final section, numbered XII, in which he evokes effortlessly the "gracious and picturesque" aspects of Shiloh but only with difficulty its gore and horror, and in which he says that if he could have the gold of Youth for just a moment in his current drab age he would happily yield up "an other life" than the one that he "should have thrown away at Shiloh"— all this is matchless in Civil War remembrance literature.

Bibliography: Daniel Aaron, *The Unwritten War: American Writers and the Civil War* (New York: Oxford University Press, 1973); James Lee McDonough, *Shiloh—In Hell before Night* (Knoxville: University of Tennessee Press, 1977); Schaefer.

"WHAT MAY HAPPEN ALONG A ROAD." *See* "What Occurred at Franklin."

"WHAT OCCURRED AT FRANKLIN" (1906, 1909). Essay. (Original title: "What May Happen Along a Road.") On 27 November 1864, Bierce was with General John Schofield, commanding a "little [Union] army," as they fell back north of Duck River and toward Nashville, Tennessee. The next day they saw Confederate General John Bell Hood's forces proceeding toward Spring Hill like a "fascinating and portentous pageant." Hood could have "effaced" the one insufficient Union division sent to Spring Hill to oppose him, but he did not. Wondering at this, Bierce concludes that "fools are God's particular care, and one of his protective methods is the stupidity of other fools." Union units proceeded to Franklin safely. On 29 November, Bierce was positioned to observe the two-mile plain south of town. The afternoon was "as beautiful as a day-dream in paradise." Of Hood's 40,000-man force, at first only a few heads-of-column advanced, one turning. For an hour or so, the enemy formed battle lines, then executed a frontal attack. The Union countercharge spelled horrifying defeat for the Confederates, who lost several generals amid countless other casualties. Bierce says that he cannot recollect everything that happened and wryly adds that "[p]ossibly I have not a retentive ear." But he goes on to name many gallant soldiers on both sides and concludes that "[i]t was a great day for Confederates in the line of promotion." Intermittent firing went on into the night for a while— "an affair of twinkling musketry and broad flares of artillery." Union forces went on safely to Nashville. The Confederates followed and dug in, but did not attack and were destroyed two weeks later.

Bibliography: Thomas L. Connelly, *Five Tragic Hours: The Battle of Franklin* (Knoxville: University of Tennessee Press, 1983); Joshi and Schultz; Morris; Schaefer.

"A WHITE HOUSE IDYL" (1907, 1912). Short drama. (Originally part of "Small Contributions.") Theodore Roosevelt* discusses the Panama Canal and the possibility of a third term as president. This brief piece is written in heroic couplets.

WHITNEY, MARTIN L. In "A Light Sleeper," he is the father of Mrs. John Hoskin, who lives with her husband in San Francisco. While she is in Springfield, Illinois, visiting relatives, including Whitney, she dies of heart disease. He has his daughter's corpse sent to John Hoskins. Hoskins thanks him for positioning the body like that of a sleeping child, lying on its side. But Whitney replies that the body was placed on its back, its arms at its sides. This starts a chain of suspicions and viewings by Hoskin, which results in his going insane.

"WHO ARE GREAT?" (1899, 1901, 1911). Essay. History wrongly calls men of action the greatest. The greatest American, however, is not George Washington or Abraham Lincoln. Since "the most exalted, the most lasting and most beneficial intellectual work" is fine poetry, Edgar Allan Poe may well be called our greatest American. Men of action are famous only because great writers have preserved their lives. Without Washington and Lincoln, America would still be independent and slavery would still be abolished. Omar Khayyam lives through his readers. Art and literature are more permanent than anything conquerors have wrought. His poet-friend George Sterling* felt that "Who Are Great?" was Bierce's finest essay.

Bibliography: George Sterling, "A Memoir of Ambrose Bierce," pp. xxxiii–xlvii, in Bertha Clark Pope, ed., *The Letters of Ambrose Bierce* (San Francisco: Book Club of California, 1922).

"WHY I AM NOT EDITING THE 'COWVILLE STINGER.' " *See* "Why I Am Not Editing 'The Stinger.' "

"WHY I AM NOT EDITING 'THE STINGER' " (1874, 1911). Short story. (Original title: "Why I am Not Editing the 'Cowville Stinger.' ") (Characters: Inxling, Henry Inxling, Mrs. Henry Inxling, J. Munniglut, Muskler, Peter Pitchin, William Quoin.) Here is a series of memos to and from the offices of *The Stinger*, from Monday at 9 A.M. to Friday evening, J. Munniglut, proprietor, and Peter Pitchin, editor, are worried about an article they published in *The Stinger* about a man named Muskler. Munniglut says that Muskler intends to find out who wrote it. Pitchin writes Munniglut to tell the man to go away. Munniglut says he has to be polite to Muskler. Pitchin suggests that they sue him. Munniglut says that Muskler is in the office and wants Pitchin to come meet him. Pitchin replies that he is busy. Henry Inxling, Pitchin's bookkeeper, writes Pitchin that Munniglut is absent, that a big man is in the office, and that a bull-dog is with him. When Pitchin writes Inxling to eject the man, Inxling says that the man has a revolver and that Inxling has a wife and five children. Pitchin writes Inxling that the man is Muskler, the coward that Pitchin wrote about. Inxling writes that, when told to leave, Muskler laughed, and so did his dog, and adds that William Quoin, the foreman, is calling for copy he wants to publish. Pitchin replies that he is moving, since his landlady is filthy. Quoin writes Pitchin that Inxling is absent and that he needs copy. Pitchin writes Quoin to get the compositors together and rush Muskler out but not to give him Pitchin's new address. Munniglut writes Pitchin that Muskler has positioned himself opposite the deserted *Stinger* office with a shotgun. Pitchin writes Munniglut that he is leaving and that Munniglut should hire a new editor. Bierce, the brave editor of the *Wasp*, was frequently in trouble for his stinging squibs, but never behaved like his satirically handled *Stinger* journalists—cowards one and all.

"WHY THE HUMAN NOSE HAS A WESTERN EXPOSURE" (1906, 1911). Essay. Why, when people move, do they move in a westerly direction? It is because the sunset beckoned our primitive ancestors and we have inherited their instincts. Sunrises did not beckon those ancestors because they were sluggards and did not get up early.

"THE WIDOWER TURMORE" (1891). Short story. (Characters: Sir Aldebaran Turmore de Peters-Turmore, Elizabeth Mary Johnin Turmore, Joram Turmore.) The narrator, Joram Turmore, holds a professorship of

Cats in the University of Graymaulkin, teaches only by reading lectures of predecessors to his one- or two-student classes, and receives no salary. For money, he marries wealthy Elizabeth Jane Johnin. She remains in control of her assets until her death, but according to law they would devolve upon him at her death. To cause her a death "match[ing] her social distinction," he plans to consult Turmore archives, which are located in a nicely masoned strong room in his basement. Going back to the seventh century, the room contains family robes, jewelry, swords, a wine cup made out of a king's skull, and much else—not least, records of esteemed family murders. To his surprise, everything is missing. Disappointed but proceeding regardless, he catches his wife asleep, ties her up, takes her down to his basement, and bricks her into a snug corner near his rifled treasure room, the contents of which he never revealed to her. He goes to a judge, swears as to her death, and blames a servant for building the wall. He inherits Elizabeth's estate, but it is worth far less than his missing treasures. Six months later, rumors reach him that her ghost has been seen, far from Graymaulkin, in costly raiment and being driven about. He orders his wall torn down, so as to find Elizabeth's corpse, bury it properly, and thus lay her ghost. But not a vestige of her is within! The narrator turns feverish for months. When summer comes, he visits his wine cellar for some Madeira and finds two big bricks out of place in its wall, next to where his "lamented wife" was. Pushing them out, he determines that much earlier she must have slipped through that available opening and taken every treasure of value along with her; she hid four worthless items, including the king's skull, behind some wine casks. She must have sold everything she took and is now "enjoy[ing] her infamous gains in distant parts." When the narrator tries to get a warrant for her arrest, he is told that she is legally dead. So he must suffer because his Elizabeth was "devoid alike of principle and shame."

"The Widower Turmore" may well have owed its inception to Edgar Allan Poe's "The Cask of Amontillado." There could also, however, have been a more sinister, personal inspiration. Bierce was obsessed by the topic of wife murder and wrote two unpleasant little essays on the subject (*News Letter*, 26 December 1868 and 20 January 1872).
Bibliography: Miller, Morris.

WILLIAM. In "Perry Chumly's Eclipse," he tries to warn Ben that he is pointing his spectroscope at a chambermaid instead of at a comet, by telling him, and his friend Thomas, the narrator, about Perry Chumly. That stupid fellow, wanting to observe a solar eclipse, climbed down a well, looked up, and briefly mistook the aperture for the sun and a black man's face for the moon. He screamed, fainted, and drowned when he realized his mistake. William has to tell Ben to check where he has been pointing.

WILLIAMS, LIEUTENANT. In "The Affair at Coulter's Notch," he is the officer whom Captain Coulter's colonel orders forward to congratulate

Coulter on the accuracy of his artillery fire. When Williams does so, he is killed.

WILLIAMSON. In "The Difficulty of Crossing a Field," he or she is mentioned as the child of Williamson and his wife. The child does not figure in the action.

WILLIAMSON. In "The Difficulty of Crossing a Field," he is a planter living near Selma, Alabama. One day he walks through his lawn, crosses the road beyond, and proceeds into his pasture. He intends to tell Andrew, his overseer, about some horses. Williamson disappears and is never heard from again.

WILLIAMSON, MRS. In "The Difficulty of Crossing a Field," she is the wife of Williamson. The two and their child live near Selma, Alabama. One day while crossing into their pasture, Williamson disappears. Mrs. Williamson rushes out, saying that he is gone and that his disappearance is "an awful thing!"

WINTER. In "Killed at Resaca," he is a friend of Marian Mendenhall. Perhaps through jealousy, Winter told her that her closer friend, Lieutenant Herman Brayle of the Union Army, behaved in a cowardly manner during a battle in Virginia, where Winter was hurt. She writes Brayle that, while she will hate Winter for the comment, she would rather hear of Brayle's death than of his cowardice.

"A WIRELESS ANTEPENULTIMATUM" (1905, 1912). Short drama. (Original title: "A Wireless Ultimatummytummy.") President Theodore Roosevelt* is griping to his secretary of state, John Hay* and to Herbert Wolcott Bowen (1856–1927), his minister to Venezuela. He orders Bowen to put pressure on the Venezuelan president, Cipriano Castro (1858–1924)— who is, however, asked to reply slowly, by mail. The work is written in cute heroic couplets. Thus, Roosevelt says, " 'Twixt Castro and the Doctrine of Monroe, /My fears are nimble and my wits are slow." Hay replies, "If needful show your teeth." In reality, Castro's administration was corrupt and plagued by foreign financial claims. Roosevelt intervened to obtain arbitration. Castro was overthrown and left permanently for Europe (1905). Roosevelt curtly dismissed Bowen (1905).

"A WIRELESS MESSAGE" (1905). Short story. (Originally part of "Some Uncanny Tales.") (Characters: Holt, Holt, Mrs. William Holt, William Holt.) In the summer of 1896, William Holt, a wealthy manufacturer, is visiting his brother in central New York state. A year earlier, certain "infelicities" cause him to leave his wife and child. Behold Holt now, walking out of town. Suddenly he is surrounded by a glowing red light. His watch tells him it is 11:25 P.M. He sees his wife and child, apparently in the air and white. They vanish in a flash. The next morning, back in town, he looks gray and haggard to his brother. An hour later by telegram he learns of the death by fire of both wife and child, in their Chicago home, at 11:25 the night before.

WISE, BARHAM. In "An Unfinished Race," he is a linen draper living in Leamington, England. He, Hamerson Burns, and an unnamed man follow James Burne Worson, who has bet the unnamed man he can run to Coventry and back. On the way the three see Worson suddenly vanish. Back in Leamington, they tell about his disappearance but are not universally believed.

"WIT AND HUMOR" (1890, 1903, 1911). Essay. We laugh at humor. We do not laugh at wit but may smile at it. Wit at its best has the precision of a headsman's stroke. The French, especially Rochefoucauld and Rabelais, are witty; Americans, for example, Mark Twain,* are merely humorous. "Humor is tolerant, tender; its ridicule caresses. Wit stabs, begs pardon—and turns the weapon in the wound."

"THE WIZARD OF BUMBASSA" (1892, 1912). Essay. (Original title: "Rabid Transit.") It is to be lamented that George Westinghouse (1846–1914) says that he cannot invent an air-brake effective enough to slow a railroad train going a hundred miles an hour quickly enough to prevent accidents. When the King of Bumbassa, eager to help civilize the Dark Continent, ordered an inventor to devise an instantaneous train-stopper, the effect was successful, but passengers were killed and the cars all burned up. This should give pause to anyone seeking to travel fast by train from New York to Chicago. But who should wish to do so anyway?

"WORD CHANGES AND SLANG" (1889, 1903, 1907, 1911). Essay. Some words devolve from standard to slang; others, vice versa. Slang is tasteless and lacks originality. Bierce mentions John Camden Hotten,* who published a book of slang edited by George Augustus Sala,* who was an "accomplished scholar."

"WORKING FOR AN EMPRESS" (1882, 1909). Essay. (Original title: "How I Worked for an Empress: A Singular Bit of Literary History.") Bierce explains that while living in Leamington, England, in 1874, he wrote for several London newspapers, including The *Figaro*. It was edited and published by James Mortimer, who had known the Emperor (Napoleon III, 1808–1873) until his death and was still a friend of Empress Eugénie (1826–1920). When Mortimer established a new journal, to be called *The Lantern*,

Bierce reluctantly agreed to write all of its contents—provided "it should be irritatingly disrespectful of existing institutions and personages." Bierce venomously skewered General Sir Garnet Wolseley (1833–1913) for plunder during the Ashantee campaign (1873–1874). Bierce soon aimed his barbs at Henri Rochefort, le Conte de Lucay (1830–1913), an anti-imperialist journalist, the title of whose newspaper *La Lanterne* Mortimer had taken. Rochefort had recently escaped from a French penal colony in New Caledonia and was threatening to editorialize in England. The Empress was terrified; so Bierce did what he could to denigrate Rochefort, not least when he remarked that the fellow was "suffering from an unhealed wound. It was his mouth." Fortunately, Mortimer had copyrighted his new title, the French version of which Rochefort had never registered; he therefore left London and set up shop in Belgium. Relieved, the Empress invited Bierce to visit her at Chiselhurst in England; but since her invitation by protocol was in the form of a royal "command," Bierce, being of republican sentiments, declined. Still, he says, he enjoys thinking that he was the only American journalist ever paid by an empress to attack another journalist.

Bibliography: Alyn Brodsky, *Imperial Charade: A Biography of Emperor Napoleon III* (Indianapolis and New York: Bobbs-Merrill, 1978); Morris.

WORSON, JAMES BURNE. In "An Unfinished Race," he is a shoemaker in Leamington, England. He drinks too much and also boasts of his athletic ability. On 3 September 1873, he bets an unnamed man the sum of a sovereign that he can run to Coventry and back, a distance of forty miles. Hamerson Burns, Barham Wise, and the unnamed man get a cart or wagon and closely follow Worson. He runs well for a time but then suddenly pitches forward, falls, and vanishes without hitting the ground. The three witnesses look about for a while, then return to Leamington, and tell their story, which is not universally believed. Did the three have something to conceal?

WREN, ARMOUR. In "The Difficulty of Crossing a Field," he is Williamson's neighbor. They live on adjoining plantations. Wren has sold some horses to Williamson, and their delivery is delayed. As he goes to tell Williamson so, he and his son, James Wren, see Williamson and then never see him again.

WREN, JAMES. In "The Difficulty of Crossing a Field," he is the son, thirteen, of Armour Wren. The two see Williamson, and then the man disappears forever.

WRIGHT, BERNICE (1842?–?). She was a native of Warsaw, Indiana, Bierce's classmate there, and his first sweetheart. Her nicknames were Bernie, Fatima, and Tima. Fatima's nickname for Bierce was Brady. Her father ran a boardinghouse. Bierce sent Bernice an anonymous love poem, about kissing her twice and only twice. She did not identify the timid author at first. While on leave from the U.S. Army (December 1863–February 1864), he returned to Warsaw; she mentioned the poem, and he acknowledged his authorship. The two enjoyed a brief engagement, ended by her airheadedness and his prickliness. Bierce sent her a bitter poem, but he also wrote Bernice's sister Clara Wright to express his love for both girls; this letter (8 June 1864) is the only extant one by Bierce written during the Civil War. When Bierce was wounded in the head (23 June 1864), he returned on furlough to Warsaw (through September 1864); but he and Bernice evidently argued, probably over their carelessness in writing, perhaps because of his already-forming adverse opinion of females. Bernice destroyed all of his letters to her.

Bibliography: Fatout; Joshi and Schultz; Carey McWilliams, "Ambrose Bierce and His First Love," *Bookman* 35 (June 1932): 254–259; Morris; O'Connor.

WRIGHTMAN, WILLIAM C. In "That of Granny Magone," he is a witness confirming the story that Sarah Magone, though pronounced dead, fought a black cat off her face. Four days later, never reviving, she was buried.

WRITE IT RIGHT: A LITTLE BLACK LIST OF LITERARY FAULTS (1909). Book. In a prefatory statement, Bierce says that his "main purpose . . . is to teach precision in writing" and defines "good writing . . . [as], essentially, . . . clear thinking made visible." His handling of controversial matters of grammar and semantics, even while he strays into unnecessary wittiness, makes evident his ultraconservative stance. His secondary aim, as usual, is to blast positions of which he disapproves. Here are a few examples. "Aggravate" means to augment disagreeableness or badness of something, not "irritate." Don't say "I feel badly." Don't say "continually" (part of the time) if you mean "continuously" (without interruption). A sentence is "executed," whereas a person is "hanged." The word "gentleman" should not be regarded as a synonym for "man." If one says "got married," one can also say "got dead." Horses are not "horseflesh." The word "literally" is often senseless, as when, for example, one says "His eloquence literally swept the audience from its feet." If a criminal strikes a woman "over the head," he misses her. If one says "roomer" instead of "lodger," then, Bierce adds, "See *Bedder* and *Mealer*—if you can find them." If one says "I will try and see him," one's effort will be successful, which is not the actual meaning; one should say "try to see." The adjective "unkempt" properly describes the hair only. The word "[w]ell," when used to begin a sentence, "is overtasked." One "sees" something, but "witnesses" it only if one observes it and "tell[s] afterward." Bierce takes pains to excoriate the word "gubernatorial," when he exhorts the reader to "[e]schew it; it is not English, is needless and bombastic." He goes on: "Leave it to those who call a political office a 'chair.' 'Gubernatorial chair' is good enough for them. So is hanging." In his short story "Jupiter Doke, Brigadier-General," he has the phony Doke apply "for the Gubernatorial Chair of the Territory of Idaho," which, according to Bierce's view here, would make him a poor writer. Modern dictionary definitions of both "gubernatorial" and "chair" would trouble Bierce if he were alive today. One wonders if Bierce, professing some knowledge of Latin, knew the meaning of the Latin word "gubernator" (steersman, helmsman, pilot). One knows, however, what he would think of these current academic neologisms: "chair," "chairone," "chairperson," and especially "chairwoman."

Bierce's rigid, austere stance in *Write It Right* is hard to square with the implications of his definition of "lexicographer" in *The Devil's Dictionary*. In it, he avers that "the bold and discerning writer . . . , recognizing the truth that language must grow by innovation if it grow at all, makes new words and uses the old in an unfamiliar sense." Bierce deliberately excluded *Write It Right* from his *Collected Works*, even though he wrote Walter Neale,* his publisher, that he was uniquely proud of it. Bierce even published his critical reply to a 1909 reviewer of *Write It Right* (in *Army and Navy Journal*, 1 January 1910).

Bibliography: Howard W. Bahr, "Ambrose Bierce and Realism," pp. 150–168 in Davidson, *Essays*; Grenander; Hopkins; Joshi and Schultz.

"WRITERS OF DIALECT" (1892, 1895, 1896, 1899, 1903, 1912). Essay. A writer of dialect should (1) already speak the dialect used and (2) also write "in the larger tongue." Robert Burns is an example. His poetry is hard to read. Humorous or satirical writings may acceptably be in dialect. Serious fiction writers should avoid dialect. *David Harum: A Story of American Life*, an 1898 bestseller in "loutly" dialect (by Edward Noyes Westcott [1847–1898]), is stupid and vulgar. Mary E. Wilkins Freeman and Mary Murfree are no better; their works are neither attractive nor picturesque. Heroes speaking in dialect are "an affront." John Hay* was a good poet, but in his dialect poems he "pander[ed] . . . to peasants." Rudyard Kipling's "Gunga Din" is wrongly considered great. James Whitcomb Riley's poetry in dialect "affects the sensibilities like the ripple of a rill of buttermilk falling into a pig-trough." Using dialect to describe fine thoughts, loving sentiments, and deep feelings "defile[s]" them. By contrast, Herman George Scheffauer* writes natural, simple, and beautiful poetry.

Y-Z

YOUNTSEY, SAM. In "The Stranger," he is one of the gentlemen hunters. He confronts the stranger and would like to kill him, until the Captain explains that the stranger, who is Berry Davis, is already dead.

ZEL'Y. In "Hades in Trouble," he or she is evidently the subject of a scandal that Nick would tell the devils in Hades about but for the fact that he passes out drunk before he can do so.

General Bibliography

Aaron, Daniel. *The Unwritten War: American Writers and the Civil War*. New York: Oxford University Press, 1973.

Bahr, Howard W. "Ambrose Bierce and Realism." *Southern Quarterly* 1 (July 1963): 309–331.

Beer, Thomas. *The Mauve Decade*. New York: Alfred A. Knopf, 1926.

Berkove, Lawrence. "Ambrose Bierce's Concern with Mind and Man." Ph.D. dissertation, University of Pennsylvania, 1962.

———. "The Man with the Burning Pen: Ambrose Bierce as Journalist." *Journal of Popular Culture* 15 (February 1981): 34–40.

Brazil, John R. "Behind the Bitterness: Ambrose Bierce in Text and Context." *American Literary Realism* 13 (Autumn 1980): 225–237.

Brooks, Van Wyck. *Emerson and Others*. New York: E. P. Dutton, 1927.

De Angelis, Valerio Massimo. "Ambrose Bierce's War Wonders." *Letterature d'America: Revista Trimestale* (1952–1953): 43–79.

Dyal, Donald H. *Historical Dictionary of the Spanish American War*. Westport, Conn.: Greenwood Press, 1996.

Fadiman, Clifton, ed. *The Collected Writings of Ambrose Bierce*. New York: Citadel Press, 1946.

Fatout, Paul. *Ambrose Bierce and the Black Hills*. Norman: University of Oklahoma Press, 1956.

Faust, Patricia, L., ed. *Historical Times Illustrated Encyclopedia of the Civil War*. New York: Harper & Row, 1986.

Field, B. S., Jr. "Ambrose Bierce as Comic." *Western Humanities Review* 31 (1977): 173–180.

Follett, Wilson. "Ambrose Bierce—An Analysis of the Perverse Wit That Shaped His Work." *Bookman* 68 (November 1928): 284–289.

Foote, Shelby. *The Civil War: A Narrative*. New York: Random House, 3 vols. 1958–1974.

Francedese, Janet M. "Ambrose Bierce as Journalist." Ph.D. dissertation, New York University, 1977.

Fuentes, Carlos. *The Old Gringo*. New York: Farrar, Straus and Giroux, 1985.

Fusco, Richard. *Maupassant and the American Short Story: The Influence of Form at the Turn of the Century*. University Park: Pennsylvania State University Press, 1993.

Grattan, C. Hartley. *Bitter Bierce: A Mystery of American Letters*. New York: Doubleday, 1929.

Grenander, M. E. "California's Albion: Mark Twain, Ambrose Bierce, Tom Hood, John Camden Hotten, and Andrew Chatto." *Papers of the Bibliographical Society of America* 72 (1978): 457–462.

Guelzo, Allen C. "Ambrose Bierce's Civil War." *Civil War Times Illustrated* (September 1981): 36–45.

Hartwell, Ronald. "What Hemingway Learned from Ambrose Bierce." *Research Studies* 38 (December 1970): 309–311.

Hayden, Brad. "Ambrose Bierce: The Esthetics of a Derelict Romantic." *Gypsy Scholar* 7 (1980): 3–14.

Hopkins, Ernest Jerome, ed. *The Complete Short Stories of Ambrose Bierce*. Lincoln and London: University of Nebraska Press, 1970.

Hoppenstand, Gary. "Ambrose Bierce and the Transformation of the Gothic Tale in the Nineteenth-Century Periodical," pp. 220–238, in Kenneth M. Price and Susan Blasco Smith, eds., *Periodical Literature in Nineteenth-Century America*. Charlottesville: University Press of Virginia, 1995.

Joshi, S. T., and David E. Schultz. *Ambrose Bierce: An Annotated Bibliography of Primary Sources*. Westport, Conn.: Greenwood Press, 1999.

Klein, Marcus. "San Francisco and Her Hateful Ambrose Bierce." *Hudson Review* 7 (August 1954): 392–407.

Knight, Melinda. "Cultural Radicalism in the American Fin de Siècle: Cynicism, Decadence and Dissent." *Connecticut Review* 14 (Spring 1992): 65–75.

Linderman, Gerald F. *The Mirror of War: American Society and the Spanish-American War*. Ann Arbor: University of Michigan Press, 1974.

Mariani, Giorgio. "Ambrose Bierce's Civil War Stories and the Critique of the Martial Spirit." *Studies in American Fiction* 19 (Autumn 1991): 221–228.

Millard, Bailey. "Personal Memories of Ambrose Bierce." *Bookman* (New York) 40 (February 1915): 643–658.

Oliver, Lawrence J., and Gary Scharnhorst. "Charlotte Perkins Gilman v. Ambrose Bierce: The Literary Politics of Gender in Fin-de-Siècle California." *Journal of the West* 32 (July 1993): 52–60.

Pope, Bertha Clark, ed., with a memoir by George Sterling. *The Letters of Ambrose Bierce*. San Francisco: Book Club of California, 1922.

Rather, Lois. *Bittersweet: Ambrose Bierce and Women*. Oakland, Calif.: Rather Press, 1975.

Reed, Ishmael. "On Ambrose Bierce's *Tales of Soldiers and Civilians*," pp. 37–43 in *Classics of Civil War Fiction*, David Madden and Peggy Bach, eds. Oxford: University Press of Mississippi, 1991.

Rolle, Andrew. *California: A History*. 5th ed. Wheeling, Ill.: Harlan Davidson, 1998.

Saunders, Richard. *Ambrose Bierce: The Making of a Misanthrope*. San Francisco: Chronicle Books, 1985.

Schaefer, Michael Wingfield. " 'Just What War Is': Realism in the Civil War Writings of John W. DeForest and Ambrose Bierce." Ph.D dissertation, University of North Carolina, 1990.

Sheller, Harry Lynn. "The Satire of Ambrose Bierce: Its Objects, Forms, Devices, and Possible Origins." Ph.D. dissertation, University of Southern California, 1945.

Solomon, Eric. "The Bitterness of Battle: Ambrose Bierce's War Fiction." *Midwest Quarterly* 5 (1963–1964): 147–165.

Starrett, Vincent. *Ambrose Bierce*. Chicago: Walter M. Hill, 1920.

Stevens, Louis. *Here Comes Pancho Villa: The Anecdotal History of a Genial Killer*. New York: Frederick A. Stokes, 1930.

Suhre, Lawrence R. "A Consideration of Ambrose Bierce as Black Humorist." Ph.D. dissertation, Pennsylvania State University, 1972.

Walker, Franklin. *Ambrose Bierce: The Wickedest Man in San Francisco*. San Francisco: Colt Press, 1941.

———. *San Francisco's Literary Frontier*. New York: Alfred A. Knopf, 1939.

Woodruff, Stuart C. *The Short Stories of Ambrose Bierce: A Study in Polarity*. Pittsburgh: University of Pittsburgh Press, 1980.

Index

Note: Peripheral and incidental names and titles are omitted. Original titles later changed are omitted. Page references to main entries are in **boldfaced** type.

About the Author

ROBERT L. GALE is Professor Emeritus of English at the University of Pittsburgh. His previous books include *A Dashiell Hammett Companion* (2000), *A Sarah Orne Jewett Companion* (1999), *An F. Scott Fitzgerald Encyclopedia* (1998), *A Herman Melville Encyclopedia* (1995), *A Cultural Encyclopedia of the 1850s in America* (1993), *Cultural Encyclopedia of the 1850s in America* (1993), *The Gay Nineties in America* (1992), *A Nathaniel Hawthorne Encyclopedia* (1991), and *A Henry James Encyclopedia* (1989), all available from Greenwood Press.